Ruining Revolution

COLUMBIA STUDIES IN TERRORISM AND IRREGULAR WARFARE

COLUMBIA STUDIES IN TERRORISM AND IRREGULAR WARFARE
Bruce Hoffman, Series Editor

This series seeks to fill a conspicuous gap in the burgeoning literature on terrorism, guerrilla warfare, and insurgency. The series adheres to the highest standards of scholarship and discourse and publishes books that elucidate the strategy, operations, means, motivations, and effects posed by terrorist, guerrilla, and insurgent organizations and movements. It thereby provides a solid and increasingly expanding foundation of knowledge on these subjects for students, established scholars, and informed reading audiences alike.

Marta Furlan, *Inside Salafi-Jihadist Governance: The Strategies and Characteristics of Islamist Insurgent Rule*

Alexandra Rachel Phelan, *The Combination of All Forms of Struggle: Insurgent Legitimation and State Response to FARC*

Erica L. Gaston, *Illusions of Control: Dilemmas in Managing U.S. Proxy Forces in Afghanistan, Iraq, and Syria*

Andreas E. Feldmann, *Repertoires of Terrorism: Organizational Identity and Violence in Colombia's Civil War*

John Horgan, *Terrorist Minds: The Psychology of Violent Extremism from Al-Qaeda to the Far Right*

Harrison Akins, *The Terrorism Trap: The War on Terror Inside America's Partner States*

Rita Katz, *Saints and Soldiers: Inside Internet-Age Terrorism, From Syria to the Capitol Siege*

Tricia L. Bacon and Elizabeth Grimm, *Terror in Transition: Leadership and Succession in Terrorist Organizations*

Daveed Gartenstein-Ross and Thomas Joscelyn, *Enemies Near and Far: How Jihadist Groups Strategize, Plot, and Learn*

Boaz Ganor, *Israel's Counterterrorism Strategy: Origins to the Present*

For a complete list of books in the series, please see the Columbia University Press website.

RUINING REVOLUTION

How International Islamist and Salafi Forces
Have Held Libya Hostage Since 2011

INGA K. TRAUTHIG

COLUMBIA UNIVERSITY PRESS *NEW YORK*

Columbia University Press
Publishers Since 1893
New York   Chichester, West Sussex

Library of Congress Cataloging-in-Publication Data

Names: Trauthig, Inga, author.
Title: Ruining revolution : how international Islamist and Salafi forces have held
Libya hostage since 2011 / Inga Trauthig.
Description: New York : Columbia University Press, 2025. | Series: Columbia studies in
terrorism and irregular warfare | Includes bibliographical references and index.
Identifiers: LCCN 2024047285 (print) | LCCN 2024047286 (ebook) | ISBN 9780231219945
(hardback) | ISBN 9780231219952 (trade paperback) | ISBN 9780231562980 (ebook)
Subjects: LCSH: Ikhwān al-Muslimūn—Libya. | Salafīyah—Libya. | Islam and state—Libya. |
Libya—History—Civil War, 2011–
Classification: LCC DT236.5 .T73 2025 (print) | LCC DT236.5 (ebook) |
DDC 961.205—dc23/eng/20241231

Cover design: Milenda Nan Ok Lee
Cover photo: Giles Clarke/Getty Images

GPSR Authorized Representative: Easy Access System Europe, Mustamäe tee 50,
10621 Tallinn, Estonia, gpsr.requests@easproject.com

Contents

CONTENTS

Figures and Tables

Acknowledgments

THIS BOOK IS closely related to my research at King's College London. For this research, I received mentorship from Shiraz Maher and Peter Neumann. I am immensely grateful that they saw potential in me and took me on as a research fellow at the International Centre for the Study of Radicalisation. At ICSR, I was fortunate enough to be surrounded by brilliant minds who challenged me regularly and with that advanced my academic thinking tremendously. Dounia Mahlouly, Inna Rudolf, Haid Haid, Gina Vale, and Joana Cook, thank you for being the best colleagues and now friends.

The School of Security Studies at King's College London has been my home for the years in which I worked on this book, and I am incredibly proud to call King's my alma mater. There are too many people there to thank, but Jonathan Hill, Magda Long, Francesca Ghiretti, Devorah Margolin, Daniela Richterova, and Nick Kaderbhai, in particular, have guided me through the years, read various parts or previous versions of this manuscript, and motivated me to keep going. I am also indebted to Bruce Hoffman and Caelyn Cobb of Columbia University Press, who worked with this first-time author and included my book in a series I've always admired. Thank you for your incredible patience.

For this book, I have spoken to many Libyans as well as people from the government, academic, and corporate sectors who have worked on or in Libya. I am grateful to anyone who spared a few minutes of their time to meet with me. Over the years, I have encountered several individuals who continue to inspire me. Unfortunately there are too many to name, but Daniel Gerlach, Zora Hauser, Khadeja Ramali, Aaron Zelin, and Martyn Frampton are among them.

I could not be more thankful to my family: my parents, who have always supported me, my siblings, who have always provided distractions when I got too much into my head, and my patient, generous, and ingenious husband, whom I met in the last year of my PhD and who miraculously stayed by my side.

Finally, to everyone I have engaged with over the last several years, thank you for listening to me talk about Libya for probably far too many hours.

Acronyms

GNA	Government of National Accord
GNC	General National Congress
GNU	Government of National Unity
HNEC	High National Election Commission
ISL	Islamic State Libya
JCP	Justice and Construction Party
LIFG	Libyan Islamic Fighting Group
LNA	Libyan National Army
LPDF	Libyan Political Dialogue Forum
NFA	National Forces Alliance
NFSL	National Salvation Front for Libya
NTC	National Transitional Council
PIL	Political Isolation Law
SDF	Special Deterrence Force
SSC	Supreme Security Committee
SSR	Security Sector Reform
UNSMIL	United Nations Support Mission in Libya

Ruining Revolution

Introduction

IN 2011, LIBYAN Islamists were surprised that local protests in Benghazi grew into a national revolution.[1] Libyan quietist Salafis were shocked to witness open defiance to the country's dictatorial leader, Muammar al-Gaddafi—whom they considered the *wāli al-amr* (legitimate ruler).[2] Neither the Islamists nor the Salafis played a central role in the onset of the revolution—yet, over a decade later it is clear that both shaped contemporary Libya immensely.[3] This book aims to show how. It draws on a range of sources, including in-depth interviews and propaganda shared on social media, to examine the descent into violent confrontation and unruliness in Libya after the removal of its longtime head of state.

For this, it focuses on two key but underestimated movements: the Libyan Muslim Brotherhood and Libyan Salafi-Madkhalis. It argues that these Islamist and Salafi movements played a bigger role than previously assumed for Libya's descent from a hopeful candidate of the "Arab Spring" into a decade of political turmoil and regular violence: that the groups failed to work for the common good of Libya by seeking compromise. It aims to elevate the argument that militant Islamist or Salafi groups are dangerous per se to a more sophisticated understanding of how and why some actions by those groups are dangerous and can have major consequences, and to explain what drives these harmful behaviors.

With this, *Ruining Revolution* suggests ways forward for Western policy makers as it outlines how crucial it is to untangle the contribution of specific movements to Libya's recent developments instead of understanding the country as one convoluted mess. The book also underlines the centrality of examining how groups talk and behave toward each other and the local population rather than what they tell themselves or Western policy makers.

From "Arab Spring" to "Arab Winter"

Libya has turned into a headache for many policy makers due its intractable conflicts and corruption. Further, it has become an infamous reference point for anyone arguing that the "Arab Spring" turned into an "Arab Winter."[4] While the 2011 international intervention by the North Atlantic Treaty Organization has been heavily discussed, explanations that bring together international *and* local factors are far less elaborate.[5] Whereas Libya under Gaddafi represented a case of totalitarian control and suppression of any non–state sanctioned activities, postrevolutionary Libya is an active playing field of various forces that either came out of the shadows (and prisons) inside Libya or to the country from abroad.[6] Crucial among them are the Libyan Salafi-Madkhalis and the Libyan Muslim Brotherhood.

The Libyan uprisings in February 2011 were embedded within a regional wave of protests against authoritarian regimes.[7] Rapidly, however, and for a number of reasons, the Libyan case set itself apart from other revolutions and attempted revolutions in the Middle East and North Africa (MENA) Region.[8] It was the only country where

- a Western-led military intervention was conducted under the NATO umbrella;
- the previous head of state was captured and brutally murdered by the rebel fighters; and
- it fractured over time in a manner that makes it impossible for outside observers to identify fault lines that surpass small social circles, such as tribes or families.[9]

The internationalized character of the Libyan revolution, the brutality and (re-)surfacing of grievances, and the emancipation of groups and beliefs long suppressed under Gaddafi have set the stage for the two groups at the heart of this book to embark on power quests. The political turmoil—which has claimed more than twenty thousand lives and frustrated international partners since 2011—is an immensely intricate power play.[10] Its actors include an ample collection of politicians often backed by military groups, both Libyan and international. Between 2014 and 2024, the key actors can be roughly characterized with three broad strokes:

1. Affiliated before March 2021 with the Government of National Accord (GNA) and/or the Government of National Unity (GNU) after that point; or
2. Affiliated with the so-called Libyan National Army (LNA)[11] and the House of Representatives; or
3. Independent.

These three categories broadly align geographically with (1) western Libya, (2) eastern Libya and some of southern Libya, and (3) eastern, southern, and western Libya. Some independent groups can be found in all of these regions. However, in eastern Libya, where the LNA is strongest, unaligned groups and individuals are less common, given leader Khalifa Haftar's demand for loyalty and submission, especially with regard to armed actors.[12]

Libyan key actors include armed groups and their individual leaders and political representatives who are potentially aligned with but not directly part of an armed group. Affiliations in Libya are often feeble. In other words, politicians and armed groups have been switching sides, even crossing previous enemy lines in search of power. Fathi Bashagha, for example, is a Libyan politician who hails from Misrata. Misrata was among the cities that vehemently stood up against Gaddafi and where several powerful armed groups formed during and after the 2011 uprisings.[13] Misratan civilians were likely victims of war crimes, while Misratan armed groups were accused of brutality under the veneer of revenge in regime-loyal parts of Libya. The latter were also involved in the battles around Sirte that finished off Gaddafi in October 2011.[14] The city's influence in post-2011 Libyan parliamentary politics was not so brutal but had an equal impact.

Fathi Bashagha was an influential Misratan who worked his way into powerful political positions via establishing military credentials and commitment but combined this with legitimacy via elections. In 2014, he was elected to the House of Representatives for the city of Misrata. However, the country slid into civil war following those elections and his position became ineffective. In October 2018, the GNA made him Minister of the Interior. In February 2022, after eleven years of continued alignment with western Libyan forces, Bashagha lobbied successfully to be selected as prime minister–designate by the eastern-based authorities. In effect, he set up a breakaway government propped up by the eastern Libyan political forces (the House of Representatives) and the LNA.[15]

Affiliations in Libya are two-way rather than top-down relations. While several armed groups rely on payments from Libyan authorities and therefore follow some command of ministers, these politicians also rely on locally embedded armed groups for legitimacy—and survival.[16] For example, in 2016, the prime minister selected to head the looming GNA, Fayez al-Sarraj, did not feel safe traveling to Tripoli by plane. Instead, he traveled from Tunisia by sea to Tripoli's Abusita naval base. Once in Tripoli, Sarraj was guarded by armed actors who subsequently benefited from state resources.[17] Hence, official heads of state and ministers in Libya needed to regularly align themselves with locally embedded armed actors to consolidate their actually powerful positions.

While imperfect, the three categories and their geographic counterparts listed above can help readers who follow Libya infrequently. Since the summer of 2014 political power there has been split between rival authorities, specifically, western-based authorities in Tripoli and eastern-based ones in Benghazi and Tobruk. With the creation of the GNU in March 2021, this division was supposed to have been overcome—but, de facto, the dividing lines among Libya's elites persisted and were again institutionalized in March 2022, when Bashagha declared a rival Government of National Stability (GNS) in Sirte, which was supported by the LNA.[18] Therefore, it is imprecise to describe the GNU as a successor to the GNA because it reshuffled alliances. However, when scrutinizing Libya's political divides today, the lines still broadly fall under the three defined strokes, with individual people and groups occasionally switching them up.[19]

In the chapters that follow, Libya's key actors will resurface and they are embedded into the book's analysis. More importantly, however, the discussion of the Libyan Muslim Brotherhood and Libyan Salafi-Madkhalis concurrently shows how some ideological movements operate and entrench themselves on opposite sides of the Libyan political divides and hence grow even more important. Binding factors beyond ideology, such as tribal bounds, also connect some actors and surpass geographical boundaries.

But how did Libya's "Arab Spring" turn into almost a decade of civil war? And which roles have Islamist and Salafi forces played in this development?

The conviction that the Libyan Muslim Brotherhood would capitalize on the removal of the Gaddafi regime and the attempt to establish a democracy defined early analysis of the revolution.[20] There are three reasons for this. The Libyan Muslim Brotherhood is an avowedly political movement and its ideological backdrop points toward inclusion in decision-making.[21] It is part of a transnational movement with experience of political organization.[22] In addition, the organization is defined by exiled structures: Many members spent significant amounts of time in Western countries and are therefore well-versed in influencing democratic processes.[23] However, as this book demonstrates, these characteristics played out detrimentally for the Libyan Muslim Brotherhood because they were incongruous with many Libyans' experiences and expectations. Overall, a mix of internal factors, such as conflated self-perception, together with external factors, such as the inexperience of many Libyans with parliamentary politics, explain why the Libyan Muslim Brotherhood gained influence shortly after the fall of Gaddafi but has lost influence over the years since then.

No analysis appears to have been published in 2011 referencing the Libyan Salafi-Madkhalis as a post-Gaddafi force with potential burgeoning influence. The movement is part of the quietist tradition and therefore considered politically quiet and inert.[24] Hence, its ideological backdrop would point toward noninvolvement in institutions of a nascent democracy.[25] Libyan Salafi-Madkhalis were a marginal force with a poorly understood relationship to the Gaddafi regime. They were intimately tied to their Saudi founder, Rabi bin Hadi al-Madkhali, who only emerged as an influential cleric in the 1980s and did not gather followers in Libya until the late 1990s.[26] Most observers agree that Libyan Salafi-Madkhalis did not participate in the revolution at all.[27] This book demonstrates that these convictions are mistaken: that the Libyan Salafi-Madkhalis' marginal nature was in fact helpful for their role in the formation of security institutions by former Gaddafi officials in postrevolutionary Libya, and that they have political impact despite their quietist tradition, given that the group managed to exploit the chaotic Libyan situation for their own benefit, relying on violence and cooperating with ideological enemies. In short, the post-2011 Libyan Salafi-Madkhalis remained quietist despite transforming and having political impact. They never entered institutional politics.[28]

Instead, their rise took place in terms of practices of contentious,[29] force-ful,[30] and "extraordinary" politics.[31]

Purpose and Aims of the Book

Because violent Salafi–jihadi groups often grab the headlines, academics and policy makers have studied these groups in Libya to a greater extent than they have the "mainstream" Islamists of the Muslim Brotherhood and the quietist Salafi-Madkhalis.[32] But the insights presented in this book are pertinent for an understanding of the descent of Libya's Arab Spring into almost a decade of civil war. It demonstrates how internal decisions and behaviors by both the Libyan Muslim Brotherhood and the Libyan Salafi-Madkhalis were central to the failure of a political system that was intended to be built on nonviolence, cooperation, and compromise. These actors sabotaged the nascent democracy Libya attempted after the removal of the Gaddafi regime, using their influence in an exclusionary manner to promote their own people and objectives.

Mapping out crucial junctions of Libya's recent history and tying in the movements' pasts, the book argues that these ideological forces have been of greater importance than previously assumed. While the 2011 Libyan revolution was not a religious one, Islamist and Salafi actors proved surprisingly well-prepared to capitalize on different fissures inside the country as well as draw in international support for their respective agendas. Understanding the movements' activities and motivations has significant policy implications for regional engagement and also illuminates underlying workings found in a range of radical groups.

Against the backdrop of social movement theory, this book showcases how the developments of two key movements largely negated behavioral and ideological moderation—and with that contributed heavily to Libya's instability. For instance, the Libyan Muslim Brotherhood pursued exclusionary politics, relying on violence after it reached positions of political dominance, while the Libyan Salafi-Madkhalis pursued discriminatory policing and violently attacked institutions and individuals they deemed heretical after assuming control as security forces in pivotal parts of the country. In both instances, the groups failed to seek compromise for the common good of Libya. Moreover, both movements also failed to moderate with regard to ideology: Their principal figures frequently relied on violent rhetoric in their framing of events and engaged in exclusionary identity formation. The book demonstrates how the Libyan Muslim Brotherhood and Libyan Salafi-Madkhalis fluctuated but ultimately abandoned moderating behaviors and framing. Throughout this analysis, it explains how historical and external factors, such as copious amounts of weaponry or Gaddafi's eradication of civil society, thwarted attempts of movement moderation—and with it a peaceful, potentially even democratic Libya.

The two movements turned less moderate the more they became incorporated into postrevolutionary political and security structures. This book shows how hardliners trumped moderate members at key junctions, outlining that a different path for the movements and the nation could have been possible. By investigating the contemporary trajectories of the Libyan Muslim Brotherhood and the Libyan Salafi-Madkhalis, it identifies the conditions that facilitated or impeded the country's postrevolutionary descent into instability and violence. These and other movements with a religious ideology that achieved positions of power and were presented with the potential for expansion pursued uncompromising, potentially violent actions to secure their positions vis-à-vis other parts of the population.

The book fills a lacuna not just on contemporary Libya but also on international Islamist and Salafi movements. Given that acute recent concerns about continuous violence and ideological hardening have given rise to fears of a revival of the "Libyan strong man" (a figure embedded in counter-Islamist and counterterrorism rationales who relies on violent groups among his ranks), *Ruining Revolution* is particularly timely.

Libya may seem far away for some of this book's readers, but existing grievances there, the security vacuums, and the nation's geographic proximity will continue to serve as pull factors for extremist groups aiming to cause harm in Europe.[33] This unstable country's negative impact on international security can be witnessed in the Christmas Market terror attack in Berlin in 2016, the assassination of U.S. Ambassador Christopher Stevens in Benghazi in 2012, and the infiltration of Russian Wagner mercenary troops into parts of the country. Its vast territory, bridge between Africa and Europe, history of Salafi–jihadism and Islamism, and various armed groups make Libya a powder keg with international influence.

While many forces have been competing for positions and power in post-Gaddafi Libya, few movements managed to entrench themselves as thoroughly as the Libyan Muslim Brotherhood and Libyan Salafi-Madkhalis. (These and other ideological movements have been undervalued in analysis on Libya.) Similarly, while there is a vast body of literature on Islamism and Salafism generally and an increasing number of researchers now rely on social movement theory, important gaps remain in our understanding about specific local groups, with Libya a glaring example. This book therefore has three goals:

1. It directs attention to Islamist and Salafi forces in order to deepen understanding of how Libya descended into over a decade of political turmoil and regular violence after the 2011 revolution.
2. It shows that the two movements under study became greatly involved in the post-Gaddafi Libyan system by obtaining key political positions and inserting themselves into the security institutions of the postrevolutionary environment. In so doing, it reveals why they both failed to moderate: They refused to operate according to parameters necessary for establishing a political system originally intended to be built on nonviolence, cooperation, and compromise.
3. It resolves the paradox of how Islamist parties such as the Muslim Brotherhood–affiliated Justice and Construction Party underperformed in elections but still developed into the main political forces in the elected political body, as well as how an allegedly apolitical movement of quietist Salafis became crucial for Libyan politics.

Specifically, this book challenges the conventional wisdom that Islamist groups are best prepared to rise in influence in the Middle East and North Africa after the overthrow of authoritarian regimes by showing the incongruence to the Libyan population of the Libyan Muslim Brotherhood's ideas and behaviors and the Libyan Salafi-Madkhalis' rise to nationwide importance due to their emphasis on establishing local security.

Theoretical Parameters: Social Movement Theory and Moderation

Social Movement Theory (SMT) is an interdisciplinary body of literature that has arguably become the dominant theoretical corpus for scholars seeking to explain continuity and changes within Islamist and Salafi movements' ideology, strategies, and behavior.[34] Different social movement scholars rely on different aspects of SMT, including historical path dependencies in resource allocation, systemic collapse, and internal division—often subsumed as "political opportunities"[35]—when explaining a particular movement, a revolution, or shifts in social movements' strategies, rhetoric, and practice.[36]

Mario Diani defines a social movement as "a network of informal interactions between a plurality of individuals, groups and/or organizations, engaged in a political or cultural conflict, on the basis of a shared collective identity."[37] This book uses the terms "movement" and "group" interchangeably to analyze the Libyan Muslim Brotherhood and Libyan Salafi-Madkhalis, because most scholars agree that a social movement at its core is a "collectivity of individuals" with a loosely defined goal, while the term "organization" is contested.[38]

Many scholars devote themselves to what Donatella della Porta identifies as the three focus areas of SMT—namely, (a) social movements as potential expressions of social conflict, (b) the origins of social movement cultures, and (c) the process through which values, interests, and ideas are turned into collective action. This book focuses on a fourth: (d) how a certain social, political, and/or cultural context affects social movements' chances of success, the forms they take, and the impact they have—in this case, the development of a country.[39]

Both the Libyan Muslim Brotherhood and Libyan Salafi-Madkhalis established themselves as social movements before 2011. Scholars sometimes neglect the origin of movements and their initial mobilization in favor of elaborating on their more recent successes or decline.[40] But SMT scholars such as Hein-Anton Van der Heijden have analyzed how the opening of institutions in former authoritarian regimes provides social movements with the opportunity for growth.[41] Such insights are generally subsumed under the umbrella terms "political opportunity structures" and "democratization" when applied to the study of social movements.[42] This book relies on those insights and then engages with the inclusion-moderation hypothesis developed by Jillian Schwedler.[43] In essence, Schwedler argues that social movements that become included in political and societal institutions that aspire to democratic principles are likely to turn moderate in their behavior and ideology. However, the established inclusion-moderation hypothesis for the study of Islamist and Salafi movements needs to be updated for postrevolutionary environments; even more, the previous conceptualizations lose their relevance as an analytical framework the more a country tilts toward revolution. In other words, the loss of control of centralized institutions following revolutionary actions has significant impact on the hypothesis's logic because it was originally designed for authoritarian openings, such as the small-scale reforms by King Hussein in Jordan, and its rationale weakens when applied in environments with less centralized control.[44]

Along those lines, the removal of the head of state signals a major change in authoritarian nations, as was the case in Tunisia in January 2011. However, the death of Gaddafi and the breakdown of the entire Libyan system he had established represents extreme structural change for an authoritarian system—in the words of Hannah Arendt, a "successful" revolution—and hence different structural conditions.[45]

The inclusion-moderation hypothesis argues that the inclusion of Islamist and Salafi movements in these structures (as has been described in Jordan) would lead to the moderation of movements previously operating outside the established institutions by giving them incentives to broaden their appeal to a larger part of the population: to suggest they would grow by popular mandate.[46] On the flip side, small-scale democratic reforms such as allowing previously repressed groups to compete in elections are driven by the regime's objective to neutralize potentially threatening opposition forces by co-opting them into the existing institutions and establishing better oversight.[47]

Some scholars, such as Khalil al-Anani, insist that more holistic examinations of Islamist movements are necessary to better understand their development.[48] Al-Anani's main criticism of the inclusion-moderation hypothesis is that it concentrates on outcomes. Instead, he argues, an analysis should be centered in an examination of the processes and dynamics of Islamists' inclusion to capture all nuances and explain the developments of Islamist and Salafi movements more comprehensively, without the limitations of a normative focus on moderation.[49] However, by engaging in a theoretical conceptualization that includes a focus on outcomes, the analysis of movements' developments benefits from clear points of comparison that emerge along the way. A social movement approach always incorporates both internal and external processes and dynamics without including those influences in the primary lens of analysis.[50]

This book's conceptualization of broad categories within which the groups are assessed is crucial when juxtaposing divergent or similar developments. For example, the reliance on weapons by both movements to protect existing influence in 2013 highlights the overbearing effect of external factors, namely the outbreak of civil war. The divergent behavior with regard to the months following the 2012 national election highlights how the Libyan Muslim Brotherhood favored exclusionary politics over cooperation in parliament. By contrast, the Libyan Salafi-Madkhalis in Tripoli adopted behavior such as recruiting outsiders into their neighborhood security forces and cooperating with other local groups. These differences in behavior led the Libyan Muslim Brotherhood to lose influence in the longer term, with the Libyan Salafi-Madkhalis increasing their influence because they were able to cooperate with and even integrate outsiders.

This book therefore identifies three aspects of comparison: (1) abandonment of violence; (2) cooperation; and (3) compromise. Despite the previously described discrepancies between the origins of the inclusion-moderation hypothesis (authoritarian openings) and the structures of the environment under examination in this book (revolution and its aftermath), the analytical tradition is still of value because it remains the most meaningful way of relying upon both: an established analytical framework flexible enough to have been used for different Islamist and Salafi groups in different environments.[51]

This book establishes that the expected development of Islamist and Salafi movements after inclusion into state institutions and structures did not lead to the anticipated moderation that had been established by previous scholars focusing on authoritarian openings elsewhere. This was due to the loss of regime control and controlled inclusion. Therefore, updated frameworks are necessary, including for the regional landscape following the 2011 Arab uprisings: Many countries suffered a loss of centralized control, albeit to different degrees, with Libya likely being the most extreme example.[52]

With the surprising and sudden exit of the Gaddafi regime in 2011, the ruler's idiosyncratic political and social system, which he called the *jamāhīriyah,* vanished.[53] However, ever since he seized power in 1969, Gaddafi had used his clout and Libya's oil revenues to foster his authority, thus creating a system in which all areas of the state were his prerogatives, includ-ing the social sphere.[54] Thus, all actors in post-Gaddafi Libya carry advanta-geous or disadvantageous structural, perceptive, and ideological "baggage," including the Libyan Muslim Brotherhood and Libyan Salafi-Madkhalis.

While the Libyan Muslim Brotherhood was characterized as the coun-try's "most vilified opposition group" during Gaddafi's forty-two years in power, the Libyan Salafi-Madkhalis were partially promulgated by the regime in the 1990s.[55] This is because the Islamist Libyan Muslim Brother-hood embarked on attempts to dethrone the Gaddafi regime.[56] The Libyan Salafi-Madkhalis, however, had been invited into the country in the 1990s, as the followers of Shaykh Rabi bin Hadi al-Madkhali had been deemed an inert and therefore a more "acceptable" version of Islam to counteract what Gaddafi called derivative influences, such as the Libyan Muslim Brother-hood and the Libyan Islamic Fighting Group (LIFG).[57] However, Gaddafi tasked one of his sons, Saadi Gaddafi, with becoming close to and reporting on the Madkhalis, demonstrating that he hardly trusted the group either.[58] The dismantling of the Gaddafi regime presented a unique opportunity for formerly suppressed groups such as the Libyan Muslim Brotherhood to position themselves in the process of the construction of new elites and for groups already partially accepted in the system, such as the Libyan Salafi-Madkhalis, to expand their influence.[59]

Some existing studies, such as Sumita Pahwa's research on the Egyptian Muslim Brotherhood (MB), began to criticize the discrepancy between those environments for which that the inclusion-moderation hypothesis was orig-inally designed and the realities of the case study in question. Pahwa explains that while the MB's transition from religious movement to majority-seeking party in Egypt's post-2011 democratic experiment offered a key test of the hypothesis, the movement's increasing "religious and organiza-tional conservatism" challenged it.[60] Pahwa offers an initial criticism of the inclusion-moderation hypothesis in postrevolutionary environments by arguing that, while her study affirms the relevance of the political learning mechanisms it predicts, the divergent outcomes of this learning suggest the need to focus on the contexts and motivations that set movements along one of multiple possible adaptive pathways.[61] However, she stops short of adapt-ing the inclusion-moderation hypothesis to be more functional for the tran-sitionary environment of her case study.

Ruining Revolution is one of the few studies examining Islamic movements along the inclusion-moderation hypothesis that has been led by a deductive approach: It first theorizes the three aspects of moderation rooted in the existing literature on which the two movements will be compared and then undertakes the comparative analysis.[62] The pursued deductive approach allows for less predisposed analysis, meaning that the analytical framework is more robust and not entirely reliant on the two cases examined; further, it increases the chances of the framework being used and transferred to the study of other post–Arab Uprisings Islamic movements, enhancing its value in terms of a comparability framework.[63] The book engages with two ideologically different groups that also chose two different pathways of behavior. While the Libyan Muslim Brotherhood focused on reaching influential positions in the country's political institutions, such as parliament, the Libyan Salafi-Madkhalis focused on protecting their local influence in Tripoli's mosques and with presenting themselves as a reliable local security provider with no broader political vision.

By analyzing these groups' strategies along the three aspects of abandonment of violence, cooperation, and compromise, the book shows how both failed to moderate. The range of their analyzed behavior is vast and captures the introduction of exclusionary legislation aiming for the expulsion of oppositional members of parliament by the Libyan Muslim Brotherhood and the destruction of Sufi shrines by the Libyan Salafi-Madkhalis. The book shows how the three categories can work as a framework for the study of other Islamic movements in the contemporary MENA region by offering flexibility alongside a well-defined blueprint that relies on a defined goal and benchmarks for moderation.[64]

Unsurprisingly, "moderation" is a very contested term. In essence, the dividing line for Islamic movements is between scholars who draw the line when a group commits to nonviolence and those extending moderation to include adherence and promotion of liberal views.[65] This book argues for a middle ground for an environment such as Libya. First of all, it agrees with scholars such as Douglass North that the commitment to nonviolence is a necessary but insufficient condition for moderation.[66] At the same time, including liberal views when studying moderation of Islamist and Salafi groups in such a conservative country is largely alien to the context and hence futile in its theoretical usefulness. Therefore, this book understands the abandonment of violence as the first aspect of moderation but then expands the framework to include cooperation and compromise, both of which are derived from Schwedler's approach comparing the Islamic Action Front (IAF) party in Jordan and the Islah party in Yemen and including "tolerance for opposing views, respect for pluralism, and openness to cooperation" in its definition of moderation.[67] With this, *Ruining Revolution* agrees with scholars who demand establishing an actor's commitment to nonviolence as a main characteristic of moderation but also argue that the abandonment of violence is only a first step, as movements that are supposed to function in nascent democratic systems also need to display cooperation and compromise. (For more discussion, see this book's appendix.)[68]

The aims of these theoretical parameters are to answer these two questions: How did Libya's Arab Spring turn into almost a decade of civil war? Which roles have Islamist and Salafi forces played in this development? Social movement theory generally, and the updated inclusion-moderation hypothesis in particular, are crucial to show that the Libyan Muslim Brotherhood and Libyan Salafi-Madkhalis played bigger roles than previously assumed for the nation's descent from a hopeful candidate of the Arab Spring into a decade of political turmoil and regular violence. The groups' commitment to peaceful means was patchy, their attempts at cooperation with other Libyan forces short-sighted, and they entirely failed to work for the common good of Libya by seeking compromise. This book therefore elevates the argument that militant Islamist or Salafi groups are dangerous per se to a more sophisticated understanding of how and why some of their actions are dangerous and can have major consequences.

Still, a few explanations of moderation and movements are in order. Drawing on the work of Jillian Schwedler, Manfred Brocker and Mirjam Künkler explain that

> moderation may of course vary across issues, and it is important to outline the realms in which parties do moderate and in which they do not. Second, moderation is not irreversible [See figure 0.1] and, as a related issue, new radicalisms may emerge even in long-standing democracies. Third, 'moderation' is not a category, but a process. It entails change that should be understood as a movement along a continuum from radical to moderate. Fourth, political parties are not unitary actors. They may moderate positions at the centre but

not in the periphery, or vice versa, the elite may become moderate in its positions but not the larger membership, or vice versa, and there will be differing levels of moderation across party factions. Party change is not necessarily an all-encompassing process and may comprise simultaneous moderation and immoderation processes.[69]

However, with these caveats in mind, this book follows the established scholarly tradition when examining religious movements that argues that moderation can principally occur in two dimensions: ideology and/or behavior.[70]

Behavioral moderation, according to Güneş Murat Tezcür, refers to "the adaptation of electoral, conciliatory, and nonconfrontational strategies that seek compromise and peaceful settlement of disputes at the expense of non-electoral, provocative, and confrontational strategies that are not necessarily violent but may entail contentious action." Ideological moderation can be defined as "a process through which political actors espouse ideas that do not contradict the principles of political pluralism . . . and limits on arbitrary state authority."[71]

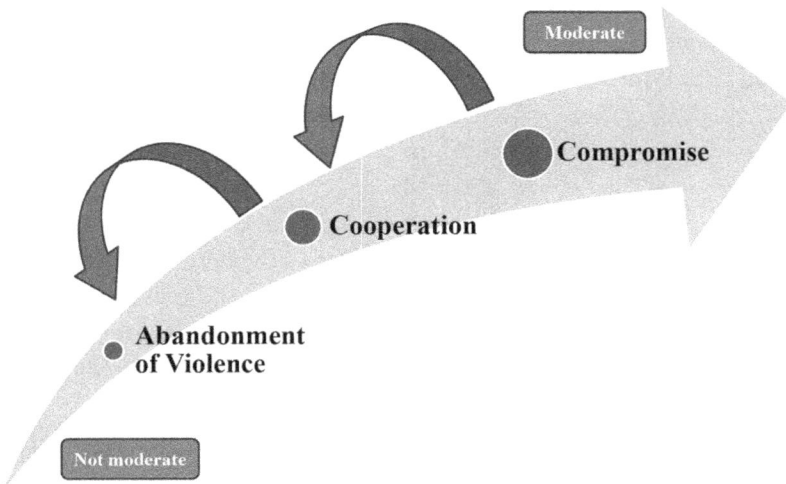

Figure 0.1 Three aspects of moderation. The arrow is not supposed to represent a binary categorization into a beginning or end but a process of change that is not linear and can also develop backward again. Image by author.

Abandonment of violence, cooperation, and compromise will account for both behavioral and ideological change as chapters 2–4 assess the adaptation of nonconfrontational strategies and also the espousal of ideas that do not contradict the principles of political pluralism with framing analysis. While behavioral moderation largely captures steps toward establishing procedural democracy, such as participation in elections, it is ideological moderation that determines whether Islamic movements will not undermine a mid-to-long-term development of a country toward liberal democracy.

Research Design

This book draws on eighty-five interviews carried out by the author and a large number of primary sources, coupled with contributions from the secondary literature. Methodologically, it employs frame analysis of primary sources and qualitative comparative analysis utilizing grounded theory regarding the interviews, providing opportunities to examine cases in depth and to uncover nuances.[72] The dual case study approach allows for a comparison between the two groups and ultimately leads to a more detailed understanding of failed moderation by social movements.[73] In addition, the insights from this comparative approach allow the development of a more sophisticated analytical contribution than one case study would permit, thereby facilitating more meaningful adaptations for the inclusion-moderation hypothesis after the Arab Uprisings.[74] Although other Islamist or Salafi groups in Libya (e.g., Islamic State or Ansar al-Sharia) are not the prime focus of the book, it acknowledges their relevance and will refer to them throughout by highlighting their impact at crucial junctions.

The interviewees are subdivided into three groups. The first comprises 72 percent of the total sample (sixty-one people) and includes individuals who were or are part of the Libyan Muslim Brotherhood and/or its affiliated Justice and Construction Party or identify as Libyan Salafis who consider Rabi bin Hadi al-Madkhali a key scholar or are part of the political, military, and societal institutions that emerged in Libya after 2011. Participants span the generational spectrum, ranging from nineteen to seventy-nine years in age. They include senior leaders who remain faithful party members, as well as former members who declare they have absconded. The second group of interviewees makes up 16 percent of the total sample (fourteen people) and comprises members of Libyan civil society groups with a history of opera-tion inside the nation's networks of power, as well as local journalists, United Nations employees, and other international government officials working on Libya. The final group of interviewees makes up 12 percent of the total sample (ten people) and includes senior experts and researchers in the field focusing on Libya. The findings at the core of this book therefore go beyond the usual pool of members who act as the interface and public voice of an organization to include the views, actions, and strategies of members who traditionally are more in the shadows.

The primary sources consulted include online public materials such as press releases, election manifestos, statements, sermons, press interviews, and self-produced videos. These documents have been gathered in a personal database, and were combined with various sources, including the author's contacts inside Libya, Libyan and regional news websites (among them al-Akhbar, al-Wasat, infoLibya, Libya Herald, and the Libya Observer), and social media platforms and applications (mostly Facebook, but also Telegram, Twit-ter, Viber, and WhatsApp).

While acknowledging and factoring in the structural strains of the theoretical framework, this book also builds a counterpoint to a widespread sentiment that in post-Gaddafi Libya individual actors' and movements' developments are deterministically decided by the overarching evolution of the country (for example, the belief that, with the start of civil war, actors are forced to take up arms or engage in otherwise contentious behavior such as exciting their members rhetorically).[75] However, this book will por-tray the variety of choices that movements still had as the Libyan Muslim Brotherhood and Libyan Salafi-Madkhalis exhibited antithetical behavior and/or framing. For instance, the latter group's growth into one of the main security forces in Tripoli accelerated at a time when the country was under-going attempted democratic transformation and they were not threatened in any way. However, the framing at the time by the movements' local leader, Abdulraouf Kara, focusing on neighborhood concerns and the scaling up of the alleged need for self-protection, convinced many members to interpret the ongoing structural developments through his interpretative lens.[76]

Within the analyzed time period Libya underwent three structural phases: collapsing authoritarian regime, nascent democracy, and civil war. This book examines how the two groups adapted and changed over a period of protests and intense fighting (regime opposition, revolution from

January through October 2011), relatively peaceful months and elections (democratic phase November 2011 through May 2013), and disintegrating authority and renewed fighting (passing of the political isolation law and civil war from June 2013 through March 2021).

In March 2021, Libyan stakeholders convened by the United Nations Support Mission in Libya (UNSMIL) in the Libyan Political Dialogue Forum selected a Government of National Unity, which was supposed to be a provisional government to unify the rival Government of National Accord in Tripoli and the House of Representatives with a connected government in the east of the country, based in Tobruk. However, the GNU still exists in 2025 as this book goes to press, and its interim prime minister, Abdul Hamid Dbeibeh, has developed a strong taste for power.[77]

The first scheduled attempt to hold elections, on December 24, 2021, failed. UNSMIL and Special Representative of the Secretary-General (SRSG) Abdoulaye Bathily doubled down on their efforts to have the elections take place at the end of 2023.[78] Regarding the continuous failure of credible, national elections to produce stability, Vito Todeschini explained in 2023:

> While a first attempt to hold elections on December 24, 2021 has failed, since the beginning of 2023 the UN Support Mission in Libya (UNSMIL) and the Special Representative of the Secretary-General (SRSG), Abdoulaye Bathily, have doubled down on their efforts to have the elections take place at the end of this year. One of the factors that has hindered the electoral process is the absence of a constitutional framework that clearly defines the form of government and division of powers in Libya.[79]

In the summer of the following year, elections and a peaceful transfer of power still seemed remote. While Libya's election process is caught up in legal lack of clarity, this book will help readers to understand that twelve years of uncompromising politics in the country presents the biggest hurdle for a political system legitimately representing the Libyan people and working for the good of the entire country.

Internal factors driving actions that diverted these two movements from a potentially moderating course included (1) the hunger for power by both individual members and leaders, as demonstrated by the Libyan Muslim Brotherhood refusing to take up their role as the main opposition leader in parliament but instead working to establish themselves in government,

TABLE 0.1
Book findings overview

THEORETICAL FRAMEWORK	HYPOTHESIS	(1) REVOLUTION	(2) NASCENT DEMOCRACY	(3) CIVIL WAR
Assumption A ("political opportunities" and social movements, Della Porta, Tilly)	If "democratization" and increased access to national institutions occurs, then social movement benefits	Libyan Muslim Brotherhood		
		Yes	Yes	No
		Libyan Salafi-Madkhalis		
		No	Yes	Yes
Assumption B ("inclusion-moderation hypothesis," Schwedler, Cavatorta and Merone)	If included in national institutions, social movements become more moderate because they want to broaden base/appeal to more people	Libyan Muslim Brotherhood		
		Yes	No	No
		Libyan Salafi-Madkhalis		
		Yes	No	No

Note: This table is based on the literature review and findings of chapters 2–4. The way in which the inclusion-moderation hypothesis is combined with the tradition of studying "political opportunities" is shown. These concepts are only presented as separate dimensions for analytical purposes, while in reality they affect, interact, and overlap with one another.

despite being the party with only the second-greatest number of votes;[80] (2) conflated self-perception, as when the Libyan Muslim Brotherhood insisted throughout their election campaigning that they were the only party able to translate Islamic principles into politics; (3) fear of rivals' ascent, as when Libyan Salafi-Madkhali members joined a military offensive against Islamist forces despite the warning against doing so by Rabi al-Madkhali; (4) exclusionary identity formation, such as the Libyan Salafi-Madkhalis relying on defining themselves against allegedly heretical but popular Libyan traditions such as the *hadra*, a ceremony involving recitation and music; and (5) frames justifying violence, as when influential cleric Sadeq al-Gharyani declared in 2011 that picking up arms was the right response to Gaddafi's repression and that dying for the cause of the revolution would be martyrdom. A pair of external factors had the same effect: the inexperience of Libyans with democratic politics leading to widespread skepticism about organized political bodies such as political parties, which

Gaddafi had condemned and warned of, and the high penetration of weap-onry in the country after spring 2011. These two lists are not extensive; instead, they provide an overview of the most important dynamics that define the movements' developments over the course of this book when assessing their failures to moderate.[81]

Structure of This Book

The following chapter outlines various Islamist and Salafi groups that have been and/or are still operating in Libya. This chapter is vital to under-score the dividing lines between these groups. It would be unhelpful to subsume all actors and groups that conduct occasional violence and rely on religious language into the same category, employing terms like "Islamist" or "Jihadi" in broad strokes. Instead, the chapter will outline several rele-vant differences that characterize ideological groups relying on Islam. Dis-cussing these groups in some depth helps to explain intra-Islamist ideo-logical competition in Libya and with that some of the behavior that followed, with all groups being convinced that their ideology and methods were the "right" ones. Chapter 1 therefore starts with al-Qaeda and then unpacks contemporary competitors such as Ansar al-Sharia, as well as the notorious terrorist group Islamic State's offshoot in Libya (ISL). It also explains how quietist Salafis differ from their jihadi counterparts and introduces understandings of Islamism and Salafism.

Chapter 2 turns to the two movements in focus and explains the lead-up to and the months of the 2011 revolution. Both were surprised by the local developments and were forced by the violent character of the Libyan revo-lution to take a stance on militia participation. This was a paradigm shift for both the quietist Salafis and the Muslim Brotherhood. Individual mem-bers found themselves at odds with the movements' leaderships, who argued against violent participation in the uprisings.

Chapter 3 shows how the Libyan Muslim Brotherhood and the Libyan Salafi-Madkhalis exploited new opportunities for growth in a nascent sys-tem, mainly by capitalizing on most Libyans' lack of political experience and profiting from reverberating insecurities respectively. After setting up a political party and dominating parliament, the Libyan Muslim Brother-hood pursued exclusionary politics in which they regularly sabotaged political institutions while seeking to expand their own influence and place their people in top positions. The Salafi-Madkhalis exploited influential positions in neighborhood armed groups and started amassing resources from the new Libyan institutions for their own purposes. They also began damaging Sufi shrines that they deemed heretical and often promoted the destruction on social media. They feared no governmental backlash because their militias were relied upon to prop up government structures. Both movements hurt Libya, as they regularly sabotaged attempted compromise and consensus-building. Their actions were ideologically underpinned by key leaders in the movements who enforced exclusionary identity formation and superiority on religious grounds.

Chapter 4 shows how the negative implications for Libya grew worse and how the Libyan Muslim Brotherhood and Libyan Salafi-Madkhalis contributed to this perpetual instability, including their regular acts of violence. The chapter also explains how ISL's rule in Sirte came about and ended, and the roles played by Islamists and Salafis. Overall, it shows how both the Libyan Salafi-Madkhalis and Libyan Muslim Brotherhood have held Libya hostage and become main hindrances to a peaceful future for the country.

The final chapter addresses the question of what can be expected next. It concludes by commenting on Libya in 2024, which has continued to suffer violence and political failures since 2014. The chapter summarizes key insights based on the study's empirical findings and reflects on the challenges the two movements pose for the MENA region, where unrest and potential revolutions can break out in unpredictable ways due to varying levels of suppression and fluctuating external interventions. It also outlines policy implications for Western engagement in Libya and the MENA region, specifically with regard to Islamists and Salafists.

ONE

Who Are Libya's Islamists and Salafists?

THIS BOOK FOCUSES on the Libyan Muslim Brotherhood and Libyan Salafi-Madkhalis. However, these are not the only movements with an Islamist or Salafi ideology that have been operating in Libya. To define analytical boundaries and help the reader follow the book's analysis, this chapter introduces some other ideological groups. It is important to keep in mind that definitions and categories imposed by academics often struggle to capture the quickly changing dynamics on the ground. Similarly, individuals whom externals consider as being part of a movement might disagree or define their relationship to the movement differently. Still, this book relies on various terms designating political and religious meaning to people and movements, such as Islamists, Salafists, quietist Salafists, and Salafi-jihadists. Some explanations are therefore in order.

According to Shiraz Maher and Martyn Frampton:

> Islamism (or 'Political Islam') is a worldview which teaches its adherents that Islam is a comprehensive political ideology and must be treated as such. Its proponents believe that Islam must be placed at the centre of an individual's identity, as either the overriding or the only source of that identity. The Islamist outlook is one that essentially divides the world into two distinct spheres: 'Muslims' and 'the rest'.[1]

Further, adherents consider Islam and its written sources as models after which to design a political system and constitution, preferably in the form of a "Caliphate."[2] They engage in activism on multiple levels to achieve these goals. The activist Muslim Brotherhood, founded by Hasan al-Banna in 1928 in Egypt but now an international movement, is the most renowned example of an Islamist group.[3]

Salafis are generally understood to be a puritanical movement who advocate for the "return" to the origins of Islamic belief and practice. These origins hark back to the time of the Prophet Muhammad and the first three generations of Muslims (*al-salaf al-salih*). Salafis therefore disregard the majority of Islamic sources outside this period and condemn later practices, usually declaring them un-Islamic, sinful innovations (*bida*). In other words, they consider the only legitimate sources of Islam to be the Qu'ran, the sayings of the prophet (the *hadith*), and the consensus of the Salaf.[4]

Scholars argue that whereas a broadly uniform *'aqida* (religious doctrine) fleshes out the content of Salafism, there is intra-Salafi disagreement over *manhaj* (method): how to apply the absolute sources of Islam to, inter alia, political authority,[5] politics, society, *da'wa* (proselytization), and worship.[6] Still, useful as a baseline is Quintan Wiktorowicz's classification of what he considers the three major Salafi factions: purists, politicos, and jihadis.[7] These are characterized by interpretative differences dividing the movement along the question of which faction is best equipped to address modern challenges. Wiktorowicz believes that these differences chiefly occur between the senior (older) purists and the younger "politico and jihadi" scholars. Purists focus on da'wa and worship; politicos involve themselves in various forms of political engagement; for jihadis, jihad is the most important and legitimate method. Hence, despite the notoriety of Salafi-jihadism due to atrocities committed by groups of this ilk, traditional Salafism oscillates between quietism and activism. Even more, "quietist Salafis are the largest subgroup within, and in many ways the true heart of, Salafism."[8]

Thomas Hegghammer and Shiraz Maher have pointed out the need to scrutinize the movement further in order to better understand the political preferences of the "actors described as Salafis" because "although Salafism is a theological distinction, divisions within the tradition are best understood with reference to its fault lines, which principally cut across cleavages of power."[9] This underlines how Islamism and Salafism are sometimes conflated: Islamist ideology is fused with Salafi theology. However, the two have different historical roots and diverge in their approaches to studying and interpreting Islam: While many Islamist movements call for a return to the scriptural foundations of Islam like their Salafi counterparts, Islamists do not shun, but rather actively seek to reinterpret and update them, with the attempt of making them most useful for solving modern social and political issues.[10]

In Libya, a plethora of groups have been and are still operating. These range from Salafi-jihadis to quietist Salafis but also include a range of Islamists. Arguably the most well-known in recent memory is the Islamic State in Libya (ISL), an offshoot of ISIS (or IS), the notorious Salafi-jihadi group that formed in Iraq and Syria in the early 2010s and has not only wreaked havoc in those countries but also brought terror to Europe.[11] Next to ISL, the second most infamous Salafi-jihadi group is al-Qaeda, which continues to operate in the country. It includes affiliated groups that operate under a global banner but are deeply rooted locally, such as Ansar al-Sharia in Benghazi.[12]

The plethora of Salafi and Islamist groups in Libya has its backdrop in four structural factors. First, the Libyan people are culturally conservative. Theirs was the only country where the introduction of *sharia* as the basis of a political system and legislation was *not* disputed after the "Arab Spring." This means that Islam plays an important role for almost any Libyan. While different Islamic groups hold differing objectives, they compete for the minds of a big pool of potential recruits. Second, Islamic groups were the only real challenge to the Gaddafi regime over its forty-two-year rule. The roots of the nation's Salafi-jihadi groups can be traced back to the 1990s, when the Libyan Islamic Fighting Group (LIFG) and the Libyan Muslim Brotherhood developed into among the biggest challenges to the Gaddafi regime. After the 2011 revolution, Islamist and Salafi groups repeatedly tried to tie their legitimacy—as being the true heirs of a post-Gaddafi Libya—to the history of Islamic revolt against Gaddafi by these two organizations.

Third, the Libyan revolution and the resulting state breakdown were particularly violent. Salafi-jihadi groups were neither the main drivers nor the initiators of the uprising against Gaddafi, which induced hundreds of thousands of people to take to the streets across the country, demanding justice and an end to corruption.[13] However, among the forces fighting were hardline Islamist militias, which prospered the longer the fighting continued and were aided by its violent nature, which had been fueled by the hardhanded, brutal response of the regime.[14] In addition, the revolutionaries freed many jailed regime opponents, among them Islamist militants, while simultaneously Salafi-jihadi groups such as alQaeda actively began deploying senior members to Libya and Libyans who had traveled to fight with al-Qaeda in Iraq (for instance, after the 2003 US invasion) returned to the country.[15] The collapse of governance and security that followed the overthrow then created beneficial conditions for Islamist and Salafi groups to reemerge relatively undisturbed. Moreover, Libya has exhibited a significant availability of weaponry since 2011; in recent years the situation has been exacerbated due to blatant but welldocumented breaches of the UN arms embargo.[16] The porous borders that have resulted from the nonexistent national state authority—which would in any case normally have faced challenges in controlling such an extraordinarily large territory—allow for local actors to negotiate the terms of border management.[17]

This leads to the last and final structural point: the location of Libya as an intercontinental bridge.[18] The country's geographical location will always remain attractive for radical groups because it facilitates the recruitment of African fighters, intersects with relevant trading and smuggling routes,[19] and is close to the shores of Europe.[20] Sub-Saharan Africans have come to constitute a large part of Libya's foreign fighters, a new trend, since prior to 2011 East and West Africans had mostly stayed preoccupied with local insurgencies in their home countries. The international danger from these groups is now felt regularly, from local assassinations of diplomats to terrorist attacks in Western countries such as the 2016 Christmas market attack in Berlin and the 2017 Manchester Arena bombing in the UK, both perpetrated by young men with ties to Libyan Salafi-jihadis.[21] Post-uprising Libya has entered the annals of history as "the fourth-largest foreign fighter mobilization in global jihadist history, behind only the [ongoing] war in Syria, the Afghan jihad of the 1980s [and 1990s], and the 2003 Iraq war."[22]

Al-Qaʿida, Ansar al-Sharia, and the Islamic State in Libya

The roots of Salafi-jihadism in Libya run deep. The main global movement that captured Libyan jihadis was what came to be known in 1988 as al-Qaʿida, with its leader, Osama bin Laden.[23] Al-Qaʿida is the heir to Libyan Salafi-jihadism, which emerged in the LIFG and developed networks of fighters. Among the most significant events in very recent history was the involvement of Libyans in al-Qaʿida's militant battles in Iraq after the 2003

U.S. invasion. Those fighters—returnees from abroad or prisoners freed from the infamous Abu Salim prison in Tripoli—then joined the Salafi-jihadis who fought alongside national forces in the 2011 Libyan revolution.[24]

However, there were different paths to take from those early days of the Salafi-jihadi movement, and two Libyan brothers epitomized those choices. Abdelwahhab Mohamed Gaid and Mohamed Hassan Gaid both grew up in Libya's southern desert town of Sebha and became involved in Islamic activism linked to the LIFG in the 1980s, with the goal to oust Muammar Gaddafi. Fast-forward to 2023 and Abdelwahhab Gaid is a Libyan politician who cofounded the *al-Umma al-Wasat* Party (Central National Party), a small Islamist splinter group. While he has turned to parliamentary politics, his actions there have been controversial and he is regularly accused of being involved with more radical groups outside parliament, most prominently al-Qaʿida.[25] However, in his own words: "I still make mistakes, but I am also learning . . . what I know is violence is not the solution and Libya needs democracy . . . [but] we have been harmed by Gaddafi . . . it is hard to trust [anyone] in Libya."[26] At the time he said, this, his brother Mohamed Hassan Gaid had been dead for eleven years, killed in an American drone strike in Pakistan in 2012. By that time, he had risen to become a leading figure within al-Qaʿida with the nom de guerre Abu Yahya al-Libi.[27]

Opposition to Muammar Gaddafi was the spark that ignited both of their involvements with the global jihadi movement. But while Abdelwahhab Mohamed was captured by Gaddafi's border guards in 1995 as he tried to cross into Libya on an LIFG mission and spent sixteen years in prison, until the eve of the 2011 revolution, Mohamed Hassan was imprisoned in Afghanistan by U.S. forces in 2001 and infamously escaped his prison cell only to radicalize further and become al-Qaʿida's deputy leader.[28] Retrospectively, Abdelwahhab insists that, although he was a militant and willing to use violence to oust Gaddafi, he never joined al-Qaʿida or subscribed to its ideology that saw the West as an enemy as well.

This family story highlights the various degrees of entanglement of Libyans with the global jihadi movement, which traces its steps back to the Muslim mobilization of the 1980s, in which Islamism rose to become the main ideology of defiance against Gaddafi.[29] Abdelwahhab Mohamed Gaid stands as an example of the hundreds of Libyan Islamists who turned against the country's leader and either ended up in prison or in exile. Mohamed Hassan Gaid was one of the hundreds of Libyan Islamists who saw local leaders as their main enemies at first but radicalized further abroad and turned their primary scorn toward the West, the United States in particular after the 2001 invasion of Afghanistan. Albeit to different degrees, both brothers were in touch with al-Qaʿida and tangled up in the global jihad from which the movement ultimately emerged as the strongest.[30]

Prior to the 2011 revolution, stories such as these meant that al-Qaʿida was in a prime spot to coordinate individual stragglers of Libyan militant groups. Although the LIFG as a group never adopted al-Qaʿida's ideology fully or pledged allegiance to Osama bin Laden, some members did.[31] The LIFG as a group renounced violence and officially disbanded in 2010; however, many individual members were discontent with this development and renounced the group's renunciation.[32] Returning or released foreign fighters and disgruntled militants, many of whom were linked to both al-Qaʿida and the LIFG, played a fundamental role in the reconstitution of an al-Qaʿida-linked presence and network inside the country during 2011.[33] They leveraged relationships with other members of the network to start and enlarge military and training camps in the vast, ungoverned Libyan space.[34]

The U.S. Library of Congress's Federal Research Division identified Abu Anas al-Libi as the "the builder of al-Qaeda's network in Libya." At the same time, the Federal Research Division acknowledges that "the extent of its [al-Qaʿida's] network and organization is largely . . . unknown."[35] The Libyan revolution was a huge opportunity for al-Qaʿida, which its leadership duly recognized. Aaron Zelin quotes a letter that senior leader Atiyah Abd al-Rahman al-Libi wrote to Osama bin Laden in May 2011: "Brothers from the Libyan [Islamic] Fighting Group and others are out of jail. There has been an active jihadist Islamic renaissance under way in Eastern Libya (Benghazi, Darnah, Bayda, and that area) for some time, just waiting for this kind of opportunity. We think that the brothers' activities, their names, and their 'recordings' will start to show up soon."[36] The exiled LIFG members came back to Libya from various places, including Ireland and the United Kingdom, to serve in these groups.[37] Among them were Salman and Hashem Abedi, the brothers responsible for the 2017 Manchester Arena terrorist attack.[38]

After the killing of Gaddafi, the al-Qaʿida-linked networks pursued three main tactics. First, they grew their presence in Libya and bolstered Al-Qaʿida in the Islamic Maghreb (AQIM) as a flexible network of Salafi-jihadi groups affiliated with al-Qaʿida.[39] These included Salafi-jihadi umbrella organizations such as the Benghazi and Derna Mujahedin Shura Councils.

Next, they created local fronts under different names, most prominently Ansar al-Sharia. Those groups were especially targeted at new members and recent recruits to jihadism, many of whom started their radicalization online or when talking to prior jihadist generations. Hand in hand with this, they established themselves locally with extensive da'wa and potentially some governance work, such as policing. The latter was one of the key differences that Zelin defined in 2012 when comparing contemporary jihadi groups to those of the 1990s: "[They are] now more ideologically homogenous—in the 1990s, jihadis thought locally and acted locally, while many now talk globally and act locally. These newer groups are also more interested in providing services and governance to their fellow Muslims."[40] This evolution was particularly pertinent with regard to Ansar al-Sharia and later the ISL.

The goal that underlined all three tactics was the boycott of elections and opposition to democracy. This put these groups at odds with broader structural dynamics happening in Libya at the time, namely the move toward elections. However, it is important to keep these jihadi strands in Libyan society in mind. Different sections of militants intervened or occasionally even collaborated with the moderate Islamists of the Muslim Brotherhood or the Umma party of Abdelwahhab Gaid. "Moreover," notes Zelin, "the shared excitement of overthrowing the regime resulted in shortsightedness among more-nationalist forces, which failed to marginalize the jihadists" and even gave them space to collaborate and grow. "For example, former LIFG members helped found or became key figures in a number of insurgent forces—including Katibat Shuhada Abu Salim, Katibat Umar al-Mukhtar . . . Katibat Rafallah al-Sahati, and Katibat al-Nur"—that would eventually affiliate with Ansar al-Sharia.[41] This already foreshadows the influence of Islamists and Salafis on local and international developments and the often-blurred boundaries between some of the groups.

But al-Qa'ida did not have free rein in Libya in 2011. Instead, the world and the region had developed into a field of jihadist competition where it was only one of the bidders, with its biggest rival being ISIS.[42] One of its main tactics to expand influence and keep ISIS at bay in Libya was the proliferation of Ansar al-Sharia groups similar to others that had already successfully formed in Yemen and Tunisia.[43] In Libya, Ansar al-Sharia became the most powerful jihadi group until ISL managed to establish governance in Sirte in 2015.

Ansar al-Sharia in Libya: Local Da'wa and the Killing of an American Ambassador

Ansar al-Sharia in Libya was part of a Salafi-jihadi trend after 2011: Instead of adopting unique names, groups would refer to themselves as *ansa*, Arabic for "supporters." Ansar al-Sharia—supporters of Islamic law—was the most popular label, as it underlined an appealing goal: to establish an Islamic state (Caliphate). Groups calling themselves Ansar al-Sharia formed in Tunisia, Yemen, and Libya. While they shared a name and group members were often previous al-Qaʿida affiliates, they did not have a leader or transnational organizational structure.[44]

In Libya, groups calling themselves Ansar al-Sharia first formed in Derna and Benghazi. The latter rose to international prominence after it was accused of perpetrating the September 2012 attack on the U.S. consulate in Benghazi and killing ambassador Christopher Stevens.[45] Ansar al-Sharia in Derna was led by former Guantánamo Bay and Abu Salim prison inmate Abu Sufyan bin Qumu and established itself as an important force in the city after the death of Gaddafi in October 2011.[46]

While these groups were initially independent from one another, they united under the name Ansar al-Sharia Libya in late 2012. Their ideology had already been aligned on key matters such as unambiguously disavowing elections and related democracy. Any form of democracy as well as elections, forming political parties, and other democratic procedures was considered heretical and antithetical to Islam.[47] This set them apart from many other Islamist militant groups and political parties operating in Libya after 2011, who saw their chance to gain power by playing ball with the supporters of elections and a democratic system.

Ansar al-Sharia had different ideas of governance and implemented them by capitalizing on local power vacuums. Popular efforts to expand locally would rely on da'wa campaigns, which included aspects such as delivering aid to the poor, cleaning roads and public places, and providing security to hospitals and other local infrastructure, as well as religious teaching.[48] Still, the group's ideology was intolerant and strictly Salafi-jihadi, with its primary goal to establish an Islamic state in Libya with shariʿa as the sole source of legislation—and the group espoused violent jihad to achieve this aim.

The group's ideological intolerance was never in doubt for citizens of Derna, one of its main strongholds. A twenty-year-old student there vividly remembers how most books of the local library were burned: "I never understood why. They said they [the books] were against shariᶜa and promoting Western ideas, but I knew some of the books . . . they were just books." Her friend expressed: "I did not like the book burnings but what was most awful was that because of them our city turned toxic . . . no one could be trusted anymore . . . we could not vote . . . and then everything got destroyed by Haftar."[49]

Derna and Benghazi had developed spatial pockets in which Salafi-jihadi groups largely did what they wanted. The killing of U.S. Ambassador Stevens on September 11, 2012, was crucial for the mobilization of international support for Libyan forces trying to defeat Salafi-jihadi forces in Libya.[50] In May 2014, General Khalifa Haftar, a retired military officer who had defected in 1983 while fighting in Chad, returned from his home in the United States for the 2011 revolution and launched a military offensive with the so-called Libyan National Army (LNA) to rid Benghazi of "terrorist groups." With that, the degradation of the group was on the horizon.[51] However, the general relied on militias from all over the country that he organized under the banner of the LNA—some of them Salafi-Madkhalis who themselves had radical views and behaviors. While wreaking local havoc, killing many innocent citizens, and lumping together any opposing individuals and groups under his definitions of radical Islam and terrorism, Haftar managed to diminish the influence of Ansar al-Sharia. The group was forced to focus almost all of its efforts on military activity, eliminating daᶜwa work to a skeleton of what it had been before. It officially dissolved in 2017.[52]

Independent of which war propaganda Libyans listened to, all parties claimed to be the true heirs of the Libyan revolution and the opposing side resultingly were enemies of the 2011 revolution.[53] This claim to legitimacy was utilized across the ideological spectrum and to the dismay of Libyans who suffered under continuous violence. Simultaneously to Ansar al-Sharia's battles with Haftar's forces, the intra-Salafi competition in Libya picked up speed in June 2014 when the IS declared a "Caliphate." This made IS very appealing to Libyan Salafi-jihadis alongside other Salafi-jihadis from around the world.[54]

ISL and Its Brutal Rule in Sirte

The Islamic State barged into Libya with aggression, as they had in Iraq and Syria.[55] Their behavior was brutal and their inclination for cooperation and compromise close to zero. One barbaric image that came to stand for some of IS's viciousness was a video from Libya in February 2015 that showed masked fighters beheading a group of Egyptian Christians.[56] As Zelin points out, "After [Salafi-jihadi] fighters streamed from Libya to Syria in 2012–13" to support the Syrian jihad after the removal of Gaddafi, "the trajectory reversed itself in spring 2014, aimed at bolstering the Islamic State's attempt to establish a base in Libya." Ultimately, "the Islamic State in Libya [ISL] was formed by a combination of pro-IS individuals based in Darnah [Derna], returning Libyans and other foreign fighters in Syria's Katibat al-Battar al-Libiyah," and defectors from Ansar al-Sharia.[57]

However, after having established some presence in Derna, ISL's breakthrough came when they managed to establish governance in the coastal city of Sirte—and for that, they needed to exploit existing power struggles and gather local support. Operation Karama (or Dignity) ultimately involved the entire country. The military operation's title was chosen by Haftar to signal that he was aiming to bring back "dignity" to Benghazi first and then Libya as a whole. While his forces had grown influential in eastern parts of Libya (such as Benghazi and Derna), he was also pushing westward. In the early months of 2015, the fighting was concentrated over the crucial oil facilities of the Sirte Basin. In geographical terms, the city of Sirte was deeply entrenched in this battle. With the dominant military forces of the east and west focused on fighting each other, IS managed to exploit the ensuing power vacuum.[58]

Other local jihadi competitors, most prominently Ansar al-Sharia members in Sirte, started fearing the encroachment of Operation Dignity fighters and sought to align themselves with stronger forces.[59] Ultimately, ISL managed to portray itself as what it longed to be: a jihadi force not characterized by gradualism and with clear support from the IS core that pushed for an unambiguous vision of governing.[60] Ultimately, IS outmaneuvered Ansar al-Sharia in Sirte and many members pledged allegiance (*baya*) to the selfproclaimed Caliph Abu Bakr al-Baghdadi.

The city of Sirte carries its own significance. In this hometown of Muammar Gaddafi, many local tribes were allied with the regime and Sirte became an emblem, a focal point for ire, for many in postrevolutionary Libya. It was also the literal target of anti-Gaddafi forces and NATO airpower.[61] Following the overthrow, it was clear that Sirte had ended up on the wrong side of history. The victorious forces (many of them from Misrata) enacted revenge, such as detentions and executions, disrupting the existing social fabric of the city.[62]

IS's offer of violent rule provided local forces with retribution mechanisms for what they considered unfair treatment after 2011. This rationale by local tribes and communities was not driven by a bona fide alignment with IS's goals and ideology: It was an opportunistic cooperation focusing on short-term benefits.[63]

ISL took over the city step by step: the radio station, the Wataniya television studio, the immigration center, Ibn Sina Hospital, the University of Sirte, and local government buildings. After controlling large swaths of the city, they installed a local leader: Usamah Karamah, a relative of a former senior Gaddafi intelligence officer.[64] By August 2015, the group had turned Sirte into its largest stronghold outside of its core territory in Iraq and Syria—an achievement that is still unmatched today.

The immense ideological pull of the Caliphate acted as its main recruitment tool. ISL propped up their ranks with foreigners. In the eighth issue of IS's English-language magazine *Dabiq* in March 2015 Libya featured prominently. In one piece called "The Libyan Arena," IS denounced the nation's parliaments and referred to Libya as the "ideal land for Hijra [immigration]" for those who could not come to Syria, such as adherents from Libya's neighboring countries or sub-Sahara Africa. The article emphasized that ISL was prospering and expanding. This would have been extremely appealing to Salafi-jihadis from countries such as Tunisia or Kenya, because it meant that they did not need to go all the way to Syria and Iraq to fight for the Caliphate.[65] Many foreigners were part of the local leadership: Mostly Iraqis and Tunisians have held top positions, maintaining close ties between the Libyan branch and the core group in Iraq and Syria.[66]

IS's presence in Sirte ended in 2016 when the group was militarily defeated by Libyan forces under the umbrella of the al-Bunyan al-Marsous operation room (which translates to "solid, well-built structure/construction/wall" and was a coalition of Libyan forces, many from Misrata), with U.S. airstrikes from Operation Odyssey proving crucial for the Libyan ground offensive. Members of the Libyan Muslim Brotherhood as well as Libyan

Salafi-Madkhalis were part of this anti-ISL coalition (more about which in chapter 4). By December 2016, IS's sixteen-month reign in Libya was over and the group had lost all its territories due to the coalition as well as its own eradication of local support with its brutality.[67]

After that territorial defeat in Sirte, ISL shifted. The group became known as a refuge for IS forces under pressure in Iraq and Syria; what little property remained to it was viewed as a possible staging post to threaten Europe due to Libya's geographical proximity to one of the main migrant routes.[68] It also established a network of sleeper cells waiting for the right opportunity to rise again.[69]

But the group has been unable to build a proper base or even to govern in Libya. Instead, the group has been chased around the country: Following the loss of its base near Ghodwa, in the south of the country, the group moved to Haruj and began operating again in April 2019, until it was expelled again by the LNA. Overall, ISL is trying to portray itself in a hyperbolic way. While its activity over the years has been relatively weak, the volatility and geography of the country as well as prevailing grievances remain pull factors for ISL, which makes it potentially threatening, even if the organization is currently negligible.[70]

The horrors of having lived under ISL's rule, however, are still haunting people in Sirte, many of whom had fled the city and came back to only rubble.[71] One local councilwoman described how she tried to envision a better future but "Daesh [IS] ruined everything."[72] She also explained how ISL had become a point of reference for groups within the country to discredit those they were fighting, a way of identifying the "enemy" by calling "anyone you don't like 'Daeshi.'" This way of signaling detestation was heavily employed by Haftar and forces of his LNA, which worked to further conflate any opponents with Islamist extremists.[73] But this narrative is also employed inside Islamist and Salafi circles.[74] As another symbol of the polarized Libyan discourse, especially since Haftar's Operation Dignity, another curse word for an (alleged) enemy in Libya emerged: "Ikhwani" (member of the Ikhwan, the Arabic term for the Muslim Brotherhood).

Ansar al-Sharia and ISL both managed to dominate and de facto govern parts of the country in 2012–2013 and 2015–2016, respectively. However, in contrast to the Libyan Muslim Brotherhood and Libyan Salafi-Madkhalis, these groups were not as successful in surviving the different challenges they faced. Despite their ability to create local governance models, their successes were comparatively short-lived, largely due to their alienation of local and international forces. Still, much has been written about Ansar al-Sharia and ISL's structures, operations, and the threats they present to Libya and further afield.[75] This is due in part to their brutality, which captured headlines around the world. Much less has been written about the Libyan Muslim Brotherhood and Libyan Salafi-Madkhalis, who had a substantial impact on Libya after 2011 and continued to do so for years.

The Libyan Muslim Brotherhood and Salafi-Madkhalis

After the 2011 revolution, Salafi-jihadis were quick to capture headlines due to their violence and competition for attention. However, two other groups are more pertinent for the current Libyan state, as they have had a more long-lasting impact: the Islamists of the Libyan Muslim Brotherhood and the quietist Salafi-Madkhalis. As already outlined, the most notorious Salafi-jihadi groups are violent and intolerant in their ideology and behavior. However, some of them are also quite invested locally and have constructed their own ways of governance. The latter never included elections. Quite the contrary: The groups boycotted the ongoing Libyan elections and violently kept Libyan citizens away from ballot boxes in localities such as Derna.[76]

By contrast, the reformed successors of the LIFG and Libyan Muslim Brotherhood were interested, invested, and participants in elections in post-revolutionary Libya. This set these groups apart from Salafi-jihadis and brings us back to the activist Islamism described earlier. In the words of Abdelwahhab Gaid, who formed the Umma party together with the LIFG's former spiritual leader Sami al-Saadi: "We wanted to do the right thing for Libya . . . [and] we wanted people to vote for us."

The Muslim Brotherhood founded the Justice and Construction Party in March 2012. Other well-known Islamists also opted to participate in Libya's 2012 elections, some running as individual, nonparty candidates and others who formed their own political parties. These included leaders of the LIFG. Overall, Libya's existing Islamist networks fragmented during this electoral process. While existing networks were activated, those were repurposed for political aims of some leaders and parties.[77]

However, Libya's Islamist movements needed to react to the revolution *after* the main developments had occurred, rather than the revolution being an event in which they led the way. Both the Libyan Muslim Brotherhood and the LIFG had engaged in reconciliation efforts with the regime shortly before the revolution. Now they were taken by surprise as they had to conceptualize their identity faced with the new realities of post-Gaddafi Libya. Having defined themselves as anti-Gaddafi for decades but then embarking on conciliation with the Gaddafi regime, they were now confronted with deciding what they stood for *independent* of Gaddafi.[78]

By 2011, these groups were either forced into exile (with some having settled in the United Kingdom or the United States) or were coopted by the Gaddafi regime under the "Repent and Reform" program, led by Gaddafi's second son and rumored heir Saif al-Islam. This program was purported as a de-radicalization program, which mainly targeted Islamist prisoners. In exchange for relinquishing any political activity in Libya, prisoners could secure a release.[79] Members of both these Islamist organizations emerged from the revolution collectively burdened by Gaddafi's decades-long efforts to demonize and ostracize them within Libyan society. Above all, each of them, as well as the group, was required to deliberate the role they could fill in post-Gaddafi Libya. Since their previously unifying factor of opposing Gaddafi had vanished, internal unity suffered.

It would be a misconception to believe that Libya's Islamist political milieu is cohesive. Instead, it includes the Muslim Brotherhood and networks drawn from members of the LIFG who regularly disagree with each other. Within these orbits, Islamists operate who have influence in their towns or regions or are linked to certain militias and join alliances with the former when deemed useful.

Explaining the Libyan Muslim Brotherhood

The Libyan Muslim Brotherhood has a long and tumultuous history in Libya, one linked to the global Muslim Brotherhood movement founded in 1928 in Egypt. In fact, the Libyan Muslim Brotherhood has been called the "country's oldest Islamist group."[80] Although the group was initially welcomed by King Idris in the 1940s, matters quickly changed after the military coup of 1969 that brought Colonel Muammar al-Gaddafi to power.

Severe repression and meager reprieves under Gaddafi's *jamāhīrīyah* meant that the Libyan Muslim Brotherhood could only carry out a string of incoherent, choppily executed activities in the country. In the early 2000s, however, it participated in the Repent and Reform program. By doing so, the Libyan Muslim Brotherhood left behind its status as a persecuted group but remained a shadow of what its founders intended it to be—namely a deeply entrenched and influential Islamist group. Before 2011, it consisted of a negligible congregation of people, denoted by its exiled membership. It offered only futile daʿwa work, which meant that by the time of the revolution, its goals were widely unknown among Libyans. If anything, the Libyan Muslim Brotherhood was considered a murky force with negative connotations thanks to Gaddafi's decades-long propaganda against it.[81]

The decision about how to react to what appeared to be an indomitable revolutionary stimulus in eastern Libya in 2011 put the organization in a conundrum. Even when it began active support of the revolution, the Libyan Muslim Brotherhood still appeared open to the possibility of making a deal with the very regime it was fighting.[82] These moves did not go unnoticed by the Libyan people. However, after internal discussions among the largely exiled leadership in Switzerland, the Libyan Muslim Brotherhood decided to take the side of the revolutionary forces and turn its back on the regime. Chapter 2 will show us how and why.

The Muslim Brotherhood's Ideological Cousin and Libyan Competition—the LIFG

The Libyan Islamic Fighting Group originated when Libyans returning from battles against the Soviet Union in Afghanistan chose Gaddafi as their next target. After the regime discovered an LIFG cell in 1995, the group found itself prematurely caught up in a confrontation with Gaddafi and most of its members wound up in prison, to be released about ten years later as part of the Repent and Reform Program.

The regime killed over a thousand prisoners in the Abu Salim prison the same year, among them many members of the Libyan Muslim Brotherhood and the LIFG, in response to their protests about abysmal detention conditions. Eyewitnesses reported that regime forces rounded up hundreds of inmates in the prison's military courtyards and fired at them with Kalashnikovs from rooftops before finishing off the survivors with pistols.[83] The victims' bodies were never found. This unforgotten massacre planted the seeds of Libya's uprising fifteen years later, with grievances over the cold-blooded murders galvanizing widespread protests against the regime. The Abu Salim massacre is still referenced today to point out the brutality of Gaddafi's regime.[84]

Ironically, Abu Salim's last prisoners were released in February 2011, just as the revolution started in eastern Libya, empowering some former LIFG members to feature in the conflict from the start. These men developed into an organized cohort and, realizing the importance of getting into key positions in the emerging political apparatus, decided to run for office.[85] This newly developed political class, however, faced a crucial struggle against Ansar al-Sharia groups, IS affiliates, and other jihadis who rejected any form of political participation.

The LIFG sought to overcome suspicions about its past in Afghanistan and hence affiliation with al-Qaʿida that questioned the very notion of democracy. Diverging approaches emerged as to how the rebranding would be achieved. For over two decades, the LIFG had defined itself as a group whose aim was to remove Gaddafi and establish an "Islamic State" in Libya. Gaddafi's killing in October 2011 triggered an identity crisis.[86] The fact that the dictator's death was the culmination of a revolution in which LIFG members were actors—and not necessarily protagonists—forced the group to revise its purpose. Moreover, establishing an Islamic State seemed to stand at cross purposes with democratic aspirations, which most other revolutionary forces espoused. In a ceremony in Tripoli's Tobactus Hotel in November 2011, some four hundred LIFG members met to discuss the group's future.[87] They reached a consensus to respect Libya's nascent democratic process, with key LIFG leaders inspired by other Muslim-majority countries' approaches to governance to believe that democracy was no longer to be viewed as irreconcilable with Islamic values.

Ahead of the 2012 elections, the previous LIFG emir, Abdelhakim Belhadj, announced the establishment of a new political party, al-Watan (The Homeland). Al-Watan brought together an amalgamation of figures that called for moderate Islamic democracy: Islamists—including ex-LIFG members and Libyan Muslim Brothers—businessmen, youths, civil society activists, even more liberal voices. Belhadj's move caused tension with his previous LIFG peers, particularly Abdelwahhab Gaid and Sami al-Saadi, who had not been informed about his plan. They subsequently established al-Umma al-Wasat, an explicitly Islamic party with a more conservative agenda and a clearer stance on shari'a's role in governance. Neither al-Umma al-Wasat nor al-Watan secured any party list seats in the 2012 elections. Gaid, however, who ran separately in his hometown of Murzuq in southern Libya despite being part of al-Saadi's party, secured a seat at the General National Congress. Ironically, ex-LIFG candidates hung their banners adjacent to his. Some ran independently and others under al-Watan or al-Umma al-Wasat. All in all, the consecutive rounds of fragmentation that the LIFG experienced, its inability to collectively strategize against the new revolutionary backdrop, and the opportunism of its own members rendered the group politically ineffectual. The Libyan Muslim Brotherhood had more success.[88]

Explaining the Libyan Salafi-Madkhalis

The Libyan Salafi-Madkhalis belong to the tradition of quietist Salafism. Joas Wagemakers argues that quietists avow obedience to incumbent regimes and stay aloof from or refrain from actively participating in institutional and oppositional politics. Madkhalis specifically—what Wagemakers calls "propagandist" quietists in the context of Saudi Arabia—support incumbent regimes as an "article of faith."[89] Crucially, while Madkhalis may claim to shun politics, they "use instruments of power to obtain hegemony in the transnational Islamic movement and ultimately become . . . a political movement, proving resistance and ultimately fostering internal strife."[90]

Salafi-Madkhalis are intimately tied to their namesake, Rabi bin Hadi al-Madkhali, an octogenarian Saudi scholar who held positions at the Islamic University of Medina. His messages have spread across the world, due in part to the support of well-funded Saudi religious charities and promulgation of his sermons via satellite television.[91] Specifically, Madkhali became more prominent in Saudi Arabia during the time of the Iraqi invasion of Kuwait in August 1990. He was a stringent custodian of the royal family's support for "Operation Desert Shield," which included the stationing of U.S. troops in the country. Madkhali argued that this was just, since the ruler's decisions with regard to the 1990-1991 Gulf War belonged to *ta'at wālī al-amr* (obedience to the ruling authority according to this conceptualization is, to a great extent, removed from how just or pious said ruling authority is deemed).[92] This will be referred to below simply as *wālī al-amr*, or "righteous ruler."

The security apparatus of the Gaddafi regime had unequivocal instruc-tions to interpret any religious behavior that differed from Gaddafi's inter-pretations as suspicious. Therefore, first appearances of Libyans adhering to Madkhali in the 1990s alerted the regime. Salafi-Madkhalism had made its way to Libya from Saudi Arabia via Libyans who had visited Saudi Arabia or Yemen while on hajj (pilgrimage) or for religious studies.[93] Madkhalism, however, is usually vocal against political opposition (due to wālī al-amr). This objection of political activism against the ruler was something Gad-dafi wanted to take advantage of. Resultingly, he supported the spread of Madkhalism in Libya.[94] Salafi-Madkhalis were allowed to preach some of the Friday sermons in Libyan mosques. In some places, Gaddafi authorized Salafi-Madkhalis to commence prayer rooms and religious educational centers, in which locals were encouraged and instructed to memorize the Qu'ran. These institutions also shared Islamic books and tapes with religious sermons from Saudi Arabia. In addition to some local popularity related to the mentioned institutions, Madkhalism also spread in Libya due to its presence on satellite TV and the internet–just as other Salafi currents.[95]

The Gaddafi regime deemed Madkhalism an inert and therefore more acceptable version of Islam to counteract what the dictator called deriva-tive influences, such as the Libyan Muslim Brotherhood and the LIFG.[96] In their sermons and literature, Salafi-Madkhalis warned against such politi-cal Islamist movements. It is possible that Gaddafi employed Salafi-Madkhalis as part of regime efforts to surveil religious places (mosques and prayer rooms). However, these efforts have not been proven and existing publica-tions on Salafi-Madkhalis in Libya mention them as rumors.[97] What is clear, however, is that Saadi Gaddafi, one of Gaddafi's sons, became close to the movement and grew into an aspiring Salafi-Madkhali.[98]

Scholars focusing on these movements differ in their interpretation of their doctrinal distinctions. Joas Wagemakers argues that Salafi politicos diverge from quietists because they participate in parliamentary politics or, where they do not or indeed are prevented from doing so, they instead undertake contentious political debate and activism and set out their views on how the country should be run through letters, organizations, and petitions. Khalil Al-Anani, however, lays out a broader notion of what he terms "political" Salafis: actors who voice their opinion in the public sphere through participation in formal politics or by mobilizing informal networks (protests, social activism, and media appearances). Other scholars argue that quietists, including Madkhalis, are distinct from Salafi-jihadis because, inter alia, they reject the latter's use of violence with the specific goal of unseating incumbent regimes (via "revolutionary jihad"). Frederic Wehrey and Anouar Boukhars query this distinction, reasoning instead that the participation of Libyan Madkhali militias in "factional battles" and violence demonstrates "the inadequacy of terms like 'quietism' in the Libyan context." Elsewhere, Zoltan Pall and Stéphane Lacroix argue that even Salafi groups who participate in running for office, political activism, or other party politics (al-hizbiyya) in pursuit only of "reactionary" goals and single issues such as implementing shariᶜa and protecting their freedom to proselytize, *remain quietists*.[99]

However, these definitional quandaries are not the focus of this book. I have argued in other pieces that discussions of quietist Salafi politics with regard to Libya should focus on mobilizing a notion focused not simply on formal, institutional arenas but rather on a broader set of practices that help to capture the political and militant potential of Libyan Madkhalis.[100] This book is interested in how and why Salafi-Madkhalis influence contemporary Libya, independent of their definitional designation.

Existing Literature on the Libyan Muslim Brotherhood and Salafi-Madkhalis

Literature on the Libyan Muslim Brotherhood is scarce, particularly in comparison to the plethora relating to the Egyptian Muslim Brotherhood. Existing scholarship can be divided into three categories: works that (1) examine Libyan politics generally (before, during, and after Gaddafi's regime); (2) dissect the Libyan Islamist spectrum (mostly to differentiate between radical groups and individuals); and (3) explore the regional and international entanglements of the Muslim Brotherhood, including the Libyan offshoot, at least in part.

With regard to the first category, Dirk Vandewalle has paved the way with monographs and edited volumes that examine Libya's trajectory and how Islamism features, although the Libyan Muslim Brotherhood appears only marginally in general accounts of Libya under Gaddafi.[101] During the dictator's forty-two-year rule, the exiled Libyan Muslim Brotherhood almost vanished from Libya and hence is analyzed and featured in studies that examine opposition to the Gaddafi regime generally.[102] It tends to be referenced in accounts by political scientists applying an identity lens when analyzing the state.[103] Research on Libya and the Libyan Muslim Brotherhood changed significantly during and after the 2011 revolution. Since then, scholarship has tended to focus on the Libyan Muslim Brotherhood within the postrevolutionary dynamics of a rearranging, competitive social and political field.[104] However, given the high militarization of the society due to the violent nature of the revolution and the emerging fragmentation of the country, scholars rarely treat the group as a focal point of analysis, instead, the focus is on armed actors of different backgrounds.[105]

The second category of research saw an increase after 2011 because policymakers have wanted to know with whom they were to deal in post-Gaddafi Libya.[106] However, research spiraled further following 2013, when Salafi-jihadi groups, including the ISIS, gained a foothold in the country. Most research in this regard is done either by terrorism studies scholars or think-tanks. Again, few terrorism studies scholars focus on Libya exclusively but rather tie in Libyan connections to other studies. Omar Ashour, for instance, has undertaken numerous attempts to analyze the Libyan Muslim Brotherhood within the broader, international Islamist spectrum as well as the Libyan scene. Ashour tends to apply elements of social movement theory, especially to explain de-radicalization. Journalists have contributed invaluable research on the freed Libyan political space after 2011, with some, like Mary Fitzgerald, focusing on Islamist groups and contributing their accounts to publications such as Brian McQuinn and Peter Cole's seminal volume *The Libyan Revolution and Its Aftermath*.[107] While journalistic accounts are less theoretical than academic studies, one aspect unites the various approaches: their emphasis that the Libyan Islamist spectrum is amalgamated. This insight carries significance for this book, which, while it concentrates on the Libyan Muslim Brotherhood, also factors in affiliated Islamists as well as ex-members who are still part of the Libyan Islamist scene, even if officially detached from the Libyan Muslim Brotherhood (e.g., Ali al-Sallabi).

A variety of scholars have contributed with regard to the third category—literature on the regional and international spread of the Muslim Brotherhood that also features the Libyan Muslim Brotherhood. Alison Pargeter has studied the Muslim Brotherhood in Egypt, Tunisia, and Libya from an area studies perspective, contributing important details about the Libyan

Muslim Brotherhood's trajectory from Libya to exile and back to Libya.[108] Research tying the Libyan Muslim Brotherhood into broader Muslim Brotherhood research usually focuses on the Middle East–North African (MENA) region and hence analyzes the former either as a regional group with regional importance and impetus or the powerhouse and mothership of the Egyptian Muslim Brotherhood, with assessment of the Libyan Muslim Brotherhood concentrated within the context of broader developments of repression or freedom of Islamist movements in Egypt and the region.[109]

These two trends were already apparent before 2011 and continued to exist after the Arab uprisings that swept the region. However, with regard to the Libyan Muslim Brotherhood, one quality changed significantly: namely, that Libya almost capsized its position from a repressive country to a safe haven for Islamist forces.[110] Therefore, more recent writings, such as those by Haala Hweio, assess "Libya as the last resort for the continued existence of the global movement [the Muslim Brotherhood]."[111] Overall, the Libyan Muslim Brotherhood features little in general analyses of Islamism or the Muslim Brotherhood vis-à-vis the Arab uprisings and their aftermath.[112] Works by scholars who have examined the Muslim Brotherhood outside their region of origin are of particular value.[113]

As outlined previously, many scholars of Islamism have not limited their scope to an exclusive school of thought, but rather employed combinations of these.[114] With this in mind, the next section will map and discuss prevailing studies on Salafism and the Salafi-Madkhalis.

Research focusing on the Libyan Salafi-Madkhalis is scarce for a number of reasons. The Libyan Muslim Brotherhood is part of a movement that aspires to be politically active and influential and enters the spotlight almost naturally. By contrast, the Libyan Salafi-Madkhalis belong to a strand of Salafism that is avowedly apolitical and better known among the cognoscenti than the general public. The Muslim Brotherhood emerged as a movement in the 1930s and has decades of national, regional, and international history. The Libyan Salafi-Madkhalis are a much younger movement, whose namesake emerged as an influential cleric in the 1980s and only managed to gather followers in Libya in the late 1990s. With regard to Libyan dynamics specifically, the Libyan Muslim Brotherhood was mostly repressed by the totalitarian Gaddafi regime and hence no force of relevance in the country at the time of the revolution. At that point, the

Libyan Salafi-Madkhalis were a more mercurial but not very influential force that were featured in Gaddafi propaganda.[115]

Literature on the Libyan Salafi-Madkhalis can be divided into two categories: (1) studies on Salafi thinkers and movements with a natural focus on Saudi Arabia that also incorporate Rabi al-Madkhali's thinking; and (2) research on Libya that mostly focuses on security aspects and features the post-Gaddafi Libyan Salafi-Madkhalis in the time they have grown in power, especially after Libya descended into civil war in spring of 2014.

With regard to the first category, it is important to mention that these writings cover all three kinds of literature that deal with Salafism generally.[116] Most insightful with regard to quietist Salafism and the difficulties in putting Salafi thinkers, groups, and individual adherents into clear-cut categories are Joas Wagemakers' *A Quietist Jihadi*, about Abu Muhammad al-Maqdisi, as well as Stéphane Lacroix's studies.[117] In addition, Gilles Kepel's *The War for Muslim Minds* includes Madkhalism, with the aim to clarify the central variable of pro- or anti-regime standing with regard to the Middle East, which gained increased traction after the emergence of the ṣaḥwa movement in Saudi Arabia.[118] Jacob Olidort and Richard Nielsen have categorized Salafi-Madkhalis as "non-jihadists," which carries particular pertinence for this book as it also addresses the engagements of the Libyan Salafi-Madkhalis with violence through framing.[119]

Some research that concentrates on particular geographic areas also carries relevance here, as it adds contextual understanding and insight on local adaptations of Salafi adherents and shaykhs to broader trends. Alexander Meleagrou-Hitchens' study on Salafism in the United States has particular pertinence, because Salafi-Madkhalism grew to have significant influence over American Salafism. Recent research on Salafism in the Maghreb is acutely salient for followers of Libyan Salafi dynamics, as it offers new insights into Salafi ideological and practical adaptations depending on their local environments.[120]

The second category of literature comprises a solid body of papers from think tanks and shorter analyses by scholars, most published after 2013 and focusing on Libyan developments after that date.[121] Some writings, such as those by Virginie Collombier, focus on a contrast between the Libyan Salafi-Madkhalis and "political Salafis,"[122] while others reference the first group in broader research about developments in Libya after Gaddafi. The latter research predominantly addresses (in)security challenges from a security sector reform lens; it conceptualizes the ideology of Salafi-Madkhalism as a threat to local attempts to build an army due to the alleged challenge of overseeing groups that derive their legitimacy from outside communal lines.[123]

These writings often confuse quietist Salafism with an implied mandate to remain quiet; however, quietist Salafism does contain activism. For instance, it empowers followers by urging them to join the Salafi mission and the spread of the call (da'wa). It therefore has an immediate social function of members not only showing their superiority but also exerting it in the public and private domains by means of walā' wa-l-'barā' (loyalty and disavowal) and hisba (community morals), or in even stronger terms by taking part in jihad (struggle). This chapters that follow describe how Libyan Madkhalis have been incorporated into the Libyan system and how this affected their development on a scale of possible moderation.

The Libyan Salafi-Madkhalis, like all religious movements, can rely on ambiguity and flexibility because, although they claim to be clear and rigid in their doctrine and their striving for purity, in practice they are malleable; this ambiguity allows adherents to be politically supportive of regimes as well as to reject them.[124] Different forms of walī al-amr are practiced by different Salafi-Madkhali groups in different parts of Libya. That being said, Libyan Salafi-Madkkhalis' military involvement in Libya's factional struggles and their willingness to take up arms to enforce Salafi norms have been successful since 2012. They look likely to continue to grow as a force.[125]

Framing of Ideological Enemies and Its Consequences

Libya has been and is defined by a plethora of Islamist and Salafi movements that are sometimes overlapping and occasionally defined by individuals switching from one to the other, both inside the Islamist and Salafi spaces and across them.

While Islamist groups have competed against each other by forming different parties, as occurred in the Libyan elections of 2012, the underlying bonds between Libyan Islamists are high. This may be unsurprising to anyone who has followed Islamist developments in the twenty-first century, but it is particularly noteworthy for Libya, which lived through multiple decades of severe repression under Gaddafi.[126] The resilience of these bonds is attributable in part to the shared experiences of oppression, with actors exhibiting solidarity with one another whether in exile or prison (most notoriously in Abu Salim).

For Western observers, the Gaid brothers and the Manchester Arena bombing are examples of how different generations of Libyan Islamists influenced one another and how radicalization can turn out differently even within a family. The Gaids initially turned to Islamism for the same reason (opposition to Gaddafi's regime) but ended on very different trajectories, with Abdelwahhab becoming an MP in the Libyan parliament and Mohamed Hassan acting as al-Qaʿida's second-in-command until his death in an American drone strike. These different journeys underline the dangers of treating the many strands of political Islam as a single radical threat. Violent jihadism is not an automatic result of becoming an Islamist.

Salman Abedi, the perpetrator of the Manchester Arena attack, became radicalized during a visit to his father in Libya at the age of sixteen and engaged in fighting alongside Islamist groups against Gaddafi. However, while his father was solidly embedded in the Islamist milieu of the LIFG and Libyan Muslim Brotherhood, Salman became attracted to more radical Salafi-jihadi forces. Ultimately, like many youngsters, Salman would reject the ideology of his father's generation in favor of IS-styled jihadism due to local but also international factors, such as the ongoing Syrian civil war and related Salafi-jihadi mobilization.[127]

Next to these practical insights into the international threat landscape that are captured when following Libyan developments, the Islamist and Salafi trajectories in the country have challenged existing conceptualizations around affiliated groups, such as the ongoing discussion about whether Salafi-Madkhalis are "quiet" and "apolitical." Most importantly for this book, Ansar al-Sharia and ISL had little interest in working with and through emerging political and social structures but instead pursued their own. This means that the groups were less receptive to Libyan developments and local concerns and failed to gather local support, at least in the mid to long term. These factors explain why Ansar al-Sharia and IS may be good case studies for scholars examining Salafi-jihadi governance models or the Salafi-jihadi threat landscape in Libya but do not lend themselves as well to a social movement theory–driven analysis examining two movements that both had an impact on Libya but were also affected by the society and structural strains around them.

It is worth noting that the capacity of both the Libyan Muslim Brotherhood and Libyan Salafi-Madkhalis to survive in a civil war environment that many analysts claim is largely defined by tribal loyalties makes both of them a significant part of the counterargument that in Libya, ideological fault lines matter.[128] The following chapters will show the significance of framing the enemy as threatening to movements' identities and survival to mobilize members into action. Even more, it pushed the Salafi-Madkhalis to expand their reach to new frontiers, such as supporting local service provision in parallel to their security enforcement in Sirte after the defeat of IS in December 2016.

Given all that has been described in this chapter, a comparison of a quietist group (Libyan Salafi-Madkhalis) with an Islamist group (Libyan Muslim Brotherhood) is useful because the focal point of the analysis is not their different ideological backdrops but rather their varying adaptations to the ongoing developments in (post-) revolutionary Libya. This book treads a fine line between acknowledging the importance of ideology, values, and meaning and demanding a sociological analysis of two movements that scholars of Islamic Studies might find counterintuitive to compare. At the same time, the Libyan Muslim Brotherhood and Libyan Salafi-Madkhalis share crucial characteristics that contribute to their comparability from an SMT perspective. They are both religious Islamic groups. They are both part of transnational movements. Both have history in Libya before 2011. And both were surprised by the 2011 revolution but sought to take advantage of following developments.

TWO

Surprised by Libya's Revolution

THIS CHAPTER EXPLORES how the Libyan Muslim Brotherhood and Libyan Salafi-Madkhalis took advantage of the declining state repression and increased access to political, security, and societal institutions with the removal of Gaddafi's regime. It homes in on the time of the revolution (January 2011–October 2011) as well as the first months of a nascent democracy (until spring 2012).

Both groups began by inserting their own members into existing structures and built new institutions where the fall of Gaddafi's regime left a tangible void, such as in the policing sphere.[1] The Libyan Muslim Brotherhood followed the anticipated trajectory for nonstate actors in previously repressive regimes after declining state repression and subsequent access to institutions, often subsumed under the umbrella term "democratization": They re-established themselves inside Libya and quickly founded a political party.[2] However, the Libyan Salafi-Madkhalis only benefited marginally at this point, as the group initially kept largely on the side of the Gaddafi regime, which ended up losing to the revolutionary forces. Interestingly, in this first phase, both movements behaved in a moderate manner by largely refraining from violence.

This chapter introduces evidence that aligns with Aisha Ahmad's theoretical thinking by demonstrating how the Libyan Salafi-Madkhalis' involvement in security institutions has grown more in importance than the Libyan Muslim Brotherhood's involvement in political institutions, in part because of the rise in importance of security institutions in postrevolutionary environments.[3] Overall, this chapter, along with chapters 3 and 4, shows the distinct contribution of social movement theory vis-à-vis political science: the emphasis on informal modes of participation and on the social and cultural embeddedness of formal institutions. By relying on social movement theory, chapters 2 through 4 demonstrate how the Libyan Salafi-Madkhalis' successes and the Libyan Muslim Brotherhood's loss of influence are related to the postrevolutionary environment in which, as David Meyer and Suzanne Staggenborg have argued, politics and the influence of the "state" permeate areas of life not usually considered political.[4] This explains in part why a quietist movement achieved political significance by October 2020, with its centrality in Libya's security apparatus, while an Islamist movement almost withered to irrelevance as it lost political positions and was blamed for the subsequent civil war.

The history of the Libyan Muslim Brotherhood's political involvement until the dissolution of the first postrevolutionary parliament in early 2014 confirms Arturo Escobar's argument concerning the importance of democratization as a facilitating factor for the growth of social movements.[5] John Markoff reasons that democratization provides opportunities for involvement in decision-making institutions, essential for the ability of a social movement to expand.[6] As mentioned, the Libyan Muslim Brotherhood was of marginal size in Libya until the fall of the Gaddafi regime. The group had mainly focused on escaping Gaddafi's surveillance and surviving thanks to the help of exiled members at the expense of establishing themselves and doing social work (daʿwa) inside Libya.

Notably, the reason for delaying its project (ruling over their nation) was not the absence of a clear ideological objective. Instead, the movement was calculating either to enter or reenter Libya under a reformed government led by Gaddafi's son and heir apparent, Saif al-Islam Gaddafi, or to wait until Gaddafi's potential downfall, when the regime would be removed altogether. While the Libyan Muslim Brotherhood was testing the waters with regard to the first option when they engaged in conversation with Saif al-Islam about the release of political prisoners in exchange for repentance for all engagement in Libya in 2005, the latter option was deemed so unrealistic that little preparation had been made. However, when this scenario did materialize, the Libyan Muslim Brotherhood was quick to return and mobilize its support structures in Tunisia and Egypt, eager to capitalize on the political plans to develop Libya into *their* version of a democracy.

During the 2011 uprisings and shortly after the new political system developed in Libya, the organization worked to get as many members as possible positioned in the new political structures of the transitionary council and the first parliament. This included building alliances with ideologically opposed factions and individuals such as Mohammed al-Magariaf, a Libyan politician who had lived in exile in the United States since the 1980s.

The movement acted in a calculating manner, weighing the advantages and disadvantages of advancing their influence in Libya and putting aside their ideological ideals of the country being ruled exclusively by Islamists. This supports Frances Fox Piven's and Richard Cloward's assertions that Islamist movements act according to system constraints and adapt instead of pushing for their ideological end goals and disregarding realistic deliberations about how to get there.[7] The declining repression after the fall of the Gaddafi regime and the increased access to political security and societal institutions for nonstate actors were game-changers for all Libyans, who had been ruled by a totalitarian pervasion of virtually all aspects of the state and society under Gaddafi.[8] The Libyan Muslim Brotherhood engaged in alliance-building and compromise in 2011 and early 2012. They saw this as a means to an end, the end being an Islamist-governed Libya that was part of an Islamist-governed region stretching from Egypt to Morocco.

The Libyan Muslim Brotherhood is part of an Islamist movement with previous experience in armed revolt. By contrast, the Libyan Salafi-Madkhalis, as a quietist movement, did not participate in uprisings against the ruling authority and therefore the abandonment of violence in behavior is largely anticipated and hence acts as control variable (see chapter 1).

For the movements' framing attempts, this chapter will focus on two key Libyan Muslim Brotherhood figures, Sadeq al-Gharyani and Nizar Kawan, and the central Libyan Salafi-Madkhali figure Rabi al-Madkhali. Diagnostic, prognostic, and motivational framing will be examined to provide a comprehensive analysis of whether or not the two groups exhibited ideological moderation over the course of the revolution. However, given the inherent call for action that the pursuit of violence entails, motivational framing is central to this chapter.

As noted in the introduction, ideological moderation includes accepting legitimacy in holding an alternative view. This chapter demonstrates that both groups considered their interpretation of the unfolding events and subsequent call for action supreme. Their framing leaves little room for alternative interpretations, so, while the call for violence was not the primary motivational frame for either the Libyan Muslim Brotherhood or the Libyan Salafi-Madkhalis, the groups' simultaneous intolerance toward opposing views indicates the grim prospects for further moderation over the following time periods. By including framing attempts of the movements' leaders, this book also shows how their vision can diverge from some members' actions—foregrounding the ongoing internal struggles between hardliners and more moderate members.

Utilizing Negotiation Skills and Existing Islamist Networks

The Libyan Muslim Brotherhood had refrained from establishing their own armed groups over the course of the revolution. In early 2011 they focused on negotiations with the Gaddafi regime, subsequently inserting members into the hastily established interim political institution the National Transitional Council (NTC).[9] Following Gaddafi's death in October 2011, they continued this path of moderation by founding a political party in order to align with the systemic requirements of a nascent democracy and by not violently opposing developments such as taking up arms to fight for an exclusively Islamist government. Therefore, and largely throughout the analyzed timeframe from January 2011 to summer 2013, the Libyan Muslim Brotherhood favored negotiations over violence.

This organization was largely in line with the first aspect of potential moderation—the abandonment of violence—as it worked with and through the existing structures by negotiating simultaneously with the Gaddafi regime and opposition politicians. It exploited existing resources in order to strategically position itself in anticipation of different outcomes for the protests. These included personal connections formed during the negotiations with Saif al-Islam Gaddafi from 2005 to 2008 as well as with opposition politicians, such as Mohammed al-Magariaf, during decades of exile in the United States.[10]

These negotiations varied, depending on the progress of the revolution and internal discussions among Libyan Muslim Brotherhood members about the brutality of the Gaddafi regime.[11] Often they took place outside of Libya, for instance in the UK, Turkey, and Switzerland, or via letter, as when in late January 2011 they mailed Saif al-Islam a "genuine reform agenda" for Libya in order to avoid a rebellion.[12] They also relied on phone diplomacy as described in the book by former higher education minister Aqeel Mohamed Aqeel, a relative of senior member Abdulrazzak al-Aradi. Aqeel called Saif al-Islam Gaddafi on February 15, 2011, warning of brewing violence and asking for dialogue. However, in this instance Saif Gaddafi allegedly responded by switching off his phone line.[13] On February 5, 2011, the group published a letter based on its meeting in Zürich, demanding that the Gaddafi regime "hold a comprehensive national conference adopting the demands of Libyans" and emphasizing their conviction that change was needed and could be achieved via discussion and gradual reform.[14]

In May 2011, four months after the start of the revolution, some Libyan Muslim Brotherhood members were still supportive of trying to find a compromise with the Gaddafi regime. Gaddafi's general secretary, Baghdadi Mahmoud, publicly stated that the government was "ready for dialogue" in June 2011—this after months of murdering protesters. He also revealed that the regime had been in dialogue with opposition members during talks in Egypt, France, Norway, and Tunisia.

For the revolutionaries on the ground in Libya, these claims were infuriating. In their eyes, all actors involved in these negotiations were discredited. Hence, Mustafa Abdeljalil, the former regime member turned leading revolutionary and one of the quoted members in those negotiations, quickly denied participation. Suleiman Abdelkader, former general guide of the Libyan Muslim Brotherhood, likewise told the *Asharq Al-Awsat* newspaper that Gaddafi was aiming to "drive a wedge in the national ranks."[15] Yet despite the denials, Ali al-Sallabi, an Islamist scholar, politician, and early member of the Libyan Muslim Brotherhood imprisoned under Muammar Gaddafi but central to the negotiations with Saif al-Islam Gaddafi about releasing Islamists from prison in the early 2000s, continued to engage with the regime. His contacts included a meeting in Cairo in May 2011 with regime representatives, including Abuzaid Dorda, a former Libyan ambassador to Italy. Sallabi claimed that he had the consent of Abdelkader, Nizar Kawan, later spokesperson for the Libyan Muslim Brotherhood's political party, and Ismail Gritli, a former Libyan Muslim Brother who now lives in Istanbul but emphasized his disengagement from the group when contacted for this book. (However, he had been particularly active in setting up the group's media channels.)[16]

A former senior member of the Gaddafi regime who defected in July 2011 stated in an interview that he was convinced that the Libyan Muslim Brotherhood was able at negotiating because the group apparently kept their cards close to their vest: "During the revolution I was convinced they wanted to compromise with us . . . only when it was all over did I realize that they were against us from the start."[17] What was identified as a negotiation tactic, however, was partially linked to internal discussions, as the group was initially reluctant to support the demonstrators in Libya.

This reluctance is in line with what Fang Deng describes as the "information gap," which creates an extra obstacle for individuals and groups to participate in what is deemed risky behavior, where the outcome and consequences for participants are uncertain (e.g., demonstrations calling for the fall of a regime).[18] For the Libyan Muslim Brotherhood, this information gap was intensified because the movement was largely missing informants on the ground. In January 2011, Suleiman Abdelkader defined the organization as having "no one inside the country and no more than 200 outside." Their initial reaction to the protests was reluctance due to lack of strength and uncertainty locally.[19] This was tied to their previous moderation in the early 2000s after largely futile attempts of Islamist coalitions attacking the Gaddafi regime in the previous decade, a stance still defining large parts of the Libyan Muslim Brotherhood in 2011. While former leader Mahmoud Nacua, who became ambassador to the UK in 2012, emphasized that their activities in the 1990s were marginal and focused on social events with little political vision or involvement in violence, the Gaddafi regime saw this differently and persecuted all Islamist opposition groups with the same vigor.[20] The regime arrested 152 members in 1998, including those in its leadership who did not escape abroad.

A few figures stand out in the Libyan Muslim Brotherhood's period of exile. Ashur Shamis, an early immigrant to the UK, became active in connecting like-minded Libyans and Muslim Brotherhood (MB) members exiled across Europe.[21] The Muslim Welfare House, which he founded in London in the 1970s, became vital in the growth of the international networks of the

MB, which tried repeatedly to venture back into their home countries.[22] Mohamed Abdelmalek played a crucial role for the Libyan Muslim Brotherhood over the decades. In contrast to Ashur Shamis, he only came to join the MB in the UK in 1983. Abdelmalek is a British national of Libyan origin and became a member of the organization's Shura council, its spokesperson, and its European representative. He represents a Westernized version of the MB. He was granted UK citizenship and "benefitted greatly from the democratic system that existed in this country and adopted it as [his] own within [his] organization."[23]

Abdelhakim Belhadj serves as a prominent example of the interconnectedness of Libyan expatriates and their Islamist commitment.[24] He helped to establish the Muslim Association of Britain, which brought together Islamists in the UK[25] In the years leading up to the 2011 revolution, the Libyan Muslim Brotherhood was thus present and active in Europe—probably more so than it was in Libya. At home, it was weakened to the point where it decided not to partake in the Libyan opposition conference in London in 2005 because it considered attendees' demands, such as the removal of Gaddafi, to be *too radical*.[26] Their persecution by the Gaddafi regime and entrenchment in democratic societies had given the movement a largely moderate disposition on the eve of the Libyan revolution.

Interviewees for this book who were asked about behavioral adaptations to internal structural changes in Libya that represented political opportunities expressed what seemed to be the primary sentiments of the Libyan Muslim Brotherhood at the beginning of the revolution: an abandonment of violence and a focus on negotiations to secure as many influential positions as possible as a response to the opening political system. The group would first negotiate with the waning regime, then engage with an emerging parallel political institution, the National Transitory Council (NTC).[27]

The First Revolutionary Political Body

The NTC was established on February 27, 2011, in Benghazi, Libya's largest eastern city and cradle of the uprisings. Mustafa Abdeljalil created the council, which was chaired by Mahmoud Jibril. Shortly before, both men had defected from their positions in the Gaddafi regime (as justice minister and head of the National Planning Council, respectively).[28] The NTC acted as an interim political body and was tasked with steering the transition, communicating with international actors on behalf of the Libyan people, and drafting concrete plans, such as a constitution for post-Gaddafi Libya.[29]

The significance of this council meant that the Libyan Muslim Brotherhood needed to have a foothold within it in order to stand a chance in implementing their vision of a Libyan government based on Islamic principles.[30] Instead of forcefully imposing themselves on the NTC, the group relied on negotiation again, albeit using quite aggressive tactics at times. Ali al-Sallabi appeared regularly on Al-Jazeera, a regional news channel devoted to covering the Libyan and regional uprisings in detail and that had international reach.[31] He heavily criticized the composition of the NTC as "illegitimate." Not only had it not been chosen by the Libyan people, he declared, but it was also not representative of Libya because it was dominated by representatives from the east, many with alleged secular backgrounds.[32]

The resulting implication—that Islamists were not represented on the NTC—was understood not only across Libya but also by outside observers. A senior UK diplomat emphasized as much: "We were really hoping at the time that at least some Islamists would be included . . . they seemed annoyed and aggressive and at the time we thought if they got involved in political bodies, they would refrain from violence . . . that was probably naïve."[33] Baron David Richards of Herstmonceux, former chief of the British defense staff, confirmed this opinion in 2016, reporting to the British Foreign Affairs Committee that while "the Muslim Brotherhood's participation in . . . Libya had only been indirect, or ambivalent," in hindsight the idea that Islamists were not participating and benefitting from the rebellion "was wishful thinking at best."[34]

Internally, the Libyan Muslim Brotherhood was quick to devise a strategy: In early March fifteen Libyan Islamists, representing the Libyan Muslim Brotherhood and the Libyan Islamic Fighting Group (LIFG), convened in Istanbul for consultations led by Ali al-Sallabi. Two participants—Abdulrazzak Al-Aradi, a senior Libyan Muslim Brother, and Nizar Kawan, later spokesperson for the Libyan Muslim Brotherhood's Justice and Construction political party—confirmed that the meetings were defined by lengthy and sometimes heated discussions and that all participants were in agreement that the NTC was not the right body for Libya. However, they decided that, for the time being, the Islamists should influence and work through the NTC rather than confront it.[35]

With its stance in favor of negotiation and working with and inside existing institutions rather than violence and direct confrontation, this behavior is in line with moderating behavior. It also confirms the theories of Francesco Cavatorta and Fabio Merone describing Islamist movements as rational calculators who are able to adopt a mid- to long-term vision; these groups do not push to enforce their end goals in a risky manner, but instead choose the most promising means—in this case, simultaneously negotiating and pressuring existing institutions while refraining from attacking them with violence.[36]

In May 2011, Abdeljalil confirmed that two Libyan Muslim Brotherhood representatives had been invited to join the political institution. The organization decided to send Alamin Belhaj, a senior Libyan Muslim Brother who had been involved with the movement for decades, together with al-Aradi. Both were also regional representatives of the capital Tripoli, a region proportionately underrepresented in the NTC when compared to population size.

Shortly after this, the Libyan Muslim Brotherhood was also able to secure representation by two senior members on the NTC's core body, the executive board, which was devised as the de facto government for the Libyan opposition. Abdullah Shamia, an economics professor, took charge of the economy portfolio, while scholar Salim Sheikhi was appointed to head up the *awqāf* (Islamic endowments) portfolio.[37] A female former NTC member confirmed, "As far as I'm aware the Ikhwan did not need to use violence [to attain positions in the institution, but when they joined] . . . I never felt like they were really part of it . . . they seemed to be their own organization . . . [but] wanted also to be included with us."[38]

This lingering suspicion foreshadows what will be uncovered throughout this book: that the Libyan Muslim Brotherhood's behavioral adaptations regarding cooperation and compromise foregrounded the movement's turn toward exclusionary politics. In this chapter, the findings largely confirm both Donatella della Porta and Charles Tilly's theories that social movements benefit from the opening of previously authoritarian systems by inserting members into key positions.[39] These findings are also largely in line with moderation.

Not all Libyan Muslim Brotherhood members were in agreement with the advocation of nonviolence or the predominant tactic of negotiation. Some regarded working with the Gaddafi regime as treacherous and the relatively small-scale support for the attacked demonstrators as insufficient.[40] There-fore, several Libyan Muslim Brothers on the emerging frontline in Beng-hazi decided to join the revolution's armed fight. Abdulrazzak al-Aradi was conceptually very uncomfortable with a violent revolution and pointed out that gradual change through society would be the movement's ideal sce-nario.[41] Ismail al-Sallabi, the brother of Ali al-Sallabi, who described him-self simply as "a student and businessman" (an understatement), was among the Islamist militia leaders. He started the Rafallah al-Sahati militia, named after one of the first protesters who died from Gaddafi fire, and turned it into one of the three most powerful armed groups in eastern Libya over the course of the revolution.[42]

Although the Libyan Muslim Brotherhood did not create its own militias during the 2011 revolution, multiple members participated in what Abu Kitef called "individual capacity."[43] The overarching militia structure under which many Brotherhood members joined the armed fight was the 17 February Martyrs Brigade. Kitef, a leading Libyan Muslim Brotherhood figure who was jailed for almost twenty years under Gaddafi, was a key leader of another large group, the Revolutionary Brigades Coalition.[44] One of the founders emphasized his conviction in an interview for this book that this military grouping was supposed to exist "solely to get rid of Gaddafi and his brutal regime"; however, it was "difficult to disband after the revolution."[45]

While several Libyan Muslim Brotherhood members confirmed in inter-views that they were hoping to produce change in a nonviolent manner and through negotiation, when pressed they also affirmed that having some members involved on the battlefield put the group in an advantageous posi-tion where they could secure key positions, such as Abu Kitef becoming deputy defense minister in the NTC.[46] These calculations were particularly prevalent in Tripoli.[47] The two central attempts at unifying various groups under a single authority failed. With the formation of the transitional government in November 2011, these attempts were derailed by emerging rival militia conglomerates whose affiliated governmental representa-tives handed them official status and salaries.[48] One of the leading actors in this shuffle was the Deputy Minister of the Interior, Omar al-Khadrawi, a Libyan Muslim Brother from Zawiya, a town west of Tripoli.[49] At the seat of the NTC in Benghazi, attempts at uniting fighting forces proved futile. Command structures were characterized by a divide between the defecting units of the former army, headed by Abdelfattah Younes, and the Islamist

Revolutionary Brigades. These dynamics exacerbated during the next analyzed timeframe. The Libyan Muslim Brotherhood's partial involvement
in armed groups fueled the competition.[50]

Making Islamist Sense of Libya's Political Turmoil:
From Jihad to Indecisiveness

In the months in and around the revolution, Libyan Islamists did their best
to interpret the changes for their members and neighbors. Shaykh Sadeq al-
Gharyani, a Libyan Muslim Brotherhood associate, was vocal on regional
and local news channels in attempts to explain and assign meaning to ongoing developments and to suggest solutions to the identified problems. In
Robert Benford and David Snow's terms, Gharyani exerted diagnostic and
prognostic framing attempts.[51]

The importance of Gharyani in Libya was highlighted in a survey in 2014:
Participants were asked to "name the most influential leaders in Libya, positive or negative," and Gharyani's name was mentioned in 60 percent of
responses. His dominance in Libya had become institutionalized in 2012
when he became Grand Mufti.[52] Other Libyan Muslim Brothers joined framing attempts, such as Nizar Kawan, who became a frequent guest on regional,
national, and international radio and television channels as well as in the
group's channels on social media. During the revolution, Kawan embarked
on a journey of becoming "one of new Libya's most recognizable faces." His
words carried meaning for many Libyans who opposed Gaddafi, and particularly for Libyan Muslim Brotherhood members.[53]

By March 2011 Kawan was spokesperson of the so-called 17 February
Coalition, composed of Libyan Muslim Brotherhood members and members
of the National Salvation Front for Libya (NSFL). He repeatedly used his political connections outside the country, as when formally announcing the
creation of the 17 February Coalition on Al-Jazeera in early April 2011.[54]

The importance of movements' formal and informal leaders for successful framing has been highlighted by Enrique Laraña, Hank Johnston, and
Joseph R. Gusfield, who have emphasized that individuals often join groups
or movements to express deeply held commitments, values, and beliefs and
are thus frequently motivated by more than just self-interest and a desire
to obtain benefits. As a consequence, movement leaders can mobilize

individuals to violent or nonviolent action by issuing a call to arms or a normative rationale for collective action ("motivational framing").[55]

With regard to high-risk activism, such as joining a revolution, which could result in a heavy potential backlash, movement leaders' ability to motivate people is paramount.[56] The promise of martyrdom has proven a potent prognostic and motivational framing by various scholars of Islamists and Salafists in the Middle East and the West.[57] In a framing attempt from late February 2011 that was analyzed for this book, Gharyani inserted additional meaning into the uprisings against Gaddafi with his declaration of a fatwa for jihad against the dictator on live television. To justify this call to action, he built his diagnostic frames on two foundations, the same ones that Nizar Kawan employed: the corruption of the Gaddafi regime and the physical support provided to it by external forces. But while Gharyani referenced religious sources (such as *hadiths*) in order to compare and relate moments from the early history of Islam with the present situation for Libyan Muslims, Kawan often relied on more recent historical accounts. Both worked to create a narrative that placed the violent oppression of the country's population by the Gaddafi regime in a broader context of Muslims struggling against unjust rulers. However, the solutions they offered following this analysis differed: Gharyani declared the right response to be picking up arms and dying for the cause of the revolution, while Kawan, at that time representing the Libyan Muslim Brotherhood leadership, remained indecisive. When Kawan did offer a solution, it was usually given in vague terms, such as "building a coalition" or "sticking together as Libyans."[58]

Some of the Libyan Muslim Brotherhood members interviewed for this book participated in violence and others refrained from it. Reviewing their responses, the different ways in which Gharyani and Kawan influenced group members become apparent. Overall, the analysis concludes that while the Libyan Muslim Brotherhood as an organization and especially its leadership largely refrained from calling for violent opposition against Gaddafi, figures such as Gharyani who were influential for many members filled this void and were key in mobilizing some Libyan Muslim Brotherhood members on the ground in Libya against the regime.

In his broadcasts and writings, Gharyani expressed the belief that Gaddafi had conducted a direct ideological attack on Islam by deliberately diluting and damaging the religion and Islamic identity of Muslims, and hence most of Libya.[59] Like many Islamic theologians in Libya, Gharyani needed to come to terms with the country's ideology under Gaddafi: that is, the dicta-tor's *Green Book* and his Islamic interpretations.⁶⁰ On the one hand, Ghary-ani agreed with one of Gaddafi's principal narratives, namely that Western secular culture was a threat to Islam and Muslims. On the other, he differed from Gaddafi and Islamic theologians in his approach to engage openly with politics. This was something his quietist counterparts pointedly avoided. Islam, according to Gharyani, was standing up to the Imperialist West. This attitude reverberates with Islamist thinking that views Islam as an all-encompassing political ideology forming the basis for opposition to the West.⁶¹

Gharyani was also comfortable making references to current political developments, such as the physical support of Gaddafi's regime by external forces, which he blamed for its survival in the summer of 2011. This helps us to comprehend further the reasons behind Gharyani's mass appeal to Liby-ans in those tumultuous months. He was addressing modern political issues and engaging with the outside world in a way that would attract people beyond the core audience and readership of his religious students.⁶²

Building on these foundations, Gharyani managed to elicit participation in the Libyan uprisings as a response to a perceived moral responsibility or commitment. In late February, two weeks after the first protests, Gharyani reportedly issued his live television anti-Gaddafi fatwa for jihad.⁶³ Joining the uprisings was now framed as the solution to the previously described problems (diagnostic frames), employing jihad as a prognostic frame and turning it into a motivational frame for some Libyan Muslim Brother-hood members who joined the violence in an individual capacity. One man who joined the uprisings against Gaddafi in March 2011 explained in an interview how these arguments had convinced him of his "duty" to take up arms, which Gharyani had "explained very well." However, the inter-viewee expected this episode to be unique and was hoping that after "we defeated the unjust Gaddafi regime . . . everything [would] be better."⁶⁴

Gharyani claimed this moral duty by arguing that "what the regime is now commanding and doing, using thousands of foreign mercenaries, most of whom are non-Muslims . . . is a matter that no one disputes . . . as [one of] the greatest sins."⁶⁵ With this he also expanded on his previous modes of explanation: namely, blaming foreign/external actors and Gaddafi for Lib-ya's ills. This rationale was a popular one, particularly in Libya where Gad-dafi had been fearmongering for decades, warning of foreign invasions.⁶⁶

Fighting Gaddafi and his foreign backers was mentioned by several interviewees who participated in the 2011 revolution. When questioned about the fact that the revolutionaries also had considerable support from foreign actors, the interviewees claimed that this was different, without much elaboration.[67] Gharyani had also declared the glory of dying for the cause of the revolution, which he explained as citizens demanding their rights peacefully and acting in legitimate self-defense after the violent response of the regime. He affirmed in his fatwa that "whoever was killed by the ruler . . . was at the highest levels of martyrdom."[68]

Gharyani's comments in 2011 hint at what turned into a crucial framing competition between Islamists, activist Salafis, and quietist Salafis in Libya until the current day over the right Islamic response to ongoing developments. That spring, this amounted to the ongoing protests and rebellion against the Gaddafi regime.

Gharyani's reference to quietist Salafi preachers and especially Rabi al-Madkhali, whose teachings are renowned for their steadfast belief in the ruling authority (wālī al-amr), was relatively unconcealed when he warned of "politicized fatwas . . . [also] from outside the country . . . under the pretext of obedience to the ruler and the inadmissibility of disobeying them." Again, he relied on religious sources and quoted the hadiths, explaining that the described interference was wrong because their prophet commanded listening to and obeying the ruler, but that the nature and limits of this obedience were defined by being in favor of the ruled: "There is no obedience to a creation if it is in disobedience to the creator." With this, he also argued that obeying Gaddafi's orders was impermissible because "obedience is only known, and anyone who shoots a single bullet at his countrymen is considered a deliberate murderer." Gharyani further aimed his address at quietist Salafism students when he cited fatwas by Shaykh Abdel Aziz bin Baz and Shaykh al-Albani on "those who denied the Sunnah and mocked their prophet . . . [such was the case of Gaddafi] in many of his sermons and recorded in some books, such as his saying 'Muhammad is nothing but a postman,' wondering: 'Is this the guardian who must be obeyed'?"[69] While none of the Salafis interviewed for this book claimed that Gharyani's discussion of wālī al-amr had any effect on them or had even influenced them to join the rebellion, the discourse around conditions for wālī al-amr as well as the designation of the "right" wālī al-amr heightened over the years, with

Libya losing its authoritarian leader and splintering into regions with different authorities.[70]

A central concept in this regard is Madkhali's conceptualization of wālī al-amr, which states that the fact that a person is in power proves Allah's desire for them to possess ruling authority. This argument makes the cleric a natural ally for any system with a player who is determined to stay in power. For Madkhali, this determination to obey the ruling authority comes from the threat of *fitna* (chaos), with violent uprisings being one of the main initiators. Indeed, we will see this inter-movement framing competition turn into an intra-movement competition, one increasingly defined by referencing local sources and circumstances instead of religious framing coming from Rabi bin Hadi al-Madkhali in Saudi Arabia.

Nizar Kawan's approach to framing is driven by more recent history than Gharyani's religious sources and historic tales of their prophet. As well as referencing Libyan history, during the revolution Kawan also relied on other instances of Muslim suppression and corruption of a state, such as in Tunisia under Ben Ali.[71] His narrative placed the contemporary Libyan developments of violent oppression by the Gaddafi regime in a broader context of Muslims struggling against unjust rulers.

Kawan's main diagnostic frames aligned with Gharyani's. The repression and violent revolution in Libya, he noted, evolved around two core topics: the cultural and ideological corruption of the Gaddafi regime and its physical support by external forces that had worked to suppress local expressions of disaffection with the Gaddafi regime.[72] Here, Kawan was firmly in line with many exiled Libyan Islamists who believed that Islam in Libya was deeply corrupt under Gaddafi's "final authority" on all matters in the nation, including religion. Kawan had been considering a return to Libya for years; however, the near-extinction of the Libyan Muslim Brotherhood there meant that overthrow of the regime was highly unlikely, verging on impossible.[73] This practical assessment seemed detached from the conviction of the righteousness of removing Gaddafi for the sake of a new, just Islamic system.

On the Turkish-based media channel Al-Manara Media, established on YouTube in October 2010 with over nine thousand followers to advance reform in Libya, Kawan was featured several times during the revolution. There, he emphasized that Libya and Islam in Libya were under attack and had been for several decades under Gaddafi. Libyans needed to be freed of oppression just as their neighboring North Africans were demanding in Tunisia.[74] He was also comfortable accusing the external forces of backing the Gaddafi regime for their own reasons and disregarding Libya's best interests. However, Kawan seemed aware in his messaging that there was a fine line between blaming these outsiders for Libya's problems and relying on other external forces to drive the reform agenda forward.[75]

Inside the Muslim Brotherhood generally, discrepancies emerged in what was considered the correct external support for the Libyan rebels. In early March 2011, a prominent member of the Egypt-based group's Executive Bureau, Essam al-Erian, demanded that "the Arab League and Arab countries" needed to step up their game in Libya "to end the crisis" while simultaneously warning Western countries away from "interfering in Libya's affairs." He argued that interference from beyond the Arab world was "motivated by interest," whereas Arabs were better equipped to help each other. However, key members of the Libyan Muslim Brotherhood, such as Kawan, endorsed opinions such as the Muslim Association of Britain's declaration that they were "in agreement with the enforcement of the no-fly zone in Libya, by Britain and its allies in order to protect Libyan civilians from being murdered by its cruel dictator Gaddafi."[76]

This ambivalent picture helps us to better understand the issues the Libyan Muslim Brotherhood was dealing with in early 2011. These hampered their success in creating compelling prognostic and motivational frames, therefore diminishing their persuasion of many Libyans to join the revolution with the group's visions in mind. It is unclear whether this persuasion was the aim at this stage or if the mainly exiled members of the Libyan Muslim Brotherhood were more cautiously watching the protests and trying to figure out how best to insert themselves, a reversal of the direction of influence from the movement's framing influencing the protests. Given the Libyan Muslim Brotherhood's initial remoteness from Libya, the latter appears to be the case.

Still, in order to escape the unfair nature of Gaddafi's current regime, Kawan was in accordance with other Islamic thinkers, including Gharyani, that a new system should be established that was built on Islam. As already noted, the men's proposed solutions differed, with Gharyani calling for armed revolution and martyrdom and Kawan hesitant in arguing for a clear course of action. Instead, Kawan largely was stuck in condemning the violence. He accused Saif al-Islam Gaddafi of spreading disinformation and stoking fear and identified the alleged roots of Libya's ills, but rarely moved from this diagnostic framing into more proactive prognostic or motivational framing attempts.[77] Many Libyan Muslim Brotherhood members at the time were acutely aware that in order to continue lines of communication and cooperation with Western countries, many of which had been havens for them in previous years, they would need to avoid the detrimental call for violence and terms like "jihad."[78]

This could be considered a unique feature of the Libyan branch of the Muslim Brotherhood due the dominance of its exiled members. Just two years earlier Mohamed Mahdi Akef, chairman of the MB, was adamant that in Palestine, "jihad is the path" and that the Muslim Brotherhood would continue to "diligently advise the entire Muslim nation . . . [how] to do their part for the liberation of the blessed land of Palestine and Al-Aqsa Mosque."[79]

James Jasper and Jane Poulsen have called instances such as the Libyan protests and the regime's response "moral shocks" of the type that can trigger armed mobilization, irrespective of the costs and benefits that could affect those involved.[80] A progression toward high-risk activism was often a result of successful framing (such as Gharyani's making it a moral obligation that also demanded self-sacrifice). The positive reception of Gharyani's message was not entirely a consequence of the frame's intrinsic appeal. Rather, it hinged on a set of conditions removed from, and hence external to the content itself. Examples include (1) the brutal crackdown by the Gaddafi regime, which made violent resistance necessary for the mere survival of any protests; (2) the credibility and effectiveness of Libyan Muslim Brotherhood agents and modes of transmission; and (3) the organization's reinforcement through militia leaders and members at the grassroots level.

As Carrie Wickham has described with regard to mobilization of Egyptian students in Cairo, framing "successes" like these helps to "set the groundwork for riskier political contention," such as violence.[81] The Libyan Muslim Brotherhood's ideological moderation by the time of the Libyan revolution was quite strong and intertwined with the movement's closeness to some Western forces. This worked to inhibit calls for violence from their leadership. In her studies of Islamists in Jordan, Janine Clark names what seem to be red lines for movements in their framing "ideological roadblocks."[82]

It can be argued that the call for violence was an ideological roadblock for large parts of the Libyan Muslim Brotherhood, at least in this first time-frame under analysis. However, influential figures were key to mobilizing other members on the ground in Libya against Gaddafi.

When "Staying Quiet" Turns Into Support for Violence

For the Libyan Salafi-Madkhalis, involvement in the initial protests against Gaddafi would have been very surprising behavior: This strictly quietist group considered him their ruling authority (wālī al-amr). As a matter of fact, one Libyan Salafi-Madkhali in Tripoli was convinced that "not only myself but many of us thought the protesters would go away . . . I mean they were crazy . . . what did they even want? . . . we didn't trust any of them . . . we wanted stability and that was with Gaddafi."[83]

Most Libyan Salafi-Madkhalis' behavior in 2011 was in line with their quietist ideology, which warns against violence and emphasizes the belief in stability and social order. Their leaders at the time included founder Rabi bin Hadi al-Madkhali and Majdi Hafala, also known as Abu Musab, a prominent but not senior shaykh who epitomized the movement inside Libya to a certain extent. These men sprang into action at the start of the conflict, assuring their members that disobedience or rebellion against the ruling authority created strife and chaos (fitna). The group's behavior was pointedly captured by the acquired nickname "stay-at-homers."[84]

Whereas Islamists, such as the Libyan Muslim Brotherhood, and Salafi-jihadis, such as Ansar al-Sharia, were jostling about how to best maneuver in a changing Libya and employed both violent and nonviolent tactics, Libyan Salafi-Madkhalis were largely trying to ignore the uprisings and hence shut their door to the outside world. This, however, was not what the Gaddafi regime had in mind; instead, they contacted quietist Salafis both inside and outside the country in attempts to deny the protesters religious legitimacy and to advocate for stability, which could presumably only be secured if Gaddafi remained in power. In Libya, the regime's hopes for success in this quest were largely centered on Gaddafi's son, Saadi Gaddafi, who had previously aspired to be the de facto arbiter for Salafism in Libya. Repercussions of this are still felt today, as some Libyans refer to the Libyan Salafi-Madkhalis as "Saadi's Faction" (Jamaʿat Saadi).[85]

One Libyan Salafi shaykh based in Tripoli stated in our interview that Saadi Gaddafi began attending the Issa al-Awsi mosque in Mansoura and the Bennabi mosque in the early 2000s; both are popular among quietist Salafis in Tripoli.[86] In addition, the shaykh emphasized, Saadi seemed "personally committed to the Salafi way." The younger Gaddafi traveled to Saudi Arabia (where he allegedly also met Shaykh al-Madkhali) and Jordan many times and hosted Saudi and Yemeni quietist scholars in Libya.[87]

In the eyes of another Libyan Salafi scholar in Tripoli, it was partially clear at the time and obvious retroactively that Saadi Gaddafi becoming Salafi was part of the regime's agenda: Among the brothers, Saif al-Islam was supposed to "control the Islamists" and Saadi to "control us [quietist Salafis]" so "in case there [was] any problem brewing with the Ikhwan, Saif al-Islam should hear about it and if there was anything with regard to us, Saadi [was] going to hear about it."[88]

Gaddafi Coopting the Madkhalis

In 2011, the Libyan government began to exploit this nurtured relationship. The official Gaddafi regime channels began broadcasting Salafi-Madkhali voices, such as Majdi Hafala's.[89] However, the majority of Libyans did not consider Salafi-Madkhalis to be main religious authorities. In the previously mentioned 2014 survey in which participants were asked to "name the most influential leaders in Libya, positive or negative," Sadeq al-Gharyani dominated in the responses, identified by 60 percent. After him came Ali al-Sallabi (32 percent), followed by Abdelhakim Belhadj (13 percent). No fewer than 162 other religious leaders were mentioned as having influence at a local or national level, but most of these were mentioned by fewer than ten interviewees.

Hafala's authority was much more strongly based on other figures, particularly non-Libyan Islamic scholars with whom he had personal links.[90] Unofficial biographies on Salafi online fora highlight the main source of his authority as a preacher as his embeddedness in networks linked to Saudi Arabia and Yemen. This is characteristic of the Salafi trend, which is largely based on the informal relationship between the teacher and the student.[91] Either way, in 2011, Hafala and al-Madkhali made sure to proclaim the unrighteousness of participation in the protests, which would contribute to instability and fitna.[92]

Saadi Gaddafi himself tried hard to show his quietist credentials and commit to further support of quietist Salafis in Libya, painting the regime in a pious light. One video circulated widely on regime channels as well as YouTube shows him emphasizing the emerging importance of the Salafi daʿwa (call), which he claims had been "chained." He praises books about *tafsir* (exegesis), particularly those by Shaykh Muhammad Nasir al-Din al-Albani and Muhammad bin Uthaymin.[93] Al-Albani, considered "one of the greatest hadith scholars" of the twentieth century, is credited with a revolutionary interpretation that insisted (in opposition to the Salafi religious establishment in Saudi Arabia) on studying all existing hadiths. This led him to proclaim fatwas that ran counter to the wider Islamic consensus.[94]

In an effort to shore up support, the regime also relied on external quietists, such as Yaḥya al-Hajuri, head of the Dar alHadith institute in Dammaj (Yemen), who broadcast on his website his answer to a telephone call that he received in late May 2011 from Gaddafi's son. In this conversation, the Salafi cleric's stance: He highlighted that the Arab uprisings were a "crime" controlled by "Freemasons . . . and Jews."[95] Therefore, the behavior and framing of quietist Salafis in Libya and abroad were in line with the Gaddafi regime. They refrained from protesting and advocated for the rest of the country to do the same, relying on a mixture of religious sources and drawing a line between historical enemies of Islam and alleged current ones.

Harsh Criticism of Protests Against Gaddafi

The framings by Rabi bin Hadi al-Madkhali and other Salafi-Madkhali leaders were clear-cut. Involvement in the demonstrations was out of the question. Diagnostic framing was central to the shaykh's framing attempts, with prognostic and motivational framing secondary. The centrality of Madkhali for quietist Salafis is discernible up to the present day, with quietist preachers still traveling to Saudi Arabia to meet him and to ask for advice.[96] Therefore, Shaykh Madkhali falls into the category of what Laraña et al. call "formal leaders" of social movements, who have proven particularly successful in attaching meaning to ongoing developments due to an inherent legitimacy and authority that precedes their respective utterances.[97]

As mentioned, quietist Salafis were employed by the regime and so Shaykh Madkhali was featured on Libyan media. In addition, he populated his own home page and associated social media channels with sermons and opinions. In his 2011 framing attempts, Madkhali was steadfast in his condemnation of the protests against Gaddafi as *fitna* and *miḥna*; both terms invoke troubling, divisive times for Muslims from early Islamic history.[98] Furthermore, he showed no signs of ideological adaptation or reflection even when the violence of the Gaddafi regime increased exponentially. In order to justify these interpretations, he built his diagnostic frames on two foundations: (1) the categorical misdeed of revolting against the ruling authority; and (2) the misguidedness of the protesters, who were corrupted by the West.

Similar to Sadeq al-Gharyani, Rabi bin Hadi al-Madkhali often referred to religious sources, but at the same time compared and related moments from the early history of Islam to the situation of contemporary Libyan Muslims. In addition, he proved apt at referencing current developments and painting them in a harrowing light, creating a narrative of dark times that awaited Libya if the protests continued. However, the solutions he offered were uninspiring in the sense that there were few options other than refraining from participation. In my interviews with Libyan Salafi-Madkhalis, very few of whom participated in the violence, with the majority refraining from joining the revolution in any capacity, it was obvious that Madkhali's clear guidance was always well understood. However, for some group members, developments on the ground pushed them to the breaking point, causing them to act in a manner that they saw as being in discordance with the religious guidance. (A few of these even claimed not to have been advised on this subject.)

Madkhali believed that, by revolting against the Gaddafi regime, the protesters were also attacking Islam (not to mention their categorical misdeed of disobeying the ruling authority). Their extremely loyal devotion to walī al-amr has been described as setting followers of Madkhali apart from those of other quietist preachers.[99] The Libyan developments of 2011 are a case in point. On the one hand, his orders to refrain from participation in the protests are unsurprising, as his previous quietist teachings foreshadowed them.[100] On the other hand, the demonstrations were a new challenge for Madkhali because they were the first large-scale popular uprisings in many North African countries for decades.[101] However, he believed that staying loyal to the ruling authority was paramount and announced that "the people never benefited from revolting against the rulers . . . and the people of Madinah's revolt against [their ruler] resulted in great evils." In a sermon published on his website on March 17, 2011, Madkhali reiterated the righteousness of "the ruler," who "must advise . . . the nation to apply the rulings of God and implement the law of God." Potential wrongdoing by the ruler should not be for the people to judge and act upon, but instead, "if the ruler does not advise the nation, then God has forbidden him from paradise."[102]

The protests and rebellion in Libya were therefore misguided in his estimation and participation was to be seen as a deviation from the will of God, who would judge the ruler himself. Madkhali took this general sentiment further and evoked a grim future for Libya if its leader was deposed by relying on the allegedly abysmal state of Iraq after Saddam Hussein's removal. In addition, he reminded his followers that "the ruler of Tunisia left [but] chaos remains . . . [and only] God knows how things will end. I don't think it will end with the rule of Islam." In other words, he told his listeners, exposing the existing ruling authority might not lead to the ultimate desired outcome: the word of God ruling the land of Islam.[103]

Madkhali also condemned the protesters for being misguided and corrupted by heretical ideas from the West. In another sermon, published on October 4, 2011, titled "Warning Against Sedition and Democracy and Its Derivatives," he alerted his listeners that "one of the most dangerous innovations coming to the lands of Islam is democracy and the call for freedom that was invented by the atheists of the West and their followers."[104] In this sermon, Madkhali achieved two things: He painted democracy (and with it a whole plethora of liberal concepts and practices such as freedom, a civil state, and elections) as innovation (bida') and thus foreign to the Muslim world. Any innovation was misguided because, he argued, democracy was inherently tied to moral and practical corruption. He elaborated that "the West exported this democracy . . . based on lies, betrayals, and bribes." He was concrete on who to blame for these unholy uprisings as "this act of theirs is only a service from them to their masters, the Masons, and the atheists of the West, whether they feel it or not."[105]

Building on these foundations, Madkhali managed to draw a line between participation in the Libyan uprisings and simultaneous support for the West and un-Islamic principles and practices.[106] The resulting solution (prognostic frames) to the constructed meaning of the protests (diagnostic frames) was therefore straightforward: Stay away and return to studying Islam.

Picking up one of the most popular demands of the protesters—"justice"—Madkhali argued that in democracy, there was no justice, only "injustice and darkness on top of each other, as true freedom in Islam liberates a person from all the slavery permitted by democracy and other pre-Islamic legislation."[107] Therefore, calling for democracy meant simultaneously calling for injustice. With this statement, he managed a strategic framing attempt. Some Libyan Salafi-Madkhalis could identify with the calls for justice while being skeptical of demands for democracy. By linking the two, Madkhali ensured that his followers felt further discouraged from joining the protests as they would not want to advocate for democracy.[108]

In early October (just three weeks before Gaddafi was killed in Sirte), Madkhali answered questions via his website about the correct, virtuous behavior in the current Libyan circumstances. He began with a rhetorical question, asking if the fighters were better than Ali ibn Abi Talib, the Prophet's cousin, whose closeness to the Prophet and marriage to his daughter Fatimah inspired some followers to see him as their leader after Muhammad's death.[109] He added that the Prophet's companions would not have joined in these types of fighting and elaborated on the questions of whether "the Brothers should go and fight in Sirte" and if there was a wālī al-amr over Libya and if that wālī al-amr required them to defend Gaddafi in Sirte and Bani Walid and Sebha (where they would be fighting fellow Salafis and Muslims). Shaykh Madkhali believed there was no reason to fight, as the "only objective of fighting that is permitted in Islam is to fight to raise the word of God." However, the Libyan situation portrayed a mixture of other objectives that were earthly (and hence of minor motives, including democracy promotion). In Madkhali's estimation, no true Salafis would take up weapons.[110]

Implicit in this framing was also his proposed solution: studying Islam. For Madkhali, taking refuge in Islam meant to concentrate on prayers asking God for help, guidance, or forgiveness (du'a) according to the obligations (farā'idh) and the optional prayers (rawatīb) so that "Allah removes from you what has afflicted you of the fitna." Furthermore, if one felt threatened or even pulled into the protests, one should "stay [at] home and firmly close the doors. And whoever forces and enters upon you . . . repel him . . . with the least force and if he rejects it then repel him with what you are able." In case one was injured or even killed in this exchange, the victim (if he was Muslim) would be a martyr.[111]

Interestingly enough, Madkhali relied on blaming foreign powers and influence, just like Gharyani. However, the two leaders attributed this to opposite sides of the revolution: Gharyani blamed Libya's violence on external actors backing Gaddafi, whereas Madkhali blamed foreign forces for corrupting Libyans and fueling the protests. Both picked a popular rationale—namely, diverting attention from national ills by blaming outside forces. This frame has survived in Libya to the present day.

In George Joffé's assertion that the Libyan uprisings in 2011 set themselves apart from those in Tunisia and Egypt, one primary reason was the lack of any "incipient precursors to social movements" in Libya. The country had never adopted the liberalized autocracy pattern typical of other North African states; instead, the *jamāhīrīyah* (Gaddafi's political and social system) tolerated no competition.[112] In 2011 this meant that many Libyans for the first time were pushed toward having an opinion on the state of the country or the righteousness of the revolutionaries or were even asked to join the revolution.

While in religious terms the nonparticipation in the protests was a clear matter for Madkhali and most of his followers, the local circumstances led to a mismatch between individuals' experiences and Madkhali's guidance from Saudi Arabia. As a consequence, his framing attempts, especially prognostic framing, were only partially successful: Some Libyan Salafi-Madkhalis decided to ignore his advice and participate in different capacities in the revolution.

However, many Libyan Salafi-Madkhalis did not need convincing. Their behavior at the beginning of the uprisings was in line with the quietist predisposition to refrain from violence. A few weeks later, they were more incorporated into the regime, especially its propaganda apparatus,[113] but Libyans did not seem susceptible to "the men with beards," as several interviewees involved in the revolution described.[114] While the Libyan Salafi-Madkhalis' behavior over this timeframe was moderate, the group was not very influential during the revolution.

At this point in time, the Libyan Salafi-Madkhalis had not benefited from the opening of institutions, as they were not pursuing involvement in the potential new reality of a post-Gaddafi Libya. In addition, an analytical conundrum presented itself: While their organization's influential figures declared the rebellion wrong in their diagnostic framing and hence spoke against joining the protests (prognostic frame), they simultaneously and implicitly supported violent action, namely the brutal crackdown by the

Gaddafi regime. However, with the protests developing into a revolution and unarmed protesters subjected to indiscriminate violence, individual Libyan Salafi-Madkhalis began to participate in the uprising. These behavioral adaptations appeared in Tripoli and Zawiyya, the latter of which was hard-hit by Gaddafi's security forces.[115] Some group members also picked up arms and, similar to the Libyan Muslim Brotherhood, became part of militias formed in their respective neighborhoods. One Libyan Salafi-Madkhali who joined a revolutionary brigade in Zawiyya explained: "I joined my brothers in my neighborhood to defend ourselves . . . Gaddafi was out of control."[116]

After Gaddafi was overthrown and a nascent democracy started emerging, most Libyan Salafi-Madkhalis did not participate in the new participatory politics, either by voting in the election or joining a party to compete in the election. With this, the organization remained fiercely quietist and set itself apart from regional trends of Salafi reconfiguration, such as the Yemeni quietists who founded a Salafi party in March 2012, the Rashad Union (Ittiḥād al-Rashād).[117] Reasons for this can be found in the lack of internal organization in Libya. The Libyan Salafi-Madkhalis in 2011 were still largely made up of decentralized structures with no acclaimed and senior leaders locally; instead, they were reliant on Shaykh Madkhali in Saudi Arabia.

The actual removal of Gaddafi and with him the wālī al-amr left many group members puzzled and led to an inward turn for the movement, with a new focus on neighborhood needs instead of the organization's growth (see chapter 3).[118] Rabi bin Hadi al-Madkhali continued to warn against entanglements in democracy and Hafala to advise young Libyan not to engage in politics, saying that the best way to "do politics is to withdraw from politics."[119] In other words, these leaders advocated for an inward turn for the movement and behavior that, on the one hand, did not advocate violence but, on the other, was at odds with the demands of the existing system (a nascent democracy). Therefore, Libyan Salafi-Madkhalis stood at odds with the emerging structures in Libya; they largely refused to integrate into the new system and instead opposed it, albeit primarily in a nonviolent manner.

Libyan Salafi-Madkhalis who remained close to the Gaddafi regime can actually be seen as cooperating with a heavily violent actor, pointing to additional flaws in the inclusion-moderation hypothesis as it formulates ideal preconditions that are often difficult to realize in practice: namely, the baseline that a movement needs to be incorporated into an aspiring pluralistic system to become more moderate, which the Gaddafi regime was not.

New and Old Cleavages

This chapter engaged with what Timothy Mitchell called the "common sense distinction" between the material and the ideological world by juxtaposing the ideological sense-making (framing) of the movements' leaders with the actions of some of the members.[120] It is a puzzle how to know definitively whether actors really mean what they say. Inherent in this theoretical exercise is the possibility that behavior can be opposite to "true" ideological commitments. Here, Islamists often carry the legacy of "historical bad guys" who need to be seen with skepticism about, for example, their expressed democratic commitments.

As Jillian Schwedler explains, this then turns into a catch-22 situation because, if Islamists were irrational ideological fanatics, there would be "no way of understanding or predicting their actions; yet if they are rational and strategic—something of a promotion from being blind fanatics—then they must also be capable of deceit and therefore should not be taken at their word."[121]

This book works to remove itself from these analytical confines by adding empirical research that provides nuance in the sense that its findings do not fit well into this behavioral-ideological binary. Instead, the actions and framing attempts of the two movements show that some behaviors can be categorized as strategic and rational responses to political opportunities or incentives; others are coded more as manifestations of ideology, but many are hard to pin down to either. Furthermore, as the intra-movement framing competition of Gharyani and Kawan has shown, on both levels (action and framing) it is hard to find a consensus that would define the entire movement.

It is true that much of the literature assessing the inclusion-moderation hypothesis is defined by a normative bias in the sense that scholars *want* Islamists to become (more) moderate. This tendency heightened after the Arab uprisings in 2011, when analysts were eager to watch how different

Islamist groups would engage in "real democratic processes" and not only in the quasi-authoritarian elections that defined the region for decades. However, this hope was quickly crushed in Libya when the country descended into civil war only two years after the revolution.

Despite Francesco Cavatorta and Fabio Merone's important theoretical contribution, the Libyan Muslim Brotherhood case study suggests that the calculations of an Islamist group are limited to a relatively short timeframe and, in this case, thwarted by high-level discussions among the group's senior members instead of broader discussions and inclusion in the local population.[122] That being said, several preconditions defined the Libyan Muslim Brotherhood compared to other Muslim Brotherhood branches, including (1) its strong reliance on exiled members to survive during the Gaddafi years; (2) the corresponding gap between many experiences by its members versus other Libyans; and (3) its image as Libya's most prominent enemy that Gaddafi had nurtured.[123]

The chapter that follows adds to these points. The Libyan Muslim Brotherhood's recent history was detrimental to the movement on the ground: Many members' experiences in Western contexts did not lead to a moderate Libyan branch of the Muslim Brotherhood after 2011. Despite the risks involved, the organization vigorously pursued its strategy of disenfranchising political opponents by disrupting their political actions and pushing for exclusionary legislation, such as the Political Isolation Law. They considered it important both to dominate political institutions and to limit Libyans' options to a binary choice between the Libyan Muslim Brotherhood as the "real" alternative or corrupted former regime officials. This left people with no choice but to align themselves with one side or the other, a strategy that ultimately contributed to civil war.[124]

For the Libyan Salafi-Madkhalis, the idea that democratization leads to the moderation and related growth of a social movement seems counterintuitive, for they are ideologically opposed to participatory politics in a democratic manner. Hassan Mneimneh and Abdelghani Mimouni have demonstrated that such quietist loyalist movements benefit from being incorporated into a partially repressive regime, as occurred in Saudi Arabia and Egypt.[125] However, despite this relevant academic contribution, which explains the growth and expansion of what was originally a Saudi movement to countries like the United States and Libya, this case study of the Libyan Salafi-Madkhalis suggests that the group has benefited from local democratization not because it could help them expand into the developing political institutions, but rather because Libya's democratization was neither stable nor inclusionary. Therefore, the group's strategy of denouncing and discouraging involvement in electoral politics proved beneficial. Furthermore, its local approach concentrating on security provision has been strategically successful behavior. These steps of inclusion into what was supposed to be a democratic system, however, have not led to their adopting moderating behavior. Instead, Libyan Salafi-Madkhalis have grown more exclusionary and uncompromising the more influence in the security institutions they have amassed.

As shown in the literature review, many scholars, including Jillian Schwedler, Janine Clark, Raquel Ojeda Garcia, Günes Murat Tezcür, and Joas Wagemakers have examined whether groups turn moderate over time (such as before and after elections).[126] Some attention has been paid to examining how the groups' composition affects this development. Such factors are particularly important when the local environment is recovering from a decades-long repressive regime that often framed its policies as a fight against "imperialist outside invaders."[127]

Chapter 3 illustrates the various strategies and tactics used by the Libyan Muslim Brotherhood to entrench themselves in postrevolutionary Libya and analyzes the result as the movement lost positions and was ultimately blamed for the outbreak of civil war, a legacy from which the group continues to suffer. It uses variations of established social movement theory to assess the potential growth of a movement after democratization in the country and the related inclusion-moderation hypothesis by examining cooperation. While doing so, it highlights the impact of the group's removed approach and increasingly exclusionary politics, as well as its internal dynamics, showing that it failed to become more moderate over the course of analysis due to a mixture of wrong calculations and historical baggage.

Once part of the system, the Libyan Muslim Brotherhood was mostly concerned with protecting its own position instead of creating an inclusionary political system built on compromise. Its tactics inside the postrevolutionary political institutions align with what Lucia Ardovini observed with regard to the Egyptian Muslim Brotherhood after 2011: a largely self-absorbed movement that smelled danger at every corner and hence remains inward-looking and guarded.[128] The way the Libyan Muslim Brotherhood tried to establish itself after the fall of Gaddafi mirrors that: Instead of understanding that large parts of the population were wary of a new political elite and hence of parties, they rushed to establish a party with a big fanfare and neglected to build societal, localized support that could outlive an electoral cycle.[129]

THREE

Securing Interests While Hurting Libya

IN MARCH 2013 ARMED groups entered the Libyan parliament to force voting behavior into line with the Political Isolation Law, a major initiative led by the Justice and Construction Party (JCP). Before then, this political party of the Libyan Muslim Brotherhood had been largely detached from the enduring street violence and instead had focused on positioning itself in the nascent political institutions of post-Gaddafi Libya. The Political Isolation Law aimed to outlaw the participation of previous Gaddafi regime officials in postrevolutionary political institutions. However, the definition of this category was broad and included prominent figures of the revolution, such as Mahmoud Jibril, head of the largest party in post-Gaddafi Libya, as well as Mohamed al-Magariaf, then president of the Libyan parliament.[1] Many scholars consider this political initiative the precursor to the country's' descent into civil war.

This chapter unpacks this development as well as other key junctions by foregrounding the Libyan Muslim Brotherhood's and Libyan Salafi-Madkhalis' behavior with regard to cooperation in postrevolutionary Libya. It studies the months of the developing nascent democracy from Spring 2012 until its demise in civil war in Summer 2013. It argues that neither group showed behavioral developments toward cooperation. Instead, the Libyan Muslim Brotherhood pursued exclusionary politics, regularly sabotaging political institutions while seeking to expand its influence by placing their people in top positions. Some Libyan Salafi-Madkhalis exploited influential militia and security positions and amassed resources from the new Libyan institutions. While this behavior was an exception at the start of the analyzed timeframe, it became more widespread later on, with Libya sliding into civil war.

While acknowledging the structural strains and factoring these into the theoretical framework, this book also builds a counterpoint to a widespread sentiment that in post-Gaddafi Libya individual actors and movements' developments are deterministically decided by the overarching evolution of the country. This chapter highlights the *choices* made by movement leaders when exercising framing attempts to instill meaning into ongoing developments.

As conceptualized in the introduction, ideological moderation would also entail legitimacy in holding an alternative view. However, this chapter demonstrates how both groups considered their interpretation of the unfolding events and the resulting prognostic frames as supreme, thus hampering their potential moderation within the post-Gaddafi structures. By including framing attempts of the movements' leaders, this chapter also shows how their vision can be in disagreement with some members' actions.

The previous chapter focused on the revolution, the immediate aftermath after the fall of Gaddafi, and the freshly established political institutions of a nascent democracy in order to assess any success gained in taking advantage of opened structures. It focused analysis of the potential corresponding moderation through the abandonment of violence as the first, most basic behavior necessary for a movement's moderation. In this chapter, cooperation is analyzed. Behavioral moderation, as exemplified in cooperative behavior, goes together with the move away from conduct that is judgmental and ultimately prohibitive of any diversion from agreed-upon practices. Further, it ascribes those diverging practices as dangerous.[2] Cooperation is a second, crucial lens to trace a movement's moderation. However, while behavior exhibiting compromise implies the acknowledgment and acceptance of dropping demands or goals permanently for the common good of society, cooperation is often merely a willingness to work with other groups or individuals on a short-term basis for a shared goal.[3]

Caveats highlighted in chapter 2 prevail here: namely, the theoretical assumption of a pluralistic system as an ideal predisposition for the inclusion-moderation hypothesis. This will be critiqued further in this chapter, as Libyan structures are only partially in alignment with democratic ideals.

Evidence from the Libyan Muslim Brotherhood's and Libyan Salafi-Madkhalis' incorporation into these fragile, breaking, ultimately undemocratic structures points toward a reformulation of the inclusion-moderation hypothesis.[4] With the outbreak of civil war in Libya in 2013, both movements' behavior adapted to this internal structural change by seeking to protect their influence, also with weapons.[5] Furthermore, and in line with the theoretical backdrop of social movement theory, this chapter continues to assess whether they took advantage of the political opportunities of the opening institutions. The Libyan Muslim Brotherhood managed to benefit from these over the course of the first and second analyzed time periods but lost influence afterward due to a mixture of involvement mainly in political institutions that crumbled and internal miscalculations that focused on a top-down approach with little effort to build bottom-up support in Libya. The Libyan Salafi-Madkhalis, on the other hand, largely refrained from involvement with political institutions and hence ended up on the "right side of history" for postrevolutionary Libya. In addition, they focused on building local support and helping out with basic needs and services for the Libyan people, such as helping out with organizing hajj (pilgrimages). This led to deeper societal entrenchment of that movement compared to the Libyan Muslim Brotherhood.

Outmaneuvering Competitors

Negotiations and deliberations over how to successfully (re-)enter Libya defined the Libyan Muslim Brotherhood during the revolution months of January through October 2011. However, the focus intensified after Gaddafi was murdered on October 20 in Sirte. Now the pressure was heightened to ensure that the group would acquire relevant positions, ideally governing the country to establish their Islamist vision. In the period between the summer of 2011 and the summer of 2013, the Libyan Muslim Brotherhood managed to achieve supremacy in Libya's political institutions thanks to a mixture of ousting previous allies and capitalizing on the group's organizational experience acquired in exile. Other Libyan actors were lacking this experience, as they had lived under the repressive Gaddafi regime for decades and never learned to organize politically.[6]

The seeds for a democratic transition had been planted when the National Transitional Council (NTC) drafted a Constitutional Declaration outlining a government led by a broadened NTC. This would include representatives from all local councils and would oversee elections to a two-hundred-seat parliament, the General National Congress (GNC).[7] In order to tailor themselves to these new democratic requirements, the Libyan Muslim Brotherhood quickly established a party with its own structures and decision-making processes and launched it in March 2012. They based their Justice and Construction Party (JCP) on the Muslim Brotherhood–affiliated Egyptian Party, which is open to others with "a similar mindset" rather than being an "exclusive Muslim Brotherhood party."[8] One former Libyan Muslim Brotherhood member, who told me that he left the group in 2014, explained: "We wanted to be influential [in post-Gaddafi Libya] and of course for that we needed a party ... but it was important that we were in control ... looking back this was a recipe for disaster: on the one hand we wanted to get as many members and votes as possible, but on the other hand we were incapable of sharing control."[9]

Implicit in this description is the founders' reluctance or unwillingness to cooperate mid- to long-term or to enter power-sharing agreements. This exemplifies two behaviors identified in this research related to the Libyan Muslim Brotherhoods' party foundation: (1) the group's abandonment of the cooperative Islamist umbrella movement that had formed in April 2011 and (2) its dominance in the JCP, which contradicted the stated goals of an independent party. The Libyan Muslim Brotherhood departed from the previous cooperation that had existed between its members and other Islamists. The National Gathering (al-Tajammu' al-Watani) had been founded at the meeting of the fifteen Libyan Islamists convened in Istanbul by Ali al-Sallabi, who agreed to participate in the NTC. In order to entrench themselves in Libya, these participants decided to establish their own civil society organization, which they envisioned would later become a political party.[10] Indeed, at this point in time, Nizar Kawan, a Libyan Muslim Brotherhood member and later independent member of the first Libyan parliament, confirmed that "cooperation was key" in order to re-enter Libya.[11]

However, over the course of the next few months, this National Gathering failed to build societal support. Many different strands of Islamists were involved, from Libyan Muslim Brotherhood members such as Nizar Kawan and Libyan Islamic Fighting Group (LIFG) leaders such as Abdelhakim Belhadj to eminent Islamists of unclear affiliation, such as Ali al-Sallabi.[12] These men became preoccupied with pursuing their own personal agendas, such as securing a position in the emerging political institutions, leading a militia in Benghazi, or capitalizing on Qatari connections to transmit the Libyan revolutionary cause to a wider audience.[13] Only months after the founding, the Libyan Muslim Brotherhood officially detached itself from the movement, according to Kawan because it "was seen as linked to jihadis . . . we didn't want to be associated."[14] The National Gathering crumbled within months of the fall of Tripoli in autumn 2011.

This explanation is surprising given that the core members of the National Gathering did not change; however, it does signal the Libyan Muslim Brotherhood's fear of being considered radical Islamists who were stirring up Libyan society. In September 2011 Ali al-Sallabi accused Mahmoud Jibril, a popular revolutionary, Gaddafi defector, and chair of the NTC's executive board, of being "an 'extreme secularist,' and Libya's new 'tyrant.' "[15] So when the national sentiment toward the National Gathering, and specifically some of its members from the LIFG, began to change, the Libyan Muslim Brotherhood quickly wanted out. Some of them recognized the toxicity of an "Islamists versus secularists" discourse.

Bashir al-Kebti, the freshly elected leader of the Libyan Muslim Brotherhood's Shura Council, was born in Benghazi but had spent over thirty years in exile in the United States. Having left behind plans of forming a political party based on the National Gathering, he and other senior members tried to downplay their organization's de facto solo run: "The Muslim Brotherhood, in partnership with others, can form a national political party with an Islamic reference . . . [but] this partnership should be on an individual basis and not on a bloc basis."[16] In other words, he said in polite terms that the Libyan Muslim Brotherhood was leaving former allies behind to form its own party. This was a surprise to others in the Islamist camp who had expected the different Islamist groups to pool their resources after the revolution to create an Islamist political party.[17] However, al-Kebti's remarks ruled that out; instead, the Libyan Muslim Brotherhood was planning to start a party that others could join individually—or not.

Thus, while the Libyan Muslim Brotherhood had calculated to join forces with others, such as al-Sallabi, the group was now convinced that it was well-prepared for the nascent democratic developments and envisioned itself in a dominant position, unrestrained by more radical Islamist baggage.[18] These behavioral adaptations are in line with social movement scholarship such as Peter Mandaville's stipulation that Islamists are calculating actors, just as other social movements are. By the time the Libyan Muslim Brotherhood decided to establish its own party, its main considerations were the controlling of the party and detaching itself from what many of their leaders considered negative connotations with more radical Islamist groups (even when their ideological goals aligned).[19] The organization focused on its own success and quickly abandoned previous allies, aspects that do not align with cooperative behavior.

The Libyan Muslim Brotherhood was unwilling to genuinely open itself to other Libyans, even the JCP, and was hesitant about cooperation early on. While the details of its political party were heavily debated internally, it was quick to decide to exclude other Islamist groups.[20] The discussion at its Libyan summit in November 2011 revolved around three options, all based on other Muslim Brotherhood movements' decisions: transforming the movement (jamā'a) into a political party as the Tunisian Ennahda had done decades before; following the Jordanian example to establish a party under the control of the movement; or following in the footsteps of the Egyptian Muslim Brotherhood by creating a supposedly independent party. Almost 70 percent of members present at the conference supported the option of an independent party.[21] One participant later recalled: "We wanted an open party, to be open to all Libyans . . . I was excited for people to join; like this we could convince people how our way is the right way."[22]

However, this open, inclusive, and hence moderate basis did not materialize in the way the quoted member had hoped. Instead, senior leaders in the movement seemed convinced that the Libyan Muslim Brotherhood should work to dominate Libyan politics despite its long absence from the country. It threw all its weight behind the JCP. This attitude provoked serious resentment among other Islamist groups, and political bickering that was defined by reproach rather than cooperation. The Libyan Islamic Movement for Change, started by LIFG members, issued a statement claiming that the Libyan Muslim Brotherhood was trying to control party creation in Libya. The latter group quickly refuted this and blamed the necessity to establish its own party on the LIFG. In the words of Alamin Belhaj, a senior Libyan Muslim Brotherhood member who was part of the NTC: "I invited people [to join] but not the LIFG, as we could not work with them."[23] The organization's quest for control over the JCP was evident. It backed the successful campaign of Muhammad Sawan, a former political prisoner from Libya's economic powerhouse Misrata and head of the Shura Council. In addition, most founders of the JCP were Libyan Muslim Brothers.[24]

While the organization appeared publicly ready to define itself as committed to democracy, a civil state, and cooperation for the common good, the Libyan Muslim Brotherhood's suspicions stood in the way of such an approach. Members rationalized that they *needed* to be in key positions because they simply did not trust JCP party members who were not part of the movement—or even newcomers to their own group.[25] Members' behaviors toward cooperating for the common good of the country were negligible; instead, the Libyan Muslim Brotherhood was increasingly looking after itself.[26]

Trust issues were at the heart of the group's dominance over the JCP. The latter was administratively, financially, and organizationally separate, but, in senior member Abdulrazzak al-Aradi's nebulous confirmation, the Libyan Muslim Brotherhood was "still important to the JCP."[27] On a local level, the party branches headed by Libyan Muslim Brotherhood members were considered more successful because they were more active. Belhaj explained that this was due to the experience members had gathered by being part of the movement and learning how to organize.[28] The Libyan Muslim Brotherhood representative in Europe, Mohamed Abdelmalek, insisted that while many members joined the party, some were asked "to leave the leadership of the party and others were asked to leave their leadership positions in the jama'a."[29] Overall, however, the independence of the party remained unclear.

The influence of senior Libyan Muslim Brotherhood members disheartened new JCP members, such as a young man from Misrata: "I joined as soon as possible, I think in April 2012 and was so excited . . . As a Muslim, I was convinced the JCP was the right party for me . . . [but] I realized there was so much going on in the background I never understood . . . in the end, I felt like an outsider in my own party."[30] Instead of fully integrating new members and cooperating with other Islamist groups to pursue behavioral moderation with the aim of broadening its appeal—as expected by social movement scholar Sam Marullo—the Libyan Muslim Brotherhood focused on existing members and exclusively pushing them into leading JCP positions with the aim of ruling Libya.[31] This approach exacerbated power rivalries and, ultimately, hurt the common good.[32]

The next step of this doomed trajectory was the Libyan Muslim Brother-hood's and JCP's behavior inside Libya's first parliament, the General National Congress (GNC). At the end of August 2011, Tripoli was taken over by the rebel forces and Gaddafi and his family fled the capital. Now the NTC's plans for a democratic transition could begin. The Libyan Muslim Brotherhood was euphoric. The group had been repressed and persecuted in Libya for decades but could now maneuver freely. They were keen to capitalize on an organizational experience that other aspiring political actors in Libya lacked.[33] The group received confidence-building international support from external actors, such as when Qatar financed a relevant network of Libyan TV stations largely based in Tripoli as well as Istanbul in 2011 and 2012.

The Libyan Muslim Brotherhood was convinced that its political vision was the right fit for the traditional nature of Libyan society, which was conservative even by regional standards and made key demands such as shariʿa as the basis for any political system and legislation unproblematic.[34] But its behavior inside the GNC continued the trajectory of lack of cooperation, further negating the movement's moderation. Quite the contrary: The more it became incorporated into political institutions in post-Gaddafi Libya, the less moderate (cooperative) it became.

The Only "True Muslims" in Libya?

Overall, the Libyan Muslim Brotherhood was trying to find its place among Libya's many shades of Islamists after Gaddafi's removal.[35] On the one hand, some members, such as Nizar Kawan, became suspicious of what they considered more radical elements and therefore advocated forming a separate political party and designing a program in line with democratic ideals.[36] On the other, the JCP's newly elected leader, Sawan (who conducted it from its start until spring 2021) was focused on the need to distinguish the JCP from other newly formed political parties in order to have a good chance in the upcoming elections.[37] These calculations translated into the Libyan Muslim Brotherhood's framing attempts at the time.

Islam in general and shariʿa specifically did not feature much in the JCP's election program. Instead, the focus was on topics in line with a moderate agenda, such as education policies that relied on the principle of mandatory basic education to expand the quality of "all the Libyan people on all the

Libyan land." Sawan's rhetoric turned increasingly exclusionary when he advocated for the JCP as the *only* party able to govern Libya "in line with Islam."[38]

An internal framing competition defined this side of the party. The identified priorities of the leadership were at odds with those identified by JCP members on the periphery in smaller towns and cities across Libya. The leadership identified their main political adversaries as the allegedly secular National Forces Alliance (NFA)—in their view, the main threat to Libya's future during the 2012 election campaign. By contrast, individual members running for Congress instead aligned with their local constituents in declaring local Islamist militias as the principal threat. Therefore, the Libyan Muslim Brotherhood's group identity was contested internally at the same time that Libya was trying to find a new national identity.

It is possible to construct meaning around these ongoing developments and the Libyan Muslim Brotherhood's reactions to them. One individual stands out in importance. A key JCP figure for over nine years, Muhammad Sawan was vocal when featured on the Libyan Muslim Brotherhood's social media channels, his own Facebook and other social media pages, where he had thousands of followers, and on local and regional news channels,[39] many based in Turkey.[40] The JCP's election program and statements published on its website allow us to identify the main framing attempts of the Libyan Muslim Brotherhood's leadership during the time period of Libya's nascent democracy.[41] In order to analyze the intra-movement framing disputes about the JCP's main political adversaries, interview data with JCP politicians who ran for the GNC has been factored into the framing analysis.

This approach is in line with Gary Alan Fine's examination of social movements, where he argues that they consist of an "ideological primary core" that finds itself in regular competition with other movement members. In order to identify these framing competitions in the Libyan study, interviewing different movement members is most enlightening.[42] One factor unites them in their framing attempts: employing recent but potent Libyan history, such as the fight against Gaddafi, but also older stories such as the myths about Omar al-Mukhtar, Libya's foremost independence fighter against Italian colonization from eastern Libya. Interestingly, religious sources are being barely relied on.[43]

The preamble to the JCP's election program stresses the group's commitment to pluralism by saying that Libya needs a road map that captures "all the desired paths for the future." In the section addressing the future Libyan constitution, the JCP emphasizes that they "aim to establish a civil state based on the Constitution which guarantees the rule of democracy and peaceful transfer of power for which the revolution of 17 February [2011] has erupted and made great sacrifices." The Constitution itself is supposed to "derive its content from principles and values of Islam." The conviction that "Islamic law is the main source of legislation" is argued to mean "sticking to the beliefs of the Libyan people and community values."[44] In other words, the election program is a masterful stroke attempting to assure Libyans of the Libyan Muslim Brotherhood's commitment to the country and its values and traditions, including Islam, without defining how these would play out in actual policies.

On the one hand, this vagueness can be interpreted as a general symptom of election programs, especially those that are only ten pages long.[45] On the other hand, this program is very much representative of the JCP's main framing challenges at the time: namely, appealing to international observers wary of Islamist takeovers after the Arab Spring and to a Libyan population wary of a previously absent and therefore unknown movement.[46] In interviews, foreign government officials explained how meetings with the Libyan Muslim Brotherhood went very smoothly. While other Libyan politicians would regularly show up late or forget meetings altogether, the JCP was "always on time and usually in suits," as one British official described.[47] A Libyan NTC member referenced these same dynamics but interpreted them as "suspicious."[48]

The assessment of the election program reverberates with the strategic moderation of party stances or a movement's agenda in virtually every study of moderation, although its centrality varies. In her study of Islamists in Yemen and Lebanon, Stacey Philbrick Yadav conceptualizes the notion of behavior to encompass the "public framing" of arguments, explaining how Islamists, operating within a political context of greater inclusion and thus competition, must self-consciously moderate both their speech and actions to appeal to a broader audience.[49] Charles Kurzman and Ijlal Naqvi, analyzing election programs, find that many Islamist groups have similarly adjusted their public rhetoric.[50] Other studies of Islamist groups emphasize different mechanisms for ideological change, but still tend to acknowledge that groups strategically moderate their behavior as well as their rhetoric in order to take advantage of new political opportunities.[51]

The JCP followed this established pathway of Islamist parties by tailoring their election program to Western readers and government officials who could identify all the important buzzwords. (They even outlined the importance of gender equality.). At the same time, the JCP referenced shariʿa as the basis of legislation, committing to a core issue for the Islamist group that was also undisputed in Libya at the time. It is important to examine how Islamist groups actually behave locally as well as how they address (alleged) competitors instead of focusing on what they tell Westerners or put in public statements.

In his attempts to construct meaning, Sawan was preoccupied with portraying the Libyan 2012 election as a development for which there was a right and a wrong outcome. However, he faced two challenges. First, Libyans are overwhelmingly conservative and hence the role of shariʿa was never really disputed; this was unlike circumstances in Egypt or Tunisia, where shariʿa's role was a major debate topic in political discussions and the election campaigns following Zine el-Abidine Ben Ali and Hosni Mubarak's removal.[52] The almost complete absence of truly secularist forces, coupled with Libyans' innate conservativism, meant that there was a broad acceptance inside Libya that shariʿa should be the main source of legislation. In his first public speech in Tripoli in September 2011, the head of the NTC, Mustafa Abdeljalil, stated: "As a Muslim country, we have adopted the Islamic Sharia as the main source of law. Accordingly, any law that contradicts Islamic principles with the Islamic Sharia is ineffective legally."[53]

This is the context in which Sawan applied framing attempts, painting the identified main adversaries (NFA politicians) as supposedly secular and un-Islamic. He tried to frame a vote for the JCP as the only vote for "true Islam" by relying on a narrative that described the years under Gaddafi's rule as a dire time because the political system was in discordance with Islam.[54] The problem that needed to be solved in this diagnostic framing attempt was therefore clear: Libya had to move toward a better future while relying on politics informed by shariʿa.[55] The prognostic frame offering the solution to this identified situation was straightforward: Vote for the JCP.[56] However, the sources with which Sawan justified his rationale were relatively weak and he relied mostly on insinuating or stating explicitly that the JCP's opponents were not sincere in their commitment to Islam. He also tried to imitate previous successful framing attempts by the Libyan Muslim Brotherhood leadership during the revolution that justified calls to action by building

diagnostic frames on the foundation that the Gaddafi regime was culturally and ideologically corrupt. Sawan now tried to argue that the JCP's
opponents were largely remnants of the Gaddafi regime and hence both
not committed Muslims and corrupted.

In a Facebook post on March 3, 2012, Sawan argued that the JCP was "the
first and only party with Islamic reference" in Libya and therefore the
right solution for the country, which had been repressed by "Gaddafi's hea-
then beliefs."[57] These statements were supported by messaging on the JCP's
and the Libyan Muslim Brotherhood's official Facebook sites in March
and April 2012, emphasizing how the JCP knew Islam best and hence was the
best leader for Libya.[58] In that way, Sawan also worked to create a narrative
that placed the Libyan elections into a broader context of meaning by referring to other elections in the region where Islamist parties were successful
after many years of repression, such as in Tunisia. This he interpreted as
the true will of the people finally coming to fruition, as when he elaborated
on the Egyptian people finally being freed "of the chains from Mubarak" in
a Facebook post in March 2012.[59]

However, Sawan's framing attempts were ultimately not convincing. He
was alternating between confirming that the JCP was a liberal democratic
force to please Western representatives and painting it as the most authen-
tically committed party to Islam in Libyan politics. This dual incentive hurt
the potency of his framing attempts, as they were incoherent.[60] Sawan's
description of the NFA as un-Islamic and therefore unsupportable for people who cared about Islam in politics was not convincing for many Libyans
who knew NFA party members and were convinced of their religiosity.[61]

Sawan's framing attempts backfired, as several Libyans interviewed
for this book expressed. They did not need the JCP to define their Islamic
identity. One Libyan activist from Benghazi said: "It was unnecessary to
explain to me that I should vote for an Islamic party. All parties for me were
Islamic because in Libya we are all Muslims. The JCP was being arrogant . . .
they can't tell me that I am only a good Muslim if I vote for them."[62] While
Sawan was trying to speak to Libyans' commitment to Islam by creating
framing attempts to "fit" with a person's beliefs, the frame did not resonate
with many Libyans; hence, the sender appeared to lack credibility.[63]

After many years in exile and Gaddafi's relentless denunciation of the
group, most Libyan Muslim Brotherhood representatives and especially
those in the JCP were seen with skepticism by many Libyans who were wary

of their broader goals attached to an international Islamist movement.[64] In addition, the JCP's opponents were astute enough to remain aware of the Libyan Muslim Brotherhood's attempts to frame them as secular.[65] Neither the NFA nor other parties worked toward a secular group identity, nor did they campaign with a focus on secular policies such as the separation of religion and state. Once Mohammed al-Magariaf, leader of the National Front, was quoted claiming that Libya should become a secular state. Both NFA and JCP politicians were quick to denounce him.[66] Like the JCP, the NFA recognized democracy generally and shariᶜa as the main source of law.[67] However, the NFA had a strong advantage for potential framing success. Sawan was largely unknown to Libyans, but the front-runner of the NFA, Mahmoud Jibril, had emerged as one of the most prominent figures of the 2011 revolution.[68]

While Sawan was focused on defining the JCP's identity as Islamic and juxtaposing it to the allegedly secular NFA, other JCP candidates were portraying themselves as committed to local issues, such as neighborhood security.[69] Therefore, while its leadership was focused on constructing the JCP's group identity on Islam, other members were willing to downplay this aspect and focus instead on policy issues, such as the difficulties of ensuring security without a monopoly of force in Libya's postrevolutionary environment.[70] One JCP member who ran for election in 2012 explained: "I wanted to work on a lot of things that people I spoke to raised . . . [among them] their fear of militias. But there was never room in our meetings . . . instead the focus was on always saying the right things, if you know what I mean."[71] Another former JCP member who was helping in an election campaign in Sebha said: "Honestly, I did not understand why we [the JCP] kept talking about Islam . . . the things I was worried about weren't about Islam . . . and I know we are all Muslims, but this is what we talk about in the mosques."[72]

Overall, the described framing attempts exemplify two things: First, they foreshadow the unwillingness of the Libyan Muslim Brotherhood to cooperate with the NFA once elected to parliament.[73] Second, they show how parts of the JCP leadership were detached from concerns in the local constituencies. By trying to implement political campaigning that focused on separating the JCP from other groups in the country by emphasizing their Islamic identity, the JCP actually appeared to alienate many Libyans (including some members of their own party).

The interplay of external and internal factors can be observed here: The external factors hampering Sawan's success were the denunciation of the Libyan Muslim Brotherhood, as well as political parties and democratic inexperience under Gaddafi, which left a lasting imprint on many Libyans wary of a broader agenda of political organization attached to an international movement. The internal factors were the Libyan Muslim Brotherhood's hunger for power related to their conviction to be the righteous force to lead Libya. Finally, by putting emphasis on their Islamic identity and constructing that identity in juxtaposition to other, allegedly secular forces, the JCP claimed the right to judge what was right or wrong and hence ruled out the possibility for a group to see validity in the views of others—a key component of moderation of social movements.[74]

Sawan tried to employ a previously successful narrative by Islamists that the true path to development and success was outlined in the sources of Islam and therefore the correct adherence to Islam would remove all ills and reward society for their faithfulness.[75] But in Libya in 2012, he was not successful due to his lack of credibility as an agent, in addition to the outlined ambivalence about the frame's intrinsic appeal.

The Muslim Brotherhood Engineers Libya's First Elected Body

The Libyan 2012 election law reserved only eighty of the two hundred seats in the GNC for political parties; the rest were to be filled by individual candidates.[76] The first elections in the country since 1965 were held in July 2012 to great enthusiasm, and received a big turnout of 65 percent.[77] The election results, however, were a disappointment for the Libyan Muslim Brotherhood, as the JCP won only seventeen of the eighty party seats.[78] However, in order to have the best chances of dominating the GNC, the organization fielded several locally rooted members considered popular, already-established candidates as individual contestants.

In conjunction with its individual candidates and a revived interest in cooperation by other Islamists, the Libyan Muslim Brotherhood therefore managed to dominate Libya's political institutions for a limited time. This was due to, first, the necessity of the biggest party (the NFA) to cooperate with others, and, second, the resulting shrewd negotiations in which the Libyan Muslim Brotherhood relied on sabotaging political cooperation and pitted members of parliament against each other. In contradiction to what Western media described as an election victory for the "liberals" (the NFA) over the Islamists, the Libyan Muslim Brotherhood and smaller Islamist and Salafi parties together gained a bigger proportion of formally independent representatives. And the Libyan Muslim Brotherhood managed to control this amalgamation of Islamists in their voting behavior for some time.

The NFA, the strongest political party in the first post-Gaddafi parliament (GNC), was led by Mahmoud Jibril. It was a loosely organized group that is best described in the words of a previous deputy head: "We were a party with chance for success that was not Islamist . . . [that] is also why I joined."[79] However, with thirty-nine of the two hundred seats secured, the NFA was reliant on cooperation with other political parties and individually elected candidates in order to form a majority coalition and hence government. Fully aware of the NFA's predicament and still bitter about its election results, the JCP played hardball when invited to negotiations about leadership posts. They managed to sabotage the election of Jibril, the natural candidate for head of the GNC and de facto Libyan head of state as he was leader of the biggest party. Instead, the Libyan Muslim Brotherhood convinced individual candidates and MPs from smaller Islamist parties to vote against him.

Mustafa Abu Shagur, MP of the National Front, a small party with three seats in the GNC, won the office (although his turn only lasted a few weeks).[80] Because Shagur was unable to satisfy the demands of his backers—for instance, the JCP demanding eleven ministries but only receiving four—he knew that his time was over when he was reading out the names of the government and a large number of GNC members walked out before he had even finished. The next day, he was removed following a no-confidence vote.[81]

This opened the same political process for the second time in just four months. The Libyan Muslim Brotherhood then aimed to get one of its members (Mohamed al-Harari) into the country's highest office, despite its relatively poor showing in the party election results. By now, the NFA had accepted that it needed to cooperate with other political parties and individuals. This time it did not field Jibril but instead backed Ali Zeidan, an independent, who won by ninety-three votes to Harari's eighty-five.

The Libyan Muslim Brotherhood relied on excuses to explain Zeidan's success, with senior member Abdulrazzak al-Aradi explaining that some JCP members were on pilgrimage in Mecca at the time of the vote and therefore unable to cast their ballots. This explicitly questioned the legitimacy of the new prime minister and also asserted that, if the movement and its allies had been present in full force, they would have averted this election of a candidate not supported by the their leadership instead of succumbing to cooperation. However, notably, a number of JCP MPs from Fezzan had voted for their townsman Zeidan, suggesting that regionalism and the desire to have strong representation on a national level for a historically marginally region of Libya broke party discipline.[82]

While the Libyan Muslim Brotherhood did not manage to secure the post of prime minister in the second election, the movement still dominated the GNC and continued to sabotage the success of their rival parties and political candidates. They relied on sabotaging political cooperation and pitting members of parliament against each other, none of which would have been possible without Islamist or Salafi-leaning groups together gaining a greater share of the nominally independent members than the NFA.[83] Hence despite its lackluster performance at the party level, the JCP can be understood as having had the allegiance of around sixty individual candidates. Some were prominent members who stood as independents, realizing that this increased their chances to enter parliament, such as Nizar Kawan. These individual candidates helped to push through Decision Number 7, an initiative originated and driven by the JCP, which legitimized a controversial military offensive on Bani Walid. Therefore, the depicted strength in party seats should be regarded as approximate; instead, as Wolfram Lacher explains: "The real size of parliamentary groups varies, with the Alliance [NFA] in particular lacking internal discipline."[84]

The Libyan Muslim Brotherhood, however, could rely on much greater internal cohesion than other parties: Many of its members spent years in prison or exile together and were therefore well attuned to the need for closing ranks and sticking together.[85] Those who entered the GNC as independents exhibited stronger loyalty than did the NFA associated independents.[86] In the person of Nizar Kawan, a formally stated independent was even elected head of the JCP's parliamentary group.

In addition, Islamist or Salafi-leaning MPs were estimated at twenty-seven members, with ten associated with the al-Asala ("authenticity") movement closely allied with Grand Mufti Sadeq al-Gharyani in Tripoli.[87] A second group was made up of individuals close to Sami al-Saadi, formerly the LIFG's religious authority, and Abdelwahhab Gaid, a former leading LIFG member and founder of the al-Umma al-Wasat ("umma") party.[88] Other MPs were linked to Salah Badi, who was not officially part of the LIFG but was close to many members. Five independents were associated with the al-Watan ("homeland") Party of

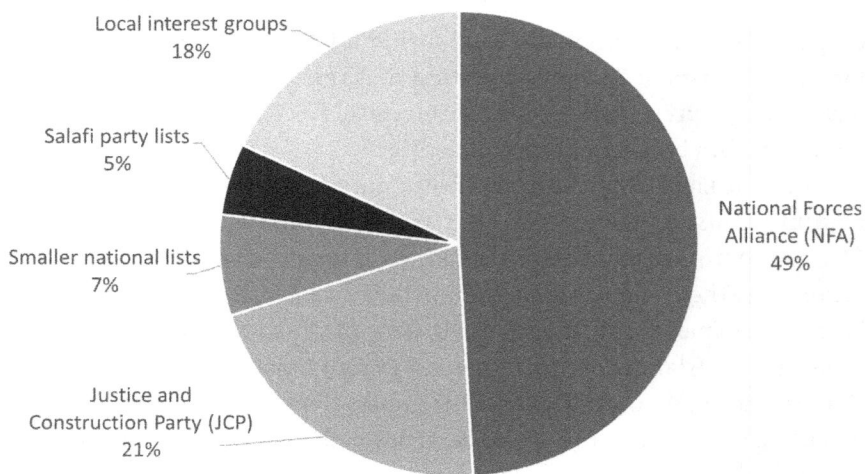

Figure 3.1 GNC party seats (80 out of 200). *Source:* Wolfram Lacher, "Fault Lines of the Revolution: Political Actors, Camps and Conflicts in the New Libya." Research Paper 2013/RP 04. *Stiftung Wissenschaft und Politik*, May 7, 2013, 9.

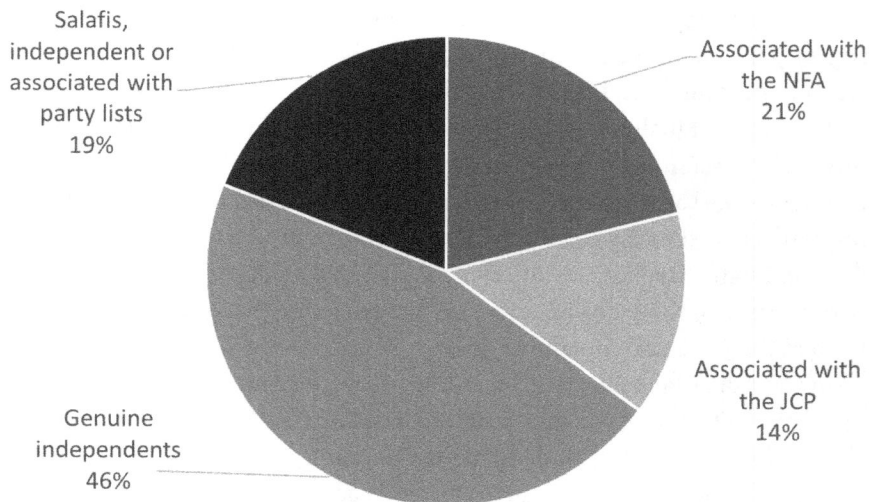

Figure 3.2 GNC independent seats (120 of 200). *Source:* Wolfram Lacher, "Fault Lines of the Revolution: Political Actors, Camps and Conflicts in the New Libya." Research Paper 2013/RP 04. *Stiftung Wissenschaft und Politik*, May 7, 2013, 9.

Abdelhakim Belhadj, who founded it after his disagreements with the Libyan Muslim Brotherhood leadership over the National Gathering.[89] These four groups are subsumed under "Salafi Party Lists" in figure 3.1.

These two dynamics show how the Libyan Muslim Brotherhood was able to act in a dominating manner over the nascent democratic institution of the GNC and hence exploit the presented political opportunities successfully through relentless negotiation and sabotaging political wins by their biggest rival (the NFA). The organization also relied on allies in the Islamist spectrum who were not official members of the JCP but could align themselves with some of the JCP's goals, such as averting a government dominated by alleged secularists.

The Libyan Muslim Brotherhood successfully grew into Libya's postrevolutionary political system, but this did not result in their following behavioral moderation. Instead of cooperating with other political actors for the common good of all of Libya, as Kenneth Roberts theorized about moderation in a different country context,[90] the Libyan Muslim Brotherhood was led by pride, its conviction of superiority and, when entering cooperative agreements, relentlessly asking for returns.[91]

When the NFA, under Jibril's leadership, approached the JCP, the group did not enter negotiations in a cooperative and open manner but instead resented that these negotiations were part of a larger meeting that included other political parties. According to Alamin Belhaj, this was humiliating.[92] The Libyan Muslim Brotherhood's previous rhetoric had been to "rebuild Libya . . . for everyone," as Suleiman Abdelkader had proclaimed at the November 2011 summit and various other members repeated over the following months. This now seemed increasingly shallow because the movement was focused on securing high-level posts in the new government or at least barring their main rivals.[93]

The organization was infuriated by the NFA's suggestion that Jibril and Ali Zeidan, neither of whom they favored, fill the roles of prime minister and head of the GNC, respectively. The movement cut all contact with the NFA and put forward its own candidates (Awad al-Barassi and Mohamed al-Harari) instead.[94] With its pride hurt, and still convinced of its superiority, the Libyan Muslim Brotherhood was determined to deny Jibril a top position, even if it meant displaying uncooperative and self-centered behavior.

The organization did enter some cooperative agreements—for example, with Mohammed al-Magariaf, the leader of the National Front, whose party had won just three seats in the elections. However, even then, the Libyan Muslim Brotherhood insisted on unreasonable returns. After the two groups struck a deal to vote Magariaf into the position of GNC head, the Libyan Muslim Brotherhood demanded that the National Front vote for Barassi, an engineer from Benghazi elected as JCP MP, to be prime minister in return.

The National Front agreed, then broke its promise and cast its votes for its own candidate, Mustafa Abu Shagur. Barassi was eliminated in the first round. The Libyan Muslim Brotherhood subsequently had to choose between Shagur and Jibril in the second round, leaving them in a situation where they needed to support Shagur to hold back their biggest competitor.[95] Shagur's victory left post-Gaddafi Libya in a situation where the two most senior posts were held by a party that had won only three seats in the elections, while the most popular party had not secured a single high-level position. The Libyan Muslim Brotherhood subsequently demanded eleven portfolios for the JCP from Shagur's government. Shagur recounted in an interview in 2012: "As soon as I won, I contacted the party to ask for their nominations. They sent me their first list seven days later. They asked for the [post of] deputy prime minister and ten ministries."[96]

Retroactively, some Libyan Muslim Brotherhood members tried to distance themselves from this obvious power grab. Abdulrazzak al-Aradi, for example, insisted that the Libyan Muslim Brotherhood "didn't demand any portfolios from Abu Shagur," instead blaming certain JCP members.[97] However, given the previously outlined domination of the Libyan Muslim Brotherhood over the JCP, especially in those early days, it seems very likely that the Libyan Muslim Brotherhood was aware of the events and behaviors of its members; one former senior member simply stated in our interview: "Of course, we knew what was going on in the GNC."[98]

The Libyan Muslim Brotherhood's behavior must be seen as part of its environment. Libya in 2012 was defined by political bickering, little trust, and little cooperation. The NFA, similar to the JCP, demanded nine portfolios from Shagur, claiming that they were the party with the largest popular mandate and should be represented in the government's constellation; when this failed, the NFA joined the no-confidence vote.[99] At the same time, however, the NFA, in contrast to the JCP, had legitimate reasons to demand these portfolios, given its size in the GNC.

Theoretically, this section has highlighted additional caveats for the inclusion-moderation hypothesis related to the ideal preconditions under which the hypothesis operates: namely, that of a pluralistic system. These ideal conditions are difficult to achieve, and this seems to have an impact upon the movement's trajectory as evidenced by how less moderate the Libyan Muslim Brotherhood turned as it became increasingly part of the post-Gaddafi Libyan political system. This can be seen as aligning with what Benedetta Berti formulated when she argued that "as political parties institutionalize, they . . . consequently become more prone to seek adaptation to the environment."[100] In this case, the Libyan Muslim Brotherhood's recalcitrance can also be interpreted partially as part of an uncooperative environment with its uncooperative stance being part of its accommodation-seeking tools. This section has also shown differences between members of a movement, which is always a challenge when analyzing social movements' trajectories as a whole.[101]

From Quietists to Powerful Militia Members

Libyan Salafi-Madkhalis were able to capitalize on opportunities originating from the opening of the political system, largely because they refrained from participating in the central political institution, the GNC. Instead, the group focused on adjacent institutions, such as the militias-cum-social-wings that sprang up after Gaddafi's removal. In retrospect, this turned out to be a strategic move. Libya's political institutions disintegrated in 2014 and the country slid into civil war, which was blamed on the uncooperative political institution of the GNC and its inability to govern the country and meet citizens' needs. In an environment in which Libyans were looking for safety in their immediate surroundings and hoping for actors to substitute basic services or run prisons, Libyan Salafi-Madkhalis managed to cater to many of these needs.

With this, the movement became influential in Libya's post-Gaddafi security institutions, specifically in parts of Tripoli as well as Sirte. With Libya split between two governing authorities from 2015 (the Government of National Accord in Tripoli and the House of Representatives in Tobruk), Libyan Salafi-Madkhalis managed to entrench themselves in security institutions aligned with both sides by integrating members into the Libyan

National Army (LNA) allied with the House of Representatives and dominating some neighborhoods in Tripoli with the Radaa or Special Deterrence Force (SDF) and Nawasi brigades on which the GNA relied for security in the capital.[102]

They became influential because they followed a locally based approach of organization. However, the movement did not become more cooperative and hence moderate in their behavior once they were part of Libyan institutions. Like the Libyan Muslim Brotherhood, they only exhibited moderate behavior for a limited time, until they felt themselves to be in a dominating position. Libyan Salafi-Madkhalis relied on tactical cooperation in order to gain influence, but when relatively secure in its position, the group transgressed into exclusionary behavior and cut cooperation with previous allies.

Shaykh Madkhali and other key Libyan Salafi-Madkhali figures framed the attempts to establish a democratic system based on elections as foreign to Libya and un-Islamic. This was a continuation of the framing attempts that Madkhali had established around his perceived illegitimacy of the protests in 2011. However, his framing attempts were partially unsatisfactory for Libyan followers, who felt local pressure to participate in the election. In addition, the conundrum of having lost their walī al-amr and not being sure how to replace this ruling authority led some Libyan Salafi-Madkhalis to believe that successful elections were the solution.

At the same time, local leaders such as Abdulraouf Kara became confident in their standing and employed framing attempts aimed at identity construction to create stronger coherence within their districts. Kara's framing attempts focused on neighborhood concerns and scaled up the alleged need for self-protection. This convinced many of his readers and listeners to see the ongoing structural developments through his interpretative lens. He relied on current developments and linked struggles in his neighborhood to previous struggles faced by Muslims in the Qur'an. This connection made his frames strong and the neighborhood group he started in 2012 became considered "one of Tripoli's most organized factions" by 2021, highlighting the influence that ideology, social roots, and leadership can have on an armed group's cohesion and its potential role as a security provider.[103]

While post-Gaddafi Libya as a whole was attempting a democratic trajectory, Libyan Salafi-Madkhalis were largely unaffected and uninvolved in the actions toward this goal. They were not involved in setting up political parties, participating in elections, or sending individual representatives to parliament. However, while Libyan Salafi-Madkhalis opposed electoral politics, the group was still cooperating with the new state and its institutions, especially at the local level.[104] They capitalized on opportunities linked to the removal of the Gaddafi regime, such as the collapsed security sector and the ideological void following the demise of Gaddafi's *Green Book*, which was no longer the main "religion" of the country. In so doing, they cooperated with a variety of actors—from the Souq al-Jouma revolutionary brigades and other militias formed during the uprisings to representatives of the new state, such as Hashim Bishr from the Supreme Security Committee (SSC). Interestingly, the first reason why they were successful in capitalizing on the internal structural changes was the movement's recognition of the importance of cooperation.

The Libyan Salafi-Madkhali movement aligned itself with local fault lines along neighborhoods and tribes and participated in the SSC and with that cooperated with rival elements, such as Islamists. Abdulrazzak al-Aradi, a leading Libyan Salafi-Madkhali and NTC representative, helped to set up the SSC in Tripoli. The group also strategically managed to cater to palpable needs and tangible solutions for Libyans in the transition away from a totalitarian system. In other words, instead of focusing on setting up a political party and securing leadership positions in the country's nascent political institutions as did the Libyan Muslim Brotherhood, Libyan Salafi-Madkhalis focused on gathering support locally that the group could rely on independent of the institutional setup governing Libya. This allowed them to thrive in the Libyan environment of transition.

During this successful trajectory, Libyan Salafi-Madkhalis relied in part on cooperation with other Libyan actors and hence exhibited moderate behavior as they put commitment to their ideology on the back burner when recruiting new members. However, they were quick to leave behind such cooperative behavior and turn away from previous allies when a position of perceived superiority was reached. This happened, first, when the SSC was dissolved, after which Libyan Salafi-Madkhalis cut cooperation with other armed groups in Tripoli, and, second, when the Libyan Salafi-Madkhalis achieved supremacy among Tripoli's armed groups after July 2015 and the installment of the GNA was achieved.

The group's behavior supports Mark Woodward et al.'s argument that Salafi groups are apt at adaptation along pragmatic lines. The pages that follow offer further empirical evidence for the de-exceptionalization argument of social movement scholar Olivier Roy, who emphasizes that the Salafi movement should be examined just like other social movements.[105] Empirical research engages critically with the existing inclusion-moderation hypothesis needs to be reexamined in the contexts following the Arab uprisings in North Africa that are defined by transitionary political environments, as Jillian Schwedler and Marc Lynch have pointed out.[106] This is because the distinction between political and nonpolitical spheres is blurred without a well-established monopoly of force and political institutions.

The Cradle of Tripoli's Souq al-Jouma

The Libyan Salafi-Madkhalis were successful in capitalizing on the internal structural changes because they built upon previous linkages and resources. For instance, in Tripoli's eastern suburb of Souq al-Jouma, the organization had established their presence under Saadi Gaddafi. These former links to the regime helped Libyan Salafi-Madkhalis to build local support. They were privileged compared to other groups under the Gaddafi regime: The group had received some resources to establish da'wa work and could operate relatively freely.[107] One Libyan Salafi-Madkhali, who had spent time in Yemen with Salafi preacher Muqbil al-Wadi'i but returned to Libya in 2001, explained: "It was clear that Gaddafi did not leave us alone. Every few weeks I would get interviewed . . . but they asked normal questions: what we were saying in the mosque, who is coming to the sermons . . . that was ok . . . they [the Gaddafi regime] were still protecting us."[108]

After the removal of the Gaddafi regime, Libyan Salafi-Madkhalis in Souq al-Jouma needed to prove their commitment to the neighborhood as the organization was still viewed as linked to the previous regime and hence suspicious.[109] They managed this largely by employing previously gathered financial resources to scale up da'wa work and by forming neighborhood vigilante groups focusing on averting lawlessness in the local society.[110] The latter effort came to be appreciated by locals, who saw other parts of their country, such as Benghazi, struggling to assert law and order. Libyan Salafi-Madkhalis were central in establishing regular patrols aimed at creating a sense of local law enforcement that was supposed to deter crime but generally made sure that Souq al-Jouma would not devolve into street shootings or looting, as happened regularly in parts of Benghazi in 2012.

In an attempt to recruit more members to these security-enforcing groups, local Libyan Salafi-Madkhalis emphasized their local embeddedness more than their religious alliance with the movement. In interviews for this book, three local Libyan Salafi-Madkhalis explained their rationales, but also how they considered themselves to be sincere in their local commitment. They confirmed the importance of religion and the centrality of Rabi bin Hadi al-Madkhali and his sermons, while simultaneously emphasizing their commitment to their neighborhood and their conviction that all neighbors should come together to protect each other.[111]

Abdulraouf Kara was able to motivate people to join his neighborhood groups by capitalizing precisely on this outlined duality. By employing frames that created an in-group defined by local characteristics, Kara designed motivational frames that aided his success. He emphasized the importance of securing local institutions such as neighborhood mosques from influence by Salafi-jihadis and reserving the important Friday sermons for quietist preachers, as well as religious sources such as the Qur'an.[112]

Kara also stressed the need in his neighborhood, Souq al-Jouma, for self-protection. Gaddafi had developed Tripoli into the main anchor of his regime and expanded the Bab al-Azizia military compound, in which he hid until the last weeks of the revolution.[113] The capital city had seen intense fighting during the revolution and after Gaddafi's fall, and now the feeling of insecurity was spreading. One SDF member from Tripoli explained how he found assurance in joining Kara's group in late 2012: "There was a major difference between my fears before and after I joined . . . after joining I had a goal and a purpose: I wanted to protect my neighborhood . . . [and] I was doing it in the name of God."[114]

With Kara embedding the role of his group within a bigger purpose, he responded to existing fears of the post-Gaddafi uncertainty that prevailed among Libyan Salafi-Madkhalis and Libyans more generally. Many Libyans were struck by the seeming unwillingness of some revolutionary forces to give up their weapons.[115] Some witnessed revolutionary fighters they had admired a few months earlier committing petty crimes with impunity, such as violating traffic laws.

Against this perceived reality of a society of several individuals pursuing their selfish aims, joining Kara's neighborhood group also offered the chance for action in a community with a shared moral purpose acting in accordance with God's precepts. The framing's diagnostic and prescriptive dimensions—simultaneously unfolding the causes of corruption of some parts of society and pointing the way to solutions—resonated in particular with young people in Souq al-Jouma faced with finding their place in a society unknown to their parents, who had grown up under Gaddafi and were unable to provide guidance. At the same time, Kara's framing attempts were rooted in Madkhali ideology, such as his unwavering contempt for democratic politics. With this, he offered a new conceptual language for understanding the predicament of contemporary Libyan society and an agenda for change.[116]

Central to these framing successes was Kara's approach to the topic of wālī al-amr, which had many Salafis in Souq al-Jouma puzzled. By relying on the Qur'an, he explained, "one is obligated to follow the strongest political authority in whatever territory one sits."[117] This explanation did two things: First, it allowed room for interpretation, which was and continues to be necessary in such a fast-changing environment; second, it instilled moral purpose in the support of the strongest political authority, superseding accusations of personal enrichment or interest. As Kara explained, supporting anyone who was not the strongest local authority caused fitna (chaos). Kara's early attempts at persuasion proved potent: by 2013, when they joined Khalifa Haftar's side in Libya's civil war ("Operation Dignity"), Libyan Salafi-Madkhalis in eastern Libya had begun to frame their actions as support for the authorities in the field of security and order while refraining from seeking official political positions.[118]

Kara's framing successes in 2012 Tripoli, however, were also related to him personally, for "the credibility of information is judged in part by the credibility of the source, [so] we would expect speakers with greater social legitimacy to succeed more often at persuading others." Legitimacy is particularly strong for those "to whom society has already allocated a special protective or interpretive role," such as religious men or local leaders.[119] In Souq al-Jouma, Gaddafi's appropriation of quietist Salafis had made them authorities in local mosques, paving the way for local Muslims to be susceptible to Kara's interpretations even if they did not consider themselves followers of Shaykh Madkhali.[120]

In this instance, the Libyan Salafi-Madkhali movement had been successfully adapting its behavior after the fall of Gaddafi and managed to carve out local influence; in addition, they proved open to cooperating with other neighborhood groups and hence exhibited moderate behavior. This approach was in line with the majority of Libyan actors who identified and organized at a local or regional basis in late 2011 and early 2012 (with the Libyan Muslim Brotherhood an outlier).[121] This represented a shift for a movement that had been tied to the Gaddafi regime until the very end. Now its members were listening to local grievances and cooperating with neighbors in order to achieve the joint goal of local security.

Retrospectively it is difficult to say if more members joined Libyan Salafi-Madkhali-led neighborhood groups independent of or because of their religious background. The former seems more likely. Recall that Libyan Salafi-Madkhalis were known for their success in starting and recruiting neighborhood groups and that these groups had always benefited from state resources, which became much more abundant after 2011.

The SSC and Failed Security Sector Reform

The still developing groups in Souq al-Jouma benefited from the appointment of religiously conservative Hashim Bishr to a leadership role in the most important post-Gaddafi security institution: the Supreme Security Committee (SSC).[122] The SSC was established with the mandate to organize the various militias and their respective supervising mechanisms that were created during the revolution under the umbrella of the post-Gaddafi authorities. Thanks to Bishr, the Salafi-Madkhali-led groups from Souq al-Jouma were granted special access to new resources. One such group was led by the aforementioned Abdulraouf Kara, a former metalworker, Libyan Salafi-Madkhali, and member of a locally influential family.[123] Kara became the main person in charge of all local "support branches" of the Tripoli branch of the SSC and was able to fill this role successfully, as he had plenty of resources at his disposal. He also employed social capital gained from his upbringing in Tripoli's residential neighborhoods.[124] In 2013 the SSC was dissolved, as it had become too powerful and, crucially, too independent from political oversight by the GNC and its appointed ministers. Embedded in the principle of security sector reform efforts, the existing support groups reorganized. Many Salafis from Souq al-Jouma followed Kara, who went on that year to found and command the Special Deterrence Force (SDF or Quwat al-Radaa al-Khassa, commonly known in Tripoli as Radaa).[125]

While his group was renamed and restructured, Kara still pursued his proven approach: working to impose order in local society in a bottom-up manner, collaborating with municipalities and neighborhood leaders, and continuing to uphold his reputation for leading the armed actors best able to work in the populated areas of Tripoli.[126] Officially now directly supervised by the Ministry of the Interior under Libya's SSR efforts, Kara's Radaa reached a point of superiority where the Tripoli-based ministry was reliant on the force to ensure security in large parts of the capital. This, paired with the Salafi-Madkhali adherence of Kara and many of the group's members, pushed back against the government's attempts to impose a more regular hierarchy.

In 2013, therefore, the modus operandi (and hence behavior) of Libyan Salafi-Madkhalis with Radaa at their forefront was shifting from relatively easily cooperating with other forces of different background and origin in the SSC to becoming more exclusionary in its recruitment and favoring cooperation with other Libyan Salafi-Madkhalis rather than local groups. Identifying with Salafi-Madkhali ideology became more important for interested Libyans; furthermore, this affected the SDF's organization internally because, among other things, leadership was approached through the model of consultation (*shura*) instead of the hierarchical mechanisms suggested by the ministry.[127] By this time the civil war had split the country. The GNA now ruled in western Libya and the House of Representatives, supported by the LNA, in the east. The SDF began to cooperate more with other Libyan Salafi-Madkhali brigades in different parts of Libya, despite the fact that many of these regions were actually commanded by the LNA and other eastern forces not aligned with the SDF's ruling authorities in Tripoli.

Overall, Radaa was immensely successful by adapting its behavior following the internal structural changes related to Gaddafi's removal. At its inception, it comprised about fifty breakaway members from the Souq al-Jouma "support groups" and was based at Tripoli's Mitiga Airport.[128] By 2020, it had ballooned to a seven-hundred to nine-hundred-member force, now partitioned into policing units and combatants. The local links to its neighborhood are central to the SDF and over half of its members are believed to be practicing Salafi-Madkhalis.[129] This success has helped Libyan Salafi-Madkhali religious figures to gain reputation and influence; for example, Majdi Hafala's following greatly increased after 2011, notably among members of local armed groups, and his Friday sermons in Tripoli's mosques progressively attracted hundreds of followers.[130]

Salafi shaykhs were also central in connecting different Libyan Salafi-Madkhali armed groups across the country, but especially in northwest and central Libya, beginning in 2014. As one interviewee, himself a shaykh in Tripoli, explained: "Communication amongst us [religious leaders] already existed [as Gaddafi had allowed it] so we knew about each other . . . after we had met abroad and sometimes, we could meet in Libya as well . . . After 2011 it was important for us to connect and also to bring people together."[131]

In sum, the Libyan Salafi-Madkhalis' success in exploiting the opened-up system largely boils down to the fact that "mostly the problem was the [post-Gaddafi's] state's inability to back agreements negotiated by tribal leaders by deploying security forces and prosecuting crimes."[132] This is precisely the gap that Libyan Salafi-Madkhalis aimed to fill and Radaa successfully did so by cooperating with local neighborhood and tribal leaders and making security and crime prosecution its priorities.

This situation is different from popular arguments that the Libyan Salafi-Madkhalis were "against the state" because the movement largely refrained from voting and their religious leaders rhetorically railed against elections and democracy. The movement was in fact largely in line with quietist convictions that typically reject political activism.[133] However, Libyan Salafi-Madkhalis became emancipated from the typical focus on religious education and learning by shifting their emphasis to law enforcement. The movement therefore largely cooperated with the nascent state institutions, especially at a local level and with regard to its security infrastructure, such as the SSC.[134] Its behaviors have proven pragmatic and shrewd because it adapted and cooperated on a tactical level. It also continued to prove relatively moderate in its behavior during the analyzed timeframe: The violence against polling stations was largely undertaken not by Libyan Salafi-Madkhalis but instead by Salafi-jihadis such as Ansar al-Sharia in Benghazi. Instead, Libyan Salafi-Madkhalis cooperated with elected politicians and institutions. Nevertheless, group members did begin to attack Sufi shrines and exhibited uncompromising and violent behavior. This will be analyzed in chapter 4 as part of an assessment of the final aspect of potential behavioral moderation: compromise.

Elections Take a Back Seat to Armed Groups

Madkhali's framing attempts with regard to the election are a continuation from 2011 when he built his diagnostic frame on the foundation that the protesters were corrupted by the West (see chapter 2). In a sermon from October 2011 titled "Warning Against Strife and Democracy and Its Derivatives," Madkhali warned that "one of the most dangerous innovations coming to the lands of Islam is democracy and the call for freedom that was invented by the atheists of the West and their followers."[135] In this sermon, he aimed to convince his followers of the dire times ahead in case a democracy based on the rule of the people was implemented.

This inescapability of a dark democratic future for Libya is based on two main points, with one being more general and the other more practical: First, Madkhali interprets democracy, especially elections that determine the sovereign of the state, as foreign to the Muslim world, as innovation (*bida'*). Second, he stated, democracy would lead to practical disadvantages for all Libyans as it was inherently tied to corruption.[136] As a consequence, Madkhali advised against participation in the planned elections and declared that anyone supporting them supported un-Islamic powers. Instead, his followers should take refuge in Islam and pray for the emergence of a righteous leader.[137] Shaykh Hafala reinforced these teachings and condemned any participation in the elections, employing the same justifications as Madkhali.[138]

In the aftermath of the revolution and during Libya's still euphoric phase of potential democratic transition between October 2011 and the spring of 2013, Madkhali and Hafala's advice was out of touch with the larger sentiment in the country. But, more importantly, it was out of touch with some of their followers. For instance, on May 12, 2012 one person who identified himself as Libyan asked Madkhali in an online forum: "In Saudi Arabia, they say that elections are forbidden . . . [but] when parliament is established, they said that parliament is your guardian [wālī al-amr], so how does this come together? Is it not forbidden to have elections?"[139] This reflected a confusion between beliefs and the difficulty to identify new wālī al-amr, connected to seemingly discordant developments in a new Libya not led by an authoritarian top-down leader but with democracy and opportunities for anyone to be elected as leader of the state.

As one Libyan Salafi-Madkhali from Tripoli explained, "Everyone was talking about the elections and about voting . . . [and] while I was not a supporter, I still wanted to be part . . . but I knew elections were not right."[140] This gap between Madkhali's belief and what some Libyan Salafi-Madkhalis in Libya were challenged with decreased the potency of Madkhali's frames. A frame's potency is not solely connected to its intrinsic appeal. Rather, it hinges on a set of conditions removed and hence external to the content itself, like the dominant attitude to pursue elections in Libya in late 2011 and early 2012.[141]

The grim predictions Madkhali made for Libya if it tried to adopt a system of popular sovereignty and aspire to "Western creations" such as popular sovereignty, however, stuck with Libyan Salafi-Madkhalis.[142] The analyzed sermon would be picked up again after 2014 when Libya slid into a bloody civil war from which the country is still suffering. Madkhali's warnings gave many members validation and reinforced their conviction of the wrongness of democracy.[143] In addition, Libyan Salafi-Madkhalis and local preachers such as Hafala started to promote a narrative of vindication arguing that they and the propagated warnings of democracy had proven right because Libya had become insecure.[144]

By contrast, involvement in one faction of the civil war ("Libya Dawn") was seen as a way for some Libyan Muslim Brotherhood members to preserve the privileged access and control over state institutions that they had gained since 2011. While this had a negative impact on the group's popular legitimacy in the following months and years, there was an increasing sentiment that the electoral democracy had ultimately divided the country, causing fitna, insecurity, and fear of impacts on everyone's livelihoods.[145] Libyan Salafi-Madkhalis were among the biggest winners of this sentiment: They had largely kept out of the processes of electoral democracy and had ideological underpinnings from their main leaders that relied on religious sources to frame democracy as the wrong path for Libya.

The GNA, which was installed in Libya after the 2015 United Nations-led peace processes, proved a boon to the Libyan Salafi-Madkhalis in western Libya and Radaa, as this government born out of diplomatic negotiations in the Moroccan city of Skhirat was heavily reliant on Libyan Salafi-Madkhali–imprinted armed groups to protect itself and its authority. This dynamic was abetted by the GNA's international supporters.[146] Beginning in early

2015, the capital's security arrangements morphed into what Lacher calls "Tripoli's militia cartel," which amassed enormous wealth and privileges and was close to capturing the state. Local armed actors were well aware of their crucial position and most GNA representatives could not move around the capital without their protection.[147] Radaa has been at the center of this militia behemoth, with national and international partners relying on its efficacy. During the turmoil of civil war, Radaa continued this work.

As Virginia Collombier notes:

> In particular, they [Radaa] continued to work on ensuring security and order for residents at the local level, using their interventions to further build links with state institutions, particularly the Ministry of the Interior. Their work on organised crime helped them increase their links with the prosecutor general's office in the Ministry of Justice.[148]

Radaa also arrested Hashem Abedi, brother of suicide bomber Salman Abedi, who killed twenty-two people at an Ariana Grande concert in the English city of Manchester on May 22, 2017.[149]

This chapter largely focuses on Radaa as a prime example of the Libyan Salafi-Madkhalis' behavioral adaptation after the fall of Gaddafi. The next section will include Libyan Salafi-Madkhali-armed groups in eastern Libya. The reliance on different examples of the Libyan Salafi-Madkhali movement in Libya is necessary because Salafis are not as centrally organized as are the Islamist movements of the Libyan Muslim Brotherhood.

Overall, this section has, first, shown how Libyan Salafi-Madkhalis started to entrench themselves in post-Gaddafi Libya in a meaningful manner, most importantly by focusing on establishing the organization as a reliable and locally embedded security provider in the capital; second, provided some support for the inclusion-moderation hypothesis given that Libyan Salafi-Madkhalis cooperated with and included outsiders in their security forces, allegedly with the aim of working for the common good in Libya—in this instance, security in the capital—by organizing neighborhood vigilante groups. In this vein, leader Kara founded Radaa, which grew into the most significant force in Tripoli, running the largest prison in western Libya for Salafi-jihadis captured during the fight against ISIS in Sirte in 2015 and Western jihadis, such as Hashem Abedi. This section has also asserted previous arguments made by social movement scholars with regard to the inclusion-moderation hypothesis: namely, that movements might adopt moderate behavior when they integrate further into a system but only on a tactical level to increase their influence until they can abandon cooperation.

Libyan Challenges

As Jillian Schwedler states, one of the "most important effects of political inclusion" is that it "create[s] strong incentives for various groups to cooperate with each other, even if only at a tactical level."[150] However, most research in this vein has focused on the political openings in many parts of the Middle East–North Africa region in the early 1990s.[151] In these examples, cooperation between Islamists and their historic ideological rivals (communists and liberals) was pursued in various instances around issues of common interest.[152] Based on multiple examples from the Egyptian Muslim Brotherhood to the Palestinian Hamas, Schwedler argues that inclusion undoubtedly creates "institutional incentives for diverse groups to even consider cooperating with other groups."[153] This effect can be realized not only in meaningful democratic systems, but also through controlled political openings launched by nondemocratic regimes.[154]

However, the Libyan examples of the Libyan Muslim Brotherhood and Libyan Salafi-Madkhalis add new empirical insights and hence caveats to this theorization: While the former group certainly had institutional incentives to cooperate with their main rivals (the NFA and National Front), they did not; while the latter organization cooperated with locals and let outsiders join their neighborhood armed groups, one of the main mobilizing factors for continuing these armed groups was the identified need for protecting the neighborhood and Libya from Islamists and Salafi-jihadis.

This sheds light on what might be called negligent moderating. The trajectory of social movements in this environment is different from those in previous situations of opened-up political systems in the MENA region: The prevailing insecurity and emerging political institutions poison the nascent democratic political system, which would benefit from sincere cooperation and compromise. This brings us back to the need to explore how and why some actions by militant Islamist or Salafi groups are dangerous and what drives these harmful behaviors.

In the case of the Libyan Salafi-Madkhalis, 2015 proved a pivotal year. The support from Radaa proved determinant in allowing the newly negotiated Libyan government (GNA) to start working in the capital. By March 2017, Radaa had gradually pushed its rivals and former allies out of the capital, including armed groups linked to former LIFG leaders such as Belhaj, with whom they had previously cooperated by fully supporting the GNA, something their rivals did not pursue to the same degree. This can be seen as aligning with what Jarret Brachman formulated when he coined the term "Establishment Salafis" to refer to quietist Salafis who are incorporated into the institutions of the Saudi regime.[155] While the Salafi-Madkhalis never formally became part of the circle of "Establishment Salafists" in Saudi Arabia, Shaykh Madkhali still gave religious legitimacy to the ruling family, clearly outlining his support for the regime.

In Libya, despite the key role they played in allowing the GNA to survive, Libyan Salafi-Madkhali leaders emphasized the allegedly apolitical role of this support and focused on activities that were aimed at keeping order at the local level. They proved extremely able in exploiting the newly opened political opportunities related to the internal structural changes (disintegration of the security apparatus) following the removal of the Gaddafi regime. They consistently managed to prove themselves as loyal partners to emerging political authorities across Libya. While doing so, they stayed away from seeking high-profile political positions, instead focusing on supporting local control. These actions resulted in influence in the Ministry of Interior.[156] Madkhali and other Libyan preachers continued to argue for the incompatibility of Libya and an electoral democracy. This helped to concentrate the Libyan Salafi-Madkhalis on the development of local influence, because they were not distracted by setting up a party or engaging in the political campaigning of 2012.

The actions and framing attempts by Libyan Salafi-Madkhalis did not align with a development toward moderation because the movement focused only on tactical and not meaningful long-term cooperation. Furthermore, the framing was defined by an exclusionary vision based on keeping other viewpoints out, as when Kara emphasized the threat of Islamist preachers in mosques in Tripoli. The most important factor of the movement's framing attempts of this time was the interpretative lens: In their argument, protesting or revolting against sitting political rulers was a strategic mistake and a deviation from Islam that brought fitna. This interpretation was to grow in popularity in Libya and develop into a narrative of triumphalism by Libyan Salafi-Madkhalis in response to the widespread disappointment that followed the collapse of the GNC.

Overall, this section has offered the first explanations for the counterintuitive claim that a quietist force ended up being an influential force in post-Gaddafi Libya. The next chapter, focusing on compromise, will round off this explanation by outlining how the movement managed to expand from its traditional strongholds in western Libya (e.g., Tripoli) to other parts of the country, such as Sirte, Benghazi, and Fezzan, due to its involvement with the LNA, which has been de-facto governing in Eastern and Southern Libya to some extent since 2014. With this, different Libyan Salafi-Madkhali groups found themselves on different sides of a civil war.

With regard to the Libyan Muslim Brotherhood, this chapter has shown how the movement became active in the nascent Libyan political institutions, mostly by focusing on derailing attempts by the NFA to ascend to the most important government posts. It has demonstrated how the Libyan Muslim Brotherhood differs from previous case studies of Islamist movements that were incorporated into political institutions: Because it disregarded cooperation for the common good, the movement instead favored sabotaging political processes. This was particularly the case with the Libyan Muslim Brotherhood's demands and its favored domination of its senior members over parliamentarians; this showcased the movement's unwillingness to cooperate and give up any control to a democratic process. One reason for this dynamic was how little embedded socially the Muslim Brotherhood was in Libya in 2011. It has also highlighted additional caveats for the inclusion-moderation hypothesis related to the ideal precondition under which the hypothesis operates, namely, a pluralistic system.

Analysis of the Libyan Muslim Brotherhood's framing attempts further exemplifies the flawed moderation of the movement in 2012. Analyzing the JCP's election program is useful as a starting point but, given the extent to which democracy has become the dominant language for political legitimacy on a global scale, almost every political actor, apart from Salafi-jihadis or extreme outliers such as North Korea, now makes at least some claims of commitment to democratic norms and practices.[157] The problem is to determine when groups have made substantive commitments that align with shifting goals. In the case of the Libyan Muslim Brotherhood, they considered cooperation acceptable as long as the movement would emerge as the stronger actor. This would allow them to implement their own policy ideas contradictory to moderating positions such as those adopted by the Muslim Brotherhood in Jordan when it decided to participate in electoral democracy and take on junior roles.[158]

A group that has undergone substantive ideological moderation (as opposed to having adopted strategic behavioral moderation) can be identified in policies that might be considered ideological moderation with the help of evidence from internal party debates rather than just public statements. The examples of the Libyan Muslim Brotherhood and Libyan Salafi-Madkhalis add new empirical insights and hence caveats to the inclusion-moderation hypothesis: While the groups certainly had institutional incentives to cooperate with their main rivals, they largely chose not to. Furthermore, the Libyan Salafi-Madkhalis' cooperation with locals and allowing outsiders to join their neighborhood armed groups were primarily modes to protect neighborhoods and Libya from Islamists and Salafi-jihadis.

Previous studies have challenged the usefulness of the slogan "Islam is the Solution" for political change and concrete policies.[159] Islamist parties have been punished at the ballot box when voters believed their slogan to be empty words; instead, voters have held candidates responsible for delivering goods and services as well as policy reforms. The ineffective GNC fared badly in this regard. The Libyan Muslim Brotherhood's overall behavior was to lead to civil war and leave Libya with two competing centers of government authority until October 2020.[160]

A contributing factor to this quick unravelling of Libya's nascent democracy was the inherent weakness of the political institutions. When Gaddafi was removed, the personalistic system of power went with him, so that militias formed during and after the revolution emerged as the country's real power brokers. The GNC was therefore poised to pacify the militias or face violent backlash.[161] This points in turn toward a simultaneous development in Libya: the emergence of militias as partial governing entities given the incapability of the political system.[162]

Salafi-jihadi groups, such as Ansar al-Sharia in Benghazi, became infamously prominent while rejecting the new state and the principle of elections as polytheism (*shirk*) and innovation (*bida'*). Instead, Libyan Salafi-Madkhalis managed to morph into the local governing authority over the course of 2012–2013. Chapter 4 demonstrates the group's success in exploiting political opportunities that had opened up in post-Gaddafi Libya by starting to dominate existing militias and founding new ones.[163] The described weaknesses of the GNC also went hand-in-hand with the persistence of militias and the failure to establish a monopoly of power by the elected national state authority.[164] Chapter 4 assesses how this was undermined by both the Libyan Muslim Brotherhood and the Libyan Salafi-Madkhalis. For now, it is important to understand that this led to the dominance of security concerns in the Libyan population and therefore opened opportunities for growing assertiveness and strength among the militias.

FOUR

A Downhill Slope

BOTH THE LIBYAN Muslim Brotherhood and the Libyan Salafi-Madkhalis were able to exploit political opportunities that opened up after the removal of Gaddafi's internal structures by focusing on negotiating and shrewdly maneuvering their way into political institutions and by establishing locally grounded armed groups that benefited from state resources, respectively. This chapter elaborates on how this successful integration failed to moderate the two movements' behavior, concentrating on the third aspect of moderation: compromise. It covers the years of civil war, from the summer of 2013 to October 2020.

This third and final aspect generally signals a movement's advanced moderation, behavior that can be tracked over a longer period. Compromise not only displays a willingness to work with other groups or individuals on a short-term basis for an imminent goal (as cooperation does), but instead implies the acknowledgment and acceptance of dropping some demands or goals permanently for the common good of society.[1] Compromise can be pragmatic, as it is likely to increase the group's chance of appealing to a wider constituency and thus gain it more influence. However, the Libyan Muslim Brotherhood and Libyan Salafi-Madkhalis failed to moderate in this instance and engaged in uncompromising behavior and framing. Although both movements had managed to take advantage of the newly opened institutions and could have, according to social movement scholars, moved toward moderation, both turned to less moderate behavior the more entrenched they became in the post-Gaddafi Libyan institutions. In fact, their incorporation into these contentious, largely undemocratic structures points toward a need to reformulate the inclusion-moderation hypothesis to inclusion-radicalization. With the outbreak of civil war in Libya in 2013, both movements' behavior adapted to this internal structural change by seeking to protect their influence, employing all means at their disposal.[2]

Recall that the Libyan Muslim Brotherhood managed to benefit from these opportunities over the course of the first and second analyzed time periods, but lost influence afterward due to a mixture of being involved mostly in political institutions that crumbled and lost relevance and internal miscalculations that tried to eliminate all identified enemies (the LNA under Haftar's leadership and other less-threatening competitors such as the National Forces Alliance).[3] This aim was overstretched and ultimately led to the Libyan Muslim Brotherhood's descent into irrelevance by 2020: The movement was not strong enough to take on all their enemies while keeping up morale and commitment internally. Libyan Salafi-Madkhalis, on the other hand, largely refrained from getting involved with political institutions and hence ended up on the right side of history for postrevolutionary Libya when the General National Congress (GNC) ended up being a big disappointment. Instead, they focused on building local support and morphed into reliable members of security forces on all sides of the nation's political spectrum. This led to wider entrenchment of that movement compared to the Libyan Muslim Brotherhood because it ended up being embedded into multiple armed groups that gained in importance.

The Libyan Salafi-Madkhalis' successes were helped by their framing, which built on previously established narratives that revolting against Gaddafi and establishing an electoral democracy were strategic mistakes and deviations from Islam and would cause fitna (chaos). This view of the revolution became more widespread given the disappointment of the GNC. Next to these potent diagnostic and prognostic framing attempts, the motivational framing undertaken by local Libyan Salafi-Madkhali leaders in previous time periods when they were aiming to mobilize more members into action got a major boost in 2016 when their founder, Shaykh Madkhali, issued a fatwa circulated on Facebook, YouTube, and messaging apps that denounced the enemies of Operation Dignity as Muslim Brotherhood affiliates backed by Qatar and endorsed taking up arms and joining Operation Dignity forces.[4] His group had become central for security institutions in all parts of Libya by 2014 and hence carried more relevance as a whole than the Libyan Muslim Brotherhood, which was largely confined to the western part of Libya.

Perilous Interconnections of Parliamentary Politics and Militias

The GNC in this period was riddled with problems, such as finding a ruling coalition, agreeing on a prime minister, and overseeing security sector reform (SSR) that was supposed to integrate the various armed groups in Libya into one overarching structure. From the beginning, politicians and parties largely refrained from compromise politics. But in 2012 the Libyan Muslim Brotherhood began to push for the passage of two divisive bills, Decision No. 7 and the Political Isolation Law. These excluded large parts of the political class that was necessary to rebuild Libya, exhibiting the movement's uncompromising stance in defining the country's future. The fault lines created in these years still define Libya and make a democratic future led by compromise politics unlikely, a situation exacerbated by regional grievances, growing economic hardship, and repeated rounds of civil war.[5]

While the Libyan Muslim Brotherhood was the driving force of this exclusionary legislation, the previously described fragmentation of the Islamist spectrum over forming a political party meant that the most significant fault line in the GNC ran neither between the major parties nor between Islamists and non-Islamists. Instead, the congress was defined by rifts created by the aftermath of the 2011 revolution and ongoing violence in some parts of the country. On one side were most members of the Libyan Muslim Brotherhood, other Islamists, political Salafis, former members of the exiled opposition, and representatives of cities and neighborhoods that were strongholds of armed resistance during the revolution (including Misrata and Zawiya). On the other were members from cities or tribes that had supported the regime during the revolution, including Sirte and Bani Walid.[6]

In October 2012, the Justice and Construction Party (JCP) drove the storming of Bani Walid under Decision No. 7, following the death of a fighter from Misrata held hostage there.[7] Decision No. 7 was a directive by the GNC that gave way to military action against parts of Libya that were considered previous Gaddafi strongholds (and hence against the 2011 revolution). It was controversial, as it was seen as fueling further division and several members of the GNC deliberately abstained from voting on it. As Wolfram Lacher describes: "Only about two-thirds of GNC members were present; many left the chamber shortly beforehand in order to avoid having to vote. The resolution was accepted with 65 votes in favour, just seven against, and about 55 abstentions."[8] This directive served as a de facto trigger for military retribution against public and private sites in Bani Walid. Misratan militias, allied Dar' Libya units, and influential brigades under the Libya Shield Force, such as the al-Halbus and al-Hatin battalions, undertook most of these attacks.[9]

This decision was a harbinger for the politicization of Libya's main political institution in a way that morphed the GNC into a body purposed to acclaim legitimacy to one military offensive/camp or another. The establishment of the GNC as an independent elected political body working with actors from various backgrounds for the common good of Libya became more unrealistic day by day. Furthermore, some of its MPs, such as Salah Badi from Misrata and Mohamed al-Kilani from Zawiya, were simultaneously leading militias.[10]

The Libyan Muslim Brotherhood was supportive of this setup and worked to hamper demobilization and SSR efforts centered around a national structure. The movement asserted that Libya's armed forces should be constructed around revolutionary brigades, such as the Libya Shield Force, which had, nominally at least, been brought under the leadership of the Ministry of Defense earlier in 2012, but had become a kind of independent defense force. As Mohammed Abdelmalek asserted, "The [Libya] Shields are a must. We want a strong army, but we want it to stay in the brigades."[11] A leading reporter for the independent newspaper the *Libya Herald* who covered this story conveyed in our interview that "Everyone knew the SSC needs to go but no one was powerful enough to make that happen . . . or had ideas how to replace it."[12] This behavior was driven by the deep mistrusts among Libyan factions at the time, preventing any actor or authority from being trusted with leading a centralized army. As a consequence, various armed actors routinely employed their power, threatening MPs to align with their purported policy goals.

On the flip side, MPs also used allied armed groups. The Libyan Muslim Brotherhood employed these fighters for their uncompromising policy initiatives, such as the Political Isolation Law (PIL).[13] Post-Gaddafi Libyan politics occurred in an uncooperative environment. One GNC member, who was part of the NFA, described in our interviews that "Compromise [in the GNC] was never an option . . . it was always a win or lose situation."[14] Other GNC members described how they routinely felt threatened: The climate was defined by being either right or wrong and when one was on the wrong side, one needed to think about if a decision might be worth one's life. Two female MPs resigned in May 2013 and January 2014, respectively, as they were convinced that the GNC was run by "men with guns."[15]

Following this divisive path, the debate on the PIL or "law on political exclusion" pitted the previously described camps against each other.[16] The law defined who was ineligible for a position of responsibility in Libya in the future; more concretely, it aimed to keep former Gaddafi regime officials out of these positions of responsibility. How to define who was considered a former regime official could therefore decide the prospects of hundreds of Libyans.[17] The Libyan Muslim Brotherhood, smaller Salafi parties, and representatives of the revolutionary strongholds demanded sweeping exclusions, while the NFA and many independents from the south and center representing previous Gaddafi strongholds advocated for a more lenient version. In successive drafts circulated by the JCP, the circle of guilt expanded to include student union leaders, economists, former military officers, and even those who had broken with Gaddafi or tried to work for reform from within.[18] This was particularly concerning in Libya, even more so than in other countries where dictatorships had been removed, such as Iraq (which was still recovering from de-Ba'athification), Egypt, and Tunisia (where the idea of a political isolation law had been discussed but not enacted).[19]

In Libya, Gaddafi had nurtured a highly personalized regime. In Iraq, there was at least a ruling party to go after (the Ba'ath party), but in Libya the law basically needed to be applied on an individual basis with no party to ban and no comparable ideology to counter.[20] Inside the GNC, a "martyrs bloc" (Kutlat al-Wafa' li-Dima' al-Shuhada') was formed to promote the law. Sami al-Saadi (also known as Abu Mundher al-Saadi), the Libyan Islamic Fighting Group's (LIFG) former religious authority, considered close to the Libyan Muslim Brotherhood, was central to the campaign.[21]

Nevertheless, there were splits among Libyan Islamists: Opposition to the law came from former LIFG leader Abdelhakim Belhadj and representatives such as Abdeljalil Saif al-Nasr from southern Libya, who knew it was unpopular in his constituency. Still and overall, the Libyan Muslim Brotherhood and JCP directive was to support a draconian version of the law to free the path for Islamist policies. This would heavily affect their main contenders, who would have to leave their public mandates because these influential figures, such as the NFA's leader, Mahmoud Jibril, had held senior positions under Gaddafi. The JCP's leader, Muhammad Sawan, proclaimed on the Libyan social media channel Magdi Mokhtar that his organization was proud to be a strong proponent of the law and that he was convinced the law was what Libyan society wanted.[22]

The Libyan Muslim Brotherhood's rhetorical reasoning around these actions continued to be grounded in its conviction that only they truly understood how to create a political system in accordance with Islam.[23] The movement's behavior two years into Libya's post-Gaddafi reality stands out in this respect: While previously deferring from revolutionary behavior focusing on gradual conversion, the movement was now pushing for a top-down approach, exemplified by the PIL, which was supposed to overturn the vestiges of the old order completely.

Due to its contentious nature and a divided GNC, the body remained dead-locked between December 2012 and early May 2013, forestalling progress on any other policy issues, this in a country that urgently needed legislative initiatives to establish its envisioned democracy.[24] On March 5, 2013, approximately five hundred protesters, many of them armed, infiltrated the allegedly secret GNC session held in a meteorological institute in Tripoli and called for the law to be passed. Only twenty-six MPs had dared to show up to the session, but they were held hostage for the day and subjected to threats and physical violence.[25] Most refused to vote under such conditions.[26] Despite this disgraceful episode, the law was adopted almost unanimously on May 5, 2013. GNC members were practically blackmailed into passing it because armed groups affiliated with the martyr's bloc had placed the Ministry of Foreign Affairs, Ministry of Finance, and Ministry of Justice under siege.[27]

For the purpose of political advancement, the Libyan Muslim Brotherhood decided to forget about its obvious engagement with the regime through Saif al-Islam Gaddafi, the dictator's second son, and instead supported a harrowing political initiative that would ultimately divide the county in an irreconcilable manner.[28] With several of its opponents now removed from the GNC and some leaders replaced with its supporters, such as Mohammed Magariaf with Nouri Abusahmain, an ethnic Berber, the Islamists turned their attentions to the unwanted prime minister, Ali Zeidan.[29] In June 2013 the

Libyan Muslim Brotherhood accused the prime minister of being weak and announced that it was withdrawing confidence in his government because of its "successive failures to perform its duties."[30]

By summer 2013, the Libyan Muslim Brotherhood seemed to have become increasingly successful; however, Libya at large was losing in this uncompromising power play and by mid-2013 the organization and its allies were facing Haftar's increasingly successful mobilizations.[31]

Paranoia Entering the Fray: The Repercussions of Morsi's Removal in Egypt

Overall, the Libyan Muslim Brotherhood's behavior with regard to Decision No. 7 and the Political Isolation Law proved that it had largely abandoned its previous reliance on negotiations and continued its renunciation of cooperation. Now any sort of compromise with opposing actors was also out of the question. Instead, the Libyan Muslim Brotherhood proved just as inept at democratic politics as its Egyptian counterpart by obsessing over the elimination of alleged enemies and preferring a marriage of convenience with armed Islamists, Salafis, and local militias from Misrata rather than working with the NFA in any constructive fashion. In the words of Alison Pargeter: "If the Egyptians failed to come to terms with consensus politics, the corresponding failure of the Libyans was spectacular."[32]

In hindsight, Alamin Belhaj and other senior Brotherhood leaders, including Mohamed al-Hirazi, tried to tone down their behavior by emphasizing that their organization was always caught in the middle. Belhaj argued that they had managed to avert a coup against Zeidan by acting as a "mediator between the government and the revolutionaries."[33] These late claims, however, did not alter the result that the Libyan Muslim Brotherhood was working to rule over Libya in an exclusionary manner, driven by the conviction that the movement was superior. In March 2013 Sawan declared with regard to the PIL: "We are the elite, and we need to explain [this] to people."[34]

However, the Libyan Muslim Brotherhood underestimated Libya's volatility as well as their opponents' will to fight. The group's uncompromising behavior, paired with politicians being blackmailed by armed actors, eventually saw Libya spiral into civil war and political division for six years. A Libyan Muslim Brotherhood ally at the time and former LIFG luminary,

Abdelwahhab al-Gaid, leader of the Umma party (al-Umma al-Wasat), identified the PIL as "a main mistake we made" in our interview for this book.
He expressed that he "sincerely wants to apologize to the Libyan people,"
and wished he could turn back time.[35]

The Libyan Muslim Brotherhood's feeling of superiority suffered a blow
when Muhammad Morsi was removed from power in Egypt on July 3, 2013.
As one Libyan-based JCP member described in our interview: "We were in
shock . . . everyone [inside the Libyan Muslim Brotherhood] was scrambling
[over] what to do."[36] Two days later, the JCP announced that it was freezing
its work in the GNC; instead, its members would continue serving in individual capacities.[37] All Libyan interviewees who were consulted for this book
and several others from outside that country believed this announcement
to be meaningless. Internally, the Libyan Muslim Brotherhood was divided:
Some members were arguing that the movement needed to pull out of
politics entirely to avoid a possible coup or popular revolt against it, while
others were convinced that the previous JCP announcement was enough to
placate the populace and convince them that the Libyan Muslim Brotherhood was not interested in political domination while allowing it to hold on
to the positions it had attained.[38] The JCP never stopped using such communication channels as its Facebook page, contributing to the failure of the
party's disengagement from politics.[39]

There is one diagnostic frame that unites all Libyan political actors and
that reverberates heavily in the Libyan population: decrying external interference and connections as causes of the nation's ills. This became a grave
concern for the Libyan Muslim Brotherhood, which was dominated by exiled
structures and gained strength from being part of an international movement. This was captured in their first party congress in 2012, when they
invited many Islamists from other countries to Libya. After the Egyptian
events, the Libyan Muslim Brotherhood acted hastily to denounce any
attachment to the Egyptian Muslim Brotherhood or other international
Islamist structures, but with little success.[40] The conciliatory and compromising behavior they tried to display after the removal of Morsi was super-
ficial. Instead, they took a path of exclusionary and confronting behavior
that alienated parts of the Libyan population and opened the opportunity
for Khalifa Haftar to take on their movement and the political institutions
in Tripoli militarily after having launched his initial offensives in
Benghazi.[41]

The Libyan Muslim Brotherhood had rhetorically argued that the movement worked for all of Libya, but its crucial role in the passage of Decision No. 7 and PIL had proved the opposite. This political maneuvering stalled other legislation of which Libya was in dire need; additionally, the Libyan Muslim Brotherhood's alignment against a comprehensive security sector reform contributed to the violence that was still gripping the country. This included incidents such as "Black Saturday," in which the Libya Shield 1 Brigade, which belonged to the umbrella organization that had been declared a "must" by Muhammad Abdelmalik, opened fire on unarmed protesters outside its base in Benghazi, leaving more than thirty people dead.[42]

Libya Descends Into Civil War

After failing as part of a government to keep all Libyans safe, the Libyan Muslim Brotherhood decided to scale up its uncompromising politics. In September 2013 group members in the GNC pushed for a successful no-confidence vote in the government, which removed the prime minister. Ali Zeidan knew that his fate was sealed and fled the country to Germany.[43] The last piece of the puzzle that exemplifies the Libyan Muslim Brotherhood's uncompromising stance and power hunger was the movement's stalling of a crucial element of democratic politics: namely, the peaceful transition of power.

The GNC's mandate ended in February 2014, but the Libyan Muslim Brotherhood proved unwilling to put an end to what by now was a severely damaged body—especially given that large numbers of NFA MPs who had either been removed under the Political Isolation Law or had withdrawn. Still, due largely to public pressure, the expired GNC passed amendments to the Constitutional Declaration, allowing for elections to a two-hundred-seat House of Representatives to take place in June 2014. However, at this point, Khalifa Haftar had already called on national television for the GNC to be dismantled. In May 2014 he launched a military campaign called "Operation Dignity," which was backed by a number of retired Gaddafi army officers and militias who had fought Salafi-jihadi groups in Benghazi, such as Ansar al-Sharia.[44] They rationalized the campaign as a counterterrorism operation. Haftar relied on a broad definition of "enemies" and also targeted revolutionary brigades in Benghazi that were allied to the GNC, such as the Libya Shield Forces, which were in the pay of the state. LNA spokesperson Ahmed al-Mesmari emphasized on several occasions that the goal was to "cleanse" Libya of all Islamists.[45]

Unsurprisingly, the Libyan Muslim Brotherhood issued a statement on May 21 calling Operation Dignity a "desperate coup attempt."[46] In order to protect its influence, especially in the political institutions in Tripoli, the movement supported countermobilizations by connecting the Libya Shield Forces and other powerful brigades to launch a military campaign named "Operation Libya Dawn."[47] Muhammad Sawan explained this behavior to the Associated Press by calling Libya Dawn a "legitimate" response to Operation Dignity.[48] The Libyan Muslim Brotherhood's behavior was confrontational and the movement made use of its political infiltration of Tripoli's institutions by giving Operation Libya Dawn political cover.

The movement worked with other Islamist political forces, such as Al-Asala, to reinstate the GNC in Tripoli and a related government, despite there being no popular mandate to do so. According to senior Libyan Muslim Brotherhood member Mohamed al-Harizi, the JCP not only supported Operation Libya Dawn "politically and materially," but also played the "biggest role in bringing members of the national Congress back and voting on the formation of the [new] salvation government."[49] In addition, Shaykh al-Gharyani had employed the religious influence institutionally tied to the Dar al-Ifta' (Islamic advisory body) since 2012.

Shaykh Gharyani repeatedly took controversial, partisan stances in Libyan affairs: He supported Salafist and Islamist parties in the 2012 election, advocated for the PIL, took the side of the Islamist Martyrs Bloc in the GNC, and subsequently contributed to deepening polarization.[50] Beginning in Spring 2014, he supported the mobilizations of forces under Libya Dawn by declaring the fight against Haftar's forces a battle for Libya's survival against foreign forces.[51] Furthermore, he declared, "All people need to resist him [Haftar] and not fall for the so-called counterterrorism, because what is desired with counterterrorism . . . is to counter Islam."[52]

The reinstated GNC claimed to be Libya's sole legislative power and refused to accept the actual legislative body (House of Representatives) that had formed after hasty national elections in June 2014. With this, the Libyan Muslim Brotherhood was at the center of Libya's political division between two competing power centers, each demanding legitimacy and battling to control Libya's resources and institutions.[53]

Next to Khalifa Haftar and his patchwork of an army (LNA or Libyan Arab Armed Forces), the revived GNC was one of the main obstacles for the UN-sponsored peace negotiations launched in 2014 in the Moroccan city of Skhirat. These negotiations were planned with international vigor and scaled up as the Islamic State managed to carve out influence and ultimately govern in the Libyan city of Sirte in 2015. By this point, the Libyan Muslim Brotherhood's behavior had cornered the movement into sole alliance with one faction in Libya: the western-based political institution of the GNC and its military backup, Libya Dawn. Fear for its survival exacerbated the organization's uncompromising behavior as Haftar's forces advanced and gained crucial international support from Egypt, the United Arab Emirates, and even France.[54] Nevertheless, the Libyan Muslim Brotherhood, from a position of declining influence, engaged in tactical cooperation, accepting compromise in the form of cooperating with rivals. One example is its participation in the al-Bunyan al-Marsous (Solid Wall) coalition to defeat the Islamic State, which meant that it had to work with the Salafi-Madkhalis from Sirte.

The Government of National Accord, the result of the Skhirat process in 2014, was supposed to be a temporary compromise government able to surpass existing divided institutions in the country. However, it severely disappointed in this regard. To start with, it was led by a rather uncharismatic former GNC MP from a wealthy family in Tripoli, Fayez al-Sarraj.[55] The GNA was the result of international negotiations driven by European and U.S. powers who realized that instability was not only harmful for locals but also converted Libya into a haven for terrorist groups such as IS. The country's fragile borders allowed recruits, especially from Tunisia or Sahel countries, to enter relatively easily. In addition, the abundance of weapons was exploited by IS, as were the hardened grievances inside Libya.[56]

Sirte, the city where IS established its third-strongest province outside of its key territory of Iraq and Syria, had been a Gaddafi stronghold. Many of the city's residents were filled with desire for revenge toward some of the revolutionary forces that had attacked Sirte in the final days of the revolution and brutally murdered Gaddafi in the outskirts. As a legacy, the city was largely neglected by the postrevolutionary body of the GNC. Actors that promised some security, justice, and social benefits—even if attached to a radical ideology—stood a chance at local expansion.[57] Therefore, the first and primary goal of the GNA was to lead a coalition of forces to defeat IS as well as stop Libya from turning into a bigger menace for Europe in particular.

The al-Bunyan al-Marsous coalition was a strategic goal of the international backers of the Skhirat agreement and integral to the GNA's international legitimacy.[58] In order to improve their national and international image, which had suffered due to the Libyan Muslim Brotherhood's uncompromising behavior in the GNC, the group was quick to mobilize Libyan Special Forces and other affiliated militias to participate in the fight against IS.[59] Al-Bunyan al-Marsous stood out as a post-Gaddafi military offensive that brought together forces that had previously been fighting each other. The coalition also meant that the Libyan Muslim Brotherhood and Libyan Salafi-Madkhalis cooperated. The campaign started in May 2016 and lasted nearly seven months, during which time support was provided by U.S. air power and Western allies' military assistance. Still, it was a gruesome battle, with over seven hundred Libyan coalition fighters losing their lives.[60]

In October 2021, Libyan Muslim Brothers Nizar Kawan and Abdulrazzak al-Aradi published an account of the al-Bunyan al-Marsous operation, concluding that it set the final cornerstone for the relationship between political power and military power and made the latter subordinate to the former. At the same time, they argued that the battles "embodied the spirit of national unity exhausted by conflicts, divisions and counter-revolution through the synergy of cities, tribes, factions, trends, and regime and revolutionary formations."[61] However, this moment of unity was short-lived as, after the defeat of IS, the same political fault lines have continued to dominate Libyan politics until today.

Movements struggle to adapt to sudden developments with potential heavy repercussions, such as the removal of President Mohamed Morsi in Egypt. This offers additional evidence to contribute to Susanne Bygne's studies that analyzes the difficulty of bringing all members of a movement onto the same page, such as when the Libyan Muslim Brotherhood decided to have the movement refrain from politics while its MPs continued in the GNC citing "individual responsibility"—what this meant was not only hard to understand for outsiders, but also members of the movement itself.[62] Furthermore, the Libyan Muslim Brotherhood relied on divisive figures, such as Shaykh al-Gharyani who politicized the religious institution he was heading.

On the one hand, singling out the Libyan Muslim Brotherhood is unfair given that other political parties and MPs did not act much differently. This is in line with what Christina Steenkamp has addressed when she talks about "violent societies" that struggle to leave their violence-defined past behind.[63] On the other hand, this book focuses on the Libyan Muslim Brotherhood and Libyan Salafi-Madkhalis' potential moderation. Further research is required to address the same questions with regard to other movements in Libya. Still, the impact that the environment has on individual groups has factored into this book's analysis. The described weaknesses of the GNC also went hand in hand with the persistence of militias and the failure to establish a monopoly of power by the elected national state authority. How this was exploited by the Libyan Salafi-Madkhalis will be assessed in the next section of this chapter.[64]

For now, it is important to understand that the political institution of the GNC was a disappointment to most Libyans and this development left plenty of room for other actors, such as Libyan Salafi-Madkhalis, to fill their security, justice, and economic needs.

Expanding Across Libya and Becoming More Militant

During and in the immediate aftermath of the 2011 revolution, Libyan Salafi-Madkhalis had largely refrained from participating in political institutions and instead continued to grow in influence by entrenching themselves in security institutions. They focused on building local support and morphed into reliable members of security forces on all sides of the political spectrum. The movement then started to align itself strategically with leaderships in the newly divided Libya by identifying different individuals as wālī al-amr for their regions, such as Fayez al-Sarraj, the prime minister of the GNA government, in the west and Khalifa Haftar, leader of the LNA, in the east.

This led to wider acceptance of that movement compared to the Libyan Muslim Brotherhood, because it ended up being locally embedded into multiple armed groups that rose in importance in the instable post-Gaddafi environment. This challenged its followers repeatedly; for example, in 2016 Shaykh Madkhali changed his stance from abstaining from any fighting in Libya to calling on Salafis to join Operation Dignity.[65] This was in contradiction to the actions and beliefs about the identity of the wālī al-amr of Libyan Salafi-Madkhalis in western cities such as Tripoli.[66]

As this movement grew in influence in western Libya, thanks to affiliated groups becoming central to law enforcement in the capital, its members exhibited uncompromising behavior.[67] Libyan Salafi-Madkhalis exploited influential militia positions and began destroying religious and cultural heritage their leader deemed heretical. With Libya sliding into civil war, some Libyan Salafi-Madkhalis also became a crucial part of Haftar's Operation Dignity, while others tried to enforce their social values and conservative behavior on areas they captured.[68] The movement's militias became more assertive in enforcing their Salafi vision on the Libyan population and behaved in an uncompromising manner when they began enforcing gender segregation in Tripoli. The group demanded that women wear the *hijab* in Sirte and, in the east, banned women from traveling without an accompanying male.

Similar to the Libyan Muslim Brotherhood, the Libyan Salafi-Madkhalis' adaptations with regard to compromise can be analyzed with a focus on those who served under the SSC in Tripoli, in Operation Dignity, and in al-Bunyan al-Marsous. The movement exhibited largely uncompromising behavior, defined by an in-group versus out-group mentality as it attacked Sufi heritage, kidnapped Sufi activists, and enforced gender segregation. Contrary to existing scholarship by Vincent Durac, the system into which a movement is integrated matters immensely.[69] While Eva Wegner argues that there are incentives for cooperation and compromise in authoritarian regimes, the post-Arab uprisings environment in Libya demonstrates that for less stable postrevolutionary violent environments, the incentives for cooperation and compromise are low.[70]

The exploitation of influential positions and destruction of "heretical" heritage sites by Libyan Salafi-Madkhalis can be divided into two phases: (1) the early months of the nascent democracy (summer and autumn of 2012); and (2) the months following Haftar's renewed successful attacks in eastern Libya, which emboldened the Libyan Salafi-Madkhalis who were fighting with him (summer and autumn of 2017). The internal disorder in Libya was especially high during both phases, as actors were moving from a revolutionary momentum (removal of Gaddafi) to establishing a nascent democracy in the former and moving away from establishing governance in conquered spaces in the latter.

Emboldened Salafi-Madkhalis Destroy Libya's Sufi Heritage

Many Libyan Salafi-Madkhalis participated in the newly formed neighborhood groups that sprang up in Tripoli after the revolution. They managed to secure material support and political cover through aligned figures in the Supreme Security Committee (SSC), such as Hashim Bishr. Because the SSC was the highest military authority in this transitional period, many Libyan Salafi-Madkhalis felt encouraged to behave in uncompromising ways.[71] One Libyan Salafi-Madkhali from Misrata explained: "In those days everything was defined by who you knew and who you belonged to . . . I did not believe that there was an authority that would come after me, apart from, well, my commander." When asked about the new national institutions of the Ministry of the Interior and Ministry of Defense in Tripoli, he responded: "From Tripoli? No, no, they had no influence here . . . I mean I don't know. All I can tell you is I knew we were fine."[72]

The ideological justification for Sufi–Salafi rifts has been studied intensively, but the Libyan Salafi-Madkhalis' behavior and attacks on many of Libya's holy places stands by itself. While the movement refrained from taking leadership positions in the developing post-Gaddafi Libyan political institutions, and hence mostly operated outside the framework of the newly established parliamentary system, it was also clear that it could count on support within some institutions.[73] In practical terms, SSC elements, such as Infantry Brigade 28, which had spun off from the Tripoli Revolutionary Brigades after Gaddafi's death, sealed off the vicinity and allowed Libyan Salafi-Madkhali groups to operate with impunity when attacking Sufi heritage sites in northwestern Libya, including the al-Shaab mosque in central Tripoli in August 2012 and the tomb of Zubeida in Bani Walid in October 2012.[74]

Not only did the local Libyan Salafi-Madkhalis manage to secure political cover for their behavior, but they received an additional boost when Rabi bin Hadi al-Madkhali's brother, Mohammed bin Hadi al-Madkhali, a professor at the Islamic University of Medina, traveled to Libya to support them in their demolition of Sufi heritage.[75] In late August 2012, Mohammed al-Madkhali reportedly participated in the demolition of a Sufi shrine in Zliten, a town west of Misrata in northwestern Libya, employing heavy machinery such as bulldozers and explosives. Shortly afterward, the movement carried on, destroying the affiliated mosque and a historic library containing holy scripts.[76] They also demolished the tomb of Abd al-Salam al-Asmar, a fifteenth-century Muslim scholar, in Tripoli.[77]

These actions happened largely in broad daylight. Libyan Salafi-Madkhalis recorded them and uploaded some of the destruction footage to social media, de facto sharing their violent behavior instead of attempting to conceal it. This exemplifies the facts that most Libyan Salafi-Madkhalis were convinced of the righteousness of their behavior (ideologically) but also feared little repercussion from being attached to violent acts (practically); instead, they expected political cover or at least disregard for this unjust behavior.[78] In an interview, the deputy spokesperson of the SSC emphasized that "The shrine destructions were no secret . . . the videos [of the destruction] where everywhere in Libya at the time . . . especially in Tripoli people got scared."[79] Nevertheless, while it is clear that the Salafi-Madkhalis were given political cover and practical support for some of their actions (as when SSC forces sealed off areas to allow them to operate undisturbed), there was also significant pushback from the SSC, GNC, and local population. The president of the GNC, Mohammed al-Magariaf, condemned the actions, asserting that he was shocked by the uncovered links between the violators and the state security structures of the SSC. Public protests also took place in Tripoli demanding the GNC hold relevant people responsible.[80] One consequence of these pressures was the resignation of the interior minister, Fawzi Abdel-Al. Inside the SSC, figures such as spokesperson Abdelmoneim al-Hurr, who were strongly interested in the perceived legitimacy of their agency by the public, pushed for the arrest of seventeen participants and argued that the removal of Fawzi Abdel-Al would stop the political cover of such actions.

It was not until the months following Haftar's successful attacks in eastern Libya that demolitions of this magnitude resumed. In September 2017 a prominent Sufi activist was kidnapped, showcasing the vulnerability of adherents as well as Sufi sites. The following month, the historic Sidi Abu Gharara mosque in Tripoli was destroyed, and in November, the Zawiyat Sheikha Radiya, a sixteenth-century Sufi mosque in Tripoli, came under fire by unidentified assailants.[81] That December, armed Libyan Salafi-Madkhalis fighting with Haftar's Operation Dignity targeted the shrine and exhumed the corpse of Mahdi Sanusi, an eminent Libyan Sufi leader and father of the country's first ruler after independence, King Idris. The tomb was located in Kufra, in southeastern Libya, an area that had come under control of Hafar's LNA. Local residents assured Libyan reporters that Sobol al-Salam was responsible, a militia with a strong Libyan Salafi-Madkhali imprint.[82] On the one hand, these instances were part of a larger landscape of insecurity where not only Sufi sites and activists were attacked; on the other, these blatant and often propagated attacks underscored the growing power of Libya's Salafi-Madkhalis at the same time as showcasing the incapacity and unwillingness of the relevant authorities, such as the Ministry of the Interior security forces, to protect historic sites.

Alexander Knysh emphasizes that Salafi animosity toward Sufis often relies on underlying socioeconomic or political drivers. Discontent with Sufis sometimes falls across class-lines and reflects existing social tensions. Anti-Sufi conduct can therefore be a pressure relief for parts of society which associate Sufis with the regime or other repressive powers.[83] Katherine Pollock and Frederic Wehrey applied these insights to Libya and argued that "Salafi attacks on Sufi sites do not solely reflect an ideological clash."[84] After the removal of the Gaddafi regime, Sufis benefited from new liberties to celebrate their faith, yet they also came under immediate attack by Salafi-Madkhalis who declared them as supporters of the old regime who needed to be fought. This was a stretch, given that Libyan Salafi-Madkhalis were also courted under Gaddafi. Overall, the movement "came to dominate the policing sector through militias nominally aligned with Libya's rival authorities in the west and east," write Pollock and Wehrey, who confirm the previously made point that Libyan Salafi-Madkhalis used this new authority as a guarantee for impunity following attacks on Sufis.[85]

In 2013 Abdulraouf Kara, the leader of SDF or Radaa, the Libyan Salafi-Madkhalis' largest militia in western Libya, felt the need to address the continuous blame for attacks on Sufis in the capital and denied authorizing any while admitting that his men were involved.[86] What is most relevant, however, when addressing the question of growing Salafi-Madkhali influence in post-Gaddafi Libya is the fact that neither Radaa nor other security forces in Tripoli proved willing or able to *protect* Sufi sites over the years of analysis. Quite the contrary. The Libyan Salafi-Madkhalis managed to achieve a position of supremacy in security institutions that enabled their members to have uncompromising behavior without fearing backlash. One Libyan Salafi-Madkhali in Tripoli, asked if he feared any repercussions from attacking public sites such as Sufi shrines, answered: "Why would I? . . . We are the police . . . and I will not be punished for what is right."[87]

In eastern Libya, Salafi-Madkhali militias felt similarly emboldened. They carried out assaults on Sufis and because they were affiliated with the military authorities (Haftar's LNA), they could do so largely unpunished. The growing influence of Libyan Salafi-Madkhalis has been described by some analysts as a "Salafisation" of Libya's military and police forces that shows itself in religious conduct by those groups when on duty.[88] Still, while the group had been successful in infiltrating security institutions in the east and west of the country, many Libyans are not subservient to this and in December 2017 challenged the Salafi-Madkhali control of public spaces through parades and loud performances of the *hadra*, a ceremony involving recitation and music, in Tripoli, Misrata, and Sirte.[89]

Salafi-Madkhalis Concentrate on Tripoli and Sirte

The Libyan Salafi-Madkhali movement's behavior in western Libya can be defined in three observations: First, while they became uncompromising with regard to recruitment, it was mostly locally focused in Tripoli and hence relatively well-accepted. Second, they strategically targeted rivals (through abductions, for example) and aligned with the most relevant political institutions necessary to enact their preferred policies, such as becoming the private security force of Prime Minister Serraj. Third, they exploited the governance void in Sirte and became the city's main policing force, enforcing Libyan Salafi-Madkhali social mores after having tactically joined Islamist forces in the al-Bunyan al-Marsous coalition to fight IS.

When the Libyan civil war broke out between Operation Dignity and Libya Dawn, Libyan Salafi-Madkhalis in Tripoli used this time to scale up its local security provision. It also invested additional resources into organizing funerals and supporting Libyans with logistics related to the hajj.[90] This was in line with their previous behavior of not taking on key positions in leading state institutions, which they would need to fight to keep, but instead cooperating selectively with individuals close or sympathetic to the movement in order to guarantee resource flow or protection, as when attacking Sufi shrines.[91]

· During the summer of 2014, while Libya's political divisions were fought over militarily, Libyan Salafi-Madkhalis in Tripoli focused on publicizing their efforts via social media in combating smuggling (especially of drugs and alcohol) and fighting organized crime.[92] This behavior aimed to reassure the local population of Souq al-Jouma, Mitiga, and neighboring areas in Tripoli that Radaa was protecting their everyday lives, independent of the ongoing civil war. Two residents of Tripoli described in interviews for this book that it was "a good feeling" that they lived under Radaa, as they felt more protected in the tumultuous year of 2014.[93]

Simultaneously, Radaa turned more uncompromising in its recruitment while presenting itself as the protective force for large neighborhoods in Tripoli. To join the group, members were questioned about their religious beliefs, with students of Hafala allowed to join quickly. Sporting a beard became an easy identifier for Radaa members in the capital.[94] These recruitment dynamics relaxed slightly after 2015 with the alliance of Radaa with the GNA, when Radaa recruited experienced security officers from the Gaddafi era in order to broaden its membership for further embedment into society and political institutions.[95] Until December 2015, when the Skhirat agreement was signed and the civil war was supposedly over, residents in Tripoli seemed largely to appreciate Radaa's efforts and to forget in part the Libyan Salafi-Madkhali attacks against other religious currents. This was chiefly because Radaa was still seen as a local security force that was not openly attempting to seize control of leading state institutions, as one local politician from Tripoli explained: "They did not even participate in elections . . . [I was sure] they do not want political power."[96] Another reason was that Radaa managed an impressive internal discipline that set the group apart from others; as such, the group's relationship to quietist preachers and internal rationalizations for the pursuit of violence barely made headlines in Libya.[97] Similarly, a German professional who was traveling to Tripoli regularly described that he felt most secure under the group's protection: "I always try to hire folks affiliated with Radaa . . . they are much more disciplined than the rest."[98]

While analysts are in disagreement as to whether Radaa's internal discipline was due to its ideological bounds or because of its strict organizational setup and strong leadership, a mixture of both seems most likely. Radaa's organizational strength largely relied on local recruitment and embeddedness. However, the ideological backdrop of Salafi-Madkhalism helped to keep the group together because it carried the potential to guide the group in a legitimate, top-down manner with Hafala and al-Madkhali's sermons.[99] This argument is in line with Francisco Gutiérrez Sanin and Elisabeth Jean Wood, who examined internal cohesion and discipline related to ideology and argued that, especially in the mid to long term, a joint ideology strengthens a group.[100]

Radaa in Tripoli developed into an inspiring model for other Libyan Salafi-Madkhali militias across Libya. Libyan Salafi-Madkhalis also joined other smaller armed groups across western Libya, notably in Sabratha where the Madkhali-imprinted al-Wadi Brigade, which has ties with Haftar's LNA, gained ascendance following clashes between rival groups in September 2017. In Surman, or Kufra, the Subul al-Salam, a local Libyan Salafi-Madkhali militia affiliated with the LNA appears to have been able to recruit members from Arab tribes, as well as Tebu, who were fighting each other in southern Libya regularly, and Zawiya, focusing on the Counter-Crime Units (Mukafahat al-Jarīma), hoping to be able to follow in Radaa's footsteps.[101]

As to whether the movement managed to take advantage of the opened political opportunities and whether its integration into post-Gaddafi Libya made the movement more moderate in its behavior, the time of the Libyan civil war, from spring 2014 to winter 2015, was another phase of expansion for Radaa due to the Libyan Salafi-Madkhali focus on local policing rather than national confrontation. This expansion came hand in hand with increasingly uncompromising behavior, such as selective recruitment. After representatives from both rival governments in Libya signed a peace deal backed by the United Nations in Skhirat in December 2015, Radaa got another boon as it aligned itself with the newly announced prime minister (Serraj) of the so-called Government of National Accord (GNA), which was supposed to reunite Libya and lead the national fight against IS. This move allowed the group to target their rivals through abductions and imprisonment even more fervently because the new Libyan government could not survive without Radaa's protection.[102]

Emboldened by its centrality for the government's survival, Radaa changed its behavior with regard to planting members in leadership positions. Previously, Radaa had focused on establishing control over local mosques in Souq al-Jouma by only allowing selected preachers to give sermons; by 2016 the group was using its growing influence on state religious institutions to arrest and abduct current personnel with the aim of replacing them with affiliated preachers.

In 2015, the Dar al-Ifta', which is responsible for interpreting Islamic law and giving Islamic guidance in Libya, was under the leadership of Grand Mufti Sadeq al-Gharyani, having been re-established by the NTC in 2012.[103] Gharyani was largely despised by the Libyan Salafi-Madkhalis, who considered him in the same category as other Islamist preachers, such as Sayyid Qutb.[104] Due to Radaa's previous entanglements with abductions of Dar al-Ifta' members close to Gharyani, the disappearance on October 6, 2016 of Shaykh Nader al-Umrani, a prominent figure in Dar al-Ifta' who had publicly criticized the Libyan Salafi-Madkhalis, was quickly blamed on the group.[105] A member of the committee established by the GNA to investigate the case said: "Umrani, a respected and influential scholar, was a challenge to the Madkhalis. Unlike many others, he was not afraid to criticize them openly, whether in the mosque or on TV."[106] The committee never concluded who had abducted Umrani, nor could it trace his remains. But in November 2016, an individual named Haitham al-Zintani confessed to being the assassin of Umrani in a self-recorded video that circulated widely in Libya. Zintani recalled being a member of Radaa's Crime Fighting Apparatus (CFA) and that he "wanted to kill the shaykh because he presented an ideology different from Salafi scholars and clerics, especially that of Rabi' al-Madkhali."[107] He elaborated that he was not acting alone but together with CFA leader Abd al-Hakim Amgaidish, while receiving ideological guidance from Mohammed Sa'id Raslan, a former Muslim Brotherhood member turned leading Egyptian Salafi-Madkhali preacher banned from preaching in Egypt in 2018 but still with a large following in Libya.[108] Both Radaa and Raslan were quick to issue statements denying any knowledge of Zintani or any responsibility for the abduction and alleged killing of Umrani.[109]

While Radaa was at the center of this high-level abduction, the movement did not moderate its behavior as a consequence, but instead continued to exercise pressure on religious officials, such as the head of the General Authority for Endowments and Islamic Affairs (*awqāf*), Abbas al-Gadi.[110] Gadi, who was a close associate of Gharyani, was repeatedly accused by Libyan Salafi-Madkhali preachers of "selling out" to Islamists, but ultimately the straw that broke his back was his poor management of the hajj.[111] As a consequence, the GNA replaced him with Shaykh Mohammed al-Abbani, a well-known figure among Salafi-Madkhalis.[112] With this, Libyan Salafi-Madkhalis showed their uncompromising stance and unwillingness to take on leadership positions for the expansion of the movement while simultaneously indicating the GNA's willingness to intervene in support of one of their biggest security backers.

These indications became more explicit in May 2018 when the Presidency Council, an executive body under the GNA, approved Decree No. 555. This renamed Radaa the Deterrence Unit for the Fight against Organized Crime and Terrorism and declared it a force with nationwide responsibilities. With this decree, Radaa secured new resources to expand its surveillance and intelligence work.[113] Radaa took control of Mitiga airport, the main airport of Tripoli, ran the largest prison in western Libya (Mitiga prison), and proved reliable as the personal security force of Fayez al-Serraj and Sadiq al-Kabir, governor of the Central Bank of Libya.[114] The group managed to exploit benefits linked to these aspects, such as controlling and monitoring traffic in and out of Mitiga, thus making any external support, such as reported "money boxes from Riyadh airport," impossible to trace without inside members reporting on Radaa.[115]

It made it easier as well for them to deliver benefits to residents in Tripoli's neighborhoods. One interviewee from Tripoli described how Libyan Salafi-Madkhalis intervened in problems related to cash distribution by setting up "human ATMs" next to bank machines, the latter of which tended only to release small amounts of money and to run out of cash.[116] Of course, this expansion of influence raised concerns among many other forces in Libya, not only enemies such as the Islamist Libyan Muslim Brotherhood and LIFG, but also senior officials inside the GNA. One of the latter explained: "At the beginning, we were happy they existed ... we liked their discipline and reliability ... [but] we came to realize that there were so many other factors driving them ... actually we got scared as they were so powerful."[117] Radaa's integration in Tripoli went hand in hand with the conceptualization of Serraj and the GNA as wālī al-amr.[118] This took place at the same time that Libyan Salafi-Madkhalis in Libya's east started participating in militias that belonged to Haftar's LNA. For them, Haftar was wālī al-amr.[119]

The flexibility Kara had introduced earlier with regard to deciding on the legitimate ruling authority helped, as the current situation meant that different parts of Libya were dominated by different figures. Therefore, the rationale that "one is obligated to follow the strongest political authority in whatever territory one sits" seemed sufficient.[120] Several interviewees explained that, while the current situation meant Libyan Salafi-Madkhalis in different parts of Libya believed in different ruling authorities, this situation would "come together in the future," potentially the same side as Madkhali followers in other parts of Libya.[121] A much-cited example for Madkhali support across the country and hence current enemy lines was when the Subul al-Salam brigade in Kufra, part of the LNA, received three ambulances from Radaa.[122]

Radaa's established position of influence and the group's further integration into post-Gaddafi Libya did not, however, lead to more moderate behavior. Quite the opposite happened. Radaa initiated rehabilitation programs for prisoners in Mitiga and kept those programs sealed off from any oversight.[123] Representatives of the Human Rights, Transitional Justice, and Rule of Law Division of the United Nations Support Mission in Libya (UNSMIL), as well as Western government officials trying to gain access to former IS fighters, were denied access other than a closely guarded visit with prearranged questions for the guards. Follow-up visits were denied.[124] Libyan government representatives stated facing similar issues.[125]

In short, Libyan Salafi-Madkhalis gained impunity for their behavior to a large degree and could establish Kara-approved rehabilitation programs and police Tripoli's streets in line with a conservative religious understanding. Radaa members approached male and female visitors seated together in cafés to ask if they were married; if they were not, they were sent home and warned not to meet again. They approached women walking without a male guardian in public, harassed members of Tripoli's small LGBTQ community,[126] and even disrupted Tripoli's comic book convention in November 2017 and detained its organizers in Mitiga for "a number of crimes against public morals and Islam . . . [such as] agnosticism, atheism, holding masonic ideas, believing in Halloween, distorting the minds of youth, and *kufr* [disbelief]."[127] Overall, the Libyan Salafi-Madkhalis' uncompromising behavior is captured in the fact that all Libyans interviewed for this book who were at the receiving end of such policing stated that there was no room for discussion or compromise.[128] One young Libyan woman from Tripoli put it succinctly: "They are always right and you are wrong."[129] And what was right and wrong was not established in laws but at the brigade's discretion.

Bunyan al-Marsous and Continuous Influence in Sirte

Sirte is Gaddafi's hometown and the city where he was eventually killed by revolutionaries on October 20, 2011. Many residents of the area remained loyal to his regime until the end because they were directly related to Gaddafi, were part of the same tribe (Gadhafa), or had worked closely with and received influential posts in the regime or direct benefits to the town. The Ouagadougou Conference Halls Complex, for example, was made IS's headquarters when the group controlled Sirte but was built as a landmark by Gaddafi.[130]

While the Gaddafi regime, and especially Saadi Gaddafi, had concentrated on establishing a Salafi-Madkhali presence in Tripoli, Sirte was another location of interest. The dictator worked to establish tight-knit support and control over what he considered the nation's main cities (Tripoli, Sirte) and neglected others (e.g., Benghazi, Derna). Therefore, several mosques and Qur'an learning centers were already dominated by movement members such as Khalid bin Rajab al-Farjan, a Sirte-born Salafi-Madkhali preacher. After the revolution in 2011, the Libyan Salafi-Madkhalis in Sirte concentrated on da'wa (proselytization). Their behavior was of the type usually associated with quietist Salafis, such as refraining from political participation (boycotting the elections) and instead focusing on religious learning.

This changed, however, when al-Farjan was killed by IS after he publicly criticized the group as it took control of the city. This culminated in street protests, largely led by Libyan Salafi-Madkhalis and members of the Farjan tribe, against IS in Sirte. IS cracked down with militant force.[131] As a consequence, several Libyan Salafi-Madkhalis and Farjan tribal members left Sirte, including Farjani's brother. However, leaving the city did not mean that they had given up. Instead, they deliberated next steps. Forming the 604th Infantry Battalion was the most significant one. One Libyan Salafi-Madkhali from Sirte who fought with the battalion, but insists he left the group after IS was driven out of Sirte, expressed to me: "I was so mad . . . I was ready to do anything to drive the Kharijites [IS] out of our home town."[132]

The 604th Battalion was largely formed by Libyan Salafi-Madkhalis, but they also integrated other fighters, especially ones from the Farjan tribe. However, they remained inclusive in their recruitment as long as IS was the agreed-upon enemy. Because the militia only formed in summer 2015, at a time where Radaa in Tripoli could rely on almost four years of experience working as a Libyan Salafi-Madkhali armed force, the 604th Battalion relied on Radaa for advice and also recruits.[133] Before long it had joined the al-Bunyan al-Marsous coalition, tasked with removing IS from Sirte.

Prior to their joining, the coalition was predominantly dominated by militias from Misrata, many with close links to the Libyan Muslim Brotherhood, such as Salah Badi's forces. Many fighters from both sides (Islamist and Libyan Salafi-Madkhalis) within the al-Bunyan al-Marsous coalition felt uneasy about working together. However, the common enemy drove this tactical cooperation and the coalition achieved their aim. IS was driven out of Sirte in December 2016, with the help of Western military support.[134]

While most other al-Bunyan al-Marsous militias then dispersed, the 604th Battalion returned to Sirte and rapidly morphed into the strongest security actor in the city.[135] In the words of a local politician about the majority of them: "All they cared about was Daesh [IS] . . . they did not care about Sirte."[136] On the one hand, the 604th Battalion could capitalize on Libyan Salafi-Madkhali militia capabilities by, for example, sending IS fighters to the Mitiga prison in Tripoli (considered Libya's most secure prison) and hence making the return of those fighters to Sirte unlikely. On the other hand, local citizens were largely welcoming any actor that actually showed commitment to better the situation in the city, which lost international support once IS had been defeated.[137]

The 604th Battalion now forced themselves on Sirte in a variety of ways, including replacing imams and almost exclusively inserting quietist preachers, reenforcing hijab regulations, and setting up more Salafi schools. Previous allies, such as Misratan forces, protested against these measures by expressing their discontent on social media and complaining to the GNA.[138] However, because they relied on one of the battalion's allies, Radaa, the GNA had barely any capabilities to rein in the Libyan Salafi-Madkhali policing.[139]

The 604th Battalion itself took Radaa as an example and made sure to promote their commitment to the local population and its efforts to fill a governance void in Sirte with services such as building and maintaining hospitals. They established and populated their own YouTube channel and Facebook pages related to them.[140] This behavioral trajectory aligns with similar dynamics outlined for both Radaa and the Libyan Muslim Brotherhood: short-term tactical cooperation exhibiting moderate behavior and compromise, joining and cooperating in alliances that include traditional adversary forces. However, after a position of superiority was achieved, those movements turned to increasingly radical behavior by exclusively promoting their own members and enforcing their ideological vision in an uncompromising manner.

In the 604th Battalion, this behavior was defined by targeted kidnappings and armed assaults on its critics. In March of 2018, they kidnapped military prosecutor Masoud Erhouma, who had tried to establish a paper trail documenting IS fighter and other prisoner movement between Libyan Salafi-Madkhali militias.[141] Citizens of Sirte began to complain about the moral policing the 604th Battalion pursued, with one local resident who had lived in Sirte under IS saying when interviewed in 2019:

> I feel like we are under the same regime again . . . some things are good like that they [Libyan Salafi-Madkhalis] provide us with things we need, and they seem invested in Sirte but I am scared of their agenda and I am also sometimes scared to do something wrong . . . I heard about arrests of people who did not know they were doing something wrong according to Islam . . . I also wonder are people outside . . . are they watching Sirte? Why does no one care?[142]

A local teacher, who had nominated herself to the municipality election in 2014, won, and rejoined the body after IS's defeat, added: "We need to disarm the militias, but we need support . . . why did no one stay for that?"[143]

Fighting Islamists and Salafi-Jihadis with Salafi-Madkhalis: Haftar's Libyan National Army

For the first time since 2011, the 2014 civil war meant a major military confrontation that reverberated across the country. It also meant that both the Libyan Muslim Brotherhood and Libyan Salafi-Madkhalis faced crucial choices with regard to the use of violence in a context of overall violent polarization.[144] Radaa in Tripoli decided to refrain from supporting the Libya Dawn coalition that was defending western Libya's political institutions from Haftar's assault. By contrast, Libyan Salafi-Madkhali forces in eastern Libya joined the opposing faction of the LNA and supported Haftar's Operation Dignity from the start, largely by establishing their own militias.

Structurally, this was facilitated by the fact that the LNA was (and remains) not a traditional army, but rather an amalgamation of different militias collaborating under Haftar's command. Its proclaimed goal was to fight Salafi-jihadi groups in eastern Libya and to depose the government in Tripoli in order to prevent future lawlessness, as occurred when Salafi-jihadi groups wreaked havoc in Benghazi in 2013. Instead of needing to integrate into an overarching military structure, Libyan Salafi-Madkhalis could establish their own militias, allowing them to, among other things, factor prayer times into their training schedule.[145]

The assassinations of several sympathetic Salafis in Benghazi from mid-2013 to early 2014 culminated in the killing of Colonel Kamal Bazaza, head of the Islamic Affairs department in the Benghazi Security Directorate and a well-known Salafi preacher with many followers. This spurred Libyan Salafi-Madkhalis to join Haftar's campaign.[146] Of course, this was also facilitated by the fact that their rival coalition, Libya Dawn, was prominently led by groups such as the Steadfastness Front (Jabhat al-Samud) of Salah Badi, and Misratan forces, such as al-Halbus and al-Hatin, all allied with Islamists. By early 2014 Benghazi's Libyan Salafi-Madkhalis were about to take a clear turn from focusing on daʿwa to establishing and joining militias.

Foremost among eastern Libyan Salafi-Madkhali militias was the Tawhid Battalion, founded in Benghazi in June 2014 and commanded by Izz al-Din al-Tarhuni. After Tarhuni's death in battle in Benghazi in February 2015, the battalion was dispersed. Some members joined different units of Haftar's LNA, including the 302 Special Forces Battalion, the Marine Special Forces, and the 210 Brigade.[147] Some, however, left the battlefield behind when Tarhuni's death was followed by a fatwa by Shaykh Madkhali forbidding participation in the Dawn–Dignity conflict.[148]

Practically, the dispersal of many Libyan Salafi-Madkhalis into various militias led to a further increase in influence as the movement became a major power broker in Haftar's LNA. In other words, they managed to convince other LNA members not only of the superiority of their fighting skills but also that of their religion. One previous LNA member explained: "They seemed to have clear guidance . . . [and] knew what they wanted I liked that . . . I started listening . . . [and] started praying with them."[149] This is one example of some success in spreading Madkhali beliefs and practice while becoming part of the LNA.

Another influential Libyan Salafi-Madkhali involvement under the LNA umbrella was led by Ashraf al-Mayyar al-Hasi, a former field commander in the 17 February Brigade (revolutionary forces), and his deputy, Nafati al-Tajuri, who joined the Saiqa (Thunderbolt) Special Forces of the LNA and attracted many other group members to join them.[150] Mayyar was a favorite of Haftar, as he combined fighting capability with a strong devotion to Operation Dignity; hence he was regularly received by Haftar's allies at the House of Representatives in the eastern town of Tobruk.

Later in 2018, the two men would fall out and Mayyar would declare the head of the House of Representatives, Aquila Saleh, as the legitimate wālī al-amr.[151] Between 2014 and 2020, Shaykh Madkhali would only comment irregularly on whom he considered wālī al-amr in Libya. In a recording uploaded four months after the GNA's formation, he advised his listeners to "stay united" and always support those who followed Islam and advocated for the implementation of shariʿa. He did not explicitly mention the GNA or the rival government in eastern Libya. In this recording, uploaded to YouTube on April 4, 2016, one can follow an exchange after some listeners ask if they should follow the GNA or the government related to Libya's parallel structures in the east because both seem to be supporting shariʿa. Madkhali answers that he does not trust the GNA and advises to "remain with those who want the application of a shariʿa-compliant constitution." While it is unclear why this would be the government in eastern Libya, this is implicit, as he states that he does not trust the GNA.[152] This helped local Libyan Salafi-Madkhali forces with their frame potency: Their individual militia leaders or local shaykhs could interpret Madkhali's advice in different ways.[153]

Libyan Salafi-Madkhali–led forces continued to support Operation Dignity through their Tarik Ben Ziyad Brigade and by fighting with various neighborhood "protection forces" in Benghazi.[154] However, taking advantage of open opportunities related to structural change, in this case the transition into civil war, is best traced with regard to the Tawhid Battalion and the Thunderbolt forces under Mayyar's command. These turned into fierce fighting forces that some described as the "backbone" of Operation Dignity or "Haftar's shock troops."[155] One former revolutionary fighter from Benghazi who had joined Operation Dignity in its early phase stated: "They [the Salafi-Madkhalis] were very strong fighters . . . and they never seemed afraid even though I know many of them died."[156] A militia commander from

Misrata whose militia was part of Libya Dawn similarly argued: "I don't know where they [Madkhalis] learned to fight but they were relentless."[157] To acknowledge their fighting capabilities, Haftar's son, Saddam Haftar, decided to integrate Libyan Salafi-Madkhali fighters into the elite 106th Brigade (Awlia al-Dam). This furthered their influence in the LNA. The 106th was one of the best-equipped and most important brigades of Haftar's LNA, as Khalifa Haftar promoted his sons into military leadership positions to take over after his own expected rise to head of the Libyan state.[158]

In early autumn 2017, after three years of grueling conflict, Haftar declared victory in Benghazi.[159] Some Libyan Salafi-Madkhali fighters participated in offensives that followed in eastern Libya, particularly in Derna, but many assumed policing functions in the conquered area of Benghazi. But as their influence increased in the most powerful body in eastern Libya (LNA), the Libyan Salafi-Madkhalis pursued increasingly uncompromising behavior. The organization promoted its own people, who issued orders that were in line with conservative religious understanding. It enforced these orders in an uncompromising manner. It pursued the extrajudicial killings and torture of prisoners of war, a violation of international law. It also put pressure on HoR members who dared to criticize behavior by Libyan Salafi-Madkhalis.

In efforts to mirror the existing government structures in western Libya, the breakaway eastern authorities initiated an office for religious endowments in 2014. This eastern institution offered central positions to Salafi-Madkhalis.[160] The influence of Libyan Salafi-Madkhalis within the LNA can also be seen in Osama al-Otaibi, a quietist preacher from Saudi Arabia close to Rabi bin Hadi al-Madkhali, who came to Libya in early 2017 at the invitation of the LNA General Command. Otaibi was supposed to undertake a tour across eastern Libya but in some parts, such as Tobruk, local politicians and citizens protested.[161] One resident of Benghazi expressed that: "I don't recognize many preachers and our mosques and the religious center where I would go sometimes were now run by guys who seemed little different to me than Ansar al-Sharia . . . [as] they did not allow any discussion about Islam."[162]

Some Libyan Salafi-Madkhalis, including those in the 106th Infantry Battalion, joined Haftar's next offensive on the city of Derna, another previous hotspot of Salafi-jihadis in 2018. After a brutal battle over the city's control, the LNA declared victory in February 2019.[163] Subsequently, Libyan Salafi-Madkhalis targeted control of mosques. As a first step in Derna, for example, they closed the al-Sahaba mosque, preventing locals from praying at one of the city's most prominent religious centers.[164] Three lifelong citizens who still lived there at the time of their interviews in autumn 2019 described how, in late February of that year, LNA troops went through their mosques and local libraries screening for books of which they did not approve. Most of these were Western literature, although many books, such as those by Western philosophers, had already been removed or burned by Salafi-jihadi forces.[165] Even the Salafi-jihadis admitted that Libyan Salafi-Madkhalis had risen in importance as the former's situation had greatly deteriorated, with one Salafi-jihadi Libyan Telegram social media channel stating that "Madkhalis form the largest, most crucial actor in politics and daily life in the east."[166]

With regard to enforcing orders, Benghazi witnessed a stricter enforcement of Libyan Salafi-Madkhali moralities. This was largely demonstrated by limiting women's rights and youth events. The movement issued a travel ban on women traveling alone and disrupted events organized by youth groups who had started social media pages in English documenting abuses by LNA forces. One former youth group leader who now lives in exile explained: "Every day someone was either arrested or assaulted . . . and Haftar was trying to control all information . . . social media and speaking English helped us . . . [therefore] we got publicity and tried to change things, but Haftar and his forces were so powerful, and I did not see any big actors like the U.S. actually going against him."[167] In addition, the General Authority issued fatwas and directives, among them those that encouraged the destruction of Sufi heritage.[168]

As others had done in Radaa's Mitiga prison, clerics allied with the Tawhid Battalion went into LNA-controlled prisons to conduct theological "re-education" of imprisoned fighters from IS and Benghazi-based Salafi-jihadists.[169] One man interviewed by Frederic Wehrey in 2018 who contributed to these tasks as member of the 210th Brigade spoke about "ridding Benghazi of Islamic 'deviancy' and of purifying the hearts and minds of the young men who'd strayed to the 'other side,'" meaning the Muslim Brotherhood, al-Qaʿida, and Islamic State, which he considered "one and the same."[170] Given that Haftar's LNA was still caught up in fighting and that the actual reach of other potential governing actors in Libya was so low, the

Libyan Salafi-Madkhalis could roll out these programs without much competition or institutional challenge.

In June 2017 the UN Panel of Experts on Libya noted that the LNA was connected to extrajudicial killings. Salafi forces within the LNA were in charge of a "secret section" at Qarnada prison in Shahhat, in eastern Libya, supervised by two members of Tawhid, where torture regularly took place, according to witness testimonies.[171] Tying the Tawhid Battalion to torturous behavior was facilitated by the fact that members of the group took to social media to declare their enemies "apostates" and advocate for their torture.

The second most important Libyan Salafi-Madkhali militia under the LNA, the Tariq Ibn Ziyad Brigade, released a video of the execution of a suspected IS fighter from Benghazi in February 2017. This came to the attention not only of local residents disheartened by the same brutality from their new rulers that they had experienced when Salafi-jihadis were the biggest actors in town, but also of international observers. Many of the latter were ready to tie this behavior to the LNA rather than accept Haftar's claims that "some forces [have] gone rogue." An American diplomat asserted: "It was all getting too much . . . yes, Haftar did not seem like a shining democrat . . . [but] we had hoped he can bring some stability and rid Libya of these terrorists, instead he was backing other terrorists [Libyan Salafi-Madkhalis]."[172] The LNA therefore aimed to show that they were acting against such behavior. In November 2017, they detained one Libyan Salafi-Madkhali of the Tariq Ibn Ziyad Brigade, Mohammed al-Fakri, in connection with the apparent summary execution of thirty-six men in the LNA-controlled town of al-Abyar.[173]

Again, the Libyan Salafi-Madkhalis had acquired a role of superiority that enabled militias linked to the movement to act in an uncompromising manner and largely with impunity as they enjoyed political cover to a large degree. In eastern Libya, this cover came from the region's most powerful institution, the LNA.[174]

Following a series of kidnappings and forced disappearances, in July 2019 Libyan Salafi-Madkhalis also intervened in the political system by abducting House of Representatives member Seham Sergiwa, a Benghazi representative elected in 2014.[175] Witnesses blamed the 106th Brigade; its commander, Salem Rahil, had been threatening Sergiwa after her mild criticism of the LNA saying that Haftar's offensive on Tripoli should be stopped.[176] Despite multiple calls by the UNSMIL for the LNA to investigate the disappearance and the LNA's repeated denial of responsibility, Sergiwa never reappeared.[177]

Overall, the Libyan Salafi-Madkhalis managed to continue this uncompromising behavior because its members remained crucial to the LNA's fighting force in the continuing civil war being fought in eastern Libya. In Spring 2018, the Tareq Ibn Ziyad Brigade attacked Derna as part of a broader LNA offensive; when the LNA breached further south toward Sebha in March 2019, it joined forces with local Libyan Salafi-Madkhali–dominated militias, such as Battalion 116.[178] Given the movement's behavior, some scholars have begun to argue that "we may be witnessing the militarization of a movement once best known for its quietist approach to politics" in Libya.[179]

Compromise as a Distant Possibility

Compromise generally signals advanced moderation by a movement. The Libyan Muslim Brotherhood and Libyan Salafi-Madkhalis largely failed to moderate in the third analyzed time period as defined by their uncompromising behavior. In other words, while both movements had managed to take advantage of the newly open institutions and hence, according to social movement scholars, could have increasingly moved to moderation, both the Libyan Muslim Brotherhood and Libyan Salafi-Madkhalis actually turned to less moderate behavior the more entrenched they became in the post-Gaddafi Libyan institutions.

These research findings highlight an aspect explored by other SMT scholars under the "paradox of democracy." A central concern for debates about moderation is the possibility that a group can adopt what might be called behavioral moderation without substantive ideological moderation. In other words, it may behave as if it were committed to respecting pluralist and democratic political processes but continue to hold core commitments that run counter to democratic norms. Whereas behavioral moderation may well be desirable on its own, some political developments highlight the increased need for moderation. When institutions are reforming fundamentally or newly emerging with little to no checks and balances in place, the ideology of movements become extremely relevant.[180] In the places and time periods covered by this book, the behavioral moderation has already largely failed, strongly indicating that ideological nonmoderation has been driving it.

This in turn is connected to diagnostic framing. Frederic Wehrey asserts that "perhaps the most important factor has been the allure of the quietists' narrative of triumphalism in response to the widespread disappointment that followed the Arab Spring. Protesting or revolting against sitting political rulers, the quietists argue, was both a strategic mistake and a deviation from Islam that has brought only ruin and chaos, or *fitna*."[181]

While abandonment of violence and cooperation are necessary variables for a pluralistic system to function in the first place, compromise builds the third variable for it to actually survive and, ideally, run smoothly.[182] While the Libyan Muslim Brotherhood began promising moderation by largely abandoning violence and focusing on negotiations in the first time period, it turned less promising in the second, leaving behind cooperation at many instances and focusing on exclusionary behavior instead. In the third time period the Libyan Muslim Brotherhood abandoned compromise and instead failed to distinguish between politics of revenge and what was needed in a time of transition, piggybacking on forces that used violence to reach their aims.[183]

Libyan Salafi-Madkhalis mainly benefited from staying clear of attempts at parliamentary politics in post-Gaddafi Libya. Instead, they grew as local security forces and managed to build some local support. Ultimately, their militias participated in a brutal power play over Libya's vast oil resources and correlating economic wealth to increase their power. Libyan Salafi Makhdalis exploited this new influence to destroy religious and cultural heritage they deemed heretical and enforce gender-specific regulations. This was particularly the case in Sirte after the defeat of IS by a Libyan cross-ideological coalition with international support: Salafi-Madkhalis were quick to wage an ideological contest with other currents over the newly liberated public space, including schools, Friday prayers in mosques, and Islamic endowments. Nevertheless, individual members detracted from this consensus especially with regard to enforcing their ideological views with threats. Ultimately, both the Libyan Salafi-Madkhalis and Libyan Muslim Brothers have held Libya hostage and become hindrances to a peaceful future for the country.

FIVE

What Next?

AS THESE WORDS go to print in early 2025, more than fourteen years after the start of protests against the Gaddafi regime, Libya's transition into a democracy looks extremely unlikely. Analysts are divided in their assessments of why. The two prevailing explanations for Libya's dire state are the embeddedness of militias, which stands in the way of implementing civilian rule over a monopoly of force, and the interference of external actors promoting an authoritarian agenda, often connected to promoting military leader Khalifa Haftar as a savior figure.[1] Furthermore, the 2011 NATO intervention in Libya has haunted foreign policy makers such as former U.S. President Barack Obama, who declared the lack of preparation for a post-Gaddafi Libya the "worst mistake" of his foreign policy.[2] Libya continues to be a conundrum—and more, one where they can particularly quickly burn their fingers.[3]

Power Hunger and Conviction of Righteousness

The NATO intervention on the side of the revolutionaries in 2011 triggered a vast number of academic studies examining its legal standing according to International Law, its practical execution, the dearth of information on the Allied Joint Force Command Naples in Italy, and its theoretical implications for International Relations scholars, most prominently under the principle of Responsibility to Protect (R2P).[4] Far less attention has been given to the parallel recognition of the revolutionary political body of the National Transitional Council as the sole legitimate representative of Libya in the first months of the revolution.[5]

This hasty Western consensus to support the violent opposition against Gaddafi with military support, coupled with the poorly understood constellation of representatives in the NTC and revolutionary groups in the country (admitted to in, e.g., internal communications published by Wikileaks from then–U.S. Secretary of State Hillary Clinton and inquiries in the UK parliament) exacerbated the fragility of Libya's potential transition to democracy.[6] This is because the commitment to democracy by key politicians, such as the leader of the Justice and Construction Party, Muhammad Sawan, as well as claims outlined in election programs, were taken at face value, instead of more critical analysis of Libyan groups who did not act in line with moderate parameters necessary to establish a system. This assessment would likely have led to the conclusion that Western forces would need to be more engaged in Libya's transition, which was undesirable given, for instance, their existing unpopular engagement in Afghanistan.[7]

All this has resulted in a situation in which a variety of Libyan groups, many with regional links, were predominantly in charge of filling the political, social, and economic voids previously dominated by the Gaddafi regime. Consequently, over three hundred parties registered for the 2012 elections and over two thousand candidates competed for the two hundred seats. Some groups, such as Ansar al-Sharia in Benghazi, rejected elections, however, and tried to impose local governance attempts in the tumultuous aftermath of the revolution.[8]

Unlike other political and military actors, the Libyan Muslim Brotherhood and Libyan Salafi-Madkhalis proved particularly potent in taking advantage of the political opportunities present in (post-)revolutionary Libya: the former by becoming the central political party dominating the first Libyan parliament and the latter by becoming part of various militias across Libya, turning into a crucial security actor for the country.[9] But the groups failed to work for the common good of Libya by seeking compromise. Both movements also became less moderate when they reached positions of perceived dominance, as when the Libyan Salafi-Madkhalis enforced compliance with their own social norms, including gender segregation.[10] Both internal and external factors explain the developments of the Libyan Muslim

Brotherhood and Libyan Salafi-Madkhalis in a comprehensive manner. This helps to understand why, in 2025, both groups are considered hindrances to a democratic future for Libya.[11]

The main research question that has been driving this book was how and why the Libyan Muslim Brotherhood and Libyan Salafi-Madkhalis potentially contributed to Libya's descent into political dividedness and militia rule. In order to answer this question, this book examined the movements' behaviors as well as framing attempts over the course of several years, defined by abundant structural developments as Libya underwent a revolution, a nascent democratic phase, and a political collapse with ensuing civil war. It explored how the two groups adapted and changed over a period of protests and intense fighting (chapter 2: regime opposition, revolution), relatively peaceful months and elections (chapter 3: democratic attempts) and disintegrating authority and renewed fighting (chapter 4: passing of the political isolation law, civil war).

This book argues that the two groups' failure to moderate lay in their respective power hunger, fueled by the fear of rivals' ascents combined with exclusionary identity formations and external aggravating factors such as the inexperience of Libyans with democratic politics and the high penetration of weaponry. Chapters 2 to 4 examined how the exclusionary behavior the movements pursued, such as the Libyan Muslim Brotherhood working to have large parts of the elected parliament expelled under the Political Isolation Law and the Libyan Salafi-Madkhalis emphasizing recruitment of likeminded individuals after 2015, is intrinsically tied to the groups' internal convictions to be the only righteous actors for Libya in accordance with Islam. It is precisely this internal conviction of righteousness that enabled the two groups to rise in importance as they disregarded other opinions and justified tactical cooperation, only to abandon it after a position of dominance was reached.

Likewise, the groups' framing attempts, which eloquently managed to draw a line between moments from early Islamic history to the present situation of Libyan Muslims, were employed to taint contemporary developments in a harrowing light and thus create a narrative of the dark times that awaited Libya if defined solutions were not followed, such as voting for the JCP in 2012 (Libyan Muslim Brotherhood) or participating in the protests in 2011 (Libyan Salafi-Madkhalis). The Libyan Salafi-Madkhali narrative has been vindicated in that, as warned by Shaykh al-Madkhali, Libya succumbed to civil war after embarking on an attempted journey toward electoral democracy.

In addition, this book reasons that both groups operate under the assumption that there exists a binary choice between two ideological camps (Islamist versus quietist), which means that the rise of one group automatically threatens the survival of the other. This leads to the unpalatable conclusion that meaningful cooperation and actual compromise are out of the question.

Surprising Successes and Failures

The removal of authoritarian regimes in the Middle East and North Africa region was widely seen as a major chance for Islamist forces such as the Muslim Brotherhood to finally rise to power, released from the shackles of oppression under Hosni Mubarak in Egypt, Zine el-Abidin Ben Ali in Tunisia, and Muammar Gaddafi in Libya. Surprisingly, quietist Salafi groups managed deeper influence and rose to nationwide importance due to their emphasis on establishing local security. The incongruence of the Libyan Muslim Brotherhood's ideas and behaviors with those of the Libyan population, and their unwillingness to listen and truly cooperate with potential rivals, ultimately hampered their anticipated ascent. Instead of cooperating and compromising with local forces and other parties to create a good future for all of Libya, the movement was driven by its conviction to be the right political leadership for post-Gaddafi Libya.

Many Libyan actors disagreed, including the National Forces Alliance, the nation's biggest faction in parliament in 2012. Political power struggles led to the mobilizations of armed actors attached to politicians, which ultimately led to civil war in 2013. Since then, the Libyan Muslim Brotherhood has been on a downward spiral due to low popularity. They are seen as the main force to blame for the collapse of the first post-Gaddafi parliament. The Libyan Salafi-Madkhalis, on the other hand, rose to national importance over the entirety of the analyzed timeframe due to their emphasis on establishing local security. They managed to fill a void by keeping their armed actors in place when the other forces of the anti-IS coalition had left, especially in places such as Sirte, which had been ruled by IS and heavily destroyed in battles. By tracing these developments, this book explains why the developments of the Libyan Muslim Brotherhood negate expectations that existed in 2011 about the region "turning Islamist."[12] Instead, the Libyan Muslim Brotherhood fared poorly in the second round of elections in 2013 after the movement alienated many of their fellow Libyans.[13]

This behavior was led by an internal conviction that the Libyan Muslim Brotherhood was the right political leadership for Libya. They employed this rationale when justifying manipulative actions, such as plotting for the candidate of the smallest party in parliament to become prime minister instead of supporting the natural candidate. This is relevant because it provides an understanding of both internal factors, such as power hunger and conflated self-perception, as well as external factors, such as wariness by the local population of such a quick founding of a political party. (Political parties having been despised under Gaddafi and the Libyan Muslim Brotherhood's being the most vilified opposition group are more important factors than the movement's capacity to organize politically.[14])

The scarcity of literature on the two groups has limited the ability of this book to examine all aspects of this question in detail. Future research could build on these findings. One of the most notable questions to be examined in future research is the role that nonmembers of the two movements played in shaping the groups' developments.

The Libyan Muslim Brotherhood and Libyan Salafi-Madkhalis' developments against benchmarks of moderation show that, in their quests for influence in this still relatively nascent post-Gaddafi Libya, the two groups demonstrated strategical successes alongside miscalculations. An example of the former would be the Libyan Muslim Brotherhood's negotiation tactic to emphasize the proportionally low presentation of Islamist forces in the NTC, which arguably lowered its legitimacy as a body intended to represent all of Libya. An example of the latter would be the Libyan Muslim Brotherhood's ignorance and misjudgment of some of its competitors.[15] This aim was overstretched and ultimately led to the movement's descent in Libya by 2020. It has since struggled to secure influential positions in Libya's political institutions. Simultaneously, it is suffering a legitimacy crisis due to the negative connotations many Libyans have of its destructive role in the first Libyan parliament.[16]

Above all, by adjusting their behavior in Libya's political and security institutions, the Libyan Muslim Brotherhood and Libyan Salafi-Madkhalis have sought to respond to the rising influence of military actors on political institutions. This, in turn, shifted the balance of power from the Libyan Muslim Brotherhood being an influential force in the first Libyan parliament in 2012, exemplified in their potential to push through divisive legislation against the NFA, to a movement reliant on affiliated military groups that tried to defend their host institutions against assaults by Haftar, most significantly in 2014. For the Libyan Salafi-Madkhalis, the environment of instability after Gaddafi's removal outlined in chapter 2 facilitated its ascent because the movement had focused on protecting local concerns, such as safety on the streets and responsibility for Friday sermons in the mosques, by establishing armed neighborhood protection groups. By relying on religious sources when exerting framing attempts, both groups aimed to portray their actions as the only right ones, delegitimizing possible opposition and hampering the outlook of meaningful cooperation and compromise.

The preceding chapters have demonstrated the necessity for the two national movements to make adjustments. For instance, over the years analyzed in this book, multiple Libyan Salafi-Madkhalis acted in contradiction to Shaykh Madkhali's guidance, participating in the incipient civil war while Madkhali was advocating to refrain from involvement on either side. For the Libyan Muslim Brotherhood, the biggest internal discussion continues to be the poorly defined relationship between the party (JCP) and the movement (jamāʿa).[17] In November 2018, Libya's Al-Ahrar TV hosted a four-episode series that discussed the relationship of the JCP to the Libyan Muslim Brotherhood and the international Muslim Brotherhood, featuring members and external observers.[18] Eventually, in June 2021, Muhammad Sawan, previous head of the group's Shura Council before he became chairman of the JCP, had become too critical and unattainable and they replaced him with a more palatable choice, Emad al-Banani.[19] Shortly before, the Libyan Muslim Brotherhood had officially converted into a nongovernmental organization, calling itself the "Renaissance and Renewal Association" and vowing (again) to cut all ties with the international movement in an attempt to leave behind their reputation as a divisive force more interested in an international Islamist agenda than the common good of Libya.[20]

As these developments illustrate, the evolving statuses of the Libyan Muslim Brotherhood and Libyan Salafi-Madkhalis will continue to reflect how their leaders and members interpret and adapt to structural developments, such as potential new elections, which have been postponed several times but are still in planning.[21] Nevertheless, it remains very important to examine how the adjustments and tactics prioritized by the two movements have influenced the attitudes of local populations toward them and also the institutions with which they are entangled, such as the GNU and LNA.

In sum, this book argues that the ideological competition between the two movements puts them in a situation that rules out meaningful cooperation and compromise but certainly allows for tactical cooperation. This puts more recent developments into perspective, such as the 2022 alliance between Fathi Bashagha, previous interior minister of the GNA with ties to forces close to the Libyan Muslim Brotherhood, and Haftar's forces, which are well-staffed with Libyan Salafi-Madkhalis.[22] Whereas some analysts had been quick to jump to the start of a new era for Libya with forces of opposing ideological background coming together in an alliance, the findings of this book allow us to understand the temporary nature of this alliance. Consider that the Libyan Muslim Brotherhood cooperated with politicians in Benghazi who had persecuted them under Gaddafi to give the NTC more weight on the international stage and further the delegitimization of Gaddafi. The Libyan Salafi-Madkhalis fought alongside Islamist militias from Misrata in the al-Bunyan al-Marsous coalition but made targeted abductions of their previous allies after IS was defeated (see chapter 4).

While this book, as emphasized in the introduction, has focused on how and why the Libyan Muslim Brotherhood and Libyan Salafi-Madkhalis have failed to moderate in post-Gaddafi Libya, it has not addressed the extent to which nonmembers of the two movements have shaped the two groups' developments. In view of the security situation on the ground and the ethical obligations to protect individuals at risk of being targeted by armed factions, Libyan civilians were not interviewed about their general perception of the two groups or Libyan Muslim Brotherhood and Libyan Salafi-Madkhali members about their perceptibility of criticism. Given the penetration of both movements into Libya's institutions, including informants collaborating with an array of armed actors, asking civilians about their attitudes toward the Libyan Muslim Brotherhood and Libyan Salafi-Madkhalis could have potentially put them at unnecessary risk.[23] Because I am a non-Libyan researcher working on sensitive issues, such an approach could also have raised suspicions regarding the objectives of the interviews and been perceived as a foreign-sponsored attempt to build a case against the Libyan Muslim Brotherhood and Libyan Salafi-Madkhalis' claims of support in Libya or an attempt to bolster one of the groups' legitimacy by offering evidence of their popularity among the Libyan population.

Thus, interviews with current and former group members, local politicians, and international policy makers were prioritized for this research project, focusing on the behavioral changes of the two movements with regard to structural developments in the country. Accordingly, building on this book, other scholars in the field with different opportunities to embed themselves in local communities could investigate the extent to which the Libyan Muslim Brotherhood's and Libyan Salafi-Madkhalis' successes in political or military institutions correspond with their popularity or perceived legitimacy. Gaining such insights would need to move beyond surveys asking about the theoretical willingness to vote, and instead would require a long-term ethnographic approach and a carefully designed data collection methodology, allowing prospective researchers to immerse themselves in the field.[24]

After all, this book has demonstrated that the Libyan Muslim Brotherhood and Libyan Salafi-Madkhalis' failures to moderate were not determined solely by external factors, such as the high penetration of weaponry in the country, but instead by the two groups' decisions to behave in noncooperative and uncompromising manners. As Shaykh Madkhali remarked in a sermon in 2018, his followers were the only ones on the right path.[25] However, it is exactly this notion of righteousness that jeopardizes mutually beneficial developments in transitionary environments: It stands in the way of cooperation and compromise and builds the basis for frames justifying violent mobilizations and behavior.

Implications Outside Libya

The Libyan Muslim Brotherhood is only one branch of a movement that has been spreading through the Middle East and North Africa region since the 1930s and developed into diverse groups, from Hamas in Palestine to Ennahda in Tunisia. The insights uncovered in this book with regard to the movement's behavior have repercussions for other parts of the region, as Muslim Brotherhood forces might overestimate the usefulness of their internal cohesiveness and experience of organizing politically at the expense of listening and incorporating local demands and concerns.[26] Ultimately these developments left many interviewees skeptical about a democratic future for Libya, having witnessed the exploitation of political institutions by self-serving actors such as the Libyan Muslim Brotherhood when pushing for exclusionary legislation.

One thing is for certain: Islamic movements of a variety of shades and backgrounds influence political developments in the Middle East and North Africa region—and will continue to do so. Building on the lessons from this book, surprises about anticipated behavior are also in the making. For example, the military and ultimate political success of one of the strictest quietist Salafi movements in Libya (Madkhalis) was not anticipated at all. Movements that have been studied for decades, such as Hamas, defy expectations still. The terrorist attack on Israeli soil that killed over one thousand people on October 7, 2023, was a shock, even to many Hamas analysts, who had argued that international legitimacy and being seen as a true representative of the Palestinian people were among the goals of the movement.[27] This demand for international legitimacy was shattered with the brutal assault on Israeli civilians, including women and children.[28] Unrest and potential revolutions can break out in the Middle East and North Africa in unpredictable ways due to varying levels of suppression and fluctuating external interventions. Just days before the Hamas attack on Israel in 2023, U.S. president Joe Biden's national security advisor, Jake Sullivan, declared that the Middle East was the calmest it had been in two decades.[29]

The main implication for policy makers from this book is that Islamic actors should be held accountable in the same ways as other political actors. Instead of trusting representatives from the Muslim Brotherhood more than other Libyan politicians from the NFA because they appear more professional and organized or project the understanding of local embeddedness of MB actors in Egypt onto Libya, it would be most helpful if Islamists were assessed on their behavior and whether this is in line with undercurrents of liberal democracies, which rely on cooperation and compromise. These observations and attached lessons learned could go a long way and also be more helpful than designating entire groups as terrorist or not.[30]

Further Notes on the Operationalization of Moderation for This Book

Abandonment of Violence

While the notion of moderation is contested, the abandonment of violence is accepted as a first step by most scholars. As Samuel Huntington observes, the abandonment of violence and commitment to work through systemic procedures (such as elections) is a first condition of a movement's journey to moderation. Douglass North further argues that engagement with violence is the key factor when determining if societies have turned into developed, civilized nations (or what he calls "open access orders").[1] Overall, the abandonment of violence is not a recent theorization; it is a long-standing tradition in the fields of sociology and political science to assess groups' and individual actors' willingness to advance from their narrow pursuit of self-interest to become part of a collective experience built on trust and belief in mutual interests.[2] This theorization can be traced back to political philosophers, including Thomas Hobbes, outlining the possibilities of escaping the violent, anarchic "state of nature," driven by a desire to avoid the war of all against all.[3]

For modern scholars accustomed to liberal democracies and partially driven by a normative quest to help those prosper, violence is often interpreted as a spoiler to this process and is associated with "nonstate" actors, such as terrorists, harming the public order.[4] Omar Ashour explains this when he argues that behavioral moderation concerns the adaptation of electoral strategies aimed at seeking compromise and nonviolent settlement of disputes that transform radical Islamist actors to mainstream ones.[5] That violence and radicalism are increasingly viewed as illegitimate means for political participation led many Islamists to reframe their political discourse accordingly. This trend has been most visible within the context of the Arab Uprisings in 2011.[6]

For this book, the abandonment of violence is utilized as a first aspect of moderation for the Libyan Muslim Brotherhood and Libyan Salafi-Madkhalis. It acknowledges the basic foundation of this aspect for any moderation that would lend itself to building a peaceful, democratic Libya, just as previous studies asserted the abandonment of violence as prerequisites for pluralistic systems.[7] By focusing solely on nonviolent behavior, this book would have been flawed, as groups can display behavioral and ideological moderation with regard to other parameters, such as the acceptance of electoral democracy by radical parties as a means to achieve ideological goals without compromising their platforms.[8] At the same time, however, this moderation has proven to be tactical, adopted in order to, for example, achieve the aim of gaining access to state resources in order to expand the group's military wing.[9] Therefore, analyzing social movements' moderation without factoring in violent behavior and framing by some of their leadership and members falls short of comprehensively assessing their moderation.

Cooperation

Cooperation is seen as the next step in a movement's development toward moderation, with the aim of building and/or being part of a pluralistic system. Importantly, cooperation is employed as the second aspect in this book, instead of aspects used by other scholars such as adoption of liberal values or adoption of a secular constitution, to tailor it to the Libyan context, which is defined by conservative religious views that emphasize the importance of, e.g., shariʿa. Cooperation is seen as a more neutral aspect that serves as a point of comparison for groups of different backgrounds. This is because there is little normative implication apart from the belief that working together is beneficial to society and implicitly includes moderating behavior.[10] In popular discourse, virtually every Islamist group either has a claim on moderation or is being cast as an example of moderation. Examples include the PJD in Morocco, the IAF in Jordan, the Yemeni Islah Party, the Algerian Islah Party, the Turkish AKP, the Egyptian Muslim Brotherhood (MB), Ennahda in Tunisia, the Syrian MB, and the Palestinian Hamas.[11] When groups as diverse as the Turkish AKP and Hamas are branded as moderate, the analytical boundaries are inherently broad.

Scholars studying moderation demonstrate great variance in the meaning and causes of Islamist moderation. As mentioned earlier, this is largely due to the inductive nature of most studies, which identify moderation in respect to the case studies; therefore, the variations are a symptom of different types of Islamist moderation.[12] This book argues that broader categories are more useful, as the inconsistent use of the term moderation amounts to "conceptual stretching."[13] This criticism focuses on the fact that different scholars subsume various attributes to the concept, basically adding on more and more factors from accepting popular sovereignty to transparent forms of organizing. This ultimately decreases the usefulness of the concept, as it ends up being tailored to one specific group in one specific country.

Another implication is that moderation can become an instrument in ideological struggles; different factions may utilize the concept to gain legitimacy and sympathy from a broader domestic and international audience. Where moderation and democracy have become the currency of political discourse, it is crucial to understand what kind of moderation each party claims and the conditions under which such moderation comes about.

By conceptualizing cooperation as a second aspect for moderation, this book seeks to remove itself from these ideological conversations as the notion of cooperation is fundamental for any political and social system that aims to include different actors and opinions. It is therefore not normatively charged itself, as the abandonment of shariʿa as the source of legislation would be, for example. The notion of cooperation has been present in many studies that engaged with the inclusion-moderation hypothesis, such as Carrie Wickham's use of a combination of inclusion-moderation and social learning hypotheses to explain the emergence of the Al-Wasat Party in Egypt, emphasizing middle-generation Islamist leaders' interactions with people from other convictions and ideologies as a key factor in their moderation.[14] Francesco Cavatorta and İhsan Yılmaz also emphasize social learning and working with other groups when arguing for the moderation of

Moroccan and Tajik Islamists, respectively.[15] While these studies rely on cooperation to argue for or against groups' moderation, none of them explicitly conceptualizes cooperation as an aspect of moderation within which groups' behavioral and ideological adaptation over a certain timeframe are compared. This thesis brings together existing insights into movements' moderations with the realities of a postrevolutionary environment following the post–Arab Uprising period. This demands a flexible framework, especially when comparing groups as ideologically diverse as the Libyan Muslim Brotherhood and Libyan Salafi-Madkhalis.

Compromise

Compromise signals advanced moderation by a movement, especially if behavior based on it can be tracked over a longer period of time. This book employs compromise as the third aspect for assessing a movement's (further) moderation to create an analysis that is detached from ideological backdrops of movements. Instead, compromise serves as a more neutral point of reference: Behavior that exhibits it not only displays a willingness to work with other groups or individuals on a short-term basis for an imminent goal, as cooperation does, but instead implies the acknowledgment and acceptance of dropping demands or goals permanently for the common good of society.[16]

This has been understood by various scholars who argue that compromise is a consistent challenge for any movement. The temptation to act upon intrinsic beliefs, to prioritize and enact decisions or legislation in line with those beliefs that may be disconnected or harmful for other parts of society, is a long-term project for social movements that become part of existing institutions. Therefore, compromise builds the final aspect for analyzing the potential (further) moderation of the two movements under study here. In previous studies, Janine Clark challenged the inclusion-moderation hypothesis by arguing that any meaningful cross-ideological cooperation—as an observable implication of moderation—requires a "spirit of compromise" and an intra-organizational discussion of compromise. For her, inclusion and participation in a formal political structure of multiple ideological stripes is not sufficient to bring about moderation; instead, any Islamist or Salafi movement that becomes included in political or social institutions must have moderated before for cooperation and compromise to emerge. However, Clark is imprecise about what this previous moderation must entail.[17] This book argues that the abandonment of violence in behavior and ideology is the first step of a movement's moderation before elements displaying cooperation and compromise can be analyzed as serious efforts on its trajectory toward moderation.

Summary of Moderation in the Literature

Table A.1 summarizes key arguments regarding Islamist moderation. While literature on the subject is expansive at the time of writing, little agreement exists.[18] Two interrelated issues stand in the way of a generalizable theory of Islamist moderation: (1) the ways in which moderation is conceptualized and defined; and (2) the large degree of variance of moderation across different studies. While one scholar views it sufficient for an Islamist movement to participate in the democratic process for moderation to come about, another might find it insufficient because the adoption of liberal democratic norms is deemed more critical. Hence, moderation takes on different meanings, suggesting that there may be different kinds of moderation. The multitude of processes and competing explanations on moderation—that is, inclusion, participation, organizational interest, party autonomy, social learning, and socioeconomic factors—implies that varying mechanisms of moderation exist. It may be the case that for one particular kind of moderation to emerge (for example, giving up violence), a particular set of factors should exist (that is, state repression or political liberalization).

In summary, we lack a framework that systematically connects various explanations of moderation. Although most explanations deserve merit given the cases and their contexts, in the absence of a unified framework it is virtually impossible to reach a theory of Islamist moderation.[19] In order to address this conundrum, this book draws on the most extensive theoretical engagement with Islamist moderation: the inclusion-moderation hypothesis. Jillian Schwedler's model builds on previous social movement theory work by Donatella della Porta and Charles Tilly arguing that inclusion of previously excluded movements into political and social institutions is necessary for them to moderate. This book adapts the aspects for moderation by relying on more flexible categories than the ones that have largely

TABLE A.1

Overview of existing conceptualizations of moderation

SCHOLAR	CASE STUDY	INDEPENDENT VARIABLE	TYPE OF MODERATION	DEFINITION OF MODERATION
Brooks (2002)	Egypt's Islamic Jihad	Inclusion and political liberalization	Participation in democratic processes (behavioral)	—
Clark (2006)	Jordan's Islamic Action Front (IAF)	Spirit of compromise and intra-organizational discussion of compromise(s)	Cross-ideological cooperation (behavioral and ideological)	—
El-Ghobashy (2005)	Egyptian Muslim Brotherhood	Participation	Ideological transformation	Ideological moderation and democratic understanding
Nasr (2005)	Turkey's Justice and Development Party (AKP) and non-Islamist Pakistani Muslim League (PML)	Capitalism	Moderation (behavioral and ideological)	Moving away from extremism
Robinson (1997)	Jordan's Islamic Action Front (IAF)	Organizational self-interest	Endorsing democracy (behavioral)	Democracy
Schwedler (2006)	Jordan's Islamic Action Front (IAF) and Yemen's Islah Party	Inclusion	Participation in democratic processes (behavioral and ideological)	Movement from a relatively closed and rigid worldview to one more open and tolerant of alternative perspectives
Wickham (2004 "Path")	Egyptian Al-Wasat Party	Inclusion and social learning	Ideological moderation	Ideological moderation and respect for democratic processes

APPENDIX

SCHOLAR	CASE STUDY	INDEPENDENT VARIABLE	TYPE OF MODERATION	DEFINITION OF MODERATION
Zakaria (2004)	Egyptian Muslim Brotherhood, Iraqi Ba'athists, Pakistani Taliban	Economic liberalization	Ideological moderation	—

Note: This table expands upon a table by Suveyda Karayaka and A. Kadir Yildirim in "Islamist Moderation in Perspective: Comparative Analysis of the Moderation of Islamist and Western Communist Parties," *Democratization* 20, no. 7 (2013): 1322–49. It portrays key arguments on Islamist moderation in existing literature. It is not a comprehensive table and does not represent those approaches that dominate in a quantitative manner; instead, it is supposed to be a facilitation, putting outlined examples in a graphic overview.

developed recently, with the aim to transform and include Islamist movements in liberal democracies that Western scholars also envisioned in the Middle East.

List of Interviews

Few interviewees are listed with their name, according to their consent when conducting these interviews. All others wished to be anonymized and referred to in broad, nondefinable terms.

Interview 1: Former Justice and Construction Party (JCP) member, interview with author, Tunis, August 12, 2019.

Interview 2: Ashur Shamis, interview with author, London, July 30, 2019.

Interview 3: Former member of Souq al-Joum neighborhood militia, interview with author, Tunis, October 11, 2019.

Interview 4: Salafi Sheikh in Tripoli, interview with author, Skype, December 5, 2019.

Interview 5: Salafi Sheikh in Tripoli, interview with author, WhatsApp, October 28 and 31, 2019.

Interview 6: Local resident in Tripoli, interview with author, Viber, December 20, 2020.

Interview 7: Libyan researcher based in Tripoli, interview with author, Istanbul, August 21, 2019.

Interview 8: Local resident in Derna, interview with author, Tunis, September 19, 2019.

Interview 9: Local resident in Derna, interview with author, Tunis, September 19, 2019.

Interview 10: Political activist from Benghazi, interview with author, Tunis, October 14, 2019.

Interview 11: Former Libyan Ministry of Defense employee, interview with author, Tunis, September 16, 2019.

Interview 12: UK diplomat working on Libya, interview with author, Tunis, October 14, 2019.

Interview 13: Local resident in Benghazi, interview with author, Zoom, May 3, 2020.

Interview 14: Local lawyer in Tripoli, interview with author, Tunis, September 24, 2019.

Interview 15: Libyan researcher based in Derna, interview with author, Zoom, May 5, 2020.

Interview 16: Local resident in Tripoli, interview with author, Tunis, October 14, 2019.

Interview 17: Former chairman of Libyan High National Election Commission, interview with author, Tunis, September 18, 2019.

Interview 18: Former National Forces Alliance (NFA) member, interview with author, Tunis, November 1, 2019.

Interview 19: Abdelwahhab Gaid, interview with author, Istanbul, April 22, 2019.

Interview 20: Former Libyan Ministry of Defense employee, interview with author, Tunis, September 20, 2020.

Interview 21: Founder of civil society organization in Fezzan, interview with author, Tunis, September 16, 2019.

Interview 22: Former Jibril communications team employee, interview with author, Tunis, September 25, 2019.

Interview 23: Nizar Kawan, interview with author, Istanbul, April 24, 2019.

Interview 24: Abdulrazzak Alaradi, interview with author, Istanbul, April 25, 2019.

Interview 25: Mustafa Saglizi, interview with the author, Istanbul, April 30, 2019.

Interview 26: Libyan journalist based in Turkey, interview with author, Istanbul, August 15, 2019.

Interview 27: Michael Cousins, interview with author, Istanbul, August 17, 2019.

Interview 28: Local politician in Sirte, interview with author, WhatsApp, April 15, 2020.

Interview 29: Local politician in Zawiya, interview with author, Tunis, September 15, 2019.

Interview 30: Local resident in Sirte, interview with author, Skype, September 14, 2019.

Interview 31: Former inmate of Mitiga prison, interview with author, Tunis, October 25, 2019.

Interview 32: Libyan researcher based in Tunis, interview with author, Tunis, September 5, 2019.

Interview 33: Former JCP member, interview with author, Tunis, November 14, 2018.

Interview 34: Libyan militia member, interview with author, Tunis, November 24, 2018.

Interview 35: Libyan researcher focused on religious groups, interview with author, Washington DC, November 13, 2019.

Interview 36: Local resident in Tripoli, interview with author, Viber, April 23, 2020.

Interview 37: Former member of Muhammad Sawan's team, interview with author, Tunis, October 4, 2019.

Interview 38: Former JCP member, interview with author, Tunis, October 1, 2019.

Interview 39: Former NFA member, interview with author, Tunis, September 16, 2019.

Interview 40: Local politician in Tripoli, interview with author, Tunis, September 15, 2019.

Interview 41: JCP member, interview with author, Tunis, October 15, 2019.

Interview 42: Former Ministry of the Interior official, interview with author, Tunis, September 8, 2019.

Interview 43: Libyan militia member, interview with author, Tunis, November 20, 2018.

Interview 44: Local resident in Tripoli, interview with author, WhatsApp, May 13, 2020.

Interview 45: Libyan researcher based in London, interview with author, London, October 10, 2018.

Interview 46: Libyan militia member, interview with author, Viber, November 17, 2020.

Interview 47: Libyan working for international organization focusing on local governance, interview with author, Tunis, September 15, 2019.

Interview 48: German diplomat working on Libya, interview with author, Tunis, October 11, 2019.

Interview 49: Libyan ambassador Abdurrazaq Mukhtar in Turkey, interview with author, Istanbul, August 25, 2019.

Interview 50: Libyan working for international organization based in Tripoli, interview with author, Tunis, December 5, 2019.

Interview 51: US diplomat working on Libya, interview with author, Washington DC, November 17, 2019.

Interview 52: Libyan working for international organization based in Benghazi, interview with author, Tunis, November 12, 2018.

Interview 53: German businessman, interview with author, Berlin, May 4, 2018.

Interview 54: National Transitional Council (NTC) member, interview with author, Tunis, September 16, 2019.

Interview 55: Former militia member, interview with author, Tunis, September 17, 2019.

Interview 56: Libyan Salafi-Madkhali, interview with the author, Tunis, October 2, 2019.

Interview 57: Libyan Salafi-Madkhali, interview with author, Tunis, October 23, 2019.

Interview 58: Libyan Salafi-Madkhali, interview with author, WhatsApp, February 5, 2020.

Interview 59: Former militia commander, interview with author, Istanbul, August 21, 2019.

Interview 60: Former revolutionary fighter, interview with the author, Istanbul, August 18, 2019.

Interview 61: JCP candidate, interview with author, Tunis, September 17, 2019.

Interview 62: JCP candidate, interview with author, Tunis, September 13, 2019.

Interview 63: Former JCP member, interview with author, WhatsApp, February 12, 2020.

Interview 64: John Jenkins, former UK diplomat who was ambassador to several Middle Eastern countries (including Libya in 2011), interview with author, Zoom, October 27, 2020.

Interview 65: NFA member, interview with author, Tunis, September 15, 2019.

Interview 66: NTC member, interview with author, Tunis, September 16, 2019.

Interview 67: UK diplomat working on Libya, interview with author, Tunis, October 19, 2019.

Interview 68: Libyan Muslim Brotherhood member, interview with author, London, July 31, 2019.

Interview 69: Libyan Muslim Brotherhood member, interview with author, London, July 31, 2019.

Interview 70: JCP member, interview with author, Istanbul, August 15, 2019.

Interview 71: Libyan Salafi-Madkhali, interview with author, Viber, February 18, 2020.

Interview 72: Libyan militia member, interview with author, Tunis, October 4, 2019.

Interview 73: Libyan militia member, interview with author, Tunis, October 4, 2019.

Interview 74: Government of National Accord (GNA) member, interview with author, Tunis, September 17, 2019.

Interview 75: Libyan Muslim Brotherhood member, interview with author, Viber, February 12, 2020.

Interview 76: Libyan Salafi-Madkhali, interview with author, WhatsApp, March 5, 2020.

Interview 77: Former senior member of Gaddafi regime, interview with author, London, June 20, 2019.

Interview 78: JCP member, interview with author, Tunis, September 24, 2019.

Interview 79: JCP member, interview with author, Tunis, September 22, 2019.

Interview 80: Former deputy spokesperson, Supreme Security Committee, interview with author, Tunis, September 16, 2019.

Interview 81: GNA official, interview with author, Tunis, September 27, 2019.

Interview 82: Libyan Salafi-Madkhali, interview with author, Tunis, October 15, 2019.

Interview 83: Local politician in Sirte, interview with author, Viber, March 3, 2020.

Interview 84: Libyan militia member, interview with author, Tunis, September 10, 2019.

Interview 85: US diplomat working on Libya, interview with author, Tunis, September 29, 2019.

Glossary of Arabic Words

Arabic terminology has been standardized according to the *International Journal of Middle East Studies* (IJMES) guide and word list.

ālim	Islamic scholar
amīr	Religious or military leader or commander
awqāf	Islamic endowments
daʿwa	Preaching and proselytizing activities
fatwa	An opinion on a point of law, the term "law" applying, in Islam, to all civil or religious matters
fitna	Trial or test; in Islamic usage, a heretical uprising, especially the first major internal struggle within the Muslim community, which resulted in both civil war and religious schism between the Sunnis and the Shiʿah. In this book, the term means chaos or strife.
hadith	Recorded teachings and actions of the Prophet Mohammed, which add a source of law alongside the Qurʾan
ḥisba	Moral police
jamāhīrīyah	A shortened version of the Great Socialist People's Libyan Arab *jamāhīrīyah*, Gaddafi's unique

	construction of a political system, which translates to something like "state of the masses"
jihad	To struggle or exert effort; its legal meaning relates to combat and fighting
khawārij	Pejorative term referring to an early Islamic sect formed in response to a religio-political controversy over the Caliphate
majlis al-shūrā	Consultative council
miḥna	Ordeal, test
rawatīb	Daily prayers
shariʿa	Islamic legal system derived from the Qur'an, Sunnah, and supplementary sources of jurisprudence, which governs religious rituals and aspects of day-to-day life
shuhadā'	Martyrs
tālib al-ʿilm	Islamic student
wālī al-amr	Male legal guardian, but in this book refers to the legitimate ruler/ruling authority
waṭan	Country, homeland
wilayat al-faqīh	Doctrine based on the guardianship of the Islamic jurist

Notes

Introduction

1. Inga Kristina Trauthig, "Gaining Legitimacy in Post-Qaddafi Libya: Analysing Attempts of the Muslim Brotherhood," *Societies* 9, no. 3 (2019): 65, https://doi .org/10.3390/soc9030065.
2. Inga Kristina Trauthig and Guy Robert Eyre, " 'Quietist' Salafis after the 'Arab Revolts' in Algeria and Libya (2011–2019): Between Insecurity and Political Sub- ordination," *Mediterranean Politics*, October 29, 2023: 1–24, https://doi.org/10 .1080/13629395.2023.2272474.
3. Virginie Collombier, *Salafi Politics: 'Political' and 'Quietist' Salafis in the Struggle for the Libyan State*, Research Project Report 2020/15, European University Insti- tute, November 27, 2020, https://doi.org/10.2870/50645.
4. Stephen J. King, "The Arab Winter," in *The Arab Winter: Democratic Consolidation, Civil War, and Radical Islamists* (Cambridge University Press, 2020), i–ii.
5. Christopher S. Chivvis, *Toppling Qaddafi: Libya and the Limits of Liberal Intervention* (Cambridge University Press, 2013); Karin Wester, *Intervention in Libya: The Responsibility to Protect in North Africa*, new edition (Cambridge University Press, 2020).
6. Mary Fitzgerald, "Finding Their Place: Libya's Islamists During and After the Revolution," in *The Libyan Revolution and Its Aftermath*, ed. Peter Cole and Brian McQuinn (Oxford University Press, 2015), 177–205.
7. Mohammed El-Nawawy and Sahar Khamis, "Cyberactivists Paving the Way for the Arab Spring: Voices from Egypt, Tunisia and Libya," *Cyber Orient* 6 (2012): 4–27.
8. Andrew Garwood-Gowers, "The Responsibility to Protect and the Arab Spring: Libya as the Exception, Syria as the Norm?" *University of New South Wales Law Journal* 36, no. 2 (December 23, 2020): 594–618, https://doi.org/10.3316/ielapa

.565289638046147; Fawaz A. Gerges, "The Islamist Moment: From Islamic State to Civil Islam?" *Political Science Quarterly* 128, no. 3 (2013): 389–426.

9. Alan J. Kuperman, "Obama's Libya Debacle: How a Well-Meaning Intervention Ended in Failure," *Foreign Affairs* 94, no. 2 (2015): 66–77.
10. "Libya Crisis," Armed Conflict Location and Event Data blog, accessed July 20, 2023, https://acleddata.com/crisis-profile/libya-crisis/; Frederic Wehrey, "The Conflict in Libya," testimony before the U.S. House of Representatives Foreign Affairs Committee, May 17, 2019, https://carnegieendowment.org/2019/05/15/conflict-in-libya-pub-79160.
11. The more precise translation from "Al-quwāt al-musallaḥa al-ʿarabiya al-lībīya" would be Libyan Arab Armed Forces. However, they promote themselves as the Libyan National Army (LNA) and are usually referred to by this name, especially by international commentators, as it sounds more inclusive by not emphasizing its allegedly Arab character.
12. Inga Kristina Trauthig, "'This Is the Fate of Libyan Women': Contempt, Ridicule, and Indifference of Seham Sergiwa," *Conflict, Security & Development* 24, no. 2 (2024): 149–73, https://doi.org/10.1080/14678802.2024.2334832.
13. Brian McQuinn, "History's Warriors: The Emergence of Revolutionary Battalions in Misrata," in *The Libyan Revolution and Its Aftermath*, ed. Peter Cole and Brian McQuinn (Oxford University Press, 2015), 229–56.
14. "Assessments and Documentation of Mass Crimes: Assessments in Libya," Physicians for Human Rights blog, n.d., accessed July 29, 2024, https://phr.org/issues/investigating-deaths-and-mass-atrocities/assessments-and-documentation-of-mass-crimes/assessments-in-libya/; Alex Crawford, *Colonel Gaddafi's Hat* (HarperCollins, 2012).
15. Sami Zaptia, "HoR Grants Fathi Bashagha Government Vote of Confidence with Majority of 92," *Libya Herald*, March 1, 2022, https://libyaherald.com/2022/03/breaking-hor-grants-fathi-bashagha-government-vote-of-confidence-with-majority-of-92/.
16. Wolfram Lacher and Alaa Al-Drissi, "Capital of Militias: Tripoli's Armed Groups Capture the Libyan State," Security Assessment in North Africa/Small Arms Survey Briefing Paper, June 2018, https://www.smallarmssurvey.org/resource/capital-militias-tripolis-armed-groups-capture-libyan-state.
17. Tim Eaton, "Security Actors in Misrata, Zawiya and Zintan Since 2011," research paper, Chatham House, December 12, 2023, https://www.chathamhouse.org/2023/12/security-actors-misrata-zawiya-and-zintan-2011/02-misrata-zawiya-and-zintan-after-2011.
18. Abdulkader Assad, "Bashagha's Government Sworn in at HoR in Tobruk," *Libya Observer*, March 3, 2022, https://libyaobserver.ly/news/bashaghas-government-sworn-hor-tobruk.
19. Aligned groups and relevant individuals affiliated with the GNU (or GNA previously) in Western Libya include:

• The Tripoli Revolutionaries' Brigade, the Special Deterrence Force, the Abu Salim Central Security Directorate, and the Nawasi Brigade (8th Force), later known as the "Tripoli cartel"

- 301 Halboos Infantry Battalion (from Misrata)
- Zintani forces aligned with Osama Juwaili
- Tarhuna 7th Brigade (Kaniyat, after its leader, Mohamed al-Kani)
- Fayez al-Serraj, Prime Minister of the GNA
- Abdulhamid al-Dbeibah, Interim Prime Minister of the GNU

Aligned groups and relevant individuals affiliated with the so-called Libyan National Army (LNA) and HoR Groups include:

- Saiqa or Thunderbolt Special Forces
- Brigade 115, headed by Abdul Razzaq al-Nadhouri, later appointed chief of staff of the LNA
- Tariq Bin Ziyad Brigade, relevant for the LNA's expansion into Fezzan
- Tawhid Brigade (later Battalion 210), which prominently features Madkhali currents
- Khalifa Haftar, commander of the LNA
- Aguilah Saleh, Speaker of the House of Representatives

20. Corey Flintoff, "What Role Will Islamists Play In Libya?" National Public Radio, September 21, 2011, https://www.npr.org/2011/09/21/140665324/what-role-will-islamists-play-in-libya.
21. Graham Fuller, *The Future of Political Islam* (Palgrave Macmillan, 2003); Shiraz Maher and Martyn Frampton, "Choosing Our Friends Wisely: Criteria for Engagement with Muslim Groups," Policy Exchange, March 8, 2009, https://policyexchange.org.uk/publication/choosing-our-friends-wisely-criteria-for-engagement-with-muslim-groups/.
22. Tarek Chamkhi, "Neo-Islamism in the Post-Arab Spring," *Contemporary Politics* 20, no. 4 (2014): 453–68; Olivier Roy, *The Failure of Political Islam:* (Harvard University Press, 1996); Anne Wolf, *Political Islam in Tunisia: The History of Ennahda* (Oxford University Press, 2017); Thorsten Hasche, *Quo vadis, politischer Islam?: AKP, al-Qaida und Muslimbruderschaft in systemtheoretischer Perspektive* (Transcript, 2015); Richard P. Mitchell, *The Society of the Muslim Brothers* (Oxford University Press, 1993).
23. Trauthig, "Gaining Legitimacy."
24. Roel Meijer, "The Problem of the Political in Islamist Movements," in *Whatever Happened to the Islamists? Salafis, Heavy Metal Muslims, and the Lure of Consumerist Islam*, ed. Olivier Roy and Amel Boubekeur (Columbia University Press, 2012), 27–60; Thomas Hegghammer, "Jihadi-Salafis or Revolutionaries? On Religion and Politics in the Study of Militant Islamism," in *Global Salafism: Islam's New Religious Movement*, ed. Roel Meijer (Oxford University Press, 2014), 201–35; Quintan Wiktorowicz, "Anatomy of the Salafi Movement," *Studies in Conflict & Terrorism* 29, no. 3 (2006): 207–39.
25. Matt Buehler, "Ruptures, Reconfigurations and Revolutions: Political Change in North Africa After the Arab Uprisings," *Mediterranean Politics* 23, no. 4 (2018): 522–30.
26. Frederic Wehrey and Anouar Boukhars, *Salafism in the Maghreb: Politics, Piety, and Militancy* (Oxford University Press, 2019); George Joffé, "The Trojan Horse: The

Madkhali Movement in North Africa," *Journal of North African Studies* 23, no. 5 (2018): 739–44; Lisa Watanabe, "Islamist Actors: Libya and Tunisia," Center for Security Studies, 2018, https://css.ethz.ch/content/dam/ethz/special-interest/gess /cis/center-for-securities-studies/pdfs/Watanabe-06282018-IslamistActors.pdf.

27. Anna Zajac, "Between Sufism and Salafism: The Rise of Salafi Tendencies After the Arab Spring and Its Implications," *Studies on Cultures and Societies* 29, no. 2 (2014): 97–109; Frederic Wehrey and Anouar Boukhars, "Salafism and Libya's State Collapse: The Case of the Madkhalis," in *Salafism in the Maghreb*, 107–37.

28. Madkhali politicization in post-2011 Libya did not mean that they became politicos or jihadi–Salafis. Rather, they remained quietists because they undertook these new modes of politics in pursuit of core quietist goals: preserving their ability to conduct *da'wa* and purify Islamic doctrine, implementing shari'a law, securing "reactionary goals" such as challenging the power of Islamist parties, liberals, and alleged secularists, and thus disavowing oppositional politics, and rejecting revolutionary violence and public disobedience vis-à-vis incumbent regimes. Stéphane Lacroix, "To Rebel or Not to Rebel: Dilemmas Among Saudi Salafis in a Revolutionary Age," in *Salafism After the Arab Awakening: Contending with People's Power*, ed. Francesco Cavatorta and Fabio Merone (Hurst, 2015), 61–82; Roel Meijer, "Politicising *Al-Jarh Wa-l-Ta'dil*: Rabi' B. Hadi Al-Madkhali and the Transnational Battle for Religious Authority," in *The Transmission and Dynamics of the Textual Sources of Islam: Essays in Honor of Harald Motzki*, ed. Nicolet Boekhoff-van der Voort, Kees Versteegh, and Joas Wagemakers (Brill, 2011), 375–99; Trauthig and Eyre, " 'Quietist' Salafis."

29. Charles Tilly and Sidney G. Tarrow, *Contentious Politics* (Oxford University Press, 2015).

30. Linda Nicholson, *Identity Before Identity Politics* (Cambridge University Press, 2008).

31. Andreas Kalyvas, *Democracy and the Politics of the Extraordinary: Max Weber, Carl Schmitt, and Hannah Arendt* (Cambridge University Press, 2008); Sami Zemni, "The Extraordinary Politics of the Tunisian Revolution: The Process of Constitution Making," *Mediterranean Politics* 20, no. 1 (January 2, 2015): 1–17, https://doi.org /10.1080/13629395.2013.874108; Trauthig and Eyre, " 'Quietist' Salafis."

32. Valuable work has been undertaken to explore the various strands of Salafism in North Africa, such as Wehrey and Boukhars, *Salafism in the Maghreb*, but the Libyan Muslim Brotherhood and Libyan Salafi-Madkhalis have never been the combined focus of analyses.

33. Inga Kristina Trauthig, "Assessing the Islamic State in Libya," paper presented at the 3rd Conference of the European Counter Terrorism Centre (ECTC) Advisory Network on Terrorism and Propaganda, April 9–10, 2019, https://www .europol.europa.eu/publications-events/publications/assessing-islamic-state -in-libya.

34. Roel Meijer, ed., *Global Salafism: Islam's New Religious Movement* (Columbia University Press, 2009); Alexander Meleagrou-Hitchens, *Incitement: Anwar al-Awlaki's Western Jihad* (Harvard University Press, 2020); Mohammed Hafez, *Why Muslims Rebel: Repression and Resistance in the Islamic World* (Lynne Rienner, 2003); Jeffry

Halverson and Nathaniel Greenberg, *Islamists of the Maghreb* (Routledge, 2017); Ziad Munson, "Islamic Mobilization: Social Movement Theory and the Egyptian Muslim Brotherhood," *Sociological Quarterly* 42 (2001): 487–510.

35. Ayef Bayat, "Islamism and Social Movement Theory," *Third World Quarterly* 26 (2005): 891–908; Ayef Bayat, *Making Islam Democratic: Social Movements and the Post-Islamist Turn* (Stanford University Press, 2007); Graeme Chesters and Ian Welsh, "Rebel Colours: 'Framing' in Global Social Movements," *Sociological Review* 52, no. 3 (2004): 314–35; Benjamin Lamb-Books, *Angry Abolitionists and the Rhetoric of Slavery: Moral Emotions in Social Movements* (Palgrave Macmillan, 2016).

36. Tilly and Tarrow, *Contentious Politics*; Hanlie Booysen, *Explaining the Moderate Platform of the Syrian Muslim Brotherhood: Against the Inclusion-Moderation Hypothesis* (University of Wellington Press, 2018).

37. Mario Diani, "The Concept of Social Movement," *Sociological Review* 40, no. 1 (1992): 8, https://doi.org/10.1111/j.1467-954X.1992.tb02943.x.

38. For more, see Karl-Dieter Opp, *Theories of Political Protest and Social Movements: A Multidisciplinary Introduction, Critique, and Synthesis* (Routledge, 2009), 37. Exemptions include Mayer N. Zald and John D. McCarthy, who define social movement by a "set of certain opinions and beliefs" (instead of "a collectivity of individuals"). "Social Movement Industries: Competition and Cooperation Among Movement Organizations," Center for Research on Social Organization Paper 201, University of Michigan, 1979. According to another team of scholars, "At its most elementary level, collective action consists of any goal-directed activity engaged in jointly by two or more individuals. It entails the pursuit of a common objective through joint action—that is, people working together in some fashion for a variety of reasons, often including the belief that doing so enhances the prospect of achieving the objective." David A. Snow, Sarah A. Soule, and Hanspeter Kriesi, "Mapping the Terrain," in *The Blackwell Companion to Social Movements*, ed. Snow, Soule, and Kriesi (Blackwell, 2006), 8.

39. Donatella della Porta and Mario Diani, *Social Movements: An Introduction* (John Wiley & Sons, 2009).

40. Hamied Ansari did this in 1984 when he inquired into the nature of Islamic militancy in Egypt as a movement. "The Islamic Militants in Egyptian Politics," *International Journal of Middle East Studies* 16, no. 1 (1984): 123–44.

41. Hein-Anton Van der Heijden, "Globalization, Environmental Movements, and International Political Opportunity Structures," *Organization & Environment* 19, no. 1 (2006): 28–45.

42. Some social movement theory (SMT) scholars criticize this established wisdom and instead argue, "Contrary to the assumption that democratisation leads to the flourishing of social movements as repression is removed and new channels of participation are opened up, it is shown that in the immediate period between the end of an authoritarian regime and the initiation of a democratic one the opposite effect may occur." Christopher Pickvance, "Democratisation and the Decline of Social Movements: The Effects of Regime Change on Collective Action in Eastern Europe, Southern Europe and Latin America," *Sociology* 33, no. 2 (1999): 353. This book does not engage with the conundrum of

defining democratization or democracy but instead uses the term "democratization" as a signpost that signals the move away from a repressive regime.

43. Jillian Schwedler, *Faith in Moderation: Islamist Parties in Jordan and Yemen* (Cambridge University Press, 2006).

44. Nigel Ashton, *King Hussein of Jordan* (Yale University Press, 2008); Schwedler, *Faith in Moderation*. The opposite is the repression-radicalization hypothesis.

45. Arendt explains that the notion of a successful revolution is not a normative description but instead meant in an empirical, definitional sense: An ideal revolution is only successful if the revolutionaries succeed in not only removing the head of state but eradicating/replacing the previous political system. According to Raymond Tanter and Manus Midlarsky, "Tocqueville . . . defined it [revolution] as an overthrow of the legally constituted elite, which initiated a period of intense social, political, and economic change. Crane Brinton has continued this empirical thrust by differentiating between the coup d'état, as a simple replacement of one elite by another, and major revolutions such as the French or Russian, which were accompanied by social, political, and economic changes. These forms of revolution appear to reflect an increasing degree of change initiated by the successful insurgents and may be placed on a rank-order of increasing political or social change. "A Theory of Revolution," *Journal of Conflict Resolution* 11 (1967): 265.

46. Malik Mufti, "Elite Bargains and the Onset of Political Liberalization in Jordan," *Comparative Political Studies* 32, no. 1 (1999): 100–29; Mehmet Gurses, "Islamists, Democracy and Turkey: A Test of the Inclusion-Moderation Hypothesis," *Party Politics* 20, no. 4 (2014): 646–53. The repression-radicalization thesis asks if repression leads to a decrease in collective action or to further radicalization. Omar Ashour, *The De-Radicalization of Jihadists: Transforming Armed Islamist Movements* (Routledge, 2009); Abel Bojar and Hanspeter Kriesi, "Action Repertoires in Contentious Episodes: What Determines Governments and Challengers' Action Strategies? A Cross-National Analysis." *European Journal of Political Research* 60, no. 1 (2021): 46–68. Steven Brooke and Elizabeth Nugent demonstrate how those who voted for Morsi or his moderate Islamist rival, Abdel Moneim Abu al-Fottouh, were more likely to engage in patterns of violence following the July 2013 coup and brutal Rabaa massacre. "Exclusion and Violence After the Egyptian Coup," *Middle East Law and Governance* 12, no. 1 (2020): 61–85; Sarah El Masry and Neil Ketchley, "After the Massacre: Women's Islamist Activism in Post-Coup Egypt," *Middle East Law and Governance* 12, no. 1 (2020): 86–108.

47. Janine A. Clark, "The Conditions of Islamist Moderation: Unpacking Cross-Ideological Cooperation in Jordan," *International Journal of Middle East Studies* 38, no. 4 (2006): 539–60; Esen Kirdiş, "Similar Contexts, Different Behaviour: Explaining the Non-Linear Moderation and Immoderation of Islamic Political Parties in Jordan, Morocco, Tunisia, and Turkey," *Politics, Religion & Ideology* 20, no. 4 (2019): 467–83, https://doi.org/10.1080/21567689.2019.1698421; Sarah Salwen, "Faith in Moderation: Islamist Parties in Jordan and Yemen.," *Journal of Church and State* 49, no. 2 (2007): 353–55.

48. Khalil Al-Anani, "The Inclusion-Moderation Thesis: Muslim Brotherhood in Egypt," in *Oxford Research Encyclopedia of Politics*, August 28, 2019, https://doi.org/10.1093/acrefore/9780190228637.013.1332.

49. According to Al-Anani, the "integration of Islamist movements is not inevitably conducive to moderation, nor does it necessarily lead to democratization." In his article "The Inclusion-Moderation Thesis," he states, "Similarly, the exclusion of Islamists does not necessarily result in radicalization or extremism. Surprisingly, in some cases exclusion led to the moderation of Islamists, such as in Tunisia under Zine El Abidine Ben Ali. Therefore, it is more useful to focus on the processes and dynamics of Islamists' inclusion than focusing on the outcome of these processes and dynamics. The case of the Brotherhood after the Egyptian uprising of 2011 provides an important example for examining the limits and shortcomings of the inclusion-moderation hypothesis and to what extent it can be applied to Islamist movements."

50. Eunsook Jung, "Bringing Social Movements into the Inclusion-Moderation Thesis: The Influence of Religious Fundamentalism in Indonesia and South Korea," *Asian Survey* 61, no. 5 (2021): 797–824, https://doi.org/10.1525/as.2021.1422511; Michelle Browers, *Political Ideology in the Arab World: Accommodation and Transformation* (Cambridge University Press, 2009).

51. Overall, this book stands in the tradition of SMT scholars, including Manfred Brocker, Mirjam Künkler, and Sumita Pahwa, who argue for establishing categories as benchmarks before analyzing social movements. Manfred Brocker and Mirjam Künkler, "Religious Parties: Revisiting the Inclusion-Moderation Hypothesis," *Party Politics* 19, no. 2 (2013): 171–86; Sumita Pahwa, "Pathways of Islamist Adaptation: The Egyptian Muslim Brothers' Lessons for Inclusion Moderation Theory," *Democratization* 24, no. 6 (2017): 1066–84, https://doi.org/10.1080/13510347.2016.1273903.

52. Farhad Khosrokhavar, *New Arab Revolutions That Shook the World* (Routledge, 2016); Michael Buehler, "Revisiting the Inclusion-Moderation Thesis in the Context of Decentralized Institutions: The Behavior of Indonesia's Prosperous Justice Party in National and Local Politics," *Party Politics* 19, no. 2 (2013): 210–29; Matt Buehler, "The Threat to 'Un-Moderate': Moroccan Islamists and the Arab Spring," *Middle East Law and Governance* 5 (2013): 231–57; Elizabeth Nugent, "Rethinking Repression and Islamist Behavior After the 2011 Uprisings," in *Evolving Methodologies in the Study of Islamism*, ed. Marc Lynch, POMEPS Studies 17, Project on Middle East Political Science, 2016, http://pomeps.org/wp-content/uploads/2016/03/POMEPS_Studies_17_Methods_Web.pdf.

53. The *jamāhīrīyah* or, in its long version, the Great Socialist People's Libyan Arab *jamāhīrīyah*, was Gaddafi's unique construction of a political system, which translates to "state of the masses." The system was adapted over his forty-two years of rule and culminated (in theoretical terms) in his self-authored political philosophy as captured in the *Green Book*, first published in 1975 (six years after Gaddafi's military coup). In it, Gaddafi elaborates on "solutions" for "the problem of democracy," "the economic problem," and "the social basis of the third universal theory." Muammar Qaddafi, *The Green Book* (Ithaca, 1999), 24.

The author has formulated and used this explanation in some of her previous works, namely "This Is the Fate of Libyan Women," "Gaining Legitimacy in Post-Qaddafi Libya," and her sections in the works "'Quietist' Salafis after the 'Arab Revolts' in Algeria and Libya," coauthored with Guy Robert Eyre, and "Islamist Parties in Libya after Gaddafi: Old Networks in New Environments" in *The Rule Is For None But Allah: Islamist Approaches to Governance*, coauthored with Emad-dedin Badi (Oxford University Press, 2023).

54. In *The Green Book*, Gaddafi expresses his prerogative to create solutions for Libya in all spheres, which is very much in accordance with a totalitarian system. Hannah Arendt, *The Origins of Totalitarianism* (Houghton Mifflin Harcourt, 1973), 392.

55. Mary Fitzgerald, "Introducing the Libyan Muslim Brotherhood," *Foreign Policy*, 2 (2012), https://foreignpolicy.com/2012/11/02/introducing-the-libyan-muslim-brotherhood/; Lisa Watanabe, "Libya: In the Eye of the Storm," *CSS Analysis in Security Policy* 193 (June 2016), https://css.ethz.ch/content/dam/ethz/special-interest/gess/cis/center-for-securities-studies/pdfs/CSSAnalyse-193-EN.pdf. Also, quietist activists focus on "support of grassroots initiatives through education (*tarbiya*) and proselytising in their pursuit to purify Islam" instead of pursuing political action. Alexander Meleagrou-Hitchens, "Salafism in America: History, Evolution and Radicalisation," *Program on Extremism*, October 2018, 10.

56. In the 1990s the Libyan regime was faced with an insurgency by the LIFG, radicalized and organized mostly in Afghanistan. Overall, these challenges showed that Islam had become the predominant framework of protest in Libya; because the religious establishment had been eviscerated, the regime was now trying to co-opt the religious sphere again. The actual existence of the LIFG was not revealed until autumn of 1995, during major clashes in Benghazi and other eastern cities. Yehudit Ronen, "Qadhafi and Militant Islamism: Unprecedented Conflict," *Middle Eastern Studies* 38, no. 4 (2002): 1–16.

57. The LIFG is also known as al-Jama'a al-Islamiya al-Muqatila bi-Libya. See Noman Benotman, Jason Pack, and James Brandon, "Islamists," in *The 2011 Libyan Uprisings and the Struggle for the Post-Qadhafi Future*, ed. Jason Pack (Palgrave Macmillan, 2013), 191–228. In the 1990s, while the Libyan Salafi-Madkhali influence inside Saudi Arabia declined, its support abroad—in Kuwait, Egypt, and also Libya—began to grow, in most cases due to the appeal of its conceptualization of wālī al-amr. However, Gaddafi supported Salafi-Madkhalism not only to bolster his religious legitimacy, but to court Sufism again. Zajac, "Between Sufism and Salafism", Madawi al-Rasheed, *Contesting the Saudi State: Islamic Voices from a New Generation* (Cambridge University Press, 2007).

58. Interview 4. A list of interviews conducted for this book is included in the appendix.

59. While this book uses the terms "movement" and "group" interchangeably for both the Libyan Muslim Brotherhood and the Libyan Salafi-Madkhalis, these terms are chosen as defined by social movement theory.

60. Pahwa, "Pathways of Islamist Adaptation."

61. Charles Kurzman, "Structural Opportunity and Perceived Opportunity in Social Movement Theory: The Iranian Revolution in 1979," *American Sociological Review* 62 (1996): 153–70.

62. Bart Bonikowski, *Varieties of Popular Nationalism in Modern Democracies: An Inductive Approach to Comparative Research on Political Culture* (Cambridge University Press, 2013); David Thomas, "A General Inductive Approach for Qualitative Data Analysis," *American Journal of Evaluation* 27, no. 2 (2003): 237–46.

63. William Gamson and David Meyer, "Framing Political Opportunity," in *Comparative Perspectives on Social Movements: Political Opportunities, Mobilizing Structures and Cultural Framings*, ed. Doug McAdam, John McCarthy, and Mayer Zald (Cambridge University Press, 1996), 275–90.

64. Charles W. Anderson, "Youth, the 'Arab Spring,' and Social Movements," *Review of Middle East Studies* 47, no. 2 (2013): 150–56, https://doi.org/10.1017/S2151348 100058031; Luis Fernando Barón, "More Than a Facebook Revolution: Social Movements and Social Media in the Egyptian Arab Spring," *International Review of Information Ethics* 18, no. 12 (2012): 86–92, https://digital.lib.washington.edu:443/researchworks/handle/1773/22359; Mohamed Ben Moussa, "From Arab Street to Social Movements: Re-Theorizing Collective Action and the Role of Social Media in the Arab Spring," *Westminster Papers in Communication and Culture* 9, no. 2 (2017), https://doi.org/10.16997/wpcc.166.

65. Khalil Al-Anani, "The Young Brotherhood in Search of a New Path," *Current Trends in Islamist Ideology* 9 (2009): 96–109.

66. Douglass C. North, John Joseph Wallis, and Barry R. Weingast, *Violence and Social Orders: A Conceptual Framework for Interpreting Recorded Human History* (Cambridge University Press, 2009).

67. Jillian Schwedler, "Can Islamists Become Moderates? Rethinking the Inclusion-Moderation Hypothesis," *World Politics* 63, no. 2 (2011): 347–76.

68. This book does not aim to solve the enigma of what moderation "really" is or how "true" moderation is to be distinguished from strategic or tactical moderation. Instead, it aims to establish an adequate framework to analyze the Libyan Muslim Brotherhood and Libyan Salafi-Madkhalis' moderation in postrevolutionary Libya.

69. Brocker and Künkler, "Religious Parties," 177; Schwedler, "Can Islamists Become Moderates?" 352.

70. Menderes Çınar, "From Moderation to De-Moderation: Democratic Backsliding of the AKP in Turkey," in *The Politics of Islamism*, ed. John L. Esposito, Lily Zubaidah, and Rahim Naser Ghobadzadeh (Palgrave Macmillan, 2018), 127–57; Sultan Tepe, "Moderation of Religious Parties: Electoral Constraints, Ideological Commitments, and the Democratic Capacities of Religious Parties in Israel and Turkey," *Political Research Quarterly* 65 (2012): 467–88.

71. Güneş Murat Tezcür, *Muslim Reformers in Iran and Turkey: The Paradox of Moderation* (University of Texas Press, 2010).

72. Anja Mihr, "Semi-Structured Interviews with Non-State and Security Actors," in *Researching Non-State Actors in International Security*, ed. Andreas Kruck and Andrea Schneiker (Routledge, 2017), 65–80.

73. Robert Ying, *Case Study Research: Design and Methods* (Sage, 2009).

74. Alexander George and Andrew Bennett, *Case Studies and Theory Development in the Social Sciences* (Harvard University Press, 2005).

75. Ronald Krebs and Patrick Jackson, "Twisting Tongues and Twisting Arms: The Power of Political Rhetoric," *European Journal of International Relations* 13, no. 1 (2007): 35–66. By including framing in the analysis, this book argues that SMT scholars such as Lamb-Books, Chesters, and Welsh, who all did the same, managed to explain the developments of social movements more comprehensively. They removed themselves from the narrower explanatory mechanisms of scholars of the structural tradition by arguing that mobilizing factors can also be related to issues of identity, culture, and post-materialist concerns such as values. For scholars studying Islamic movements, these theoretical adaptations are particularly relevant: Islamic movements are intrinsically and fundamentally engaged in altercations over meaning and values. Lamb-Books, *Angry Abolitionists*; Chesters and Welsh, "Rebel Colours."

76. Next to their relationship with indigenous cultural symbols, language, and identities, the "authority of the spokesperson uttering the words is as important as the content. Ideology must therefore always be balanced by factors such as the political and cultural environment and resource mobilization and leadership." Roel Meijer, "Taking the Islamist Movement Seriously: Social Movement Theory and the Islamist Movement," *International Review of Social History* 50, no. 2 (2005): 282. If moderation was conceptualized differently than with the three aspects of abandonment of violence, cooperation, and compromise—perhaps being more descriptive by, as Marc Lynch describes, "becoming part of the system"—then a different outcome of analysis is likely. However, for the purposes of this book, the inquiry into normative moderation is crucial: The three steady aspects of moderation in an ever-changing environment can explain the movements' trajectories. This book therefore acknowledges that there is always the possibility that a group could adopt behavioral moderation without substantive ideological moderation. That is, it could behave as if it were committed to respecting pluralist processes (by cooperation and compromising) but continue to hold core commitments that run counter to these norms. In existing stable institutional contexts, such as Western democracies, behavioral moderation may well be desirable on its own, but in a fluid environment, such as post-Gaddafi Libya, where institutional checks are largely absent to prevent a single-party takeover, the underlying commitments of actors become extremely relevant, as they can shape the overall environment. Therefore, this book also assesses ideological moderation by relying on framing.

77. Angus McDowall, "Libya's Dbeibah: The Ambitious Politician Who Promised Not to Be," Reuters, February 10, 2022, https://www.reuters.com/world/africa/libyas-dbeibah-ambitious-politician-who-promised-not-be-2022-02-10/.

78. United Nations Support Mission in Libya, "SRSG Abdoulaye Bathily's Remarks to the Security Council Meeting on Libya," February 27, 2023, https://unsmil.unmissions.org/sites/default/files/srsg_abdoulaye_bathilys_remarks_to_the_security_council.pdf.

79. Vito Todeschini, "Libya: The International Community's Bet over Holding Elections in 2023," Tahrir Institute for Middle East Policy blog, July 3, 2023, https://timep.org/2023/07/07/libya-the-international-communitys-bet-over-holding-elections-in-2023/.
80. The first Libyan parliament after the fall of Gaddafi was supposed to serve in a transitional capacity with a government formed by that parliament until the new constitution was agreed upon.
81. Halil Ibrahim Yenigün, "The Political and Theological Boundaries of Islamist Moderation After the Arab Spring," *Third World Quarterly* 37, no. 12 (2016): 2304–21, https://doi.org/10.1080/01436597.2016.1227683.

1. Who Are Libya's Islamists and Salafists?

1. Shiraz Maher and Martyn Frampton, "Choosing Our Friends Wisely," Policy Exchange, March 8, 2009, https://policyexchange.org.uk/publication/choosing-our-friends-wisely-criteria-for-engagement-with-muslim-groups/, 18.
2. Mehdi Mozaffari, "What Is Islamism? History and Definition of a Concept," *Totalitarian Movements and Political Religions* 8, no. 1 (2007): 17–33, https://doi.org/10.1080/14690760601121622.
3. Victor J. Willi, *The Fourth Ordeal: A History of the Muslim Brotherhood in Egypt, 1968–2018* (Cambridge University Press, 2021).
4. Laurent Bonnefoy, "Quietist Salafis, the Arab Spring and the Politicization Process," *Salafism After the Arab Awakening. Contending with People's Power*, ed. Francesco Cavatorta and Fabio Merone (Hurst, 2015), 205–18; Laurent Bonnefoy, "Saudi Arabia and the Expansion of Salafism," Norwegian Peacebuilding Resource Centre Policy Brief, 2013; Thomas Hegghammer, "Jihadi Salafis or Revolutionaries? On Religion and Politics in the Study of Islamist Militancy," in *Global Salafism: Islam's New Religious Movement*, ed. Roel Meijer (Hurst, 2009), 201–35.
5. Zoltan Pall, *Salafism in Lebanon: Local and Transnational Movements* (Cambridge University Press, 2018).
6. Joas Wagemakers, "Revisiting Wiktorowicz: Categorising and Defining the Branches of Salafism," in Cavatorta and Merone, *Salafism After the Arab Awakening*, 17; Gilles Kepel, *Jihad: The Trail of Political Islam* (I. B. Tauris, 2002).
7. Quintan Wiktorowicz, "Anatomy of the Salafi Movement," *Studies in Conflict & Terrorism* 29, no. 3 (2006): 222.
8. Inga Kristina Trauthig and Guy Robert Eyre, " 'Quietist' Salafis after the 'Arab Revolts' in Algeria and Libya (2011–2019): Between Insecurity and Political Subordination," *Mediterranean Politics*, October 29, 2023: 78, https://doi.org/10.1080/13629395.2023.2272474;Wiktorowicz, "Anatomy of the Salafi Movement."
9. Hegghammer, "Jihadi-Salafis or Revolutionaries?, 251; Shiraz Maher, *Salafi-Jihadism: The History of an Idea* (Oxford University Press, 2016), 9.
10. Roxanne L. Euben and Muhammad Qasim Zaman, eds., *Princeton Readings in Islamist Thought: Texts and Contexts from al-Banna to Bin Laden* (Princeton University Press, 2009), 5.

11. Petter Nesser, Anne Stenersen, and Emilie Oftedal, "Jihadi Terrorism in Europe: The IS-Effect," *Perspectives on Terrorism* 10, no. 6 (2016): 3–24.
12. Henrik Gråtrud and Vidar Benjamin Skretting, "Ansar Al-Sharia in Libya: An Enduring Threat," *Perspectives on Terrorism* 11, no. 1 (2017): 40–53.
13. Kamal Eldin Osman Salih, "The Roots and Causes of the 2011 Arab Uprisings," *Arab Studies Quarterly* 35, no. 2 (2013): 184–206, https://doi.org/10.13169/arab studquar.35.2.0184.
14. Alex Crawford, *Colonel Gaddafi's Hat* (Collins, 2012).
15. Nic Robertson and Paul Cruickshank, "Islamic Militants Among Prisoners Freed from Libyan Jail," CNN, August 26, 2011, http://www.cnn.com/2011/WORLD /africa/08/26/libya.militants.analysis/index.html; Omar Ashour, "Why Does the Islamic State Endure and Expand?" *IAI: Istituto Affari Internazionali*, December 1, 2015, https://www.jstor.org/stable/resrep09845.
16. United Nations Security Council, "Final Report of the Panel of Experts on Libya Submitted in Accordance with Resolution 2644 (2022)," S/2023/673, September 15, 2023, https://documents-dds-ny.un.org/doc/UNDOC/GEN/N23/234/61 /PDF/N2323461.pdf.
17. This section explaining Libya's many weapons and its vulnerability due to large, porous borders has been developed previously by the author for her report "Islamic State in Libya—From Force to Farce?" International Centre for the Study of Radicalisation (ICSR), 2020. https://icsr.info/wp-content/ uploads/2020/03/ICSR-Report-Islamic-State-in-Libya-From-Force-to-Farce. pdf.
18. Juliane von Mittelstaedt, "German UN Envoy Martin Kobler on Spread of IS in Libya," *Der Spiegel*, February 4, 2016, https://www.spiegel.de/international /world/german-un-envoy-martin-kobler-on-spread-of-is-in-libya-a-1075475 .html.
19. Fiona Mangan and Matthias Nowak, "The West Africa–Sahel Connection: Mapping Cross-Border Arms Trafficking," Briefing Paper, Small Arms Survey, December 8, 2019, https://www.smallarmssurvey.org/resource/west-africa -sahel-connection-mapping-cross-border-arms-trafficking.
20. In January 2015, an obscure Libyan IS member, Abu Irhim al Libi, elaborated on the importance of Libya in terms of its geographical location in a work entitled "Libya: The Strategic Gateway for the Islamic State." In it, al Libi explained that "Libya looks upon the sea, the desert, mountains, and six states: Egypt, Sudan, Chad, Niger, Algeria and Tunisia . . . It is the anchor from which Africa and the Islamic Maghreb can be reached." Another IS writer, Abu Moaz al Barqawi (of Barqa), explains in a note entitled "Come to the fold of the caliphate" that IS seeks to eliminate the Tunisian, Libyan and Egyptian borders to create something along the lines of the "Euphrates Province" in Syria and Iraq. A speech released by IS controlled al Furqan Media by its recent spokesman Abu Hamza al Qurashi referred to IS being at the "thresholds of Europe"—most likely a reference to IS in Libya. Aymenn Jawad al-Tamimi, "Islamic State's Appointment of New Leader: Translation and Notes," http://www.aymennjawad.org /2019/10/islamic-state-appointment-of-new-leader.

21. Inga Kristina Trauthig, "Assessing the Islamic State in Libya," paper presented at the 3rd Conference of the European Counter Terrorism Centre (ECTC) Advisory Network on Terrorism and Propaganda, April 9–10, 2019, https://www.europol .europa.eu/publications-events/publications/assessing-islamic-state-in-libya.

22. Aaron Y. Zelin, "The Others: Foreign Fighters in Libya," Washington Institute, January 16, 2018, 1, https://www.washingtoninstitute.org/policy-analysis /others-foreign-fighters-libya.

23. Bruce Hoffman, "Al Qaeda, Trends in Terrorism, and Future Potentialities: An Assessment," *Studies in Conflict & Terrorism* 26, no. 6 (2003): 429–42, https://doi .org/10.1080/10576100390248275.

24. Omar Ashour, *How ISIS Fights: Military Tactics in Iraq, Syria, Libya and Egypt* (Edinburgh University Press, 2022), https://doi.org/10.1515/9781474438230; Thomas Hegghammer, *The Caravan: Abdallah Azzam and the Rise of Global Jihad* (Cambridge University Press, 2020).

25. For example, Gaid was a vocal advocate of the Political Isolation Law, which will be discussed in later chapters. Ibrahim Fraihat, "An Ill-Advised Purge in Libya," blog post, Brookings Institution, February 18, 2013, https://www.brookings.edu /articles/an-ill-advised-purge-in-libya/.

26. Interview 19.

27. David D. Kirkpatrick, "Political Islam and the Fate of Two Libyan Brothers," *The New York Times*, October 6, 2012, World, https://www.nytimes.com/2012/10/07 /world/africa/political-islam-and-the-fate-of-two-libyan-brothers.html.

28. Jason Burke, "Abu Yahya Al-Libi," obituary, *The Guardian*, June 6, 2012, World News, https://www.theguardian.com/world/2012/jun/06/abu-yahya-al-libi.

29. Noman Benotman, Jason Pack, and James Brandon, "Islamists," in *The 2011 Libyan Uprisings and the Struggle for the Post-Qadhafi Future*, ed. Jason Pack (Palgrave Macmillan, 2013), 191–228.

30. Hegghammer, *Caravan*.

31. Omar Ashour, "Post-Jihadism: Libya and the Global Transformations of Armed Islamist Movements," *Terrorism and Political Violence* 23, no. 3 (2011): 377–97.

32. Interviews 2, 10, and 25.

33. Salah Sarrar, "Ex-Islamists Walk Free from Libyan Jail," Reuters, August 31, 2010, World News, https://www.reuters.com/article/us-libya-prisoners-release -idUSTRE67U5U420100831.

34. Emily Estelle, "Al Qaeda and the Islamic State Will Be the Winners of the Libyan Civil War," blog post, *Critical Threats*, April 10, 2019, https://www.criticalthreats .org/analysis/al-qaeda-and-the-islamic-state-will-be-the-winners-of-the -libyan-civil-war.

35. U.S. Library of Congress, "Al-Qaeda in Libya: A Profile," August 2012, https:// freebeacon.com/wp-content/uploads/2012/10/LOC-AQ-Libya.pdf: 43.

36. Zelin, "The Others," 5.

37. Amandla Thomas-Johnson, " 'Sorted' by MI5: How UK Government Sent British-Libyans to Fight Gaddafi," *Middle East Eye*, July 11, 2018, https://www.middle easteye.net/news/sorted-mi5-how-uk-government-sent-british-libyans-fight -gaddafi.

38. Helen Pidd, "How Family and Libya Conflict Radicalised Manchester Arena Bomber," *The Guardian*, March 2, 2023, UK News, https://www.theguardian.com /uk-news/2023/mar/02/how-family-libya-conflict-radicalised-manchester -arena-bomber.

39. Lydia Sizer, "Libya's Terrorism Challenge: Assessing the Salafi-Jihadi Threat," Policy Paper 2017-1, Middle East Institute, October 2017, https://www.mei.edu /sites/default/files/publications/PP1_Sizer_LibyaCT_web_0.pdf.

40. Aaron Y. Zelin, "Know Your Ansar Al-Sharia," blog post, *Foreign Policy*, September 21, 2012, https://foreignpolicy.com/2012/09/21/know-your-ansar-al -sharia/.

41. Zelin, "The Others," 4–5.

42. Charles Lister, "Competition Among Violent Islamist Extremists: Combating an Unprecedented Threat," *Annals of the American Academy of Political and Social Science* 668, no. 1 (October 21, 2016): 53–70.

43. Zelin, "Know Your Ansar Al-Sharia."

44. Aaron Y. Zelin, *Your Sons Are at Your Service: Tunisia's Missionaries of Jihad* (Columbia University Press, 2020).

45. Robin Banerji, "Did Ansar Al-Sharia Carry out Libya Attack?" BBC News, September 12, 2012, Africa, https://www.bbc.com/news/world-africa-19575753.

46. Emily Estelle, *A Strategy for Success in Libya*, American Enterprise Institute (November 2017), http://www.criticalthreats.org/wp-content/uploads/2017/11 /A-Strategy-for-Success-in-Libya.pdf.

47. Gråtrud and Skretting, "Ansar Al-Sharia in Libya."

48. Gråtrud and Skretting, "Ansar Al-Sharia in Libya."

49. Interviews 8 and 9.

50. U.S. Senate, Committee on Foreign Relations, "The Path Forward in Libya," Hearing 114-784, March 3, 2016, https://www.govinfo.gov/content/pkg/CHRG -114shrg30552/html/CHRG-114shrg30552.htm.

51. Kristina Hummel, "Europe's True Southern Frontier: The General, the Jihadis, and the High-Stakes Contest for Libya's Fezzan Region," *CTC* [Combating Terrorism Center] *Sentinel* 10 no. 10 (2017), https://ctc.westpoint.edu/europes-true -southern-frontier-the-general-the-jihadis-and-the-high-stakes-contest-for -libyas-fezzan-region/.

52. "Libyan Islamist Group Ansar Al-Sharia Says It Is Dissolving," Reuters, May 27, 2017, EverythingNews, https://www.reuters.com/article/us-libya-security -idUSKBN18N0YR.

53. Gråtrud and Skretting, "Ansar Al-Sharia in Libya."

54. Charlie Winter, "Apocalypse, Later: A Longitudinal Study of the Islamic State Brand," *Critical Studies in Media Communication* 35, no. 1 (2018): 103–21, https:// doi.org/10.1080/15295036.2017.1393094.

55. Joana Cook, Haid Haid, and Inga Trauthig, "Jurisprudence Beyond the State: An Analysis of Jihadist 'Justice' in Yemen, Syria and Libya," *Studies in Conflict & Terrorism* (2020): 1–20, https://doi.org/10.1080/1057610X.2020.1776958.

56. David D. Kirkpatrick and Rukmini Callimachi, "Islamic State Video Shows Beheadings of Egyptian Christians in Libya," *The New York Times*, February 15,

2015, World, https://www.nytimes.com/2015/02/16/world/middleeast/islamic
-state-video-beheadings-of-21-egyptian-christians.html.

57. Zelin, "The Others," 8.

58. Frederic Wehrey and Emad Badi, "A Place of Distinctive Despair," Carnegie
Endowment for International Peace, August 8, 2018, https://carnegie-mec.org
/diwan/76997.

59. Frederic Wehrey, "When the Islamic State Came to Libya," Carnegie Endowment
for International Peace, February 8, 2018, https://carnegieendowment.org/2018
/02/10/when-islamic-state-came-to-libya-pub-75541.

60. Two years earlier, in 2013, Turki al-Binali, a renowned Bahraini preacher affiliated with IS, had delivered exhortations in Sirte's Rabat Mosque calling for the
abandonment of gradualist reform. Estelle, *Strategy for Success in Libya*.

61. Peter Bouckaert, "Death of a Dictator," Human Rights Watch, October 16, 2012,
https://www.hrw.org/report/2012/10/16/death-dictator/bloody-vengeance-sirte.

62. Lister, "Competition Among Violent Islamist Extremists."

63. Interviews 11, 28, and 32.

64. Aaron Y. Zelin, "The Islamic State's Burgeoning Capital in Sirte, Libya," Policy
Watch 2462, Washington Institute for Near East Policy, August 2015, https://
www.washingtoninstitute.org/policy-analysis/islamic-states-burgeoning
-capital-sirte-libya.

65. Dion Nissenbaum and Maria Abi-Habib, "Islamic State Solidifies Foothold
in Libya to Expand Reach," *Wall Street Journal*, May 8, 2015, https://www.wsj
.com/articles/islamic-state-solidifies-foothold-in-libya-to-expand-reach-1431
989697.

66. Cook, Haid, and Trauthig, "Jurisprudence Beyond the State."

67. Patrick Wintour, "Isis Loses Control of Libyan City of Sirte," *The Guardian*, December 5, 2016, World News, https://www.theguardian.com/world/2016/dec/05
/isis-loses-control-of-libyan-city-of-sirte.

68. Rikar Hussein and Nisan Ahmado, "Islamic State Regrouping in Libyan Desert,
Experts Warn," Voice of America, September 29, 2017, https://www.voanews
.com/a/islamic-state-regrouping-libyan-desert-experts-warn/4050753.html;
Christopher Livesay and Alessandro Pavone, "ISIS Regroups to Attack a Fragmented Libya," *PBS Newshour*, September 30, 2018, https://pulitzercenter.org
/stories/isis-regroups-attack-fragmented-libya.

69. Sudarsan Raghavan, "Libya's Civil War Creates Opening for ISIS Return as Counterterrorism Effort Falters," *Washington Post*, November 24, 2019, https://www
.washingtonpost.com/world/middle_east/libyas-civil-war-creates-opening
-for-isis-return-as-counterterrorism-effort-falters/2019/11/21/e78745c0-056c
-11ea-9118-25d6bd37dfb1_story.html.

70. Inga Kristina Trauthig, "Islamic State in Libya—From Force to Farce?"

71. Wehrey and Badi, "Place of Distinctive Despair."

72. Interview 28.

73. Stéphane Lacroix, "Social Media and Conflict in Libya," Peace Tech Lab, 2019,
https://www.icct.nl/sites/default/files/2022-12/StratComms-Report-4-Fitzgerald
-Final.pdf.

74. Frederic Wehrey, "Quiet No More?" Carnegie Endowment for International Peace, October 13, 2016, https://carnegie-mec.org/diwan/64846.
75. Trauthig, "Assessing the Islamic State in Libya."
76. Interviews 8, 9, and 15.
77. Inga Kristina Trauthig and Emaddedin Badi, "Islamist Parties in Libya After Gaddafi: Old Networks in New Shapes," in *The Rule Is for None but Allah*, ed. Joana Cook and Shiraz Maher (Hurst, 2023), 83.
78. Inga Kristina Trauthig, "Gaining Legitimacy in Post-Qaddafi Libya: Analysing Attempts of the Muslim Brotherhood," *Societies* 9, no. 3 (2019): 65, HYPERLINK "https://doi.org/10.3390/soc9030065"https://doi.org/10.3390/soc9030065.
79. Benotman, Pack, and Brandon, "Islamists"; Alison Pargeter, "Qadhafi and Political Islam in Libya," in *Libya Since 1969: Qadhafi's Revolution Revisited*, ed. Dirk Vandewalle (Palgrave Macmillan, 2008), 83–104; Trauthig and Badi, "Islamist Parties in Libya After Gaddafi," 79–101.
80. Mary Fitzgerald, "Finding Their Place: Libya's Islamists During and After the Revolution," in *The Libyan Revolution and Its Aftermath*, ed. Peter Cole and Brian McQuinn (Oxford University Press, 2015), 177–205.
81. Trauthig, "Gaining Legitimacy in Post-Qaddafi Libya."
82. Alison Pargeter, *Return to the Shadows: The Muslim Brotherhood and An-Nahda Since the Arab Spring* (Saqi, 2016).
83. "Libya: June 1996 Killings at Abu Salim Prison," Human Rights Watch, June 27, 2006, https://www.hrw.org/news/2006/06/27/libya-june-1996-killings-abu-salim-prison.
84. Jonathan Head, " 'Mass Grave' Found in Tripoli," BBC News, September 11, 2011, https://www.bbc.com/news/av/world-africa-15055804.
85. Benotman, Pack, and Brandon, "Islamists."
86. Trauthig and Badi, "Islamist Parties in Libya after Gaddafi."
87. Fitzgerald, "Finding Their Place," 198.
88. Trauthig and Badi, "Islamist Parties in Libya after Gaddafi," 100.
89. Wagemakers, "Revisiting Wiktorowicz," 17.
90. Roel Meijer, ed., *Global Salafism: Islam's New Religious Movement* (Oxford University Press, 2014), 379.
91. International Crisis Group (ICG), "Addressing the Rise of Libya's Madkhali-Salafis," *Middle East and North Africa Report* 200, April 25, 2019, https://www.crisisgroup.org/middle-east-north-africa/north-africa/libya/addressing-rise-libyas-madkhali-salafis.
92. Meijer, *Global Salafism.*
93. ICG, "Addressing the Rise of Libya's Madkhali-Salafis."
94. George Joffé, "The Trojan Horse: The Madkhali Movement in North Africa," *Journal of North African Studies* 23, no. 5 (2018): 739–44.
95. Interviews 35, 44, and 57.
96. The LIFG is also known as al-Jama'a al-Islamiya al-Muqatila bi-Libya. See Benotman, Pack, and Brandon, "Islamists." In the 1990s, while the Libyan Salafi-Madkhalis' influence inside Saudi Arabia declined, its support at home and in Kuwait and Egypt began to grow, in most cases due to the appeal of its

conceptualization of wālī al-amr. However, Gaddafi not only supported Salafi-Madkhalism to bolster his religious legitimacy, but also tried to court Sufism again: Anna Zajac, "Between Sufism and Salafism: The Rise of Salafi Tendencies After the Arab Spring and Its Implications," *Studies on Cultures and Societies* 29, no. 2 (2014): 97–109; Madawi Al-Rasheed, *Contesting the Saudi State: Islamic Voices from a New Generation* (Cambridge University Press, 2007).

97. Wagemakers, "Revisiting Wiktorowicz."

98. Interview 4.

99. Wagemakers, "Revisiting Wiktorowicz"; Khalil Al-Anani, "Unpacking the Sacred Canopy: Egypt's Salafis between Religion and Politics," in *Salafism After the Arab Awakening: Contending with People's Power*, ed. Francesco Cavatorta and Fabio Merone (Hurst, 2015), 25–42; Joas Wagemakers, *Salafism in Jordan: Political Islam in a Quietist Community* (Cambridge University Press, 2016); Frederic Wehrey and Anouar Boukhars, "Salafism and Libya's State Collapse: The Case of the Madkhalis," in *Salafism in the Maghreb: Politics, Piety, and Militancy*, ed. Frederic Wehrey and Anouar Boukhars (Oxford University Press, 2019), 107–38; Pall, *Salafism in Lebanon*; Stéphane Lacroix, "To Rebel or Not to Rebel: Dilemmas among Saudi Salafis in a Revolutionary Age," in *Salafism After the Arab Awakening*, 63.

100. Trauthig and Eyre, " 'Quietist' Salafis."

101. Dirk Vandewalle, *A History of Modern Libya* (Cambridge University Press, 2012); Pargeter, "Qadhafi and Political Islam in Libya"; John K. Cooley, *Libyan Sandstorm* (Sidgwick and Jackson, 1983); Jonathan Bearman, *Qadhafi's Libya* (Zed, 1986); John Oakes, *Libya: The History of Gaddafi's Pariah State* (History Press, 2011); Amal Obeidi, *Political Culture in Libya* (Routledge, 2001); Camilla Sandbakken, "The Limits to Democracy Posed by Oil Rentier States: The Cases of Algeria, Nigeria and Libya," *Democratization* 13, no. 1 (2006): 135–52.

102. George Joffé, "Islamic Opposition in Libya," *Third World Quarterly* 10, no. 2 (1988): 615–31.

103. Lisa Anderson, "Religion and State in Libya: The Politics of Identity," *Annals of the American Academy of Political and Social Science* 483, no. 1 (1986): 61–72.

104. Peter Cole, "Bani Walid: Loyalism in a Time of Revolution," in *The Libyan Revolution and Its Aftermath*, ed. Peter Cole and Brian McQuinn (Hurst, 2015), 283–303; ICG, "Divided We Stand: Libya's Enduring Conflicts," *Middle East and North Africa Report* 130 (2012), https://www.crisisgroup.org/middle-east-north-africa/north-africa/libya/divided-we-stand-libya-s-enduring-conflicts.

105. Wolfram Lacher, *Libya's Fragmentation: Structure and Process in Violent Conflict* (Bloomsbury, 2020); Youssef Mohammad Sawani, "Post-Qadhafi Libya: Interactive Dynamics and the Political Future," *Contemporary Arab Affairs* 5, no. 1 (2012): 1–26; Mohammed El-Katiri, *State-Building Challenges in a Post-Revolution Libya* (Strategic Studies Institute, 2012).

106. Before 2011, there were far fewer accounts about the intricacies of Libyan Islamists, first, because the Gaddafi regime was highly repressive and hence information on Libyan Islamists was almost impossible to obtain, and second, because researchers focused more on the nature of the regime in world politics. Exemptions include Marius K. Deeb, "Militant Islam and Its Critics: The Case

of Libya," in *Islamism and Secularism in North Africa*, ed. John Ruedy (Palgrave Macmillan, 1996), 187–97; Sizer, "Libya's Terrorism Challenge"; Lachlan Wilson and Jason Pack, "The Islamic State's Revitalization in Libya and Its Post-2016 War of Attrition," *CTC Sentinel* 12, no. 3 (2019): 22–31, https://ctc.westpoint.edu/islamic-states-revitalization-libya-post-2016-war-attrition/.

107. Deeb, "Militant Islam and Its Critics"; Sizer, "Libya's Terrorism Challenge"; Wilson and Pack, "Islamic State's Revitalization in Libya"; Zelin, *Your Sons Are at Your Service*; Ashour, "Post-Jihadism"; Ashour, "Why Does the Islamic State Endure and Expand?"; Omar Ashour, "Between ISIS and a Failed State: The Saga of Libyan Islamists," Working Paper, Rethinking Political Islam Series, Brookings Institution, 2015; Fitzgerald, "Finding Their Place"; Mary Fitzgerald, "Introducing the Libyan Muslim Brotherhood," *Foreign Policy* 2 (2012), https://foreignpolicy.com/2012/11/02/introducing-the-libyan-muslim-brotherhood/.

108. Alison Pargeter, *The Muslim Brotherhood: From Opposition to Power* (Saqi, 2013); Pargeter, *Return to the Shadows*.

109. David Roberts, "Qatar and the Muslim Brotherhood: Pragmatism or Preference?" *Middle East Policy* 21, no. 3 (2014): 84–94, https://doi.org/10.1111/mepo.12084.

110. Zelin, "Islamic State's Burgeoning Capital."

111. Haala Hweio, "The Muslim Brotherhood: Libya as the Last Resort for the Continued Existence of the Global Movement," *Middle East Law and Governance* 13, no. 1 (2020): 5–21.

112. Raphaël Lefèvre, "An Egyptian Scenario for Libya?" *Journal of North African Studies* 19, no. 4 (2014): 602–7; Rachel Ehrenfeld, "The Muslim Brotherhood Evolution: An Overview," *American Foreign Policy Interests* 33, no. 2 (2011): 69–85; Beverley Milton-Edwards, *The Muslim Brotherhood: The Arab Spring and Its Future Face* (Routledge, 2016).

113. Lorenzo Vidino, *The New Muslim Brotherhood in the West* (Columbia University Press, 2010).

114. Jean-François Létourneau, "Explaining the Muslim Brotherhood's Rise and Fall in Egypt," *Mediterranean Politics* 21, no. 2 (2016): 300–7.

115. Interviews 31, 32, 44, and 50.

116. The literature that covers Salafism in general includes studies that concentrate on differentiating contrasting Salafi strands via political, cultural, sociological or ideational factors (or a mix of them); literature that examines the impact, relationship, and relevance of Salafi thought on violent extremism, especially as connected to the aftermath of the September 11, 2001 attacks; and studies that define Salafism in contrast to other strands of Islam, such as Sufism, or that aim to differentiate Salafism and Islamism through actor-based research.

117. Joas Wagemakers, *A Quietist Jihadi: The Ideology and Influence of Abu Muhammad al-Maqdisi* (Cambridge University Press, 2012); Lacroix, "To Rebel or Not to Rebel"; Stéphane Lacroix, "Between Revolution and Apoliticism: Nasir al-Din al-Albani and His Impact on the Shaping of Contemporary Salafism," in *Global Salafism: Islam's New Religious Movement*, ed. Roel Meijer (Oxford University Press,

2014), 58–80; Thomas Hegghammer and Stéphane Lacroix, "Rejectionist Islamism In Saudi Arabia: The Story of Juhayman al-Utaybi Revisited," *International Journal of Middle East Studies* 39, no. 1 (2007): 103–22.

118. Gilles Kepel describes Madkhali as being one of the ideal pro-regime "court scholars" in the Middle East, as opposed to following more radical trends within the Salafist movement. Gilles Kepel, *The War for Muslim Minds: Islam and the West* (Harvard University Press, 2004), 253.

119. Jacob Olidort, "The Politics of 'Quietist' Salafism," Analysis Paper 18, Brookings Institution Project on U.S. Relations with the Islamic World, 2015, https://www.brookings.edu/wp-content/uploads/2016/07/Brookings-Analysis-Paper_Jacob-Olidort-Inside_Final_Web.pdf; Richard A. Nielsen, *Deadly Clerics: Blocked Ambition and the Paths to Jihad* (Cambridge University Press, 2017).

120. Alexander Meleagrou-Hitchens, *Incitement: Anwar al-Awlaki's Western Jihad* (Harvard University Press, 2020); Wehrey and Boukhars, *Salafism in the Maghreb*; Lisa Watanabe, "Islamist Actors: Libya and Tunisia," Center for Security Studies, 2018, https://css.ethz.ch/content/dam/ethz/special-interest/gess/cis/center-for-securities-studies/pdfs/Watanabe-06282018-IslamistActors.pdf; Joffé, "Trojan Horse."

121. ICG, "Addressing the Rise of Libya's Madkhali-Salafis"; Nathan Vest, "Heretics, Pawns, and Traitors: Anti-Madkhali Propaganda on Libyan Salafi-Jihadi Telegram," blog post, *Jihadology*, February 25, 2019, https://jihadology.net/2019/02/25/guest-post-heretics-pawns-and-traitors-anti-madkhali-propaganda-on-libyan-salafi-jihadi-telegram/; Ahmed Salah Ali, "Haftar and Salafism: A Dangerous Game," blog post, Atlantic Council, June 6, 2017, https://www.atlanticcouncil.org/blogs/menasource/haftar-and-salafism-a-dangerous-game/.

122. Virginie Collombier, "Salafi Politics: 'Political' and 'Quietist' Salafis in the Struggle for the Libyan State," Research Project Report 2020/15, European University Institute, November 27, 2020, https://doi.org/10.2870/50645.

123. Emaddedin Badi, "Exploring Armed Groups in Libya: Perspectives on Sector Security Reform in a Hybrid Environment," Geneva Centre for Security Sector Governance, December 2020, https://www.dcaf.ch/exploring-armed-groups-libya-perspectives-ssr-hybrid-environment; Emaddedin Badi, Archibald Gallet, and Roberta Maggi, "Rethinking the Road to Stability—Security Sector Reform in Libya," Geneva Centre for Security Sector Reform, November 2021, https://www.dcaf.ch/sites/default/files/publications/documents/The_Road_to_Stability11.11.2021.pdf; Taylor Luck, "Libya Crisis as Opportunity: Who Are the Madkhalis?" *Christian Science Monitor*, January 17, 2018, https://www.csmonitor.com/World/Middle-East/2018/0117/Libya-crisis-as-opportunity-Who-are-the-Madkhalis.

124. Roel Meijer, "Introduction," in *Global Salafism*, 1–32.

125. Frederic Wehrey, "As Their Influence Grows, the Maghreb's 'Quietist' Salafists Are Anything but Quiet," *World Politics Review*, December 11, 2018, https://www.worldpoliticsreview.com/articles/26962/as-their-influence-grows-the-maghreb-s-quietist-salafists-are-anything-but-quiet; Anas El Gomati, "Libya's Elections Are Around the Corner. But the Country Needs a Hard Reset," blog

post, Atlantic Council, October 13, 2021, https://www.atlanticcouncil.org/blogs/menasource/libyas-elections-are-around-the-corner-but-the-country-needs-a-hard-reset/.

126. Trauthig and Badi, "Islamist Parties in Libya after Gaddafi."

127. Nazia Parveen, "Bomber's Father Fought Against Gaddafi Regime with 'Terrorist' Group," *The Guardian*, May 24, 2017, UK News, https://www.theguardian.com/uk-news/2017/may/24/bombers-father-fought-against-gaddafi-regime-with-terrorist-group; Rukmini Callimachi and Eric Schmitt, "Manchester Bomber Met with ISIS Unit in Libya, Officials Say," *The New York Times*, June 3, 2017, World, https://www.nytimes.com/2017/06/03/world/middleeast/manchester-bombing-salman-abedi-islamic-state-libya.html; Wehrey, "When the Islamic State Came to Libya"; Kristina Pantucci, "Britain on Alert: The Attacks in London and Manchester and the Evolving Threat" *CTC Sentinel*, August 2017, https://ctc.westpoint.edu/britain-on-alert-the-attacks-in-london-and-manchester-and-the-evolving-threat/.

128. Michal Reifen Tagar et al., "When Ideology Matters: Moral Conviction and the Association Between Ideology and Policy Preferences in the Israeli–Palestinian Conflict," *European Journal of Social Psychology* 44, no. 2 (2014): 117–25.

2. Surprised by Libya's Revolution

1. These dynamics can be traced in various contexts. For examples in Niger and Mali, see Sebastian Elischer, "The Management of Salafi Activity in Africa: African State Strategies and Their Consequences in the Sahel," *ARI Newsletter* (2013): 577–97.

2. Chris Rootes, "Shaping Collective Action: Structure, Contingency and Knowledge," in *The Political Context of Collective Action: Power, Argumentation and Democracy*, ed. Ricca Edmondson (Routledge, 1997), 81–104.

3. Aisha Ahmad, "The Security Bazaar: Business Interests and Islamist Power in Civil War Somalia," *International Security* 39, no. 3 (2014): 89–117.

4. David S. Meyer and Suzanne Staggenborg, "Movements, Countermovements, and the Structure of Political Opportunity," *American Journal of Sociology* 101, no. 6 (1996): 1628–60.

5. Arturo Escobar, ed., *The Making of Social Movements in Latin America: Identity, Strategy, and Democracy* (Routledge, 2018).

6. John Markoff, *Waves of Democracy: Social Movements and Political Change*, 2nd ed. (Routledge, 2015).

7. Frances Fox Piven and Richard A. Cloward, *Poor People's Movements: Why They Succeed, How They Fail* (Vintage, 1977); Aldon D. Morris and Carol McClurg Mueller, eds., *Frontiers in Social Movement Theory* (Yale University Press, 1992).

8. In his *Green Book*, Gaddafi expresses his prerogative to find solutions for Libya regarding all spheres, which is very much in accordance with a totalitarian

system. Hannah Arendt, *The Origins of Totalitarianism* (Houghton Mifflin Harcourt, 1973), 392.

9. The National Transitional Council (NTC) was formally created on March 5, 2011. Its founding members were largely from Eastern Libya. National Transitional Council, "Founding Statement," March 5, 2011, https://web.archive.org /web/20110310051658/http://ntclibya.org/english/founding-statement-of-the -interim-transitional-national-council/.

10. Interviews 13, 26, 27 and 34; George Joffé, "Islamic Opposition in Libya," *Third World Quarterly* 10, no. 2 (1988): 615–31.

11. Interviews 26, 34, 40 and 41; Alex Crawford, *Colonel Gaddafi's Hat* (HarperCollins, 2012).

12. Salim al-Sheikhi, "Dawr al-ikhwān al-muslimīn fī 17 fibrāir" [The Role of the Muslim Brotherhood on February 17], Facebook, May 14, 2013, personal database.

13. Aqeel Hussein Aqeel, ʿAsrār wamʿlumāt min zaman al-Qadhāfī [Secrets and Information from Qaddafi's Time], N.d., personal database.

14. Alison Pargeter, *Return to the Shadows: The Muslim Brotherhood and An-Nahda Since the Arab Spring*. Saqi, 2016, 81.

15. Asharq Al-Awsat, "Libya's Muslim Brotherhood Snubs Gaddafi," June 20, 2011, https://eng-archive.aawsat.com/theaawsat/news-middle-east/libyas-muslim -brotherhood-snubs-gaddafi.

16. Aqeel, ʿAsrār wamʿlumāt min zaman al-Qadhāfī.

17. Interview 77.

18. Fang Deng, "Information Gaps and Unintended Outcomes of Social Movements: The 1989 Chinese Student Movement," *American Journal of Sociology* 102, no. 4 (1997): 1085–112.

19. Inga Kristina Trauthig, "Gaining Legitimacy in Post-Qaddafi Libya: Analysing Attempts of the Muslim Brotherhood," *Societies* 9, no. 3 (2019): 65, https://doi .org/10.3390/soc9030065.

20. Pargeter, *Return to the Shadows*, 120; Thom Westcott, "New Libyan Ambassador to the UK Presents Credentials to the British Monarch," *Libya Herald*, December 13, 2012, https://libyaherald.com/2012/12/new-libyan-ambassador-to-the -uk-presents-credentials-to-the-queen/.

21. Innes Bowen, *Medina in Birmingham, Najaf in Brent: Inside British Islam* (Hurst, 2014), 103.

22. The MWH was later run by Kamal Helbawy, a prominent and charismatic member of the Egyptian Brotherhood who settled in the UK in 1994 to create its official media center and became the organization's official spokesperson in the West. Lorenzo Vidino, *The Muslim Brotherhood in the United Kingdom* (George Washington University Press, 2015), 5. For an overview of Islamist organizations established in Britain since the 1960s, see Damon L. Perry, "The Islamic Movement in Britain," Report, International Centre for the Study of Radicalisation, September 2020, https://icsr.info/wp-content/uploads/2020/09/ICSR-Report- The-Islamic-Movement-in-Britain.pdf.

23. UK House of Commons. "'Political Islam' and the Muslim Brotherhood Review: Sixth Report of Session 2016–17," Foreign Affairs Committee report, November 1, 2016, written evidence ISL0030, http://data.parliament.uk/writtenevidence /committeeevidence.svc/evidencedocument/foreign-affairs-committee /political-islam/written/32527.html.

24. In one important study, "The Islamist groups politically and socially active in Libya during the Gaddafi regime (1969–2011)" were "classified according to different criteria: the use (or not) of violence to achieve their objectives (guerrilla, war, terrorism); attachment to the different ideological families (Salafiyya, moderate political Islam, liberal Islamism, Sufism, and so on); or whether they operated within or outside the country. However, in practice, the different groups and their individual members move fluidly across these classificatory boundaries in accordance with the regime's repressive response and the possibility of political openness." Laura Feliu and Rachid Aarab, "Political Islam in Libya: Transformation on the Way to Elitisation," in *Political Islam in a Time of Revolt*, ed. Ferran Izquierdo, John Brichs Etherington, and Laura Feliu (Palgrave Macmillan, 2017), 154.

25. The other MAB founders were Egyptian Kamal Helbawy, Iraqis Anas al Tikriti and Omar el Hamdoun, Palestinians Azzam Tamimi and Mohammed Sawalha, and Tunisian Said Ferjani. The chief goal was to influence all discussions about Islam in UK Muslim communities, Westminster policy circles, and the public sphere. Vidino, *Muslim Brotherhood in the United Kingdom*. They were vocal in 2011 in trying to influence UK policy on Libya. See, for example, "The Muslim Association of Britain (MAB) Is in Agreement with the Enforcement of the No-Fly in Libya, by Britain and Its Allies in Order to Protect Libyan Civilians from Being Murdered by Its Cruel Dictator Qaddafi," Ikhwanweb, March 22, 2011, http:// archive.today/2020.05.05-083141/https://www.ikhwanweb.com/article.php ?id=28273.

26. B. Chernitsky, "Libyan Muslim Brotherhood on the Rise," Middle East Media Research Institute, April 24, 2012, Inquiry and Analysis Series no. 828, https:// www.memri.org/reports/libyan-muslim-brotherhood-rise.

27. Interview 78.

28. Melissa Willard-Foster, *Toppling Foreign Governments: The Logic of Regime Change* (University of Pennsylvania Press, 2019).

29. The NTC was known in Arabic as al-majlis al-waṭanī al-intiqālī.

30. Paul Salem and Amanda Kadlec, "Libya's Troubled Transition," Carnegie Endowment for International Peace, June 14, 2012, https://carnegieendowment.org /research/2012/06/libyas-troubled-transition.

31. Sumaya Al Nahed, "Covering Libya: A Framing Analysis of Al Jazeera and BBC Coverage of the 2011 Libyan Uprising and NATO Intervention," *Middle East Critique* 24, no. 3 (2015): 251–67.

32. Ali al-Sallabi, "Al-Sallabi: lā yumkin-u tajāwuz-u islamiyiyy Lībīā" [Al-Sallabi: The Islamists of Libya Cannot Be Bypassed], September 15, 2011, personal database.

33. Interview 12.

34. Oral Evidence by Lord Richards given to the House of Commons Foreign Affairs Committee on January 19, 2016: U.K. House of Commons, "Libya: Examination of Intervention and Collapse and the U.K.'s Future Policy Options," Foreign Affairs Committee report, September 14, 2016, https://publications.parliament.uk/pa/cm201617/cmselect/cmfaff/119/119.pdf.

35. Interviews 23 and 24.

36. Marc Lynch, "In Uncharted Waters: Islamist Parties Beyond Egypt's Muslim Brotherhood," Carnegie Endowment for International Peace, December 16, 2016. https://carnegieendowment.org/research/2016/12/in-uncharted-waters-islamist-parties-beyond-egypts-muslim-brotherhood; Francesco Cavatorta and Fabio Merone, "Moderation Through Exclusion? The Journey of the Tunisian Ennahda from Fundamentalist to Conservative Party," *Democratization* 20, no. 5 (2013): 857–75.

37. Pargeter, *Return to the Shadows*.

38. Interview 66.

39. Donatella della Porta, "Introduction," in *Social Movements*, ed. Donatella della Porta and Mario Diani, 3rd ed. (John Wiley & Sons, 2006), 1–31; Charles Tilly, "Processes and Mechanisms of Democratization," *Sociological Theory* 18, no. 1 (2000): 1–16.

40. Alamin Belhaj tried repeatedly to justify the Libyan Muslim Brotherhood's strategy. See, for example, Alamin Belhaj, "Al-ikhwān dakhalu al-thawra mandh al-yum al-wal lakinahum tawaqʿa-u ʿan takun al-maṭālib ʿiṣlahīta" [The Brotherhood Joined the Revolution from the First Day, but They Expected That the Demands Would Be for Reform], Al-Hayat, September 24, 2011, http://archive.today/2022.03.22-101040/https://www.sauress.com/alhayat/310809.

41. Interview 24; Abdulrazzak al-Aradi, "Abdulrazzak al-Aradi fī liqāʾ khaṣin Nabil Belhaj" [Abdulrazzak al-Aradi in an Exclusive Interview with Nabil Belhaj], Wesam Media, April 26, 2013, www.youtube.com/watch?v=0jMUIrxY34M.

42. Peter Graff, "Libya Militia Leader Plays Down Shift to Military Command," Reuters, September 26, 2012, https://www.reuters.com/article/us-libya-militia-idUSBRE88P1GD20120926. A third brother, Khalid al-Sallabi, left Libya in 1996 and is an imam at a mosque in Galway, Ireland, and head of the Galway Islamic Society. Lorna Siggins, "Muslim Cleric Welcomes Irish Support for Libyan Council," *Irish Times*, September 10, 2011, https://www.irishtimes.com/news/muslim-cleric-welcomes-irish-support-for-libyan-council-1.595357; Wolfram Lacher, "Families, Tribes and Cities in the Libyan Revolution," *Middle East Policy* 18, no. 4 (2011): 140–54.

43. Qtd. in Pargeter, *Return to the Shadows*, 116.

44. The Revolutionary Brigades Coalition is referred to in Arabic as Tajammu Saraya al-Thuwwar. It was founded by Mustafa Saglizi, Ismail Sallabi, Fawzi Bukatef, and Mohammad Shaiter. Mohammed Shaiter, "Hiwār maʿ Mohammed Shaiter, āmir al-shuwun al-aʿskarīa fī Saraya al-Thuwwar" [An Interview with Mohammed Shaiter, the Commander of Military Affairs of the Revolutionary Brigades], Al-Manara, August 15, 2011, http://archive.today/2021.02.15-131315/http://almanaramedia.blogspot.com/2011/08/blog-post_5220.html.

45. Interview 25.

46. Omar Ashour, "Libya's Muslim Brotherhood Faces the Future," op-ed, Brookings Institution, March 9, 2012, https://www.brookings.edu/articles/libyas-muslim -brotherhood-faces-the-future/.

47. By early 2012, around thirty armed groups could be categorized as militarily significant in Tripoli, many of which comprised battle-hardened revolutionary fighters. Countless smaller groups also competed for territory; some were vigilante organizations while others were mere criminal gangs. Small-scale clashes were an almost daily occurrence in late 2011 and early 2012, although larger confrontations remained rare. Ala Al-Idrissi and Wolfram Lacher, "Capital of Militias: Tripoli's Armed Groups Capture the Libyan State," *SANA Briefing Paper*, June 2018.

48. The first unification attempt, known as the Tripoli Military Council, was spearheaded by former LIFG leader Abdelhakim Belhadj and the second by the Supreme Security Committee (SSC), which was formed as a direct challenge to the former by officials of the National Transitional Council (NTC). Wolfram Lacher and Peter Cole, "Politics by Other Means: Conflicting Interests in Libya's Security Sector," Working Paper 20, Small Arms Survey, October 2014, https:// www.smallarmssurvey.org/resource/politics-other-means-conflicting-interests -libyas-security-sector-working-paper-20.

49. The next most important actors were the Zintani defense minister, Usama al-Juwaili, his deputy, former LIFG member al-Siddiq al-Mabruk al-Ghithi, the Misratan interior minister, Fawzi Abdelali, and chief of staff Yussef al-Mangush.

50. "Abdel Fattah Younes' Family: Criminal Prosecution—or Revenge," Quryna News, December 5, 2012, www.qurynanew.com/45785; Karim Mezran, "Conspiracism in and Around Libya," *International Spectator* 51, no. 2 (2016): 114.

51. Robert D. Benford and David A. Snow. "Framing Processes and Social Movements: An Overview and Assessment." *Annual Review of Sociology* 26 (2000): 611–39. Gharyani also has a television channel, Tahnasu TV (https://tanasuh.tv/), which serves as his main Libyan platform, and a home page (http://www .tanasuh.com/online/index.php) and Facebook account (https://www.facebook .com/shikh.sadeg/).

52. Palwasha L. Kakar and Zahra Langhi, "Libya's Religious Sector and Peacebuilding Efforts," United States Institute of Peace, March 16, 2017, https://www.usip .org/publications/2017/03/libyas-religious-sector-and-peacebuilding-efforts; Federica Saini Fasanotti, "Libya: A Nation Suspended between Past and Future," *Studia Diplomatica* 68, no. 4 (2017): 95–104.

53. Mary Fitzgerald, "Introducing the Libyan Muslim Brotherhood," *Foreign Policy* 2 (2012), https://foreignpolicy.com/2012/11/02/introducing-the-libyan-muslim -brotherhood/.

54. The coalition is known in Arabic as I'tilaf Sab'at Ashr Fibrayir, or I'tilaf. The NFSL was a political opposition group active during the Gaddafi regime. In late 2011, it dissolved and was replaced by the National Front Party. Peter Cole and Umar Khan, "The Fall of Tripoli," in *The Libyan Revolution and Its Aftermath*, ed. Peter Cole and Brian McQuinn (Hurst, 2015), 55–105.

55. Enrique Laraña, Hank Johnston, and Joseph R. Gusfield, eds. *New Social Movements: From Ideology to Identity* (Temple University Press, 1994), 81.

56. James M. Jasper, "The Emotions of Protest: Affective and Reactive Emotions in and Around Social Movements," *Sociological Forum* 13, no. 3 (1998): 397–424.

57. Alexander Meleagrou-Hitchens, *Incitement: Anwar al-Awlaki's Western Jihad* (Harvard University Press, 2020).

58. Nizar Kawan, "Nizar Kawan fī risāla ṣawtīa min ṭarābulus" [Nizar Kawan in an audio message from Tripoli], Al-Manara, February 23, 2011, https://www.youtube.com/watch?v=cVyiO9kSe8I.

59. Frederic Wehrey and Anouar Boukhars, "Salafism and Libya's State Collapse: The Case of the Madkhalis," in *Salafism in the Maghreb: Politics, Piety, and Militancy*, ed. Frederic Wehrey and Anouar Boukhars, 107–38 (Oxford University Press, 2019).

60. See note 54, introduction.

61. Martyn Frampton, *The Muslim Brotherhood and the West: A History of Enmity and Engagement* (Harvard University Press, 2018).

62. Henrik Gråtrud and Vidar Benjamin Skretting, "Ansar Al-Sharia in Libya: An Enduring Threat," *Perspectives on Terrorism* 11, no. 1 (2017): 40–53.

63. Sadeq al-Gharyani, "Al-Gharyani: al-khuruj ʿalā al-Qadhāfi wājib" [Gharyani: Exiting Qaddafi Is a Duty], Al-Jazeera, February 28, 2011, https://archive.ph/2020.05.07-103657/https://www.aljazeera.net/news/arabic/2011/2/28/الغريان/الخروج-على-القذافي-واجب-ي.

64. Interview 60.

65. Al-Gharyani, "Al-Gharyani: al-khuruj."

66. Yehudit Ronen, "Qadhafi and Militant Islamism: Unprecedented Conflict," *Middle Eastern Studies* 38, no. 4 (2002): 1–16.

67. Interviews 46, 49, 56 and 62.

68. Al-Gharyani, "Al-Gharyani: al-khuruj."

69. Al-Gharyani, "Al-Gharyani: al-khuruj."

70. While quietists traditionally focus on the propagation of their message (*da'wa*), this means they stay away from politics and violence, which they leave to the ruler (wālī al-amr). The concept of wālī al-amr and the related submission to that ruling authority is embedded in the Qurʾan and of central importance to Madkhalism. It has been guiding debate for centuries. Rabi bin Hadi al-Madkhali became one of its most prominent defenders. The radicalness with which Madkhalis apply wālī al-amr has become a main defining feature for his strand of Salafism and his adherents are considered notorious in this regard. This also made the group infamous inside Libya: Even people with little interest in Salafi ideology proclaim, "The only thing you need to know about Madkhalis is they follow their ruler, always." The principle of wālī al-amr also explains the extremes to which noninvolvement is propagated. Madkhalism is on the extreme end of arguing for noninvolvement in politics. Furthermore, proponents are willing to designate those who oppose the ruling authority as *khawārij* and see the necessity to report persons who stray to the authorities. Jarret M. Brachman, *Global Jihadism: Theory and Practice* (Routledge, 2008).

71. Interviews 19, 36, and 50.
72. While Gharyani is considered an influential religious figure among Libyan Muslim Brotherhood members, Nizar Kawan is a younger, more politically oriented example.
73. Interviews 2, 26, and 46.
74. Kawan, "Nizar Kawan fī risāla."
75. Interview 23.
76. "MB Calls on Arab League to Intervene in Libya," Ikhwanweb, March 7, 2011, http://archive.today/2020.05.05-083626/https://www.ikhwanweb.com/article.php?id=28173.
77. Kawan, "Nizar Kawan fī risāla."
78. Interview 64.
79. "MB Chairman: We are Confident Jihad is the Path to Liberate Al-Aqsa Mosque," Ikhwanweb, November 1, 2009, http://archive.today/2020.05.05-090001/https://www.ikhwanweb.com/article.php?id=21441.
80. James M. Jasper and Jane D. Poulsen, "Recruiting Strangers and Friends: Moral Shocks and Social Networks in Animal Rights and Anti-Nuclear Protests," *Social Problems* 42, no. 4 (1995): 496.
81. Carrie Rosefsky Wickham, "Interests, Ideas, and Islamist Outreach in Egypt," in *Islamic Activism: A Social Movement Theory Approach*, ed. Quintan Wiktorowicz (Indiana University Press, 2004), 231–49.
82. Janine Astrid Clark and Jillian Schwedler, "Who Opened the Window? Women's Activism in Islamist Parties," *Comparative Politics* 35, no. 3 (2003): 293–312.
83. Interview 71.
84. ICG, "Addressing the Rise of Libya's Madkhali-Salafis."
85. Interviews 1 and 4.
86. Sean Rayment, "How the Special Forces Helped Bring Gaddafi to His Knees," *The Telegraph*, August 28, 2011, https://www.telegraph.co.uk/news/worldnews/africaandindianocean/libya/8727076/How-the-special-forces-helped-bring-Gaddafi-to-his-knees.html.
87. Interview 4.
88. Interview 5. Similar statements were made in Interviews 57 and 58.
89. Two Salafi sheikhs interviewed for this book asserted that they consider Hafala an Islamic student (*tālib al-ʿilm*) rather than an Islamic scholar (*ālim*). Frederic Wehrey and Anouar Boukhars write in *Salafism in the Maghreb* (p. 118) that "Hafala was born in the Tripoli neighbourhood of Ghut al-Shaal but tracing his roots to the western Nafusa mountains, Hafala studied in Saudi Arabia and then in Yemen with Muqbil al-Wadiʿi and briefly sided with Abu Hassan al-Maʿribi before returning to the more quietist Madkhali current. During the 2011 revolution, he issued a statement urging active Salafi support for Gaddafi as the wālī al-amr—a defense that at least one Salafi observer alleges was partly coerced. After the revolution, he became a powerful figure among various Madkhali armed groups in Tripolitania, reportedly operating a school, mosque and guesthouse on Tripoli's airport road. Another key Amazigh Madkhali figure is Muhammad Abu Sala from Nalut."

90. Although quietist Salafi preachers exist in all parts of Libya, the majority of Libyans still do not consider them the main religious voices. Kakar and Langhi, "Libya's Religious Sector and Peacebuilding Efforts."

91. Quintan Wiktorowicz, *The Management of Islamic Activism: Salafis, the Muslim Brotherhood, and State Power in Jordan* (SUNY Press, 2001).

92. While, in an unsigned International Crisis Group report, Mary Fitzgerald claims Hafala to be "the most prominent Madkhali preacher" in Libya, other research emphasizes that "no fewer than 162 religious leaders were mentioned as having influence at the local or national level, but most of these were mentioned by fewer than ten interviewees. Similarly, in 2016, a number of Madkhali and Salafi sheikhs were mentioned, but no one featured prominently," pinpointing the difficulty in determining Salafi-Madkhalis religious influence in the country until today. ICG, "Addressing the Rise of Libya's Madkhali-Salafis," *Middle East and North Africa Report* 200, April 25, 2019, https://www.crisisgroup.org/middle-east-north-africa/north-africa/libya/addressing-rise-libyas-madkhali-salafis, 5; Trauthig, "Gaining Legitimacy"; Kakar and Langhi, "Libya's Religious Sector and Peacebuilding Efforts"; Rabi al-Madkhali, "Kalimat al-shaykh Rabīʿ al-Madkhalī ʿan fitnat lībīā biʿd alQadhāfī" [Speech of Shaykh Rabi al-Madkhali on the Sedition of Libya After Qaddafi], video, October 2, 2011, http://archive.today/2019.06.12-105450/https://www.youtube.com/watch?v=sriMveeY9vA.

93. Saadi Qaddafi, "Shatm al-Salafi al-Saʿadī alQadhāfī ʿala al-hawaʾ" [The Salafi Saadi Qaddafi Is Insulted Live], video, https://www.youtube.com/watch?v=rmxnqe8ugQ.

94. Stéphane Lacroix, "Al-Albani's Revolutionary Approach to Hadith," *Isim Review* 21 (2008): 6.

95. Yahya alHajuri, "Alnaṣaḥ alwāfī lilsāʿadī b. alQadhāfī" [The trustful advice to Saadi the son of Gaddafi], recorded lecture, June 1, 2011, http://www.shyahia.net/show_sound_890.html. This is the same dynamic as the Ṣāḥ regime in Yemen. Laurent Bonnefoy and Judit Kuschnitzki, "Salafis and the 'Arab Spring' in Yemen: Progressive Politicization and Resilient Quietism," *Arabian Humanities* 4 (2015): 1–20.

96. Interviews 4 and 5. On Hafala's Facebook profile he also documents travels occasionally. See https://www.facebook.com/abu.mos3ab.magde/.

97. Laraña, Johnston, and Gusfield, *New Social Movements*.

98. *Fitna*, meaning trial or test, in "Islamic usage, is a heretical uprising, especially the first major internal struggle within the Muslim community, which resulted in both civil war and religious schism between the Sunnis and the Shiʿah. *Miḥna* literally means 'trial, ordeal, test;' it is the term coined by medieval Arabic chroniclers to describe events that took place between 833 and 847 C.E., initiated by the seventh Abbasid caliph al-Maʾmun." John Nawas, "Mihna," *Oxford Bibliographies*, last modified July 30, 2014, 10.1093/obo/9780195390155-0205.

99. On the role of the Islamic University of Medina and Madkhalism, see Michael Farquhar, *Circuits of Faith: Migration, Education, and the Wahhabi Mission* (Stanford University Press, 2016); Wehrey and Boukhars, *Salafism in the Maghreb*, 115.

100. Thomas Hegghammer, "Jihadi Salafis or Revolutionaries? On Religion and Politics in the Study of Islamist Militancy," in *Global Salafism: Islam's New Religious Movement*, ed. Roel Meijer (Hurst, 2009), 201–35.
101. Kamal Eldin Osman Salih, "The Roots and Causes of the 2011 Arab Uprisings," *Arab Studies Quarterly* 35, no. 2 (2013): 184–206.
102. Rabi al-Madkhali, "Kalimāt ʿan alʾahdāth w-almẓārāt w-alkhuruj ʿila al-hakām" [A Word about the Events, Demonstrations, and Rebellion Against the Rulers], Rabi al-Madkhali homepage, March 17, 2011, http://archive.today/2020.05.19 -155744/http://www.rabee.net/ar/articles.php?cat=11&id=285.
103. Vincent Durac, "The Role of Non-State Actors in Arab Countries After the Arab Uprisings," *IEMed Mediterranean Yearbook* 1 (2015), https://www.iemed.org /publication/the-role-of-non-state-actors-in-arab-countries-after-the-arab -uprisings/.
104. Rabi al-Madkhali, "Al-taḥdhīr min al-fitan wa min al-dimoqātiyya wa mushtaqātih" [Warning Against Strife and against Democracy and Its Derivatives], Rabi al-Madkhali homepage, March 4, 2012, http://www.rabee.net/ar /articles.php?cat=8&id=228.
105. Al-Madkhali, "Al-taḥdhīr min al-fitan."
106. Rabi al-Madkhali, "Naṣīhat al-muslimīn ʿmūmān wa-l-salafīyn khaṣata fī lībīā waghīriha min al-bilad al-ʾislamīyati" [Advice for Muslims in General and Salafis in Particular, in Libya and Other Islamic Countries], Rabi al-Madkhali homepage, July 4, 2017, http://web.archive.org/web/20210825143838/https://rabee.net/ar /articles.php?cat=8&id=319.
107. Madkhali, "Kalimāt ʿan alʾahdāth."
108. Interviews 57 and 76.
109. John L. Esposito, ed., "Ali ibn Abi Talib," *The Islamic World: Past and Present* (Oxford University Press, 2004), 26.
110. Madkhali, "Kalimat al-shaykh Rabīʿ al-Madkhalī ʿan fitnat lībīā"; Rabi al-Madkhali, "Fatwā al-shaykh Rabi al-Madkhali biʿadam alqiāl fi lībīā maʿ aiy ṭaraf" [The Fatwa of Shaykh Rabi al-Madkhali Not to Fight in Libya with Any Party], video, February 27, 2015, https://www.youtube.com/watch?v=TOyYSJnLuaA.
111. Ad-Da'watus Salafīyyah, "Shaykh Zayd Al-Madkhalī Advises the Brothers in Libya," video, May 7, 2011, https://www.youtube.com/watch?v=RQIcrO-2fYg. "Hafala also issued a fatwa urging citizens in Salafi terms to 'remain steadfast' (*ilzam baytak*—literally 'hold fast to your house') and not to 'break ranks with the legitimate ruler' (*kharuj ʿala wālī al-amr*), calling the protests the '*fitna* (strife) of al-Qaeda.'" Wehrey and Boukhars, *Salafism in the Maghreb*, 116.
112. George Joffé, "The Arab Spring in North Africa: Origins and Prospects," *Journal of North African Studies* 16, no. 4 (2011): 507–32.
113. Saadi (by now also visibly identifiable as Salafi because he had grown a full beard in the manner proscribed by Salafis) instructed and oversaw the distribution of text messages on regime-controlled mobile networks by Salafi-Madkhali Libyan sheikhs. The regime also employed automated telephone calls that broadcast recordings of Rabi al-Madkhali reiterating political protests as acts of sedition. Wehrey and Boukhars, *Salafism in the Magreb*, 119.

114. Interviews 31, 32, 44, and 50.

115. Sharron Ward, "Libya Uprising One Year On: Remembering the Zawiyah Massacre," *The Guardian*, February 16, 2012, World News, http://www.theguardian.com/world/video/2012/feb/16/libya-uprising-one-year-on-zawiyah.

116. Interview 73.

117. Omar Ashour writes, "The Salafi trend in Libya, despite being larger in size than the Islamist MB, suffers from a lack of leadership and organisation. Those Salafi political parties that currently exist—Al-Watan and Umma al-Wasat—did not gain much support during the 2012 election in Libya. This is why we may conclude that the absence of political representation in Libya led to a strengthening of the militant Salafi trend." Omar Ashour, "Libya," in *Rethinking Political Islam*, ed. Shadi Hamid and William McCants (Oxford University Press, 2017), 103. Furthermore, according to Laurent Bonnefoy and Judit Kuschnitizki, "the politicisation of Salafism and its institutionalisation through political parties is anything but a uniform, linear and one-way process; for example, quietist Salafism remains resilient in Yemen and once 'politicised' Salafis may well end up being 'depoliticised' once again." "Salafis and the 'Arab Spring,' " 3.

118. One question asked on Rabi al-Madkhali's web homepage reads: "In Saudi Arabia, they say that elections are forbidden, and when Parliament was elected, they said that Parliament is your guardian, so how does this that came to power in the forbidden elections become a guardian? How does he respond to this suspicion?" There are also questions about the use of violence after Gaddafi's removal. Personal database.

119. Madkhali, "Al-taḥdhīr min al-fitan"; Majdi Hafala, "Nasīḥa ilā al-shabāb al-salafīy li-al-shaykh Abū Musʿab Majdī" [Advice to the Salafi Youth by Shaykh Abu Musab Majdi Hafala], YouTube, November 21, 2012, https://www.youtube.com/watch?v=knimBlmycIo.

120. Timothy Mitchell, "Everyday Metaphors of Power," *Theory and Society* 19, no. 5 (1990): 545–77.

121. Jillian Schwedler, "Islamists in Power? Inclusion, Moderation, and the Arab Uprisings," *Middle East Development Journal* 5, no. 1 (2013): 1–18.

122. Cavatorta and Merone, "Moderation Through Exclusion?"

123. Lorenzo Vidino, *The New Muslim Brotherhood in the West* (Columbia University Press, 2010).

124. Frederic Wehrey, *The Burning Shores: Inside the Battle for the New Libya* (Farrar, Straus and Giroux, 2018).

125. Hassan Mneimneh, "The Spring of a New Political Salafism?" Hudson Institute, October 19, 2011, https://www.hudson.org/national-security-defense/the-spring-of-a-new-political-salafism-.

126. Jillian Schwedler, *Faith in Moderation: Islamist Parties in Jordan and Yemen* (Cambridge University Press, 2006); Joas Wagemakers, *The Muslim Brotherhood: Ideology, History, Descendants* (Amsterdam University Press, 2022); Francesco Cavatorta and Raquel Ojeda Garcia, "Islamism in Mauritania and the Narrative of Political Moderation," *Journal of Modern African Studies* 55, no. 2 (2017): 301–25; Günes Murat Tezcür, *Muslim Reformers in Iran and Turkey: The Paradox of*

Moderation (University of Texas Press, 2010); Janine Clark, "The Conditions of Islamist Moderation: Unpacking Cross-Ideological Cooperation in Jordan," *International Journal of Middle East Studies* 38, no. 4 (2006): 539–60.

127. Dirk Vandewalle, *A History of Modern Libya* (Cambridge University Press, 2006).
128. Lucia Ardovini, "The Politicisation of Sectarianism in Egypt: 'Creating an Enemy': The State vs. the Ikhwan," *Global Discourse* 6, no. 4 (2016): 579–600; Lucia Ardovini, "Stagnation vs Adaptation: Tracking the Muslim Brotherhood's Trajectories After the 2013 Coup," *British Journal of Middle Eastern Studies* 49 (2022): 187–203; Mona Farag, "Egypt's Muslim Brotherhood and the January 25 Revolution: New Political Party, New Circumstances," *Contemporary Arab Affairs* 5, no. 2 (2012): 214–29.
129. Mary Fitzgerald, "Finding Their Place: Libya's Islamists During and After the Revolution," in *The Libyan Revolution and Its Aftermath*, ed. Peter Cole and Brian McQuinn (Oxford University Press, 2015), 177–205.

3. Securing Interests While Hurting Libya

1. Eric Knecht, "The Politics of Libya's Political Isolation Law," blog post, Atlantic Council, February 28, 2013, https://www.atlanticcouncil.org/blogs/menasource/the-politics-of-libya-s-political-isolation-law/.
2. Berti Benedetta, *Armed Political Organizations: From Conflict to Integration* (Johns Hopkins University Press, 2013).
3. Manfred Brocker and Mirjam Künkler, "Religious Parties: Revisiting the Inclusion-Moderation Hypothesis." *Party Politics* 19, no. 2 (2013): 171–86.
4. The primary normative appeal of the inclusion-moderation hypothesis is that inclusion may deflate radicalism and turn revolutionaries into reformers, not that moderates may become more moderate. Jillian Schwedler, *Faith in Moderation: Islamist Parties in Jordan and Yemen* (Cambridge University Press, 2006). Tracing the Libyan Muslim Brotherhood's and Libyan Salafi-Madkhalis' failures to moderate contributes to understanding the descent of Libya from a hopeful democratic candidate in 2011 to a country riddled by violence and political noncompromise by 2021.
5. Emily Estelle, *A Strategy for Success in Libya*, American Enterprise Institute, November 2017, http://www.criticalthreats.org/wp-content/uploads/2017/11/A-Strategy-for-Success-in-Libya.pdf; Ben Fishman, "Could Libya's Decline Have Been Predicted?," *Survival* 57, no. 5 (2015): 199–208.
6. Shadi Hamid, "Political Party Development Before and After the Arab Spring," in *Beyond the Arab Spring: The Evolving Ruling Bargain in the Middle East*, ed. Mehran Kamrava (Oxford University Press, 2014), 131–50.
7. Dirk Vandewalle, "After Qaddafi: The Surprising Success of the New Libya," *Foreign Affairs* 91, no. 6 (2012): 8–15.
8. Mary Fitzgerald, "Finding Their Place: Libya's Islamists During and After the Revolution," in *The Libyan Revolution and Its Aftermath*, ed. Peter Cole and Brian McQuinn (Oxford University Press, 2015), 177–205.
9. Interview 2.

10. "Al-Sallabi, al-Sheikhi wakhrūn yuqdamūn mashruʿan limīthāq wa-ṭanīn antiqālīn" [Al-Sallabi, Al-Sheikhi, and Others Present a Draft for a Transitional National Charter], Al-Manara, March 28, 2011, http://archive.today/2021.12.15 -084548/http://almanaramedia.blogspot.com/2011/03/blog-post_3481.html.

11. Interview 23.

12. Al-Sallabi is considered part of the international Muslim Brotherhood especially close to Yusuf al-Qaradawi in Qatar, but he denies being part of the Libyan Muslim Brotherhood.

13. Wolfram Lacher, "Fault Lines of the Revolution: Political Actors, Camps and Conflicts in the New Libya," Research Paper 2013/RP 04, *Stiftung Wissenschaft und Politik*, May 7, 2013, https://www.swp-berlin.org/en/publication/libya-fault -lines-of-the-revolution.

14. Interview 23.

15. B. Chernitsky, "Libyan Muslim Brotherhood on the Rise," Middle East Media Research Institute, April 24, 2012, Inquiry and Analysis Series no. 828, https:// www.memri.org/reports/libyan-muslim-brotherhood-rise.

16. Alison Pargeter, *Return to the Shadows: The Muslim Brotherhood and An-Nahda Since the Arab Spring* (Saqi, 2016), 94.

17. This is also in line with the views of other Islamist interviewees.

18. Interviews 17, 27 and 34.

19. Peter Mandaville, *Islam and Politics*, 3rd ed. (Routledge, 2020).

20. Interviews 1, 49 and 59.

21. François Murphy, "Muslim Brotherhood Goes Public with Libya Summit," Reuters, November 17, 2011, http://web.archive.org/web/20191226163827/https:// www.reuters.com/article/us-libya-muslim-brotherhood-idUSTRE7AG2O Y20111117; Omar Ashour, "Libya's Muslim Brotherhood Faces the Future," op-ed, Brookings Institution, March 9, 2012, https://www.brookings.edu/articles/libyas -muslim-brotherhood-faces-the-future.

22. Interview 70.

23. Pargeter, *Return to the Shadows*, 100.

24. Interview 64; Omar Ashour, "Libyan Islamists Unpacked: Rise, Transformation and Future," policy briefing, Brookings Doha Center, May 2012. Sawan was removed as head of the JCP in June 2021.

25. "Ḥiwār-un maʿa al-masʾūl-I al-ʿām-i al-jadīd-i li-al-ikhwān-i al-muslimīn-a fī Lībīā" [Interview with the New Leader of the Muslim Brotherhood in Libya], video, Al-Manara, November 24, 2011, http://archive.today/2020.04.30-104402 /https://www.youtube.com/watch?v=DH57e5gqLTk.

26. Pargeter, *Return to the Shadows*, 96.

27. Interview 24.

28. Interview 64; Wikileaks, "[OS] Libya- Muslim Brotherhood, Salafist Said Moving towards Political Islamization of Libya," released on February 20, 2013, https://web.archive.org/web/20201015094650/https://wikileaks.org/gifiles /docs/15/154065_-os-libya-muslim-brotherhood-salafist-said-moving-towards .html.

29. Pargeter, *Return to the Shadows*, 102.

30. Interview 79.

31. Sam Marullo, "Frame Changes and Social Movement Contraction: U.S. Peace Movement Framing After the Cold War," *Sociological Inquiry* 66, no. 1 (1996): 1–28.
32. Frederic Wehrey, *The Burning Shores: Inside the Battle for the New Libya* (Farrar, Straus & Giroux, 2018).
33. "The Muslim Brotherhood (MB) expressed its pleasure at the announcement made by Libya that it has been completely liberated after decades under an oppressive and criminal rule . . . Reciprocated respect between all factions is necessary and recognizing Islamic and democratic independence is a must if Libya is to progress." "MB Calls on Libyan Factions to Unite and Draft Modern Constitution," Ikhwanweb, November 21, 2011, http://archive.today/2020.05.05 -082544/https://www.ikhwanweb.com/article.php?id=29080.
34. Fitzgerald, "Finding Their Place."
35. Alia Brahimi, "Libya's Revolution," in *North Africa's Arab Spring*, ed. George Joffé (London: Routledge, 2013), 101–21.
36. Interview 23.
37. Interview 32.
38. Interview 37.
39. His Facebook profile is still active at: https://www.facebook.com/mohamed .sowane.
40. As Anja Wollenberg and Carola Richter outline, the Muslim Brotherhood holds sway over important media channels for Libya from Turkey: "The Muslim Brotherhood is backing two fairly popular TV channels both with headquarters in Istanbul: Al-Nabaa and Al-Ahrar as well as the Tripoli-based Libya Panorama channel through the Anwar Libya Ltd. company. Although religious media could be part of a move toward sustainable pluralism, the current Islamist-affiliated media in Libya are characterized by a high level of polarization, and many channels appear as sources of incitement and inflammatory speech, thus reflecting the negative aspects of political parallelism." Anja Wollenberg and Carola Richter, "Political Parallelism in Transitional Media Systems: The Case of Libya," *International Journal of Communication* 14 (2020): 1181.
41. The page is still active at: http://www.ab.ly/.
42. Gary Alan Fine, "Public Narration and Group Culture: Discerning Discourse in Social Movements," in *Social Movements and Culture*, ed. Hank Johnston and Bert Klandermas (University of Minnesota Press, 1995), 127–43.
43. Hala Khamis Nassar and Marco Boggero, "Omar Al-Mukhtar: The Formation of Cultural Memory and the Case of the Militant Group That Bears His Name," *Journal of North African Studies* 13, no. 2 (2008): 201–17.
44. Justice and Construction Party, "Political Programme," accessible online at: kurzman.unc.edu/files/2011/06/LBY-2012-al-Adala-wa-al-Bina-Justice-and -Construction.pdf.
45. Elin Naurin, *Election Promises, Party Behaviour and Voter Perceptions* (Palgrave Macmillan, 2011).
46. Fitzgerald, "Finding Their Place."
47. Interview 67.
48. Interview 54.

49. Stacey Philbrick Yadav, "Understanding 'What Islamists Want': Public Debate and Contestation in Lebanon and Yemen," *Middle East Journal* 64, no. 2 (2010): 199–213.

50. Charles Kurzman and Ijlal Naqvi, "Do Muslims Vote Islamic?" *Journal of Democracy* 21, no. 2 (2010): 50–63.

51. Jillian Schwedler, "Can Islamists Become Moderates? Rethinking the Inclusion-Moderation Hypothesis," *World Politics* 63, no. 2 (2011): 347–76.

52. For example, Ennahda opposed a reference to shariʿa in the Tunisian constitution in March 2012 under Ghannouchi's leadership without previously achieving consensus inside the movement. Anne Wolf, "An Islamist 'Renaissance'? Religion and Politics in Post-Revolutionary Tunisia," *Journal of North African Studies* 18, no. 4 (2013): 560–73.

53. Dugald McConnell and Brian Todd, "Libyan Leader's Embrace of Sharia Raises Eyebrows," CNN, October 26, 2011, https://www.cnn.com/2011/10/26/world/africa/libya-sharia/index.html.

54. Facebook post by Sawan, January 27, 2012, personal database.

55. Facebook post by Sawan, March 1, 2012, personal database.

56. Facebook post by Sawan, May 20, 2012, personal database.

57. Video of Muhammad Sawan uploaded to the Libyan Muslim Brotherhood's Facebook page, March 3, 2012, personal database.

58. The official Facebook sites are at https://www.facebook.com/LYabparty/ for the JCP and https://www.facebook.com/EkwaanLibya/ for the Libyan Muslim Brotherhood.

59. Facebook post by Sawan, March 21, 2012, personal database.

60. Pamela Oliver and Hank Johnston, "What a Good Idea! Ideologies and Frames in Social Movement Research," *Mobilization: An International Quarterly* 5, no. 1 (2000): 37–54.

61. Interviews 8, 16, 41, and 43.

62. Interview 10.

63. Gwenn Okruhlik, "Making Conversation Permissible," in *Islamic Activism: A Social Movement Theory Approach,* ed. Quintan Wiktorowicz (Indiana University Press, 2004), 250–68.

64. The Libyan Muslim Brotherhood Facebook post that emphasizes the gradualist approach of MB, that no one needs to fear them, and that they have only the best for Libya in mind was made on March 12, 2012.

65. Interview 65.

66. Pargeter, *Return to the Shadows*, 110.

67. The homepage is still active at https://nfalibya.org/.

68. The NFA's candidates include young, and old figures, often from well-known families. Many of them have popular backgrounds inside Libya, albeit they are not politically experienced (such as Libyan football stars). Therefore, Wolfram Lacher argues in "Fault Lines of the Revolution," the organization "can best be understood as an unideological electoral coalition of those parts of the elites that remained in Libya during the Gaddafi era."

69. Justice and Construction Party Benghazi, "Hamlat ṭuruq alabwāb" [Knocking on Doors Campaign], video, YouTube, July 4, 2012, https://www.youtube.com

/watch?v=YYPYlk-tomw&fbclid=IwAR1Os-vJ028cFFnymdthcPrwCfii3GJpUDW8ujm6AGX_pnhA_7VfGQAL3wA.

70. Marc R. DeVore, "Exploiting Anarchy: Violent Entrepreneurs and the Collapse of Libya's Post-Qadhafi Settlement," *Mediterranean Politics* 19, no. 3 (2014): 463–70.
71. Interview 41.
72. Interview 33.
73. A lengthy statement was posted on the Libyan Muslim Brotherhood's website on September 20, 2012 (after the election) emphasizing how the JCP knew Islam best and hence was the best leader for Libya.
74. See introduction.
75. Quintan Wiktorowicz and Suha Taji-Farouki, "Islamic NGOs and Muslim Politics: A Case from Jordan," *Third World Quarterly* 21, no. 4 (2000): 685–99.
76. Gaddafi had deemed political parties modern instruments of dictatorial governments in his *Green Book*. This election law was interpreted as a legacy of lasting suspicions toward political parties as well as internal calculations by NTC members who figured they would stand a good chance as individual candidates.
77. More than 2.7 million Libyans registered to vote in the elections (85 percent of possible voters), and just over three thousand people stood as candidates. Out of these, 2,563 were independents and 649 from political parties. Laura Feliu and Rachid Aarab, "Political Islam in Libya: Transformation on the Way to Elitisation," in *Political Islam in a Time of Revolt*, ed. Ferran Izquierdo Brichs, John Etherington, and Laura Feliu (Palgrave Macmillan, 2017), 153–76.
78. The NFA won thirty-nine seats.
79. Interview 18.
80. The National Front is the successor to the National Front for the Salvation of Libya (al-Jabha al-Wataniya li-Inqadh Libya), the most important organization of the exile opposition for a long time.
81. Bani Rasheed, "Man yuṭālib bāsqāṭ al-ikhwān fālyusquṭ al-fasādi awla" [Whoever Demands the Overthrow of the Brotherhood Must Drop Corruption First], Ammon News, November 23, 2012, https://archive.md/kBmsG.
82. Interviews 19, 61, and 62.
83. Jason Pack and Haley Cook, "The July 2012 Libyan Election and the Origin of Post-Qadhafi Appeasement," *Middle East Journal* 69, no. 2 (2015): 171–98.
84. Lacher, "Fault Lines of the Revolution."
85. Interviews 12, 35, and 48.
86. Interviews 15, 18, 29, and 65.
87. "ʿAsmāʾ al-murashahīn al-dīn yadʿamuhum -tajamuʿ Al-Aṣāla" [Names of the Candidates Supported by Religion—al-Asala], Al-Asala, June 27, 2012, http://web.archive.org/web/20130315063048/http://www.alasala.ly/index.php/blog/47-أسماء-المرشحين-الدين-يدعمهم-تجمع-الأصالة; Frederic Wehrey and Anouar Boukhars, *Salafism in the Maghreb: Politics, Piety, and Militancy* (Oxford University Press, 2019), 131.
88. Lacher, "Fault Lines of the Revolution."

89. Mohammed al-Shafai, "Muasis hizb al-umat al-lībīā la al-sharq al-awsat: lam natawaqaʿ tarājuʿ al-ʾislamīyn bihadhi al-ṣuwra" [The Founder of Libyan Party al-Umma to Al-Sharq Al-Awsat: We Did Not Expect the Islamists to Retreat in Such a Way], *Asharq al-Awsat*, July 11, 2012, https://archive.aawsat.com/details .asp?section=4&issueno=12279&article=685881. Belhadj also failed to gain a single party seat.
90. Kenneth Roberts, *Deepening Democracy? The Modern Left and Social Movements in Chile and Peru* (Stanford University Press, 1998).
91. Interviews 1 and 18.
92. Pargeter, *Return to the Shadows*.
93. "Following Gaddafi's Demise, MB Warns Arab Dictators: People Always Prevail," Ikhwanweb, November 25, 2011, https://archive.ph/2020.05.05-085456/https: /www.ikhwanweb.com/article.pho?id=29079; Murphy, "Muslim Brotherhood Goes Public."
94. Interviews 45, 65, and 66.
95. Interviews 17, 25, and 51.
96. Pargeter, *Return to the Shadows*, 107.
97. Abdulrazzak al-Aradi, "Al-ṭarīq ʿila alkāritha" [The Road to Disaster], *Ean Libya*, March 1, 2015, http://archive.today/2021.12.15-111903/https://www.eanlibya .com/الطريق-إلى-الكارثة/.
98. Interview 60.
99. Interviews 29, 39, and 66.
100. Benedetta Berti, "Armed Groups as Political Parties and Their Role in Electoral Politics: The Case of Hizballah," *Studies in Conflict & Terrorism* 34, no. 12 (2011): 942–62.
101. Chris Bobel, " 'I'm not an activist, though I've done a lot of it': Doing Activism, Being Activist and the 'Perfect Standard' in a Contemporary Movement," *Social Movement Studies* 6, no. 2 (2007): 147–59; Ngai Keung Chan and Kwok Chi, "Legitimacy and Forced Democratisation in Social Movements. A Case Study of the Umbrella Movement in Hong Kong," *China Perspectives* 3 (2017): 7–16.
102. Haftar launched this operation as an offensive by the Libyan Arab Armed Forces (Al-quwāt al-musallaḥa al-ʿarabiya al-lībīya). However, they promote themselves as the Libyan National Army (LNA) and are usually referred to by this name, especially by international commentators, as it sounds more inclusive by not emphasizing the alleged Arab character.
103. Emaddedin Badi, "Exploring Armed Groups in Libya: Perspectives on Security Sector Reform in a Hybrid Environment," Geneva Centre for Security Sector Governance, December 2020, https://www.dcaf.ch/exploring-armed-groups -libya-perspectives-ssr-hybrid-environment, 30.
104. Wolfram Lacher and Peter Cole, "Politics by Other Means: Conflicting Interests in Libya's Security Sector," Working Paper 20, Small Arms Survey, October 2014, https://www.smallarmssurvey.org/resource/politics-other-means-conflicting -interests-libyas-security-sector-working-paper-20.
105. Olivier Roy, *Holy Ignorance: When Religion and Culture Diverge* (Columbia University Press, 2010).

106. Marc Lynch and Jillian Schwedler, "Introduction to the Special Issue on 'Islamist Politics after the Arab Uprisings,'" *Middle East Law and Governance* 12, no. 1 (2020): 3–13.
107. Gaddafi not only supported Salafi-Madkhalism to bolster his religious legitimacy, but also tried to cozy up to Sufism again: "Gaddafi was [also] supporting Sufism, probably in order to undermine the growing Salafi/Muslim Brotherhood influence. He was even hosting pro-Sufi conferences. The last one took place shortly before the revolution started, in February 2011." Anna Zajac, "Between Sufism and Salafism: The Rise of Salafi Tendencies After the Arab Spring and Its Implications," *Hemispheres: Studies on Cultures and Societies* 29, no. 2 (2014): 97–109. See also Brahimi, "Libya's Revolution," and Mark Woodward et al., "Salafi Violence and Sufi Tolerance? Rethinking Conventional Wisdom," *Perspectives on Terrorism* 7, no. 6 (2013): 58–78.
108. Interview 56. For more on intra-Salafi discussions, see Roel Meijer, "Politicising *al-Jarḥ wa-l-Taʿdīl*: Rabīʿ b. Hādī al-Madkhalī and the Transnational Battle for Religious Authority," in *The Transmission and Dynamics of the Textual Sources of Islam: Essays in Honor of Harald Motzki*, ed. Nicolet Boekhoff-van der Voort, Kees Versteegh, and Joas Wagemakers (Brill, 2011), 375–99.
109. Interviews 13, 15, 38, 44 and 58.
110. Wehrey and Boukhars, *Salafism in the Maghreb*; Lisa Watanabe, "Islamist Actors: Libya and Tunisia," Center for Security Studies, 2018, https://css.ethz.ch/content /dam/ethz/special-interest/gess/cis/center-for-securities-studies/pdfs /Watanabe-06282018-IslamistActors.pdf, 17.
111. Interviews 3, 57 and 76.
112. The wālī al-amr (a term identical to the one used for the legal guardian of a minor) has been transformed from an individual ruling to a modern bureaucratic and policy state in Islamic political writings without that transformation drawing notice. For an examination of how modern Islamic political thought has grappled with the nature of state authority by using and reshaping the tools of classical legal and political thought, see Nathan Brown, "Who or What Is the *Wālī Al-Amr*: The Unposed Question," *Oñati Socio-Legal Series* 4 (2019): 1–15.
113. David A. Graham, "Gaddafi's Compound: Inside Bab al-Azizya," *The Daily Beast*, August 23, 2011, https://www.thedailybeast.com/articles/2011/08/23/gaddafi -s-compound-inside-bab-al-azizya.
114. Interview 71.
115. Terrence Lyons, "Victorious Rebels and Postwar Politics," *Civil Wars* 18, no. 2 (2016): 160–74.
116. Elisabeth Wehling, "Politics and Framing: How Language Impacts Political Thought," in *The Routledge Handbook of Language and Media*, ed. Colleen Cotter and Daniel Perrin (Routledge, 2017), 133.
117. Frederic Wehrey and Anouar Boukhars, "Salafism and Libya's State Collapse: The Case of the Madkhalis," in *Salafism in the Maghreb: Politics, Piety, and Militancy* (Oxford University Press, 2019), 134.

118. Virginie Collombier, "Salafi Politics: 'Political' and 'Quietist' Salafis in the Struggle for the Libyan State," Research Project Report 2020/15, European University Institute, November 27, 2020, https://doi.org/10.2870/50645.

119. Alison Brysk, " 'Hearts and Minds:' Bringing Symbolic Politics Back In," *Polity* 27, no. 4 (1995): 577.

120. Interviews 44 and 50.

121. Sam Najjair, *Soldier for a Summer* (Hachette, 2013).

122. Hashim Bishr repeatedly tried to foreground his revolutionary credentials on his Facebook page. For example, he denied being part of the *ilzim baytak* group: that is, Salafis who followed fatwas to stay home and not join the armed forces. Personal database. For the official homepage of the now defunct SSC, see http://ssc.gov.ly/.

123. Interviews 14 and 45.

124. Lacher and Cole, "Politics by Other Means," 33.

125. Badi, "Exploring Armed Groups in Libya," 29.

126. Interviews 15, 43, and 50.

127. Interviews 36, 41, and 53; Frederic Wehrey and Peter Cole, "Building Libya's Security Sector," Carnegie Endowment for International Peace, August 6, 2013, https://carnegieendowment.org/posts/2013/08/building-libyas-security-sector.

128. As explained by Emaddedin Badi, "The SDF formed as a result of a rift within" Souq al-Jouma support groups "over a leadership dispute. Kara and the current [2021] head of the Nawasi Brigade were both leaders of clusters within" these support groups. "Kara set his sights on Mitiga and based his headquarters in the area, thus founding today's SDF. It is widely believed that Nawasi and SDF's positive (or ambivalent) relationship, and the lack of conflict between the forces in subsequent years, is primarily due to the fact that the two forces are staffed with combatants who originate from the neighborhood of [Souq al-Jouma] in Tripoli." Badi, "Exploring Armed Groups in Libya," 29.

129. Radaa is also linked to a wide-spanning and multifaceted network of Salafist preachers in Libya. Wehrey and Boukhars, *Salafism*, 130.

130. Interviews 3, 7 and 58.

131. Interview 4.

132. Lacher, "Fault Lines of the Revolution." See also International Crisis Group, "Divided We Stand: Libya's Enduring Conflicts," *Middle East and North Africa Report* 130 (2012), https://www.crisisgroup.org/middle-east-north-africa/north-africa/libya/divided-we-stand-libya-s-enduring-conflicts.

133. Inga Kristina Trauthig and Guy Robert Eyre, " 'Quietist' Salafis after the 'Arab Revolts' in Algeria and Libya (2011–2019): Between Insecurity and Political Subordination," *Mediterranean Politics*, October 29, 2023: 1–24, https://doi.org/10.1080/13629395.2023.2272474.

134. Majdi Hafala, "Nasīḥa ilā al-shabāb al-salafiy li-al-shaykh Abū Musʿab Majdī" [Advice to the Salafi Youth by Shaykh Abu Musab Majdi Hafala], YouTube, November 21, 2012, https://www.youtube.com/watch?v=knimBlmycIo.

135. Rabi al-Madkhali, "Al-taḥdhīr min al-fitan wa min al-dimoqātiyya wa mushtaqātih" [Warning against Strife and against Democracy and Its Derivatives], Rabi al-Madkhali home page, March 4, 2012, http://www.rabee.net/ar/articles.php?cat=8&id=228.

136. Madkhali, "Al-taḥdhīr min al-fitan."

137. Ad-Da'watus Salafīyyah, "Shaykh Zayd Al-Madkhali Advises the Brothers in Libya," Video, May 7, 2011, https://www.youtube.com/watch?v=RQIcrO-2fYg.

138. One example of Hafala's advice can be found in "Nasīḥa ilā al-shabāb."

139. Personal database.

140. Interview 57.

141. For the 2014 elections, which were supposed to lead the country out of confrontation but instead led to further polarization and splits, Sheikh Madkhali issued a fatwa condoning participation. These elections were supposed to create a sixty-member committee tasked with drafting the post-Gaddafi constitution. The ICG quotes this fatwa as being "something of a departure from Madkhali's views on elections in that it endorsed voting for the Constitutional Drafting Assembly—[it] was driven by concern over the role shariʿa law should be given in the constitution and how that would affect future legislation, an issue that remains fundamental for the movement." ICG, "Addressing the Rise of Libya's Madkhali-Salafis," *Middle East and North Africa Report* 200, April 25, 2019, 10, https://www.crisisgroup.org/middle-east-north-africa/north-africa/libya/addressing-rise-libyas-madkhali-salafis.

142. Interviews 3, 58 and 76.

143. Interviews 35 and 82.

144. Hafala, "Nasīḥa ilā al-shabāb."

145. Collombier, "Salafi Politics."

146. Rasmus Alenius Boserup and Virginie Collombier, *Militarization and Militiaization: Dynamics of Armed Group Proliferation in Egypt and Libya*, MENARA Working Papers 17, Instituto Affari Internazionali, October 2018.

147. Wolfram Lacher, "Tripoli's Militia Cartel: How Ill-Conceived Stabilisation Blocks Political Progress, and Risks Renewed War," *Stiftung Wissenschaft und Politik* Comment 2018/C 20, April 2018, https://www.swp-berlin.org/en/publication/libya-tripolis-militia-cartel.

148. Collombier, "Salafi Politics," 17.

149. Wehrey and Boukhars, *Salafism*, 124. In his study of Libyan armed groups, Badi writes, "While some units are specialized in raids, others act as a support force in combat or engagement situations. Some sub-units have also developed the capacity to deal with explosives and improvised explosive devices (IEDs) . . . Part-time paramedic units are also fully dedicated to the SDF." Badi, "Exploring Armed Groups in Libya," 30.

150. Schwedler, "Can Islamists Become Moderates?"

151. See table 1.

152. Wickham, *Mobilizing Islam*.

153. Jillian Schwedler, "Islamists in Power? Inclusion, Moderation, and the Arab Uprisings." *Middle East Development Journal* 5, no. 1 (2013): 1–18. See also Janine

Clark and Jillian Schwedler, "Who Opened the Window? Women's Activism in Islamist Parties," *Comparative Politics* 35, no. 3 (2003): 293–313.

154. "In Egypt, the middle-generation of Islamists in the Muslim Brotherhood increasingly sought to cooperate with their generational cohort within other political trends, just as younger Brotherhood members found that they shared many goals and values with young liberal bloggers . . . In the early 1990s, Palestine's Hamas cooperated with the Marxist Popular Front for the Liberation of Palestine, and Lebanon's Hizbullah has shown willingness to cooperate with a wide range of groups, including the rival Shi'i group, Amal, as well as various Sunni Muslim and Christian groups." Laleh Khalili, " 'Standing with my brother': Hizbullah, Palestinians, and the Limits of Solidarity," *Comparative Studies in Society and History* 49, no. 2 (2007): 279.

155. Always included in this group are Islamic scholars Bin Baz and Uthaymin. Jarret M. Brachman, *Global Jihadism: Theory and Practice* (Routledge, 2008), 63.

156. Collombier, "Salafi Politics," 17.

157. Adrian Blackledge, *Discourse and Power in a Multilingual World* (John Benjamins, 2005).

158. Schwedler, "Can Islamists Become Moderates?"

159. Mohammed Ayoob, "The Future of Political Islam: The Importance of External Variables," *International Affairs* 81, no. 5 (2005): 951–61.

160. Mohamed Eljarh, "Libya's Islamists Go for Broke," *Foreign Policy*, July 22, 2014, https://foreignpolicy.com/2014/07/22/libyas-islamists-go-for-broke/.

161. John K. Cooley, *Libyan Sandstorm* (Sidgwick and Jackson, 1983); Amal Obeidi, *Political Culture in Libya* (Routledge, 2001); John Oakes, *Libya: The History of Gaddafi's Pariah State* (History Press, 2011); Wolfram Lacher, "Is Autonomy for Northeastern Libya Realistic?" *Sada*, Carnegie Institute for International Peace, March 21, 2012, https://carnegieendowment.org/sada/47584.

162. Transnational Salafism has encountered opportunities in Libya. These organizations try to exploit the vacuum of governance in the country, taking advantage of political divisions and of the inability of political and military actors to rebuild the state apparatus. IS had a presence in Benghazi, Sirte, Derna, Tripoli, and parts of southern Libya. Lydia Sizer, "Libya's Terrorism Challenge: Assessing the Salafi-Jihadi Threat," Policy Paper 2017-1, Middle East Institute, October 2017, https://www.mei.edu/sites/default/files/publications/PP1_Sizer_LibyaCT_web_0.pdf.

163. Drawing inspiration from the rise of like-minded groups in neighboring Tunisia, Ansar al-Sharia put the teachings of Sunni scholar Abu Muhammad al-Maqdisi into practice through a program of charity and social services such as clinics, youth camps, and antidrug campaigns. As Zelin notes, "by placing democracy and Islam in irreconcilable positions, ASL undercuts Islamic democratic parties, such as the [JCP], which seek to apply Islamic principles to public policy within a democratic framework." Aaron Y. Zelin, "The Rise and Decline of Ansar al-Sharia in Libya," Hudson Institute, April 6, 2015, https://www.hudson.org/research/11197-the-rise-and-decline-of-ansar-al-sharia-in-libya.

164. Mikael Eriksson, "A Fratricidal Libya: Making Sense of a Conflict Complex," *Small Wars & Insurgencies* 27, no. 5 (2016): 817–36.

4. A Downhill Slope

1. Kenneth Roberts, *Deepening Democracy? The Modern Left and Social Movements in Chile and Peru* (Stanford University Press, 1998); Inga Kristina Trauthig, "SSR and Elections: What Role for the Security Sector in 2021?" in *The Road to Stability: Rethinking Security Sector Reform in Post-Conflict Libya*, ed. Emadeddin Badi, Archibald Gallet, and Roberta Maggi (DCAF–Geneva Center for Security Sector Governance, 2021), 29–38.
2. "Some witnesses accused the Muslim Brotherhood, in particular, of forming pragmatic alliances with Islamist militant and extremist groups during regional civil wars . . . In some places . . . , the Brotherhood and Al-Qaeda are already co-joined in armed conflict against a shared 'enemy.'" U.K. House of Commons Foreign Affairs Committee, "'Political Islam' and the Muslim Brotherhood Review: Sixth Report of Session 2016–17, November 2016, written evidence ISL0040, http://data.parliament.uk/writtenevidence/committeeevidence .svc/evidencedocument/foreign-affairs-committee/political-islam/written /32764.html.
3. The Libyan Muslim Brotherhood was therefore doubly vulnerable: First, it had alienated previous allies and second, it had neglected societal work in Libya, whereas, for example, Ansar Al-Sharia was able to attract many recruits in Benghazi and other cities in a very short time. Abdelmalek admitted that Ansar al- Sharia was smart by starting out with charity work: "They were doing what we should have been doing." Interview 78.
4. Madkhali endorsed taking up arms after a Benghazi delegation of Salafi-Madkhalis travelled to Saudi Arabia to seek support for Operation Dignity. Frederic Wehrey and Anouar Boukhars, *Salafism in the Maghreb: Politics, Piety, and Militancy* (Oxford University Press, 2019), 124–25. In another fatwa published on his website in July 2017, Madkhali again referred to the fights in Benghazi under Operation Dignity and told all true Salafis to repel the "aggression" of the Muslim Brotherhood, which he described as "more dangerous to the Salafis than the Jews and the Christians." Rabi al-Madkhali, "Naṣīhat al-muslimīn ʿmūmān wa-l-salafiyn khaṣata fī lībīā wa-ghīriha min al-bilad al-ʾislamīyati" [Advice for Muslims in General and Salafis in Particular, in Libya and Other Islamic Countries], Rabi al-Madkhali homepage, July 4, 2017, http://web.archive.org/web /20210825143838/https://rabee.net/ar/articles.php?cat=8&id=319.
5. Elie Abouaoun and Nate Wilson, "On the Road to Peace, Libya Makes Progress but Hits Pitfalls," United States Institute of Peace, July 14, 2021, https://www .usip.org/publications/2021/07/road-peace-libya-makes-progress-hits-pit falls.
6. Peter Cole, "Bani Walid: Loyalism in a Time of Revolution," in *The Libyan Revolution and Its Aftermath*, ed. Peter Cole and Brian McQuinn (Hurst, 2015), 285–303.

7. Wolfram Lacher, "Fault Lines of the Revolution: Political Actors, Camps and Conflicts in the New Libya," Research Paper 2013/RP 04, *Stiftung Wissenschaft und Politik*, May 7, 2013, https://www.swp-berlin.org/en/publication/libya-fault-lines-of-the-revolution.
8. Lacher, "Fault Lines of the Revolution."
9. Lacher, "Fault Lines of the Revolution." See also Emaddedin Badi, "Exploring Armed Groups in Libya: Perspectives on Security Sector Reform in a Hybrid Environment," Geneva Centre for Security Sector Governance, December 2020, https://www.dcaf.ch/exploring-armed-groups-libya-perspectives-ssr-hybrid-environment.
10. Lacher, "Fault Lines of the Revolution." While Salah Badi played a prominent role in the 2011 revolution, he fell from grace over the years given his increasingly uncompromising military endeavors, especially his resistance against the internationally supported GNA. In 2018 the United States finally decided to sanction him. U.S. Department of State, "The United States and UN Sanction Libyan Militia Leader Salah Badi," Office of the Spokesperson, November 19, 2018, https://ly.usembassy.gov/the-united-states-and-un-sanction-libyan-militia-leader-salah-badi/.
11. Alison Pargeter, *Return to the Shadows: The Muslim Brotherhood and An-Nahda Since the Arab Spring* (Saqi, 2016), 103.
12. Interview 27. For an example of his reporting, see Michel Cousins, "No SSC Disbandment Yet PM Declares," *Libya Herald*, December 14, 2012, https://www.libyaherald.com/2012/12/14/no-ssc-disbandment-yet-says-pm/.
13. Interviews 2, 6 and 13.
14. Interviews 18 and 29.
15. Interviews 18 and 29.
16. "Biʿda khilafi hād, al-mutamir al-waṭanī-alʿām ītifi" [After Tough Disagreements the National Congress Appoints], Al-Manara, December 26, 2012, http://www.almanaralink.com/press/2012/12/26982/بعد-خلاف-حاد-،-المؤتمر-الوطني-العام-يتف-/.
17. Haizam Amirah-Fernández, "Libya and the Problematic Political Isolation Law," Real Instituto Elcano, June 20, 2013, https://www.realinstitutoelcano.org/en/analyses/libya-and-the-problematic-political-isolation-law/.
18. "Political Isolation Law: The Full Text," *Libya Herald*, May 14, 2013, http://web.archive.org/web/20130609174823/http://www.libyaherald.com/2013/05/14/political-isolation-law-the-full-text.
19. Florence Gaub, "Libya: The Struggle for Security," *European Union Institute for Security Studies* (2013); Kora Andrieu, "Confronting the Dictatorial Past in Tunisia: Human Rights and the Politics of Victimhood in Transitional Justice Discourses Since 2011," *Human Rights Quarterly* 38, no. 2 (2016): 261–93; Michael Wahid Hanna, "Egypt's Search for Truth," *Cairo Review of Global Affairs*, Fall 2012.
20. Unlike Ba'athism, which has some ideological substance, the *jamāhīrīyah* was Gaddafi's unique construction of a political system, which translates to "state of the masses." Gaddafi, *The Green Book*.
21. Wolfram Lacher, *Libya's Fragmentation: Structure and Process in Violent Conflict* (I. B. Tauris, 2020), 31. For more information on Sami al-Saadi, see his CV on his

homepage: http://archive.today/2021.12.15-144727/https://www.samiassaadi.ly/cv.

22. Muhammad Sawan, "Raiy Sawan fī al-ʿuzl alsiyāsiy w-al-muqtarah al-adhiy ʿuriḍ ʿal-mutamar" [Sawan's Opinion on Political Isolation and the Proposal Presented to the Congress], video, Magdi Mokhtar, March 21, 2013, https://www.youtube.com/watch?v=hbBozdRGp_M.

23. Interviews 38, 40, and 60.

24. Rhiannon Smith, "Political Fault Lines Threaten Libya's Stability," OpenDemocracy, October 26, 2013, https://www.opendemocracy.net/en/north-africa-west-asia/political-fault-lines-threaten-libyas-stability/; Rhiannon Smith, "Libya's Political Isolation Law: Confusion and Charade," OpenDemocracy, May 15, 2013, https://www.opendemocracy.net/en/libyas-political-isolation-law-confusion-and-charade/.

25. On March 7, two days after the incident, an armed group attacked the offices of the al-Asema TV channel, which had taken an explicit stance against sweeping "political exclusion." The TV station's owner, Jum'a al-Usta (a leading donor to the NFA), and its executive director were abducted but later freed. Lacher, "Fault Lines of the Revolution."

26. Interviews 54 and 66. More importantly, because the law had passed with pressure from militias, it demonstrated the growing vulnerability of elected institutions to increasingly formidable armed groups, including those with an Islamist and Salafi orientation. Wehrey and Boukhars, *Salafism in the Maghreb*, 130.

27. "Libya Bans Ex-Gaddafi Officials from Office," Al Jazeera, May 5, 2013, https://www.aljazeera.com/news/2013/5/5/libya-bans-ex-gaddafi-officials-from-office.

28. "Libya: Reject 'Political Isolation Law," press statement, Human Rights Watch, May 4, 2013, https://www.hrw.org/news/2013/05/04/libya-reject-political-isolation-law.

29. Mohamed Magariaf, for example, may have headed up one of the most prominent dissident groups, but he had spent several years in the service of the regime as Libya's ambassador to India between 1978 and 1980.

30. Pargeter, *Return to the Shadows*, 107.

31. Mikael Eriksson, "A Fratricidal Libya: Making Sense of a Conflict Complex," *Small Wars & Insurgencies* 27, no. 5 (2016): 817–36.

32. Pargeter, *Return to the Shadows*, 108.

33. Libya al-Mostakbal, Al-Hirazi: Hizb al-Adalat al-dahiat al-qadīma lithawār', [JCP is the next victim of the revolutionaries], video, March 19, 2015, personal database.

34. Sawan, "Raiy Sawan fī al-ʿuzl alsiyāsiy."

35. Interview 19.

36. Interview 41.

37. Pargeter, *Return to the Shadows*, 105.

38. Interviews 2, 23, 24, 34, 40, 45, and 60. The outlined struggles faced by the Libyan Muslim Brotherhood and JCP were also discussed internally in the

movement and party, with some advocating strict disengagement of the latter from the former and some a renaming and rebranding of the JCP to leave behind its Muslim Brotherhood baggage. Still others promoted closer ties. In 2019 and 2020 a trend could be observed in Libya, with branches such as the one in Zawiya resigning. Some of these resignations were shared on social media: see the Twitter post at http://web.archive.org/save/https://twitter.com/LibyanIntegrity/status/1293941585541988352/photo/1. However, it is unclear how many people were actually part of this branch and what the "resignation" really implied. Another example is from November 2018, when Libyan TV was picking up the continuous discussion about the relationship between the JCP and Libyan Muslim Brotherhood: http://web.archive.org/web/20201201110051/https://twitter.com/libyaalahrartv/status/1067146843560251393?s=12.

39. Both the JCP Facebook and Twitter sites were still operative in 2021: https://www.facebook.com/LYabparty/ and https://twitter.com/JC2012PARTY. While the Twitter page was largely inactive at that time, the Facebook page had regular, almost daily posts.

40. Interviews 34, 36, and 45; Katherine Pollock and Frederic Wehrey, "The Sufi-Salafi Rift," Carnegie Endowment for International Peace, January 23, 2018, https://carnegieendowment.org/middle-east/diwan/2018/01/the-sufi-salafi-rift.

41. Khalifa Haftar was a retired military officer who had defected in 1983 while fighting in Chad. He lived in the United States but returned for the 2011 revolution. Sharif Abdel Kouddous, "A Q&A with Khalifa Hifter, the Mastermind behind Libya's New Revolt," *Washington Post*, May 20, 2014, https://www.washingtonpost.com/news/worldviews/wp/2014/05/20/a-qa-with-khalifa-hifter-the-mastermind-behind-libyas-new-revolt/

42. "25 qatīlan wa 45 jarīhan saqaṭū amām dirʿ lībiā 1" [25 Dead and 45 Wounded by the Libya Shield 1], Quryna News, June 8, 2013. https://archive.md/dVKKP#selection-955.0-959.154. In addition, Benghazi was shaken by high-profile attacks on foreigners. The most serious of these were an attack on the U.S. liaison office in Benghazi on September 11, 2012, in which the U.S. ambassador was killed, and a car bomb that partially destroyed the French embassy in Tripoli on April 23, 2013. For an overview of incidents until December 2012, see: U.S. Department of State, "Accountability Review Board Report," December 18, 2012, www.state.gov/documents/organization/202446.pdf, 15–16.

43. "Ousted Libyan PM Flees," *Deutsche Welle*, December 3, 2014, https://www.dw.com/en/libyan-ex-premier-zeidan-flees-to-europe/a-17492737.

44. Haftar originally announced his coup on Al Arabiya. For more information on Libya and the regional TV landscape, see Najj Abou-Khalil and Laurence Hargreaves, "Libyan Television and Its Influence on the Security Sector," United States Institute of Peace, April 2015, https://www.usip.org/sites/default/files/SR364-The-Role-of-Media-in-Shaping-Libya's-Security-Sector-Narratives.pdf. For more information on Haftar's coup attempt in 2014, see Ashraf

Abdul-Wahab, "General Hafter Announces Coup; Politicians React with Scorn, Order His Arrest," *Libya Herald*, February 14, 2014, https://www.libyaherald .com/2014/02/14/general-hafter-announces-coup-politicians-react-with -scorn-order-his-arrest/

45. "East Libyan Army Takes Rivals' Final Holdout in Benghazi," CGTN Africa, March 2017, https://www.youtube.com/watch?v=kFMQ4nrYIpA.
46. "Libya Muslim Brotherhood Statement on General Haftar's Desperate Coup Attempt." Ikhwanweb, May 21, 2014. https://web.archive.org/web/2014082 8205949/http://ikhwanweb.com/article.php?id=31656.
47. Emaddedin Badi, Archibald Gallet, and Roberta Maggi, "Rethinking the Road to Stability—Security Sector Reform in Libya," Geneva Centre for Security Sector Reform, November 2021, https://www.dcaf.ch/sites/default/files/publications /documents/The_Road_to_Stability11.11.2021.pdf.
48. This involvement was rationalized in order to prevent authoritarian rule by Haftar. Khaled al-Sharif, "Liqāʾ khāṣun maʿ Khaled al-Sharif wakīl wizārat al-difāʿ" [Interview with Khaled al-Sharif, Deputy Minister of Defense] Al-Nabaa TV, August 25, 2014. https://www.youtube.com/watch?v=FJvZz7_XIwU; Khalid Mahmoud, "Libyan Muslim Brotherhood Condemns Haftar 'Coup,'" *Asharq Al-Awsat*, May 23, 2014, english.aawsat.com/2014/05/article55332524/libyan -muslim-brotherhood-condemns-haftar-coup.
49. Libya al-Mostakbal, "Al-Hirazi: Hizb al-Adalat."
50. In a public speech broadcast on the Tanasuh channel on March 9, 2013, Sheikh al-Gharyani supported the Martyrs Bloc. Sadeq Al-Gharyani, "Al-ʿazl al-sīyāsiy w-al-mutamar al-watāniy—al-shaykh al-Sadeq al-Gharyani" [Political Isolation and the National Congress—Sheikh Sadeq al-Gharyani], Tanasuh TV, March 9, 2013. https://www.youtube.com/watch?v=hMc7aAVHNGE.
51. During the civil war, Gharyani was a key ideological supporter of Libya Dawn. Sadeq al-Gharyani, "Lībīā—muftiy lībīā al-shaykh al-Sadeq al-Gharayani bis-han al-aqtitāl al-jāriy fī ṭarābulus lībīā wa-majlis al-nuwāb al-lībiy" [Libya—Grand Mufti of Libya Sheikh Al-Sadiq Al-Ghariani on the Ongoing Fighting in Tripoli, Libya, and the Libyan House of Representatives], *Good Morning Libya*, August 5, 2014, https://www.youtube.com/watch?v=IMg0RfkjaX4 and August 24, 2014, https://www.youtube.com/watch?v=HYSFfoMsWeo.
52. Sadeq al-Gharyani, "Al-Gharyani yuftiy biwujūb qitāl quāt al-jaīsh almunḍamat taht qiādat alliwāʾ Haftar" [Al-Gharyani Issued a Fatwa That the Army Forces Joined Under the Command of Major General Haftar Must Fight], YouTube, June 9, 2014, https://www.youtube.com/watch?v=L8LsP XXqhsM.
53. Raphaël Lefèvre, "An Egyptian Scenario for Libya?" *Journal of North African Studies* 19, no. 4 (2014): 602–7; Andrea Carboni and James Moody, "Between the Cracks: Actor Fragmentation and Local Conflict Systems in the Libyan Civil War," *Small Wars & Insurgencies* 29, no. 3 (2018): 456–90.
54. Karim Mezran and Arturo Varvelli, "Libyan Crisis: International Actors at Play," *Foreign Actors in Libya's Crisis*, Italian Institute for International Political Studies (ISPI), July 26, 2017, https://www.ispionline.it/en/publication/foreign-actors -libyas-crisis-17224.

55. United Nations Support Mission in Libya, *Skhirat Agreement in English*, December 17, 2015, https://unsmil.unmissions.org/sites/default/files/Libyan Political Agreement - ENG .pdf.

56. Omar Ashour, "Between ISIS and a Failed State: The Saga of Libyan Islamists," Working Paper, Rethinking Political Islam Series, Brookings Institution, 2015.

57. Joana Cook, Haid Haid, and Inga Trauthig, "Jurisprudence Beyond the State: An Analysis of Jihadist 'Justice' in Yemen, Syria and Libya," *Studies in Conflict & Terrorism* (2020): 1–20, https://doi.org/10.1080/1057610X.2020.1776958.

58. Ziad Akl, "Militia Institutionalisation and Security Sector Reform in Libya," EuroMeSCo, June 2017, https://www.euromesco.net/publication/militia-institutionalisation-and-security-sector-reform-in-libya/.

59. Interviews 12, 48 and 52. The Libyan Muslim Brotherhood also became increasingly aggressive in their rhetoric towards Haftar, for example, calling him a terrorist who collaborated with IS. "Muslim Brotherhood Condemns Egypt Coup Regime Aggression on Libya," Ikhwanweb, May 29, 2017, https://web.archive.org/web/20190301081510/https://www.ikhwanweb.com/article .php?id=32702.

60. Holly Yan, "Libya: US Launches Airstrikes on ISIS Targets," CNN, August 2, 2016, https://www.cnn.com/2016/08/01/politics/us-libya-isis-airstrikes/index .html; Libyan Express, "Libyan Forces Lose More Fighters in Sirte as They Continue to Trap IS Radicals in 1km Area," Libyan Express, November 2, 2016, https://www.libyanexpress.com/libyan-forces-lose-more-fighters-in-sirte-as -they-continue-to-trap-is-radicals-in-1km-area/.

61. Nizar Kawan and Abdulrazzak al-Aradi, *ṣuʿud wa suquṭ tanẓīm al-dawla fī Sirte: ʿAmalīyat al-Bunyan al-Marsous* [The Rise and Fall of the Islamic State in Sirte: Operation Al-Bunyan Al-Marsous], Al Jazeera, October 10, 2021, https://studies .aljazeera.net/ar/ebooks/book-1424.

62. Susanne Bygnes, " 'We Are in Complete Agreement:' The Diversity Issue, Disagreement and Change in the European Women's Lobby," *Social Movement Studies* 12, no. 2 (2013): 199–213. In addition, a former Libyan Muslim Brotherhood member explained that, until 2021, "you will find that certain individuals who feel restricted under the MB, have left the MB, like Mustafa Saglizi, Abdulrazzak al-Aradi, but nobody believes them. This is the point . . . [in addition] some JCP members, such as Muhammad Sawan have grown to hate the MB . . . the problem is that they can't even leave the movement, if they leave it as an individual they're finished. And then as operators in the country they have no more power, no more weight." Interview 2.

63. Christina Steenkamp, *Violent Societies: Networks of Violence in Civil War and Peace* (Springer, 2014).

64. Following the 2011 revolution and its nationwide violence "local councils and militias representing the specific interests of towns, cities, and tribes [emerged]. As a result, political and military organization during and after the conflict was generally at this level, rather than regional or national." Wolfram Lacher, "Is Autonomy for North-Eastern Libya Realistic?" *Sada*, Carnegie Institute for International Peace, March 21, 2012, https://carnegieendowment.org /sada/47584.

65. Rabi al-Madkhali, "Jadīd al-ʿallama al-shaykh ʿamīr al-Madkhaliy ḥafiẓahu Allah wa raʿah li-al-salagiyyīn fī Lībīā wa ʾan yakūnū taḥt rayat Haftar" [The New Shaykh Rabi Al-Madkhali, May God Preserve Him and Protect Him—The Salafis in Libya Need to Be under the Banner of Haftar], video, February 22, 2018, https://www.youtube.com/watch?v=4HAywsUtjF4.

66. Rabi al-Madkhali, "Fatwā al-shaykh Rabi al-Madkhali biʿadam alqiāl fi lībīā maʿ aiy ṭaraf" [The Fatwa of Shaykh Rabi al-Madkhali Not to Fight in Libya with Any Party], video, February 27, 2015, https://www.youtube.com/watch?v=TOyYSJnLuaA.

67. George Joffé, "The Trojan Horse: The Madkhali Movement in North Africa," *Journal of North African Studies* 23, no. 5 (2018): 739–44.

68. Interviews 8, 9, 52, and 83. These interviewees from Derna, Sirte and Benghazi all outlined the uncompromising behavior by Libyan Salafi-Madkhali militias.

69. Vincent Durac, "The Role of Non-State Actors in Arab Countries After the Arab Uprisings," *IEMed Mediterranean Yearbook* 1 (2015): 37–41.

70. Eva Wegner, *Islamist Opposition in Authoritarian Regimes: The Party of Justice and Development in Morocco* (Syracuse University Press, 2011).

71. Interviews 71 and 76.

72. Interview 57.

73. Ronald Bruce St John, *Libya: Continuity and Change* (Routledge, 2011).

74. "Magariaf Calls Destruction of Tombs Illegal: SSC Denies Any Participation in Shrine Destruction," *Al-Watan al-Libiya*, August 25, 2012, https://archive.md /f0m4z. https://www.facebook.com/Libyantogether/posts/httpwwwalwatan-l ibyacommorephpnewsid25740catid22/220533738080846/.

75. Mohammed and Rabi bin-Hadi al-Madkhali have been in disagreement occasionally. In this instance, it seems that Rabi did not favor the destructions, but Mohammed did. Frederic Wehrey, "As Their Influence Grows the Quietist Salafis Are Anything but Quiet," *World Politics Review*, December 11, 2018, https://www .worldpoliticsreview.com/articles/26962/as-their-influence-grows-the -maghreb-s-quietist-salafists-are-anything-but-quiet.

76. "Extremists Demolish Libya's Shrines Using Bulldozers, Explosives," France24, August 29, 2012, https://observers.france24.com/en/20120829-extremists -demolish-libya-shrines-using-bulldozers-explosives-libya-mausoleum-zliten -tripoli-video-salafists.

77. "Libya Minister Quits over Sufi Shrine Attack." Al-Jazeera, August 27, 2012, https://www.aljazeera.com/news/2012/8/27/libya-minister-quits-over-sufi -shrine-attack.

78. Interviews 3 and 5.

79. Interview 80.

80. Larbi Sadiki, "Libya: Testing Tolerance," Al Jazeera, September 4, 2012, https:// www.aljazeera.com/opinions/2012/9/4/libya-testing-tolerance; United Nations, "The Destruction of Cultural and Religious Sites: A Violation of Human Rights," Human Rights Office of the High Commissioner, September 24, 2012, https:// www.ohchr.org/en/stories/2012/09/destruction-cultural-and-religious-sites -violation-human-rights..

81. "Libya: New Wave of Attacks Against Sufi Sites," Human Rights Watch, December 7, 2017, https://www.hrw.org/news/2017/12/07/libya-new-wave-attacks-against-sufi-sites.
82. "Dignity Operation Armed Groups Attack Shrine of Former King Idris Senussi's Father," Libya Observer, December 30, 2017, https://www.libyaobserver.ly/crimes/dignity-operation-armed-group-attacks-shrine-libya's-former-king-idris-senussi's-father.
83. Alexander Knysh, "Contextualizing the Salafi–Sufi Conflict from the Northern Caucasus to Hadramawt," *Middle Eastern Studies* 43, no. 4 (July 1, 2007): 503–30.
84. Pollock and Wehrey, "Sufi–Salafi Rift."
85. Pollock and Wehrey, "Sufi–Salafi Rift."
86. Pollock and Wehrey, "Sufi–Salafi Rift."
87. Interview 76.
88. David D. Kirkpatrick and Ivor Prickett, "A Police State with an Islamist Twist: Inside Hifter's Libya," *The New York Times*, February 20, 2020, World, https://www.nytimes.com/2020/02/20/world/middleeast/libya-hifter-benghazi.html; Karlos Zurutuza, "The Sect Quietly Uniting a Divided Libya—Under Salafism," *Libya Tribune*, July 4, 2018, https://en.minbarlibya.org/2018/07/04/the-sect-quietly-uniting-a-divided-libya-under-salafism/.
89. Interviews 7, 16, 21, and 35.
90. Interviews 14, 41, and 42.
91. With regard to the Libyan Civil war in 2014, initially, the Libyan Salafi-Madkhalis, especially in Tripoli, "suffered a sharp blow, and many of its figures fled to Zintan and other towns opposed to Dawn." However, over the course of 2016, this dynamic reversed and the balance of power tilted sharply in favor of the Libyan Salafi-Madkhalis, with many members returning to the capital. "The more revolutionary Islamists and Ghariani supporters (including Libyan Muslim Brotherhood members) were partially killed or imprisoned, or fled the country." Wehrey and Boukhars, *Salafism in the Mahgreb*, 131.
92. Their publicity included uploading videos showing the alleged leader of a criminal gang confessing to abducting a child in Tripoli (personal database) and presenting large quantities of hashish captured in Tripoli via their Facebook page. "Bism allah al-rahman al-rahīm hadha alfīdiu yuaḍih kaīfīat takhzīn mādat mukhadirat nawʿ hashīsh tama ẓabatuha" [In the name of God, the Most Gracious, the Most Merciful. This Video Shows How to Store a Narcotic Substance, a Type of Hashish That Has Been Seized], SDF Tripoli Facebook page, June 21, 2015, personal database.
93. Interviews 32 and 36.
94. Interviews 16, 17, 32, and 36.
95. International Crisis Group (ICG), "Addressing the Rise of Libya's Madkhali-Salafis," *Middle East and North Africa Report* 200, April 25, 2019, https://www.crisisgroup.org/middle-east-north-africa/north-africa/libya/addressing-rise-libyas-madkhali-salafis: 16.
96. Interview 40.

97. Virginie Collombier, "Libyan Salafis and the Struggle for the State," *Third World Thematics* 3, no. 6 (2022): 296–313, https://doi.org/10.1080/23802014.2022.2062442: 307.

98. Interview 53.

99. For an example critiquing the emphasis on an ideological boundary, see Badi, "Exploring Armed Groups in Libya." For an example in support, see Nathan Vest, "Heretics, Pawns and Traitors: Anti-Madkhali Propaganda on Libyan Salafi-Jihadi Telegram," *Jihadology* blog, February 25, 2019, https://jihadology .net/2019/02/25/guest-post-heretics-pawns-and-traitors-anti-madkhali -propaganda-on-libyan-salafi-jihadi-telegram/.

100. Francisco Gutiérrez Sanín and Elisabeth Jean Wood, "Ideology in Civil War: Instrumental Adoption and Beyond," *Journal of Peace Research* 51, no. 2 (2014): 213–26.

101. Providing an example of how Salafi ideology can trump tribal and ethnic loyalties, Subul al-Salam also has links with Radaa.

102. Wolfram Lacher, "Tripoli's Militia Cartel: How Ill-Conceived Stabilisation Blocks Political Progress, and Risks Renewed War," *Stiftung Wissenschaft und Politik* Comment 2018/C 20, April 2018, https://www.swp-berlin.org/en/publication/libya -tripolis-militia-cartel.

103. In February 2012 the NTC established the Dar al-Ifta' in Tripoli with decision No. 15/2012, available at https://ssf.gov.ly/wp-content/uploads/2012/09/قانون- رقم-15-لسنة-2012بشأن-انشاء-دار -الافتاء-1.pdf. Frederic Wehrey and Anouar Boukhars report, "The Madkhalis' struggle with Ghariani and his Islamist allies or sympathizers began shortly after the revolution, when Madkhalis increased their presence 'on the street'—through the establishment of private schools, the distribution of books, and their control of *manabar* (pulpits) in neighborhood mosques—sometimes through force. But al-Ghariani's adherents and sympathisers, whom the Madkhalis deride as *mukhalaf* (roughly, 'contradictory') or 'Ma'ribis' (referring to[a] schism with [a] Yemen based cleric), maintained control of the endowment offices in Tripoli." Wehrey and Boukhars, *Salafism*, 131.

104. Most Salafi-jihadis consider Madkhalis sell-outs and even *murji'a* (a derogatory term meaning "those who postpone") because of their vocal criticisms of Qutb and their rejection of violence. Brachman, *Global Jihadism*, 30.

105. Shaykh Nader al-Omrani, "Mudākhalat faḍīlat al-Shaykh Dr. Nadir al-Omrani bikhuṣūṣ al-mūqif min fatwā al-Shaykh Rabi al-Madkhali aldāʿiat lilqitāl ʾilā jānib Haftar!" [Intervention of His Eminence Shaykh Dr. Nader al-Omrani Regarding the Fatwa of Shaykh Rabi al-Madkhali Calling for Fighting alongside Haftar!], Dar al-Ifta Libya, July 11, 2016, personal database. In 2015 Radaa briefly arrested a senior member of Sadeq al-Gharyani's Dar al-Ifta for allegedly supporting IS. Michel Cousins, "Tripoli Endowments Ministry Head Released After Questioning About IS Support," *Libya Herald*, November 27, 2015, https://www .libyaherald.com/2015/11/27/tripoli-endowments-ministry-head-released -after-questioning-about-is-support/.

106. ICG, "Addressing the Rise."

107. Abdulkader Assad, "By Egyptian Fatwa and Libyan Execution, Libyan Cleric Nadir Al-Omrani Killed After 45 Days of Kidnap," *Libya Observer*, January 21, 2016, https://libyaobserver.ly/news/egyptian-fatwa-and-libyan-execution-libyan -cleric-nadir-al-omrani-killed-after-45-days-kidnap.

108. Salah el Din Hassan, "Al-salafīyūn al-mudākhalat fī miṣr (dirāsa)" [Madkhali Salafis in Egypt: (study)], blog post, December 24, 2010, http://archive.today /2012.12.10-025018/http://salaheldinhassan.blogspot.de/2010/12/blog-post _408.html.

109. "The killing of Umrani also fuelled the perception, already widespread, that elements within Radaa were sympathetic with Haftar. Yet Kara's response, in an early 2016 interview, was that he remained publicly loyal to the GNA, even if his sympathies were divided. 'I said, "God is Great!" when Haftar attacked Ansar al-Sharia,' he stated. 'But I can't support him here in the capital because that would cause *fitna*.'" Wehrey and Boukhars, *Salafism*, 132.

110. Safer Al-Harathy, "Head of Awqaf Authority Arrested in Tripoli," *Libya Observer*, August 4, 2018, https://libyaobserver.ly/news/head-awqaf-authority-arrested -tripoli.

111. Collombier, "Libyan Salafis and the Struggle for the State."

112. "This promotion, and the firing of the previous director (Abbas al-Qadi) was widely suspected to have arisen from Libyan Salafi-Madkhalis' pressure. In addition, the Libyan Salafi-Madkhalis were angered over Qadi's allowing of the public commemoration of the *mawlid* [birthday of the Prophet]." Wehrey and Boukhars, *Salafism*, 133.

113. Article 4 of the decree gave the unit broad authority to use artistic censorship to intercept all information likely to threaten the safety of the country, social safety, or national security. United Nations Security Council, "UNSMIL: Report of the Secretary General, S/2018/780," August 24, 2018, https://unsmil .unmissions.org/sites/default/files/sg-report-on-unsmil_s_2018_780_e.pdf.

114. The United Nations found that Mitiga prison held "an estimated 2,600 men, women and children, most without access to judicial authorities." This is a significant number of prisoners given that in October 2017 official prisons in Libya overseen by the GNA's Ministry of Justice were estimated to be holding some 6,500 people. "Detainees are subjected to torture, unlawful killing, denial of adequate medical treatment and poor detention conditions." United Nations Human Rights Office of the High Commissioner (OHCHR), "Abuse Behind Bars: Arbitrary and Unlawful Detention in Libya," April 2018, 3, 11, 4. https://www .ohchr.org/Documents/Countries/LY/AbuseBehindBarsArbitraryUnlawful _EN.pdf.

115. Three interviewees (42, 46, and 50) who worked under the GNC or GNA asserted they had seen money boxes coming in on flights from Saudi Arabia, which Radaa members took into their facilities at Mitiga. While this specific information is reliant on witness reporting, there are various other reports of the support of Libyan Salafi-Madkhali groups coming from Saudi Arabia. For example, see "Maṣādir takshif ziāratan qiādiy majmu'āt musalahat lībīā l-al-s'audīa" [Sources Reveal the Visit of Leaders of Libyan Armed Groups to Saudi Arabia],

Al-Araby, April 15, 2018, http://archive.today/2021.12.17-092633/ https://www .alaraby.co.uk/مصادر-تكشف-زيارة-قيادي-مجموعات-مسلحة-ليبية-للسعودية.

116. Interviews 13 and 14.

117. Interview 81.

118. Interviews 3 and 5.

119. Virginie Collombier, "Salafi Politics: 'Political' and 'Quietist' Salafis in the Struggle for the Libyan State," Research Project Report 2020/15, European University Institute, November 27, 2020, https://doi.org/10.2870/50645.

120. Wehrey and Boukhars, "Salafism and Libya's State Collapse: The Case of the Madkhalis," in *Salafism in the Maghreb*, 132.

121. Interviews 56, 58, 71, and 82.

122. Tim Eaton, "The Libyan Arab Armed Forces," Research Paper, Chatham House, last updated June 7, 2021, https://www.chathamhouse.org/2021/06/libyan-arab -armed-forces; Jalel Harchaoui and Mohamed-Essaïd Lazib, "Proxy War Dynamics in Libya," Virginia Tech, July 24, 2019, https://doi.org/10.21061/proxy-wars -harchaoui-lazib.

123. Radaa conducts a "rehabilitation" program that is partly job training and partly theological reeducation, using an array of Salafi texts from Saudi clerics including al-Albani and al-Fawzan. Wehrey and Boukhars, *Salafism*, 124.

124. OHCHR, "Abuse Behind Bars," 8.

125. Interviews 65 and 81.

126. Jamie Dettmer, "Meet the Islamic Fanatic Who Wants to Kill ISIS," *Daily Beast*, June 10, 2017, https://www.thedailybeast.com/meet-the-islamic-fanatic-who -wants-to-kill-isis.

127. Sami Zaptia, "Rada Raids Comic Con, Arrests Over 20 Organisers, Participants and Spectators," *Libya Herald*, November 4, 2017, https://libyaherald.com /2017/11/rada-raids-comic-con-arrests-over-20-organizers-participants-and -spectators/.

128. Interviews 6, 31, 33, and 38.

129. Interview 14.

130. Ahmed Elumami, "Libyan Forces Capture Sirte Convention Center from Islamic State," Reuters, August 10, 2016, World, https://www.reuters.com/article/us -libya-security-idUSKCN10L1QX.

131. ICG, "How the Islamic State Rose, Fell and Could Rise Again in the Maghreb," *Middle East and North Africa Report* no. 178, July 24, 2017, https://www.crisisgroup .org/middle-east-north-africa/north-africa/178-how-islamic-state-rose-fell -and-could-rise-again-maghreb; Cook, Haid, and Trauthig, "Jurisprudence Beyond the State."

132. Interview 82.

133. Interviews 71 and 82.

134. R. Kim Cragin, "Tactical Partnerships for Strategic Effects: Recent Experiences of US Forces Working by, with, and Through Surrogates in Syria and Libya," *Defence Studies* 20, no. 4 (2020): 318–35.

135. Some members of the dominating Misratan militias stayed in Sirte for a while but reports surfaced of abuses linked to revenge by Misratans who were still

bitter about Sirte's role in the revolution and also blamed residents for allowing IS to take hold in the city. Sudarsan Raghavan, "A Year After ISIS Left, a Battered Libyan City Struggles to Resurrect Itself," *Washington Post*, January 8, 2017, https://www.washingtonpost.com/news/world/wp/2018/01/08/feature/a-year-after-isis-left-a-battered-libyan-city-struggles-to-resurrect-itself/.

136. Interview 83.

137. UK House of Commons, "Libya: Examination of Intervention and Collapse and the U.K.'s Future Policy Options," Foreign Affairs Committee report, September 14, 2016, https://publications.parliament.uk/pa/cm201617/cmselect/cmfaff/119/119.pdf.

138. Interviews 46, 79, and 81.

139. Wehrey and Boukhars, "Salafism and Libya's State Collapse," 127.

140. See, for example, 604th Battalion, "Isdār fa hal tara lahum min bāqiya" [Issuance Do You See Anything Remaining From Them], video, January 11, 2018, https://www.youtube.com/watch?v=Ytd4sZzAzgo; 604th Battalion, "Jawlat ʿadasat katībat 604 mushāh fī mustashā bn sīnā li-al-ittilāʿ ʿlā mustajaddāt al-syāna bi-al-mustashfā" [A Tour of the 604th Infantry Battalion at Ben Sena Hospital to See the Latest Developments in the Hospital Maintenance], video, March 17, 2017, https://www.youtube.com/watch?v=RcwPd9O3yws.

141. "Armed Militants Kidnap Libya's Military Prosecutor." Alarabiya News, March 16, 2018, https://english.alarabiya.net/News/north-africa/2018/03/16/Armed-militants-kidnap-Libya-s-military-prosecutor. Another example is the attempted assassination of the deputy chief of the rival Sirte Protection and Security Force. See Abdulkader Assad, "Military Commander at Libya's Al-Bunyan Al-Marsous Operation Survives Assassination," *Libya Observer*, November 4, 2018, https://www.libyaobserver.ly/news/military-commander-libyas-al-bunyan-al-marsous-operation-survives-assassination.

142. Interview 73.

143. Interview 28.

144. Collombier, "Libyan Salafis and the Struggle for the State."

145. Interview 76.

146. The confrontation with ASL played a motivational role for some Libyan Salafi-Madkhalis to join Operation Dignity. For reference, in this sermon Bazaza explicitly takes aim at what is likely to be IS and decries the actions of a "group among us" or a "group made out of our own people" and calls that group "a bunch of evil people" with "foolish dreams" in what appears to be a quote from a *hadith*. Shaykh Kamal Bazaza, "Al-khuṭbat alatiy ightīl bisababiha al-Shaykh Kamal Bazaza min qibal majlis shūrī Benghazi" [The Sermon for which Shaykh Kamal Bazaza Was Assassinated by the Benghazi Shura Council], YouTube, May 9, 2019, https://www.youtube.com/watch?app=desktop&v=aYly1ezz-x8; "Assassination Campaign Blights Eastern Libya," *Financial Times*, December 12, 2013.

147. Andrew McGregor, "Radical Loyalty and the Libyan Crisis: A Profile of Salafist Shaykh Rabi' bin Hadi al-Madkhali," *Militant Leadership Monitor* 7, no. 12 (January 11, 2017). This was also ultimately more a rebranding than a tempering or

dilution of the Libyan Salafi-Madkhalis' military engagement. Many of them also kept up their ideological convictions and continued to propagate statements of Shaykh Rabi al-Madkhali on their social media. Personal database.

148. The following year, Madkhali issued another fatwa calling on all Salafis in Libya to counter the Benghazi Defence Brigades, an armed group formed by anti-Haftar military personnel and militiamen, including many Islamist veterans of the Benghazi Revolutionaries Shura Council. Rabi al-Madkhali, "Jadīd al-ʿallama al-shaykh ʿamīr al-Madkhaliy ḥafiẓahu Allah wa raʿah li-al-salagiyyīn fī Lībīā wa ʾan yakūnū taḥt rayat Haftar" [The New Shaykh Rabi Al-Madkhali, May God Preserve Him and Protect Him—The Salafis in Libya Need to Be under the Banner of Haftar], video, February 22, 2018, https://www.youtube.com/watch?v=4HAywsUtjF4.

149. Interview 84.

150. The Saiqa would become infamous for their brutality. One of their main commanders, Mahmoud al-Werfalli, has an International Criminal Court arrest warrant against him under Article 8(2)(c)(i) of the Rome Statute. International Criminal Court, "Case Information Sheet: The Prosecutor v. Mahmoud Mustafa Busyf Al-Werfalli," 2018, https://www.icc-cpi.int/CaseInformationSheets/al-werfalliEng.pdf.

151. Ashraf al-Mayar, "Ashraf al-Mayār yaqul inna al-ḥākim al-sharʿiy li-Lībyā howa majlis al-nuwāb wa man yakhruj ʿanh yuʿtabar min al-khwārij wa yajib qitāluh" [Ashraf al-Mayar Says That the Legitimate Ruler of Libya is the House of Representatives and Those Who Do Not Think So Are Considered Kharijites and Must Be Fought], video, October 19, 2018, https://www.youtube.com/watch?v=moocXdH4M5c.

152. Rabi al-Madkahli, "Fatwā Rabi al-Madkhali al-jadīdat ʿan lībīā" [Rabi al-Madkhali's New Fatwa on Libya], Salem Salem, April 4, 2016, www.youtube.com/watch?v=1bjR68rDGqU.

153. In a short audio recording from February 2018, Madkhali went back to supporting Haftar explicitly. Madkhali, "Jadīd al-ʿallama al-shaykh ʿamīr al-Madkhaliy."

154. Badi, "Exploring Armed Groups in Libya," 32.

155. ICG, "Addressing the Rise," 17.

156. Interview 72.

157. Interview 59.

158. Interviews with foreign diplomats (48, 52) confirmed that Saddam Haftar joined meetings or would replace his father in scheduled meetings. "Haftar's Son Visited Israel to Seek Military Support." Daily Sabah, November 9, 2021, https://www.dailysabah.com/world/africa/haftars-son-visited-israel-to-seek-military-support-report.

159. The LNA's success in the years 2016 to 2018 is also partially explained by the high levels of assistance from foreign governments, such as Egypt and the UAE, which provided arms and training. United Nations Security Council. "Final Report of the Panel of Experts on Libya Established Pursuant to Resolution 1973 (2011)," S/2018/812, https://www.securitycouncilreport.org/atf/cf/%7B65BFCF9B-6D27-4E9C-8CD3-CF6E4FF96FF9%7D/s_2018_812.pdf.

160. Collombier, "Salafi Politics."
161. Otaibi also denounced the tradition in many parts of Libya of celebrating Mawlid. "Raghm muʿāraḍat al-ʾamn w-al-baladīati. al-ʿtībiy yaṣil tibriq waṣṭ hirāsat mushadada" [Despite the Opposition of the Security and the Municipality, Al-Otaibi Arrives in Tobruk Under Heavy Security], Al-Wasat, February 14, 2017, https://web.archive.org/web/20210126002934/http://alwasat.ly/news/libya/124686.
162. Interview 13.
163. "Eyes on Jihadis in Libya," Libya Analysis, February 13, 2019, https://jihadology.net/2019/02/13/eye-on-jihadis-in-libya-weekly-update-february-12/.
164. Vest, "Heretics, Pawns, and Traitors."
165. Interviews 8, 9, and 11. This behavior is also in line with Dar al Ifta, "Speech by the Department of Mosque Affairs on the Role of Secularism in Corrupting Society by Publishing Misguided and Sinful Books and Ways of Preventing Its Evil," General Authority for Religious Endowments and Islamic Affairs Libya, January 25, 2017.
166. Vest, "Heretics, Pawns, and Traitors."
167. Interview 10.
168. "Libya: Incitement Against Religious Minority," Human Rights Watch, July 20, 2017, https://www.hrw.org/news/2017/07/20/libya-incitement-against-religious-minority.
169. United Nations. "Libya: UN Experts Call for a Swift and Rigorous Response to the Destruction of Sufi Sites," press release, Human Rights Office of the High Commissioner, September 10, 2012, https://www.ohchr.org/en/press-releases/2012/09/libya-un-experts-call-swift-and-rigorous-response-destruction-sufi-sites.
170. Wehrey, "As Their Influence Grows."
171. United Nations Security Council. "Final Report of the Panel of Experts on Libya Established Pursuant to Resolution 1973 (2011)," S/2017/466, https://www.securitycouncilreport.org/atf/cf/%7B65BFCF9B-6D27-4E9C-8CD3-CF6E4FF96FF9%7D/s_2017_466.pdf.
172. Interview 85.
173. "Libya: Mass Extra-Judicial Execution," Human Rights Watch, November 29, 2017, https://www.hrw.org/news/2017/11/29/libya-mass-extra-judicial-execution.
174. Nevertheless, and as in western Libya, some Libyan Salafi-Madkhali initiatives met with resistance. For example, restrictions on women traveling without a male relative were reversed in 2017 as a result of broad opposition in society. "Libya's Eastern Authority Freezes Women's Travel Ban," BBC News, February 22, 2017, https://www.bbc.com/news/world-africa-39053829. In April 2019, the prime minister of the interim government, Abdullah al-Thani, removed a Libyan Salafi-Madkhali figure as director of the eastern ʿawqaf and appointed a member of the Sufi sect, Abd Al-Matlub Al-Abyad, to replace him.
175. "Libya: Fears Mount for Abducted Woman Politician a Month Since She Went Missing," Amnesty International, August 16, 2019, https://www.amnesty.org/en

/latest/news/2019/08/libya-fears-mount-for-abducted-woman-politician-a
-month-since-she-went-missing/.

176. "Al-liwā' Rahil: hunāk tansīq baīn al-'irhābīyn fī madīnatiy ṭarābulus wa-derna" [Major General Rahil: There Is Coordination between the Terrorists in the Cities of Tripoli and Derna], Al-Marsad, June 3, 2019, http://web.archive.org/web /20210120063736/https://almarsad.co/2019/06/03/الإر-بين-تنسيق-هناك-رحيل-اللواء هابيين/.

177. United Nations Support Mission in Libya, "UNSMIL Deplores Enforced Disappearance of Elected HoR Member Ms. Sergewa," July 18, 2019, https://unsmil .unmissions.org/unsmil-deplores-enforced-disappearance-elected-hor -member-ms-sergewa-calling-her-immediate-release.

178. Badi, "Exploring Armed Groups in Libya."

179. McGregor, "Radical Loyalty and the Libyan Crisis."

180. Jillian Schwedler, "Islamists in Power? Inclusion, Moderation, and the Arab Uprisings," Middle East Development Journal 5, no. 1 (2013): 1–18; Lise Storm, "Exploring Post-Rebel Parties in Power: Political Space and Implications for Islamist Inclusion and Moderation," Open Journal of Political Science 10, no.4 (2020): 638–67, DOI: 10.4236/ojps.2020.104038.

181. Wehrey, "As Their Influence Grows."

182. See chapter 2.

183. "In June 2012, Salafi Jihadi brigades from across Libya held a heavily armed 'forum for the victory of sharia' in central Benghazi. The rally would not have been possible without tacit acceptance by and—in the case of elements from the Der' Libya—participation of leading brigades in the city, which are formally under defence ministry control." Lacher, "Fault Lines of the Revolution," 17.

5. What Next?

1. Tom Hill and Nate Wilson, "Foreign Interference Remains Key Driver of Libya Conflict," United States Institute of Peace, June 3, 2020, https://www.usip.org /publications/2020/06/foreign-interference-remains-key-driver-libya -conflict; Inga Kristina Trauthig, "SSR and Elections: What Role for the Security Sector in 2021?" in The Road to Stability: Rethinking Security Sector Reform in Post-Conflict Libya, ed. Emadeddin Badi, Archibald Gallet, and Roberta Maggi, DCAF–Geneva Center for Security Sector Governance, 2021, 29–38, https://www .dcaf.ch/road-stability-rethinking-ssr-post-conflict-libya.

2. "President Obama: Libya Aftermath 'Worst Mistake' of Presidency," BBC News, April 11, 2016, US & Canada, https://www.bbc.com/news/world-us-canada -36013703.

3. Interview 51.

4. Florence Gaub and Rob Weighill, The Cauldron: NATO's Campaign in Libya (Oxford University Press, 2018); Aidan Hehir, "The Permanence of Inconsistency: Libya, the Security Council, and the Responsibility to Protect," International Security 38, no. 1 (2013): 137–59.

5. Mehari Taddele Maru, "On Unconstitutional Changes of Government: The Case of the National Transitional Council of Libya," *African Security Review* 21, no. 1 (2012): 67–73.

6. Interview 64; U.K. House of Commons, "Examination of Intervention and Collapse and the U.K.'s Future Policy Options," Foreign Affairs Committee report, September 14, 2016, https://publications.parliament.uk/pa/cm201617/cmselect /cmfaff/119/119.pdf.

7. Ben Clements, "Public Opinion and Military Intervention: Afghanistan, Iraq and Libya," *Political Quarterly* 84, no. 1 (2013): 119–31; Jolyon Howorth, "The EU and NATO After Libya and Afghanistan: The Future of Euro–U.S. Security Cooperation," *Yale Journal of International Affairs* 8, no. 1 (2013): 30–39.

8. Rana Jawad, "Libya Elections: Do Any of the Parties Have a Plan?" BBC News, July 6, 2012, Africa, https://www.bbc.com/news/world-africa-18721576; Alice Alunni and Karim Mezran, "Post-Qadhafi Libya: The Electoral Dilemma," *ISPI Analysis* 114 (2012), https://www.ispionline.it/sites/default/files/pubblicazioni /analysis_114_2012.pdf.

9. Donatella della Porta, "Communication in Movement: Social Movements as Agents of Participatory Democracy," in *Social Media and Democracy: Innovations in Participatory Politics*, ed. Brian D. Loader and Dan Mercea (Routledge, 2012), 150–65; Donatella della Porta and Sidney Tarrow, "Interactive Diffusion: The Coevolution of Police and Protest Behavior with an Application to Transnational Contention," *Comparative Political Studies* 45, no. 1 (2012): 119–52; Charles Tilly and Sidney G. Tarrow, *Contentious Politics* (Oxford University Press, 2015).

10. Most existing scholarship assesses the inclusion-moderation hypothesis separately from the repression-radicalization hypothesis. However, for the Libyan Muslim Brotherhood and Libyan Salafi-Madkhalis, empirical evidence argues for an inclusion-radicalization hypothesis, as both movements become less moderate the more they integrate into the system. Scholars such as Joas Wagemakers have been making calls for systemic empirical research with regard to the repression-radicalization hypothesis, noting that, while even moderate Islamists in Jordan face quite severe repression and manipulation, they do not turn to violent resistance. The divergent interpretations of these two hypotheses challenge previously well-established rationales. Scholars studying Islamist and Salafi movements after 2011 should be particularly fine-tuned to the pitfalls of relying on conceptualizations about the very different structural environments of authoritarian openings. Marc Lynch and Jillian Schwedler, "Introduction to the Special Issue on 'Islamist Politic After the Arab Uprisings,'" *Middle East Law and Governance* 12, no. 1 (2020): 3–13; Francesco Cavatorta and Fabio Merone, "Moderation Through Exclusion? The Journey of the Tunisian Ennahda from Fundamentalist to Conservative Party," *Democratization* 20, no. 5 (2013): 857–75; Julie Chernov Hwang, *When Terrorists Quit: The Disengagement of Indonesian Jihadists* (Cornell University Press, 2018); Joas Wagemakers, "Between Exclusivism and Inclusivism: The Jordanian Muslim Brotherhood's Divided Reponses to the 'Arab Spring,'" *Middle East Law and Governance* 12, no. 1 (2020): 35–60.

11. Anas El Gomati, "Libya's Elections Are Around the Corner. But the Country Needs a Hard Reset," blog post, Atlantic Council, October 13, 2021, https://www

.atlanticcouncil.org/blogs/menasource/libyas-elections-are-around-the
-corner-but-the-country-needs-a-hard-reset/.

12. Shadi Hamid, William McCants, and Rashid Dari, *Islamism After the Arab Spring: Between the Islamic State and the Nation-State*, Brookings Institution, Project on U.S. Relations with the Islamic World Forum Papers, January 2017, https://www.brookings.edu/articles/islamism-after-the-arab-spring-between-the-islamic-state-and-the-nation-state/.

13. Inga Kristina Trauthig, "Gaining Legitimacy in Post-Qaddafi Libya: Analysing Attempts of the Muslim Brotherhood," *Societies* 9, no. 3 (2019): 65, https://doi.org/10.3390/soc9030065

14. Dirk Vandewalle, *Libya Since Independence: Oil and State-Building* (Cornell University Press, 2018).

15. The Libyan Muslim Brotherhood was doubly vulnerable, first, because it had alienated previous allies and second, because it had neglected societal work in Libya. A group such as Ansar Al-Sharia, by contrast, was able to attract many recruits in Benghazi and other cities in a very short time. Abdelmalek admitted that Ansar al-Sharia was smart to start out with charity work: "They were doing what we should have been doing." Interview 78.

16. Trauthig, "Gaining Legitimacy."

17. This discussion was also at the heart of the "resignation" of Libyan Muslim Brotherhood branches around Libya in 2019 and 2020, as happened in Zawiya. However, it is unclear how many people were actually part of this branch and what the "resignation" really implied. http://web.archive.org/save/https://twitter.com/LibyanIntegrity/status/1293941585541988352/photo/1.

18. Personal database.

19. Banani contested the elections against Suleiman Abdelkader and four other less high-profile members. Banani is considered well-embedded in the international organization of the Muslim Brotherhood. He is well-known in Europe and had returned to Libya after the revolution in 2011. "Libye: Imad al-Bannani, nouveau président du parti 'Justice et Construction,'" Anadolu Ajansi, June 20, 2021, https://www.aa.com.tr/fr/afrique/libye-imad-al-bannani-nouveau-pr%C3%A9sident-du-parti-justice-et-construction/2279695. The Libya Review, which writes the Libya briefs for the Konrad Adenauer Foundation, considers Banani "more hard-line than his predecessor, with ties to . . . Ali al-Sallabi." Konrad Adenauer Foundation, Inside Libya 12, Regional Programme Political Dialogue, July 2021, https://www.kas.de/documents/282499/282548/Inside+Libya+-+July+Edition.pdf.

20. On Sunday, May 2, 2021, the Libyan Muslim Brotherhood announced its conversion on the group's Facebook site. This account was taken down in January 2022 after being identified as linked to an influence operation. "Recapping Our 2021 Coordinated Inauthentic Behavior Enforcements," Meta, January 20, 2022, https://about.fb.com/news/2022/01/december-2021-coordinated-inauthentic-behavior-report/. Hamdi Yildiz, "Libyan Muslim Brotherhood Converts into NGO," Anadolu Agency, May 3, 2015, http://web.archive.org/web/20210615222008/https://www.aa.com.tr/en/middle-east/libyan-muslim-brotherhood-converts-into-ngo/2227616.

21. Sami Zaptia, "UN Secretary General Calls for Stability, Early Elections, and Critical Decisions to Be Taken in a Transparent and Consensual Manner," *Libya Herald*, February 25, 2022, https://libyaherald.com/2022/02/un-secretary-general-calls-for-stability-early-elections-and-critical-decisions-to-be-taken-in-a-transparent-and-consensual-manner/.

22. Jalel Harchaoui, "A Dysfunctional Peace: How Libya's Fault Lines Were Redrawn," War on the Rocks, February 24, 2022, https://warontherocks.com/2022/02/a-dysfunctional-peace-how-libyas-fault-lines-were-redrawn/.

23. Konstantin Belousov et al., "Any Port in a Storm: Fieldwork Difficulties in Dangerous and Crisis-Ridden Settings," *Qualitative Research* 7, no. 2 (May 1, 2007): 155–75.

24. United States Agency for International Development, "Libya Community Pulse: Web Survey Results," June 20, 2021, https://app.box.com/s/jw7lp254oqj4wzk1tdcu0tunbqpzurdo.

25. Rabi al-Madkhali, "Jadīd al-ʿallama al-shaykh ʿamīr al-Madkhaliy ḥafiẓahu Allah wa raʿah li-al-salagiyyīn fī Lībīā wa ʾan yakūnū taḥt rayat Haftar" [The New Shaykh Rabi Al-Madkhali, May God Preserve Him and Protect Him—The Salafis in Libya Need to Be under the Banner of Haftar], video, February 22, 2018, https://www.youtube.com/watch?v=4HAywsUtjF4.

26. Francesco Cavatorta and Stefano Torelli, "From Victim to Hangman? Ennahda, Salafism and the Tunisian Transition," *Religions* 12, no. 2 (2021): 76; Justin A. Hoyle, "A Matter of Framing: Explaining the Failure of Post-Islamist Social Movements in the Arab Spring," *Digest of Middle East Studies* 25, no. 2 (2016): 186–209; Monica Marks, "Did Egypt's Coup Teach Ennahda to Cede Power?" *Transnational Diffusion and Cooperation in the Middle East*, POMEPS Studies, August 24, 2016, https://pomeps.org/wp-content/uploads/2016/09/POMEPS_Studies_21_Transnational_Web-REV.pdf#page=54; Rory McCarthy, "When Islamists Lose: The Politicization of Tunisia's Ennahda Movement," *Middle East Journal* 72, no. 3 (2018): 365–84.

27. Beverley Milton-Edwards and Stephen Farrell, *Hamas: The Islamic Resistance Movement* (Polity, 2010); Nina Musgrave, "Hamas and the 'Trap' of Sectarianism?" *Global Discourse* 6, no. 4 (2016): 697–708; Are Hovdenak, "Hamas in Transition: The Failure of Sanctions," *Democratization* 16, no. 1 (2009): 59–80.

28. Aaron Boxerman, "What We Know About the Death Toll in Israel from the Hamas-Led Attacks," *The New York Times*, November 12, 2023, World, https://www.nytimes.com/2023/11/12/world/middleeast/israel-death-toll-hamas-attack.html.

29. Gal Beckerman, " 'The Middle East Region Is Quieter Today Than It Has Been in Two Decades,' " *The Atlantic*, October 7, 2023, https://www.theatlantic.com/international/archive/2023/10/israel-war-middle-east-jake-sullivan/675580/.

30. Inga K. Trauthig, "Is the Term 'Terrorism' Still Useful for Understanding Conflicts in Libya?" *International Affairs*, blog post, Medium, September 27, 2021, https://medium.com/international-affairs-blog/is-the-term-terrorism-still-useful-in-understanding-conflicts-in-libya-bed87ef642a7.

Appendix

1. Samuel Huntington, *The Third Wave: Democratization in the Late Twentieth Century* (University of Oklahoma Press, 1993), 190; Samuel Huntington, *Political Order in Changing Societies* (Yale University Press, 2006); Douglass North, John Joseph Wallis, and Barry R. Weingast, *Violence and Social Orders: A Conceptual Framework for Interpreting Recorded Human History* (Cambridge University Press, 2009).
2. Susanne Karstedt, "Does Democracy Matter? Comparative Perspectives on Violence and Democratic Institutions," *European Journal of Criminology* 12, no. 4 (2015): 457–81; Ludger Mees, *Nationalism, Violence and Democracy: The Basque Clash of Identities* (Palgrave Macmillan, 2003); Paul Staniland, "Violence and Democracy," book review, *Comparative Politics* 47, no. 1 (2014): 99–118.
3. Wolfgang Kersting, ed. *Thomas Hobbes: Leviathan: oder Stoff, Form und Gewalt eines kirchlichen und bürgerlichen Staates* (Akademie, 2008).
4. Alex Braithwaite, Dennis M. Foster, and David A. Sobek, "Ballots, Bargains, and Bombs: Terrorist Targeting of Spoiler Opportunities," *International Interactions* 36, no. 3 (2010): 294–305; Chris Wilson, "Ideological Motives in Spoiler Violence: Post Conflict Assam, Northeast India," *Nationalism and Ethnic Politics* 23, no. 3 (2017): 280–96; Marie-Joëlle Zahar, "Reframing the Spoiler Debate in Peace Processes," in *Contemporary Peacemaking: Conflict, Peace Processes and Post-War Reconstruction*, ed. John Darby and Roger Mac Ginty (Palgrave Macmillan UK, 2008), 159–77.
5. Omar Ashour, *The De-Radicalization of Jihadists: Transforming Armed Islamist Movements* (Routledge, 2009).
6. Suveyda Karakaya and A. Kadir Yildirim, "Islamist Moderation in Perspective: Comparative Analysis of the Moderation of Islamist and Western Communist Parties," *Democratization* 20, no. 7 (2013): 1322–49.
7. Robert S. Leiken and Steven Brooke, "The Moderate Muslim Brotherhood," *Foreign Affairs*, March/April 2007, 107–21.
8. Karakaya and Yildirim, "Islamist Moderation in Perspective."
9. Are Hovdenak, "Hamas in Transition: The Failure of Sanctions," *Democratization* 16, no. 1 (2009): 59–80.
10. Jillian Schwedler writes, "In addition to parliamentary cooperation, these groups work together around issues such as mounting demonstrations against the US war in Iraq . . . Even in Yemen, whose 1990 unification and democratic 1993 parliamentary elections stunned the region as well as the world, some Islamist trends explored links with socialists by the late 1990s and later formalized this cooperative relationship in the establishment of the Joint Meetings Party, an opposition bloc that played a significant role in the 2011 protests in Yemen." Jillian Schwedler, "Islamists in Power? Inclusion, Moderation, and the Arab Uprisings," *Middle East Development Journal* 5, no. 1 (2013): 6. See also Michelle Browers, "The Egyptian Movement for Change: Intellectual Antecedents and Generational Conflicts," *Contemporary Islam* 1, no. 1 (2007): 69–88; Nancy Davis and Robert Robinson, "Overcoming Movement Obstacles by the Religiously Orthodox: The Muslim Brotherhood in Egypt, Shas in Israel, Comunione

e Liberazione in Italy, and the Salvation Army in the United States," *American Journal of Sociology* 114, no. 5 (2009): 1302–49.

11. Michelle Browers, "Origins and Architects of Yemen's Joint Meeting Parties," *International Journal of Middle East Studies* 39, no. 4 (2007): 565–86; Francesco Cavatorta and Fabio Merone, "Moderation Through Exclusion? The Journey of the Tunisian Ennahda from Fundamentalist to Conservative Party," *Democratization* 20, no. 5 (2013): 857–75; Michael D. Driessen, "Public Religion, Democracy, and Islam: Examining the Moderation Thesis in Algeria," *Comparative Politics* 44, no. 2 (2012): 171–89; Joas Wagemakers, "Legitimizing Pragmatism: Hamas' Framing Efforts from Militancy to Moderation and Back?" *Terrorism and Political Violence* 22, no. 3 (2010): 357–77; Eva Wegner and Miquel Pellicer, "Islamist Moderation Without Democratization: The Coming of Age of the Moroccan Party of Justice and Development?" *Democratization* 16, no. 1 (2009): 157–75; Barbara Zollner, *The Muslim Brotherhood: Hasan al-Hudaybi and Ideology* (Routledge, 2009).

12. Karakaya and Yildirim, "Islamist Moderation in Perspective."

13. David Collier and James E. Mahon, "Conceptual 'Stretching' Revisited: Adapting Categories in Comparative Analysis," *American Political Science Review* 87, no. 4 (1993): 845–55.

14. Carrie Rosefsky Wickham, "The Path to Moderation: Strategy and Learning in the Formation of Egypt's Wasat Party," *Comparative Politics* 36, no. 2 (2004): 205–28.

15. Francesco Cavatorta, " 'Divided they stand, divided they fail': Opposition Politics in Morocco," *Democratization* 16, no. 1 (2009): 137–56; İhsan Yılmaz, "An Islamist Party, Constraints, Opportunities and Transformation to Post-Islamism: The Tajik Case," *Uluslararasi Hukuk ve Politika* 18 (2009): 133–47.

16. Janine Clark, "Questioning Power, Mobilization, and Strategies of the Islamist Opposition," in *Contentious Politics in the Middle East: Political Opposition Under Authoritarianism*, ed. Holger Albrecht (University Press of Florida, 2010), 117–37.

17. Janine Clark, "The Conditions of Islamist Moderation: Unpacking Cross-Ideological Cooperation in Jordan," *International Journal of Middle East Studies* 38, no. 4 (2006): 539–60.

18. Risa A. Brooks, "Liberalization and Militancy in the Arab World," *Orbis* 46, no. 4 (2002): 611–21; Clark, "Conditions of Islamist Moderation"; Mona El-Ghobashy, "The Metamorphosis of the Egyptian Muslim Brothers," *International Journal of Middle East Studies* 37, no. 3 (2005): 373–95; Vali Nasr, "The Rise of 'Muslim Democracy,'" *Journal of Democracy* 16, no. 2 (2005): 13–27, https://www.journalofdemocracy.org/articles/the-rise-of-muslim-democracy/; Glenn E. Robinson, "Can Islamists Be Democrats? The Case of Jordan," *Middle East Journal* 51, no. 3 (1997): 373–87; Jillian Schwedler, *Faith in Moderation: Islamist Parties in Jordan and Yemen* (Cambridge University Press, 2006); Wickham, "Path to Moderation"; Fareed Zakaria, "Islam, Democracy, and Constitutional Liberalism," *Political Science Quarterly* 119, no. 1 (2004): 1–20.

19. Karakaya and Yildirim, "Islamist Moderation in Perspective," 1347.

Bibliography

"Abdel Fattah Younes' Family: Criminal Prosecution—or Revenge." Quryna News, December 5, 2012. www.qurynanew.com/45785.

Abdul-Wahab, Ashraf. "General Hafter Announces Coup; Politicians React with Scorn, Order His Arrest." *Libya Herald*, February 14, 2014. https://www.libyaherald.com/2014/02/14/general-hafter-announces-coup-politicians-react-with-scorn-order-his-arrest/.

Abou-Khalil, Najj, and Laurence Hargreaves. "Libyan Television and Its Influence on the Security Sector." United States Institute of Peace, April 2015. https://www.usip.org/sites/default/files/SR364-The-Role-of-Media-in-Shaping-Libya's-Security-Sector-Narratives.pdf.

Abouaoun, Elie, and Nate Wilson. "On the Road to Peace, Libya Makes Progress but Hits Pitfalls." United States Institute of Peace, July 14, 2021. https://www.usip.org/publications/2021/07/road-peace-libya-makes-progress-hits-pitfalls.

Ad-Da'watus Salafiyyah. "Shaykh Zayd Al-Madkhalī Advises the Brothers in Libya." Video. May 7, 2011. https://www.youtube.com/watch?v=RQIcrO-2fYg.

Ahmad, Aisha. "The Security Bazaar: Business Interests and Islamist Power in Civil War Somalia." *International Security* 39, no. 3 (2014): 89–117.

Akl, Ziad. "Militia Institutionalisation and Security Sector Reform in Libya." EuroMeSCo, June 2017. https://www.euromesco.net/publication/militia-institutionalisation-and-security-sector-reform-in-libya/.

Ali, Ahmed Salah. "Haftar and Salafism: A Dangerous Game." Blog post. Atlantic Council, June 6, 2017. https://www.atlanticcouncil.org/blogs/menasource/haftar-and-salafism-a-dangerous-game/.

Alunni, Alice, and Karim Mezran. "Post-Qadhafi Libya: the Electoral Dilemma." *ISPI Analysis* 114 (2012). https://www.ispionline.it/sites/default/files/pubblicazioni/analysis_114_2012.pdf.

Amirah-Fernández, Haizam. "Libya and the Problematic Political Isolation Law." Real Instituto Elcano, June 20, 2013. https://www.realinstitutoelcano.org/en /analyses/libya-and-the-problematic-political-isolation-law/.

Anani, Khalil al-. "The Inclusion-Moderation Thesis: Muslim Brotherhood in Egypt." Oxford Research Encyclopedia of Politics. August 28, 2019. https://doi.org/10.1093 /acrefore/9780190228637.013.1332.

Anani, Khalil al-. "Unpacking the Sacred Canopy: Egypt's Salafis Between Religion and Politics." In Salafism after the Arab Awakening: Contending with People's Power, edited by Francesco Cavatorta and Fabio Merone, 25–42. Hurst, 2015.

Anani, Khalil al-. "The Young Brotherhood in Search of a New Path." Current Trends in Islamist Ideology 9 (2009): 96–109.

Anderson, Charles W. "Youth, the 'Arab Spring,' and Social Movements." Review of Middle East Studies 47, no. 2 (2013): 150–56. https://doi.org/10.1017/S2151348100058031.

Anderson, Lisa. "Religion and State in Libya: The Politics of Identity." Annals of the American Academy of Political and Social Science 483, no. 1 (1986): 61–72.

Andrieu, Kora. "Confronting the Dictatorial Past in Tunisia: Human Rights and the Politics of Victimhood in Transitional Justice Discourses Since 2011." Humanities Quarterly 38, no. 2 (2016): 261–93.

Ansari, Hamied. "The Islamic Militants in Egyptian Politics." International Journal of Middle East Studies 16, no. 1 (1984): 123–44.

Aqeel, Aqeel Hussein. ʿAsrār wamʿlumāt min zaman al-Qadhāfī [Secrets and information from Qaddafi's time]. N.p., n.d.

Aradi, Abdulrazzak al-. "Abdulrazzak al-Aradi fi liqāʾ khaṣin Nabil Belhaj" [Abdulrazzak al-Aradi in an Exclusive Interview with Nabil Belhaj]. Wesam Media, April 26, 2013. www.youtube.com/watch?v=0jMUIrxY34M.

Aradi, Abdulrazzak al-. "Al-ṭarīq ʿila alkāritha" [The Road to Disaster]. Ean Libya, March 1, 2015. http://archive.today/2021.12.15-111903/https://www.eanlibya .com/الطريق-إلى-الكارثة/.

Ardovini, Lucia. "The Politicisation of Sectarianism in Egypt: 'Creating an Enemy': The State vs. the Ikhwan." Global Discourse 6, no. 4 (2016): 579–600.

Ardovini, Lucia. "Stagnation vs Adaptation: Tracking the Muslim Brotherhood's Trajectories After the 2013 Coup." British Journal of Middle Eastern Studies 49 (2022): 187–203.

Arendt, Hannah. The Origins of Totalitarianism. Houghton Mifflin Harcourt, 1973.

"Armed Militants Kidnap Libya's Military Prosecutor." Alarabiya News, March 16, 2018. https://english.alarabiya.net/News/north-africa/2018/03/16/Armed-militants -kidnap-Libya-s-military-prosecutor.

Asharq al-Awsat. "Libya's Muslim Brotherhood Snubs Gaddafi." June 20, 2011. https:// eng-archive.aawsat.com/theaawsat/news-middle-east/libyas-muslim-brother hood-snubs-gaddafi.

Ashour, Omar. "Between ISIS and a Failed State: The Saga of Libyan Islamists." Working Paper, Rethinking Political Islam Series. Brookings Institution, 2015.

Ashour, Omar. The De-Radicalization of Jihadists: Transforming Armed Islamist Movements. Routledge, 2009.

Ashour, Omar. How ISIS Fights: Military Tactics in Iraq, Syria, Libya and Egypt. Edinburgh University Press, 2022. https://doi.org/10.1515/9781474438230.

Ashour, Omar. "Libya." In *Rethinking Political Islam*, edited by Shadi Hamid and William McCants, 110–118. Oxford University Press, 2017.

Ashour, Omar. "Libyan Islamists Unpacked: Rise, Transformation and Future." Policy Briefing, Brookings Doha Center, May 2012.

Ashour, Omar. "Libya's Muslim Brotherhood Faces the Future." Op-Ed. Brookings Institution, March 9, 2012. https://www.brookings.edu/articles/libyas-muslim -brotherhood-faces-the-future/.

Ashour, Omar. "Post-Jihadism: Libya and the Global Transformations of Armed Islamist Movements." *Terrorism and Political Violence* 23, no. 3 (2011): 377–97.

Ashour, Omar. "Why Does the Islamic State Endure and Expand?" *IAI: Istituto Affari Internazionali*, December 1, 2015. https://www.jstor.org/stable/resrep09845.

Ashton, Nigel. *King Hussein of Jordan*. Yale University Press, 2008.

"'Asmāʾ al-murashahīn al-dīn yadʿamuhum -tajamuʿ Al-Aṣāla" [Names of the Candidates Supported by Religion—al-Asala]. Al-Asala, June 27, 2012. http://web .archive.org/web/20130315063048/http://www.alasala.ly/index.php/blog/47-أ سماء-المرشحين-الدين-يدعمهم-تجمع-الأصالة.

Assad, Abdulkader. "Bashagha's Government Sworn in at HoR in Tobruk." *Libya Observer*, March 3, 2022. https://libyaobserver.ly/news/bashaghas-government -sworn-hor-tobruk.

Assad, Abdulkader. "By Egyptian Fatwa and Libyan Execution, Libyan Cleric Nadir Al-Omrani Killed After 45 Days of Kidnap." *Libya Observer*, November 21, 2016. https://www.libyaobserver.ly/news/egyptian-fatwa-and-libyan-execution -libyan-cleric-nadir-al-omrani-killed-after-45-days-kidnap.

Assad, Abdulkader. "Military Commander at Libya's Al-Bunyan Al-Marsous Operation Survives Assassination." *Libya Observer*, November 4, 2018. https://www .libyaobserver.ly/news/military-commander-libya's-al-bunyan-al-marsous -operation-survives-assassination.

"Assassination Campaign Blights Eastern Libya." *Financial Times*, December 12, 2013.

"Assessments and Documentation of Mass Crimes: Assessments in Libya." Physicians for Human Rights blog. N.d., accessed July 29, 2024. https://phr.org/issues /investigating-deaths-and-mass-atrocities/assessments-and-documentation -of-mass-crimes/assessments-in-libya/

Ayoob, Mohammed. "The Future of Political Islam: The Importance of External Variables." *International Affairs* 81, no. 5 (2005): 951–61.

Badi, Emaddedin. "Exploring Armed Groups in Libya: Perspectives on Security Sector Reform in a Hybrid Environment." Geneva Centre for Security Sector Governance, December 2020. https://www.dcaf.ch/exploring-armed-groups-libya -perspectives-ssr-hybrid-environment.

Badi, Emaddedin, Archibald Gallet, and Roberta Maggi. "Rethinking the Road to Stability—Security Sector Reform in Libya." Geneva Centre for Security Sector Reform, November 2021, https://www.dcaf.ch/sites/default/files/publications /documents/The_Road_to_Stability11.11.2021.pdf.

Banerji, Robin. "Did Ansar Al-Sharia Carry out Libya Attack?" BBC News, September 12, 2012. Africa. https://www.bbc.com/news/world-africa-19575753.

Barón, Luis. "More Than a Facebook Revolution: Social Movements and Social Media in the Egyptian Arab Spring." *International Review of Information Ethics* 18, no. 12 (2012): 86–92.

Bayat, Asef. "Islamism and Social Movement Theory." *Third World Quarterly* 26 (2005): 891–908.

Bayat, Asef. *Making Islam Democratic: Social Movements and the Post-Islamist Turn*. Stanford University Press, 2007.

Bazaza, Shaykh Kamal. "Al-khuṭbat alatiy ightīl bisababiha al-Shaykh Kamal Bazaza min qibal majlis shūrī Benghazi" [The Sermon for which Shaykh Kamal Bazaza Was Assassinated by the Benghazi Shura Council] YouTube, May 9, 2019. https://www.youtube.com/watch?app=desktop&v=aYly1ezz-x8.

Bearman, Jonathan. *Qadhafi's Libya*. Zed, 1986.

Beckerman, Gal. " 'The Middle East Region Is Quieter Today Than It Has Been in Two Decades.' " *The Atlantic*, October 7, 2023. https://www.theatlantic.com/international/archive/2023/10/israel-war-middle-east-jake-sullivan/675580/.

Belhaj, Alamin. "Al-ikhwān dakhalu al-thawra mandh al-yum al-wal lakinahum tawaqʿa-uʿan takun al-maṭālib ʿiṣlahīta" [The Brotherhood Joined the Revolution from the First Day, but They Expected That the Demands Would Be for Reform]. Al-Hayat, September 24, 2011. http://archive.today/2022.03.22-101040/https://www.sauress.com/alhayat/310809.

Belousov, Konstantin, Tom Horlick-Jones, Michael Bloor, Yakov Gilinskiy, Valentin Golbert, Yakov Kostikovsky, Michael Levi, and Dmitri Pentsov. "Any Port in a Storm: Fieldwork Difficulties in Dangerous and Crisis-Ridden Settings." *Qualitative Research* 7, no. 2 (2007): 155–75.

Benford, Robert D., and David A. Snow. "Framing Processes and Social Movements: An Overview and Assessment." *Annual Review of Sociology* 26 (2000): 611–39.

Benotman, Noman, Jason Pack, and James Brandon. "Islamists." In *The 2011 Libyan Uprisings and the Struggle for the Post-Qadhafi Future*, edited by Jason Pack, 191–228. Palgrave Macmillan, 2013.

Berti, Benedetta. "Armed Groups as Political Parties and Their Role in Electoral Politics: The Case of Hizballah." *Studies in Conflict & Terrorism* 34, no. 12 (2011): 942–62.

Berti, Benedetta. *Armed Political Organizations: From Conflict to Integration*. Johns Hopkins University Press, 2013.

"Biʿda khilafi hād, al-mutamir al-waṭanī-alʿām ītifi" [After Tough Disagreements the National Congress Appoints]. Al-Manara, December 26, 2012. http://www.almanaralink.com/press/2012/12/26982/بعد-خلاف-حاد-،-المؤتمر-الوطني-العام-يتف/.

Blackledge, Adrian. *Discourse and Power in a Multilingual World*. John Benjamins, 2005.

Bobel, Chris. " 'I'm not an activist, though I've done a lot of it': Doing Activism, Being Activist and the 'Perfect Standard' in a Contemporary Movement." *Social Movement Studies* 6, no. 2 (2007): 147–59.

Bojar, Abel, and Hanspeter Kriesi. "Action Repertoires in Contentious Episodes: What Determines Governments' and Challengers' Action Strategies? A Cross-National Analysis." *European Journal of Political Research* 60, no. 1 (2021): 46–68.

Bonikowski, Bart. *Varieties of Popular Nationalism in Modern Democracies: An Inductive Approach to Comparative Research on Political Culture*. Cambridge University Press, 2013.

Bonnefoy, Laurent. "Quietist Salafis, the Arab Spring and the Politicization Process." In *Salafism After the Arab Awakening: Contending with People's Power*, edited by Francesco Cavatorta and Fabio Merone, 205–18. Hurst, 2015.

Bonnefoy, Laurent. "Saudi Arabia and the Expansion of Salafism." Norwegian Peacebuilding Resource Centre Policy Brief, 2013.

Bonnefoy, Laurent, and Judit Kuschnitzki. "Salafis and the 'Arab Spring' in Yemen: Progressive Politicization and Resilient Quietism." *Arabian Humanities* 4 (2015): 1–20.

Booysen, Hanlie. *Explaining the Moderate Platform of the Syrian Muslim Brotherhood: Against the Inclusion-Moderation Hypothesis*. University of Wellington Press, 2018.

Boserup, Rasmus Alenius, and Virginie Collombier. *Militarization and Militia-ization: Dynamics of Armed Group Proliferation in Egypt and Libya*. MENARA Working Papers 17, Instituto Affari Internazionali, October 2018.

Bouckaert, Peter. "Death of a Dictator." Human Rights Watch, October 16, 2012. https://www.hrw.org/report/2012/10/16/death-dictator/bloody-vengeance-sirte.

Bowen, Innes. *Medina in Birmingham, Najaf in Brent: Inside British Islam*. Hurst, 2014.

Boxerman, Aaron. "What We Know About the Death Toll in Israel from the Hamas-Led Attacks." *The New York Times*, November 12, 2023. World. https://www.nytimes.com/2023/11/12/world/middleeast/israel-death-toll-hamas-attack.html.

Brachman, Jarret M. *Global Jihadism: Theory and Practice*. Routledge, 2008.

Brahimi, Alia. "Libya's Revolution." In *North Africa's Arab Spring*, edited by George Joffe, 101–21. Routledge, 2013.

Braithwaite, Alex, Dennis Foster, and David Sobek. "Ballots, Bargains, and Bombs: Terrorist Targeting of Spoiler Opportunities." *International Interactions* 36, no. 3 (2010): 294–305.

Brocker, Manfred, and Mirjam Künkler. "Religious Parties: Revisiting the Inclusion-Moderation Hypothesis." *Party Politics* 19, no. 2 (2013): 171–86.

Brooke, Steven, and Robert Leiken. "The Moderate Muslim Brotherhood." *Foreign Affairs* 86 (2007): 107–21.

Brooke, Steven, and Elizabeth Nugent. "Exclusion and Violence After the Egyptian Coup." *Middle East Law and Governance* 12, no. 1 (2020): 61–85.

Brooks, Risa. "Liberalization and Militancy in the Arab World." *Orbis* 46, no. 4 (2002): 611–21.

Browers, Michelle. "The Egyptian Movement for Change: Intellectual Antecedents and Generational Conflicts." *Contemporary Islam* 1, no. 1 (2007): 69–88.

Browers, Michelle. "Origins and Architects of Yemen's Joint Meeting Parties." *International Journal of Middle East Studies* 39, no. 4 (2007): 565–86.

Browers, Michelle. *Political Ideology in the Arab World: Accommodation and Transformation*. Cambridge University Press, 2009.

Brown, Nathan. "Who or What is the *Walī al-Amr*: The Unposed Question." *Oñati Socio-Legal Series* 10, no. 5 (2020): 985–1000.

Brysk, Alison. "'Hearts and Minds': Bringing Symbolic Politics Back In." *Polity* 27, no. 4 (1995): 559–85.

Buechler, Steven. "Beyond Resource Mobilization? Emerging Trends in Social Movement Theory." *Sociological Quarterly* 34, no. 2 (1993): 217–35.

Buehler, Matt. "Ruptures, Reconfigurations and Revolutions: Political Change in North Africa After the Arab Uprisings." *Mediterranean Politics* 23, no. 4 (2018): 522–30.

Buehler, Matt. "The Threat to 'Un-Moderate': Moroccan Islamists and the Arab Spring." *Middle East Law and Governance* 5 (2013): 231–57.

Buehler, Michael. "Revisiting the Inclusion-Moderation Thesis in the Context of Decentralized Institutions: The Behavior of Indonesia's Prosperous Justice Party in National and Local Politics." *Party Politics* 19, no. 2 (2013): 210–29.

Burke, Jason. "Abu Yahya Al-Libi." Obituary. *The Guardian*, June 6, 2012. World News. https://www.theguardian.com/world/2012/jun/06/abu-yahya-al-libi.

Bygnes, Susanne. " 'We are in Complete Agreement': The Diversity Issue, Disagreement and Change in the European Women's Lobby." *Social Movement Studies* 12, no. 2 (2013): 199–213.

Callimachi, Rukmini, and Eric Schmitt, "Manchester Bomber Met with ISIS Unit in Libya, Officials Say," *The New York Times*, June 3, 2017, World, https://www.nytimes.com/2017/06/03/world/middleeast/manchester-bombing-salman-abedi-islamic-state-libya.html.

Carboni, Andrea, and James Moody. "Between the Cracks: Actor Fragmentation and Local Conflict Systems in the Libyan Civil War." *Small Wars & Insurgencies* 29, no. 3 (2018): 456–90.

Cavatorta, Francesco. "Divided they stand, divided they fail': Opposition Politics in Morocco." *Democratization* 16, no. 1 (2009): 137–56.

Cavatorta, Francesco, and Raquel Ojeda Garcia. "Islamism in Mauritania and the Narrative of Political Moderation." *Journal of Modern African Studies* 55, no. 2 (2017): 301–25.

Cavatorta, Francesco, and Fabio Merone. "Moderation Through Exclusion? The Journey of the Tunisian Ennahda from Fundamentalist to Conservative Party." *Democratization* 20, no. 5 (2013): 857–75.

Cavatorta, Francesco, and Stefano Torelli. "From Victim to Hangman? Ennahda, Salafism and the Tunisian Transition." *Religions* 12, no. 2 (2021): 76.

Chamkhi, Tarek. "Neo-Islamism in the Post-Arab Spring." *Contemporary Politics* 20, no. 4 (2014): 453–68.

Chan, Ngai Keung, and Kwok Chi. "Legitimacy and Forced Democratisation in Social Movements: A Case Study of the Umbrella Movement in Hong Kong." *China Perspectives* 3 (2017): 7–16.

Chernitsky, B. "Libyan Muslim Brotherhood on the Rise." Middle East Media Research Institute, April 24, 2012. Inquiry and Analysis Series no. 828. https://www.memri.org/reports/libyan-muslim-brotherhood-rise.

Chesters, Graeme, and Ian Welsh. "Rebel Colours: 'Framing' in Global Social Movements." *Sociological Review* 52, no. 3 (2004): 314–35.

Chivvis, Christopher S. *Toppling Qaddafi: Libya and the Limits of Liberal Intervention.* Cambridge University Press, 2013.

Çınar, Menderes. "From Moderation to De-Moderation: Democratic Backsliding of the AKP in Turkey." In *The Politics of Islamism*, edited by John L. Esposito, Lily Zubaidah, and Rahim Naser Ghobadzadeh, 127–57. Palgrave Macmillan, 2018.

Clark, Janine. "The Conditions of Islamist Moderation: Unpacking Cross-Ideological Cooperation in Jordan." *International Journal of Middle East Studies* 38, no. 4 (2006): 539–60.

Clark, Janine, and Jillian Schwedler. "Who Opened the Window? Women's Activism in Islamist Parties." *Comparative Politics* 35, no. 3 (2003): 293–313.

Clements, Ben. "Public Opinion and Military Intervention: Afghanistan, Iraq and Libya." *Political Quarterly* 84, no. 1 (2013): 119–31.

Cole, Peter. "Bani Walid: Loyalism in a Time of Revolution." In *The Libyan Revolution and Its Aftermath*, edited by Peter Cole and Brian McQuinn, 285–303. Hurst, 2015.

Cole, Peter, and Umar Khan. "The Fall of Tripoli." In *The Libyan Revolution and its Aftermath*, edited by Peter Cole and Brian McQuinn, 55–105. Hurst, 2015.

Collier, David, and James E. Mahon. "Conceptual 'Stretching' Revisited: Adapting Categories in Comparative Analysis." *American Political Science Review* 87, no. 4 (1993): 845–55.

Collombier, Virginie. "Libyan Salafis and the Struggle for the State." *Third World Thematics* 3, no. 6 (2022): 296–313. https://doi.org/10.1080/23802014.2022.2062442.

Collombier, Virginie. "Salafi Politics: 'Political' and 'Quietist' Salafis in the Struggle for the Libyan State." Research Project Report 2020/15. European University Institute, November 27, 2020. https://doi.org/10.2870/50645.

Cook, Joana, Haid Haid, and Inga Trauthig. "Jurisprudence Beyond the State: An Analysis of Jihadist 'Justice' in Yemen, Syria and Libya." *Studies in Conflict & Terrorism* (2020): 1–20. https://doi.org/10.1080/1057610X.2020.1776958.

Cooley, John K. *Libyan Sandstorm*. Sidgwick and Jackson, 1983.

Cousins, Michel. "No SSC Disbandment Yet PM Declares." *Libya Herald*, December 14, 2012. https://www.libyaherald.com/2012/12/14/no-ssc-disbandment-yet-says-pm/.

Cousins, Michel. "Tripoli Endowments Ministry Head Released After Questioning About IS Support." *Libya Herald*, November 27, 2015. https://www.libyaherald.com/2015/11/27/tripoli-endowments-ministry-head-released-after-questioning-about-is-support/.

Cragin, Kim R. "Tactical Partnerships for Strategic Effects: Recent Experiences of US Forces Working by, with, and Through Surrogates in Syria and Libya." *Defence Studies* 20, no. 4 (2020): 318–35.

Crawford, Alex. *Colonel Gaddafi's Hat*. HarperCollins, 2012.

Dar al-Ifta. "Speech by the Department of Mosque Affairs on the Role of Secularism in Corrupting Society by Publishing Misguided and Sinful Books and Ways of Preventing Its Evil." General Authority for Religious Endowments and Islamic Affairs Libya, January 25, 2017. http://web.archive.org/web/20210308103456/www.facebook.com/AwqafLibya/posts/1388355771194970.

Davis, Nancy, and Robert Robinson. "Overcoming Movement Obstacles by the Religiously Orthodox: The Muslim Brotherhood in Egypt, Shas in Israel, Comunione e Liberazione in Italy, and the Salvation Army in the United States." *American Journal of Sociology* 114, no. 5 (2009): 1302–49.

Deeb, Marius K. "Militant Islam and Its Critics: The Case of Libya." In *Islamism and Secularism in North Africa*, edited by John Ruedy, 187–97. Palgrave Macmillan, 1996.

della Porta, Donatella. "Communication in Movement: Social Movements as Agents of Participatory Democracy." In *Social Media and Democracy: Innovations in Participatory Politics*, edited by Brian D. Loader and Dan Mercea, 150–65. Routledge, 2012.

della Porta, Donatella, and Mario Diani. *Social Movements: An Introduction.* John Wiley & Sons, 2009.

della Porta, Donatella, and Sidney Tarrow. "Interactive Diffusion: The Coevolution of Police and Protest Behavior with an Application to Transnational Contention." *Comparative Political Studies* 45, no. 1 (2012): 119–52.

Deng, Fang. "Information Gaps and Unintended Outcomes of Social Movements: The 1989 Chinese Student Movement." *American Journal of Sociology* 102, no. 4 (1997): 1085–112.

Dettmer, Jamie. "Meet the Islamic Fanatic Who Wants to Kill ISIS." *The Daily Beast*, June 10, 2015. https://www.thedailybeast.com/meet-the-islamic-fanatic-who-wants-to-kill-isis.

DeVore, Marc. "Exploiting Anarchy: Violent Entrepreneurs and the Collapse of Libya's Post-Qadhafi Settlement." *Mediterranean Politics* 19, no. 3 (2014): 463–70.

Diani, Mario. "The Concept of Social Movement." *Sociological Review* 40, no. 1 (1992): 1–25. https://doi.org/10.1111/j.1467-954X.1992.tb02943.x.

"Dignity Operation Armed Groups Attack Shrine of Former King Idris Senussi's Father." Libya Observer, December 30, 2017. https://www.libyaobserver.ly/crimes/dignity-operation-armed-group-attacks-shrine-libya's-former-king-idris-senussi's-father.

Driessen, Michael. "Public Religion, Democracy, and Islam: Examining the Moderation Thesis in Algeria." *Comparative Politics* 44, no. 2 (2012): 171–89.

Durac, Vincent. "The Role of Non-State Actors in Arab Countries After the Arab Uprisings." *IEMed Mediterranean Yearbook* 1 (2015): 37–41. https://www.iemed.org/publication/the-role-of-non-state-actors-in-arab-countries-after-the-arab-uprisings/.

"East Libyan Army Takes Rivals' Final Holdout in Benghazi." CGTN Africa, March 2017. https://www.youtube.com/watch?v=kFMQ4nrYIpA.

Eaton, Tim. "Security Actors in Misrata, Zawiya and Zintan Since 2011." Research paper. Chatham House, December 12, 2023. https://www.chathamhouse.org/2023/12/security-actors-misrata-zawiya-and-zintan-2011/02-misrata-zawiya-and-zintan-after-2011.

Eaton, Tim, Renad Mansour, Lina Khatib, Christine Cheng, Jihad Yazigi, and Peter Salisbury. *Conflict Economies in the Middle East and North Africa.* Royal Institute of International Affairs, 2019. https://www.chathamhouse.org/sites/default/files/publications/research/2019-06-21-Conflict-Economies-MENA_0.pdf.

Ehrenfeld, Rachel. "The Muslim Brotherhood Evolution: An Overview." *American Foreign Policy Interests* 33, no. 2 (2011): 69–85.

Elischer, Sebastian. "The Management of Salafi Activity in Africa: African State Strategies and Their Consequences in the Sahel." *Africa Research Initiative* 2, no. 1 (2015): 577–97.

Eljarh, Mohamed. "Libya's Islamists Go for Broke." *Foreign Policy*, July 22, 2014. https://foreignpolicy.com/2014/07/22/libyas-islamists-go-for-broke/.

Elumami, Ahmed. "Libyan Forces Capture Sirte Convention Center from Islamic State." Reuters, August 10, 2016. https://www.reuters.com/article/us-libya -security-idUSKCN10L1QX.

Eriksson, Mikael. "A Fratricidal Libya: Making Sense of a Conflict Complex." *Small Wars & Insurgencies* 27, no. 5 (2016): 817–36.

Escobar, Arturo, ed. *The Making of Social Movements in Latin America: Identity, Strategy, and Democracy.* Routledge, 2018.

Esposito, John L., ed. *The Islamic World: Past and Present.* Oxford University Press, 2004.

Estelle, Emily. "Al Qaeda and the Islamic State Will Be the Winners of the Libyan Civil War." Blog post. *Critical Threats,* April 10, 2019. https://www.criticalthreats.org /analysis/al-qaeda-and-the-islamic-state-will-be-the-winners-of-the-libyan -civil-war.

Estelle, Emily. *A Strategy for Success in Libya.* American Enterprise Institute, November 2017. http://www.criticalthreats.org/wp-content/uploads/2017/11/A-Strategy -for-Success-in-Libya.pdf.

Euben, Roxanne L, and Muhammad Qasim Zaman, eds. *Princeton Readings in Islamist Thought: Texts and Contexts from al-Banna to Bin Laden.* Princeton University Press, 2009.

"Extremists Demolish Libya's Shrines Using Bulldozers, Explosives." France24, August 29, 2012. https://observers.france24.com/en/20120829-extremists-demo lish-libya-shrines-using-bulldozers-explosives-libya-mausoleum-zliten-tripoli -video-salafists.

"Eyes on Jihadis in Libya." Libya Analysis, February 13, 2019. https://jihadology.net /2019/02/13/eye-on-jihadis-in-libya-weekly-update-february-12/.

Farag, Mona. "Egypt's Muslim Brotherhood and the January 25 Revolution: New Political Party, New Circumstances." *Contemporary Arab Affairs* 5, no. 2 (2012): 214–29.

Farquhar, Michael. *Circuits of Faith: Migration, Education, and the Wahhabi Mission.* Stanford University Press, 2016.

Fasanotti, Federica Saini. "Libya: A Nation Suspended Between Past and Future." *Studia Diplomatica* 68, no. 4 (2017): 95–104.

Feliu, Laura, and Rachid Aarab. "Political Islam in Libya: Transformation on the Way to Elitisation." In *Political Islam in a Time of Revolt,* edited by Ferran Izquierdo Brichs, John Etherington, and Laura Feliu, 153–76. Palgrave Macmillan, 2017.

Fine, Gary Alan. "Public Narration and Group Culture: Discerning Discourse in Social Movements." In *Social Movements and Culture,* edited by Hank Johnston and Bert Klandermas, 127–43. University of Minnesota Press, 1995.

Fishman, Ben. "Could Libya's Decline Have Been Predicted?" *Survival* 57, no. 5 (2015): 199–208.

Fitzgerald, Mary. "Finding Their Place: Libya's Islamists During and After the Revolution." In *The Libyan Revolution and Its Aftermath,* edited by Peter Cole and Brian McQuinn, 177–205. Oxford University Press, 2015.

Fitzgerald, Mary. "Introducing the Libyan Muslim Brotherhood." *Foreign Policy* 2 (2012). https://foreignpolicy.com/2012/11/02/introducing-the-libyan-muslim -brotherhood/.

Flintoff, Corey. "What Role Will Islamists Play In Libya?" National Public Radio, September 21, 2011. https://www.npr.org/2011/09/21/140665324/what-role-will-islamists-play-in-libya.

"Following Gaddafi's Demise, MB Warns Arab Dictators: People Always Prevail." Ikhwanweb, November 25, 2011. https://archive.ph/2020.05.05-085456/https://www.ikhwanweb.com/article.pho?id=29079.

Fraihat, Ibrahim. "An Ill-Advised Purge in Libya." Blog post. Brookings Institution, February 18, 2013. https://www.brookings.edu/articles/an-ill-advised-purge-in-libya/.

Frampton, Martyn. *The Muslim Brotherhood and the West: A History of Enmity and Engagement*. Harvard University Press, 2018.

Fuller, Graham. *The Future of Political Islam*. Palgrave Macmillan, 2003.

Gamson, William, and David Meyer. "Framing Political Opportunity." In *Comparative Perspectives on Social Movements: Political Opportunities, Mobilizing Structures and Cultural Framings*, edited by Doug McAdam, John McCarthy, and Mayer Zald, 275–90. Cambridge University Press, 1996.

Garwood-Gowers, Andrew. "The Responsibility to Protect and the Arab Spring: Libya as the Exception, Syria as the Norm." *University of New South Wales Law Journal* 36, no. 2 (2013): 594–618. https://doi.org/10.3316/ielapa.565289638046147.

Gaub, Florence. "Libya: The Struggle for Security." *European Union Institute for Security Studies* (2013).

Gaub, Florence, and Rob Weighill. *The Cauldron: NATO's Campaign in Libya*. Oxford University Press, 2018.

George, Alexander, and Andrew Bennett. *Case Studies and Theory Development in the Social Sciences*. Harvard University Press, 2005.

Gerges, Fawaz A. "The Islamist Moment: From Islamic State to Civil Islam?" *Political Science Quarterly* 128, no. 3 (2013): 389–426.

Gharyani, Sadeq al-. "Al-ʿazl al-sīyāsiy w-al-mutamar al-watāniy—al-shaykh al-Sadeq al-Gharyani" [Political isolation and the National Congress—Sheikh Sadeq al-Gharyani]. Tanasuh TV, March 9, 2013. https://www.youtube.com/watch?v=hMc7aAVHNGE.

Gharyani, Sadeq al-. "Al-Gharyani: al-khuruj ʿalā al-Qadhāfi wājib" [Gharyani: Exiting Qaddafi is a Duty]. Al-Jazeera, February 28, 2011. https://archive.ph/2020.05.07-103657/https://www.aljazeera.net/news/arabic/2011/2/28/الغرياني-الخروج-على-القذافي-واجب.

Gharyani, Sadeq al-. "Al-Gharyani yuftiy biwujūb qitāl quāt al-jaīsh almunḍamat taht qīādat alliwāʾ Haftar" [Al-Gharyani Issued a Fatwa That the Army Forces Joined Under the Command of Major General Haftar Must Fight]. YouTube, June 9, 2014. https://www.youtube.com/watch?v=L8LsPXXqhsM.

Gharyani, Sadeq al-. "Lībīā—muftiy lībīā al-shaykh al-Sadeq al-Gharayani bishan al-aqtitāl al-jāriy fī ṭarābulus lībīā wa-majlis al-nuwāb al-lībiy" [Libya—Grand Mufti of Libya Sheikh Al-Sadiq Al-Ghariani on the Ongoing Fighting in Tripoli, Libya, and the Libyan House of Representatives]. *Good Morning Libya*, August 5, 2014. https://www.youtube.com/watch?v=IMg0RfkjaX4 and August 24, 2014, https://www.youtube.com/watch?v=HYSFfoMsWeo.

Ghobashy, Mona el-. "The Metamorphosis of the Egyptian Muslim Brothers." *International Journal of Middle East Studies* 37, no. 3 (2005): 373–95.

Gomati, Anas el-. "Libya's Elections Are Around the Corner. But the Country Needs a Hard Reset." Blog post. Atlantic Council, October 13, 2021. https://www.atlantic council.org/blogs/menasource/libyas-elections-are-around-the-corner-but-the -country-needs-a-hard-reset/.

Graff, Peter. "Libya Militia Leader Plays Down Shift to Military Command." Reuters, September 26, 2012. https://www.reuters.com/article/us-libya-militia-idUSBRE8 8P1GD20120926.

Graham, David A. "Gaddafi's Compound: Inside Bab al-Azizya." *The Daily Beast*, August 23, 2011. https://www.thedailybeast.com/gaddafis-compound-inside-bab -al-azizya.

Gråtrud, Henrik, and Vidar Benjamin Skretting. "Ansar Al-Sharia in Libya: An Enduring Threat." *Perspectives on Terrorism* 11, no. 1 (2017): 40–53.

Gurses, Mehmet. "Islamists, Democracy and Turkey: A Test of the Inclusion-Moderation Hypothesis." *Party Politics* 20, no. 4 (2014): 646–53.

Hafala, Majdi. "Nasīḥa ilā al-shabāb al-salafiy li-al-shaykh Abū Musʿab Majdī" [Advice to the Salafi Youth by Shaykh Abu Musab Majdi Hafala]. YouTube, November 21, 2012. https://www.youtube.com/watch?v=knimBlmycIo.

Hafez, Mohammed. *Why Muslims Rebel: Repression and Resistance in the Islamic World.* Lynne Rienner, 2003.

"Haftar's Son Visited Israel to Seek Military Support." *Daily Sabah*, November 9, 2021. https://www.dailysabah.com/world/africa/haftars-son-visited-israel-to-seek -military-support-report.

Ḥajuri, Yaḥya al-. *Alnaṣaḥ alwāfī lilsāʿadī b. alQadhāfī* [The Trustful Advice to Saadi the Son of Qaddafi]. Recorded lecture, June 1, 2011. http://www.shyahia.net/show _sound_890.html.

Halverson, Jeffry, and Nathaniel Greenberg. *Islamists of the Maghreb.* Routledge, 2017.

Hamid, Shadi. "Political Party Development Before and After the Arab Spring." In *Beyond the Arab Spring: The Evolving Ruling Bargain in the Middle East*, edited by Mehran Kamrava, 131–50. Oxford University Press, 2014.

Hamid, Shadi, William McCants, and Rashid Dari. *Islamism After the Arab Spring: Between the Islamic State and the Nation-State.* Brookings Institution, Project on U.S. Relations with the Islamic World Forum Papers, January 2017.

Hanna, Michael Wahid. "Egypt's Search for Truth." *Cairo Review of Global Affairs*, Fall 2011. https://www.thecairoreview.com/essays/egypts-search-for-truth/.

Harathy, Safa al-. "Head of Awqaf Authority Arrested in Tripoli." *Libya Observer*, August 4, 2018. https://www.libyaobserver.ly/news/head-awqaf-authority -arrested-tripoli.

Harchaoui, Jalel. "A Dysfunctional Peace: How Libya's Fault Lines Were Redrawn." War on the Rocks, February 24, 2022. https://warontherocks.com/2022/02/a -dysfunctional-peace-how-libyas-fault-lines-were-redrawn/.

Hasche, Thorsten. *Quo vadis, politischer Islam? AKP, Al-Qaida und Muslimbruderschaft in systemtheoretischer Perspektive.* Transcript, 2015.

Hassan, Salah el Din. "Al-salafīyūn al-mudākhalat fī miṣr (dirāsa)" [Madkhali Salafis in Egypt: (study)]. Blog post. December 24, 2010. http://archive.today/2012.12.10 -025018/http://salaheldinhassan.blogspot.de/2010/12/blog-post_408.html.

Head, Jonathan. "'Mass Grave' Found in Tripoli," BBC News, September 11, 2011, https://www.bbc.com/news/av/world-africa-15055804.

Hegghammer, Thomas. The Caravan: Abdallah Azzam and the Rise of Global Jihad. Cambridge University Press, 2020.

Hegghammer, Thomas. "Jihadi Salafis or Revolutionaries? On Religion and Politics in the Study of Islamist Militancy." In Global Salafism: Islam's New Religious Movement, edited by Roel Meijer, 201–35. Hurst, 2009.

Hegghammer, Thomas, and Stéphane Lacroix. "Rejectionist Islamism in Saudi Arabia: The Story of Juhayman al-Utaybi Revisited." International Journal of Middle East Studies 39, no. 1 (2007): 103–22.

Hehir, Aidan. "The Permanence of Inconsistency: Libya, the Security Council, and the Responsibility to Protect." International Security 38, no. 1 (2013): 137–59.

Hill, Tom, and Nate Wilson. "Foreign Interference Remains Key Driver of Libya Conflict." United States Institute of Peace, June 3, 2020. https://www.usip.org /publications/2020/06/foreign-interference-remains-key-driver-libya-conflict.

"Ḥiwār-un maʿa al-masʾūl-I al-ʿām-i al-jadīd-i li-al-ikhwān-i al-muslimīn-a fī Lībīā" [Interview with the New Leader of the Muslim Brotherhood in Libya]. Video. Al-Manara, November 24, 2011. http://archive.today/2020.04.30-104402/https:// www.youtube.com/watch?v=DH57e5gqLTk.

Hoffman, Bruce. "Al Qaeda, Trends in Terrorism, and Future Potentialities: An Assessment." Studies in Conflict & Terrorism 26, no. 6 (2003): 429–42. https://doi.org /10.1080/10576100390248275.

Hovdenak, Are. "Hamas in Transition: The Failure of Sanctions." Democratization 16, no. 1 (2009): 59–80.

Howorth, Jolyon. "The EU and NATO After Libya and Afghanistan: The Future of Euro-US Security Cooperation." Yale International Affairs 8 (2013): 30–40.

Hoyle, Justin A. "A Matter of Framing: Explaining the Failure of Post-Islamist Social Movements in the Arab Spring." Digest of Middle East Studies 25, no. 2 (2016): 186–209.

Hummel, Kristina. "Europe's True Southern Frontier: The General, the Jihadis, and the High-Stakes Contest for Libya's Fezzan Region," CTC [Combating Terrorism Center] Sentinel, November, 2017, https://ctc.westpoint.edu/europes-true -southern-frontier-the-general-the-jihadis-and-the-high-stakes-contest-for -libyas-fezzan-region/.

Huntington, Samuel. Political Order in Changing Societies. Yale University Press, 2006.

Huntington, Samuel. The Third Wave: Democratization in the Late Twentieth Century. University of Oklahoma Press, 1993.

Hussein, Rikar, and Nisan Ahmado. "Islamic State Regrouping in Libyan Desert, Experts Warn." Voice of America, September 29, 2017. https://www.voanews.com /a/islamic-state-regrouping-libyan-desert-experts-warn/4050753.html.

Hwang, Julie Chernov. When Terrorists Quit: The Disengagement of Indonesian Jihadists. Cornell University Press, 2018.

Hweio, Haalo. "The Muslim Brotherhood: Libya as the Last Resort for the Continued Existence of the Global Movement." *Middle East Law and Governance* 13, no. 1 (2020): 5–21.

Idrissi, Ala al-, and Wolfram Lacher. "Capital of Militias: Tripoli's Armed Groups Capture the Libyan State." *SANA Briefing Paper*, June 2018.

International Criminal Court. "Case Information Sheet: The Prosecutor v. Mahmoud Mustafa Busyf Al-Werfalli." 2018. https://www.icc-cpi.int/CaseInformationSheets /al-werfalliEng.pdf.

International Crisis Group. "Addressing the Rise of Libya's Madkhali-Salafis." *Middle East and North Africa Report* 200, April 25, 2019. https://www.crisisgroup .org/middle-east-north-africa/north-africa/libya/addressing-rise-libyas -madkhali-salafis.

International Crisis Group. "Divided We Stand: Libya's Enduring Conflicts." *Middle East and North Africa Report* 130 (2012). https://www.crisisgroup.org/middle -east-north-africa/north-africa/libya/divided-we-stand-libya-s-enduring -conflicts.

International Crisis Group. "How the Islamic State Rose, Fell and Could Rise Again in the Maghreb." *Middle East and North Africa Report* no. 178, July 24, 2017. https:// www.crisisgroup.org/middle-east-north-africa/north-africa/178-how-islamic -state-rose-fell-and-could-rise-again-maghreb.

Jasper, James M. "The Emotions of Protest: Affective and Reactive Emotions in and around Social Movements." *Sociological Forum* 13, no. 3 (1998): 397–424.

Jasper, James, and Jane D. Poulsen. "Recruiting Strangers and Friends: Moral Shocks and Social Networks in Animal Rights and Anti-Nuclear Protests." *Social Problems* 42, no. 4 (1995): 493–512.

Jawad, Rana. "Libya Elections: Do Any of the Parties Have a Plan?" BBC Africa, July 6, 2012. https://www.bbc.com/news/world-africa-18721576.

Joffé, George. "The Arab Spring in North Africa: Origins and Prospects." *Journal of North African Studies* 16, no. 4 (2011): 507–32.

Joffé, George. "Islamic Opposition in Libya." *Third World Quarterly* 10, no. 2 (1988): 615–31.

Joffé, George. "The Trojan Horse: The Madkhali Movement in North Africa." *Journal of North African Studies* 23, no. 5 (2018): 739–44.

Johnston, Hank, Enrique Laraña, and Joseph Gusfield. "Identities, Grievances and Ideologies of Everyday Life." In *New Social Movements: From Ideology to Identity*, edited by Enrique Laraña, Hank Johnston, and Joseph Gusfield, 3–35. Temple University Press, 1994.

Jung, Eunsook. "Bringing Social Movements into the Inclusion-Moderation Thesis: The Influence of Religious Fundamentalism in Indonesia and South Korea." *Asian Survey* 61, no. 5 (2021): 797–824. https://doi.org/10.1525/as.2021.1422511.

Justice and Construction Party. "Political Programme." Accessible online at: https://web.archive.org/web/20220119171229/https://kurzman.unc.edu/wp -content/uploads/sites/1410/2011/06/LBY-2012-al-Adala-wa-al-Bina-Justice-and -Construction.pdf.

Justice and Construction Party Benghazi. "Hamlat ṭuruq alabwāb" [Knocking on Doors Campaign]. Video. YouTube, July 4, 2012. https://www.youtube.com/watch

?v=YYPYlk-tomw&fbclid=IwAR1Os-vJ028cFFnymdthcPrwCfii3GJpUDW8ujm6A
GX_pnhA_7VfGQAL3wA.

Kakar, Palwasha L., and Zahra Langhi. "Libya's Religious Sector and Peacebuilding
Efforts." United States Institute of Peace, March 16, 2017. https://www.usip.org
/publications/2017/03/libyas-religious-sector-and-peacebuilding-efforts.

Kalyvas, Andreas. *Democracy and the Politics of the Extraordinary: Max Weber, Carl Schmitt,
and Hannah Arendt.* Cambridge University Press, 2008.

Karakaya, Suveyda, and A. Kadir Yildirim. "Islamist Moderation in Perspective: Comparative Analysis of the Moderation of Islamist and Western Communist Parties." *Democratization* 20, no. 7 (2013): 1322–49.

Karstedt, Susanne. "Does Democracy Matter? Comparative Perspectives on Violence
and Democratic Institutions." *European Journal of Criminology* 12, no. 4 (2015):
457–81.

Katiri, Mohammed el-. *State-Building Challenges in a Post-Revolution Libya.* Strategic
Studies Institute, 2012.

Kawan, Nizar. "Nizar Kawan fī risāla ṣawtīa min ṭarābulus" [Nizar Kawan in an Audio
Message from Tripoli]. Al-Manara, February 23, 2011. https://www.youtube.com
/watch?v=cVyiO9kSe8I.

Kawan, Nizar, and Abdulrazzak al-Aradi. *Ṣuʿud wa suquṭ tanẓīm al-dawla fī Sirte:
ʾAmalīyat al-Bunyan al-Marsous* [The Rise and Fall of the Islamic State in Sirte: Operation al-Bunyan al-Marsous], Al Jazeera, October 10, 2021. https://studies
.aljazeera.net/ar/ebooks/book-1424.

Kepel, Gilles. *Jihad: The Trail of Political Islam.* I. B. Tauris, 2002.

Kepel, Gilles. *The War for Muslim Minds: Islam and the West.* Harvard University Press, 2004.

Kersting, Wolfgang, ed. *Thomas Hobbes: Leviathan: oder Stoff, Form und Gewalt eines
kirchlichen und bürgerlichen Staates.* Oldenburg Akademie, 2011.

Khalili, Laleh. "'Standing with my brother': Hizbullah, Palestinians, and the Limits
of Solidarity." *Comparative Studies in Society and History* 49, no. 2 (2007): 276–303.

Khosrokhavar, Farhad. *New Arab Revolutions That Shook the World.* Routledge, 2016.

King, Stephen J. *The Arab Winter: Democratic Consolidation, Civil War, and Radical Islamists.*
Cambridge University Press, 2020.

Kirdiş, Esen. "Similar Contexts, Different Behaviour: Explaining the Non-Linear
Moderation and Immoderation of Islamic Political Parties in Jordan, Morocco,
Tunisia, and Turkey." *Politics, Religion & Ideology* 20, no. 4 (2019): 467–83. https://
doi.org/10.1080/21567689.2019.1698421.

Kirkpatrick, David D. "Political Islam and the Fate of Two Libyan Brothers." *The New
York Times*, October 6, 2012. https://www.nytimes.com/2012/10/07/world/africa
/political-islam-and-the-fate-of-two-libyan-brothers.html.

Kirkpatrick, David D., and Rukmini Callimachi. "Islamic State Video Shows Beheadings of Egyptian Christians in Libya." *The New York Times*, February 15, 2015. World.
https://www.nytimes.com/2015/02/16/world/middleeast/islamic-state-video
-beheadings-of-21-egyptian-christians.html.

Kirkpatrick, David, and Ivor Prickett. "A Police State with an Islamist Twist: Inside
Hifter's Libya." *The New York Times*, February 20, 2020. https://www.nytimes.com
/2020/02/20/world/middleeast/libya-hifter-benghazi.html.

Knecht, Eric. "The Politics of Libya's Political Isolation Law." Blog post. Atlantic Council, February 28, 2013. https://www.atlanticcouncil.org/blogs/menasource/the -politics-of-libya-s-political-isolation-law/.

Knysh, Alexander. "Contextualizing the Salafi–Sufi Conflict from the Northern Caucasus to Hadramawt." *Middle Eastern Studies* 43, no. 4 (2007): 503–30.

Konrad Adenauer Foundation. *Inside Libya* 12, July 2021. Regional Program Political Dialogue. https://www.kas.de/documents/282499/282548/Inside+Libya+-+July +Edition.pdf.

Kouddous, Sharif Abdel. "A Q&A with Khalifa Hifter, the Mastermind Behind Libya's New Revolt." *Washington Post*, May 20, 2014. https://www.washingtonpost.com /news/worldviews/wp/2014/05/20/a-qa-with-khalifa-hifter-the-mastermind -behind-libyas-new-revolt/.

Krebs, Ronald, and Patrick Jackson. "Twisting Tongues and Twisting Arms: The Power of Political Rhetoric." *European Journal of International Relations* 13, no. 1 (2007): 35–66.

Kuperman, Alan J. "Obama's Libya Debacle: How a Well-Meaning Intervention Ended in Failure." *Foreign Affairs* 94, no. 2 (2015): 66–77.

Kurzman, Charles. "Structural Opportunity and Perceived Opportunity in Social Movement Theory: The Iranian Revolution in 1979." *American Sociological Review* 62 (1996): 153–70.

Kurzman, Charles, and Ijlal Naqvi. "Do Muslims Vote Islamic?" *Journal of Democracy* 21, no. 2 (2010): 50–63.

Lacher, Wolfram. "Families, Tribes and Cities in the Libyan Revolution." *Middle East Policy* 18, no. 4 (2011): 140–54.

Lacher, Wolfram. "Fault Lines of the Revolution: Political Actors, Camps and Conflicts in the New Libya." Research Paper 2013/RP 04. *Stiftung Wissenschaft und Politik*, May 7, 2013, https://www.swp-berlin.org/en/publication/libya-fault-lines -of-the-revolution.

Lacher, Wolfram. "Is Autonomy for North-Eastern Libya Realistic?" *Sada*, Carnegie Institute for International Peace, March 21, 2012. https://carnegieendowment .org/sada/47584.

Lacher, Wolfram. *Libya's Fragmentation: Structure and Process in Violent Conflict*. I. B. Tauris, 2020.

Lacher, Wolfram. "Tripoli's Militia Cartel: How Ill-Conceived Stabilisation Blocks Political Progress, and Risks Renewed War." *Stiftung Wissenschaft und Politik* Comment 2018/C 20, April 2018. https://www.swp-berlin.org/en/publication/libya -tripolis-militia-cartel.

Lacher, Wolfram, and Alaa Al-Drissi. "Capital of Militias: Tripoli's Armed Groups Capture the Libyan State." Security Assessment in North Africa/Small Arms Survey Briefing Paper. June 2018. https://www.smallarmssurvey.org/resource/capital -militias-tripolis-armed-groups-capture-libyan-state.

Lacher, Wolfram, and Peter Cole. "Politics by Other Means: Conflicting Interests in Libya's Security Sector." Working Paper 20. Small Arms Survey, October 2014. https://www.smallarmssurvey.org/resource/politics-other-means-conflicting -interests-libyas-security-sector-working-paper-20.

Lacroix, Stéphane. "Al-Albani's Revolutionary Approach to Hadith." *Isim Review* 21 (2008): 6–8.

Lacroix, Stéphane. "Between Revolution and Apoliticism: Nasir al-Din al-Albani and His Impact on the Shaping of Contemporary Salafism." In *Global Salafism: Islam's New Religious Movement*, edited by Roel Meijer, 58–80. Oxford University Press, 2014.

Lacroix, Stéphane. "Social Media and Conflict in Libya." Peace Tech Lab, 2019. https://www.icct.nl/sites/default/files/2022-12/StratComms-Report-4-Fitzgerald-Final.pdf.

Lacroix, Stéphane. "To Rebel or Not to Rebel: Dilemmas Among Saudi Salafis in a Revolutionary Age." In *Salafism After the Arab Awakening: Contending with People's Power*, edited by Francesco Cavatorta and Fabio Merone, 61–82. Hurst, 2015.

Lamb-Books, Benjamin. *Angry Abolitionists and the Rhetoric of Slavery: Moral Emotions in Social Movements*. Palgrave Macmillan, 2016.

Laraña, Enrique, Hank Johnston, and Joseph R. Gusfield, eds. *New Social Movements: From Ideology to Identity*. Temple University Press, 1994.

Lefèvre, Raphaël. "An Egyptian Scenario for Libya?" *Journal of North African Studies* 19, no. 4 (2014): 602–7.

Létourneau, Jean-François. "Explaining the Muslim Brotherhood's Rise and Fall in Egypt." *Mediterranean Politics* 21, no. 2 (2016): 300–7.

Libya al-Mostakbal. "Al-Hirazi: Hizb al-Adalat al-dahiat al-qadīma lithawār'" [JCP Is the Next Victim of the Revolutionaries]. Video. March 19, 2015. www.libya-almostakbal.org/news/clicked/65610.

"Libya Bans Ex-Gaddafi Officials from Office." Al-Jazeera, May 5, 2013. https://www.aljazeera.com/news/2013/5/5/libya-bans-ex-gaddafi-officials-from-office.

"Libya Crisis." Armed Conflict Location and Event Data blog, accessed July 20, 2023. https://acleddata.com/crisis-profile/libya-crisis/.

"Libya: Fears Mount for Abducted Woman Politician a Month Since She Went Missing." Amnesty International. August 16, 2019. https://www.amnesty.org/en/latest/news/2019/08/libya-fears-mount-for-abducted-woman-politician-a-month-since-she-went-missing/.

"Libya: Incitement against Religious Minority." Human Rights Watch, July 20, 2017. https://www.hrw.org/news/2017/07/20/libya-incitement-against-religious-minority.

"Libya: June 1996 Killings at Abu Salim Prison." Human Rights Watch, June 27, 2006. https://www.hrw.org/news/2006/06/27/libya-june-1996-killings-abu-salim-prison.

"Libya: Mass Extra-Judicial Execution." Human Rights Watch, November 29, 2017. https://www.hrw.org/news/2017/11/29/libya-mass-extra-judicial-execution.

"Libya Minister Quits over Sufi Shrine Attack." Al-Jazeera, August 27, 2012. https://www.aljazeera.com/news/2012/8/27/libya-minister-quits-over-sufi-shrine-attack.

"Libya Muslim Brotherhood Statement on General Haftar's Desperate Coup Attempt." Ikhwanweb, May 21, 2014. https://web.archive.org/web/20140828205949/http://ikhwanweb.com/article.php?id=31656.

"Libya: New Wave of Attacks against Sufi Sites." Human Rights Watch, December 7, 2017. https://www.hrw.org/news/2017/12/07/libya-new-wave-attacks-against -sufi-sites.

"Libya: Reject Political Isolation Law." Press statement. Human Rights Watch, May 4, 2013. https://www.hrw.org/news/2013/05/04/libya-reject-political-isolation-law.

"Libyan Forces Lose More Fighters in Sirte as They Continue to Trap IS Radicals in 1km Area." Libyan Express, November 2, 2016. https://www.libyanexpress.com /libyan-forces-lose-more-fighters-in-sirte-as-they-continue-to-trap-is-radicals -in-1km-area/.

"Libyan Islamist Group Ansar Al-Sharia Says It Is Dissolving." Reuters, May 27, 2017. EverythingNews, https://www.reuters.com/article/us-libya-security-idUSKBN 18N0YR.

"Libya's Eastern Authority Freezes Women's Travel Ban." BBC News, February 22, 2017. https://www.bbc.com/news/world-africa-39053829.

"Libye: Imad al-Bannani, Nouveau Président du Parti 'Justice et Construction.'" Anadolu Ajansi, June 20, 2021. https://www.aa.com.tr/fr/afrique/libye-imad-al -bannani-nouveau-président-du-parti-justice-et-construction/2279695.

Lister, Charles. "Competition Among Violent Islamist Extremists: Combating an Unprecedented Threat." *Annals of the American Academy of Political and Social Science* 668, no. 1 (October 21, 2016): 53–70.

Livesay, Christopher, and Alessandro Pavone. "ISIS Regroups to Attack a Fragmented Libya." *PBS Newshour*, September 30, 2018. https://pulitzercenter.org/stories/isis -regroups-attack-fragmented-libya.

Al-Liwāʾ Rahil: hunāk tansīq baīn al-ʾirhābīyn fī madīnatiy ṭarābulus wa-derna, [Major General Rahil: There Is Coordination Between the Terrorists in the Cities of Tripoli and Derna]. Al-Marsad, June 3, 2019. http://web.archive.org/web/20210120063736 /https://almarsad.co/2019/06/03/اللواء-رحيل-هناك-تنسيق-بين-الإر هابيين/.

Luck, Taylor. "Libya Crisis as Opportunity: Who Are the Madkhalis?" *Christian Science Monitor*, January 17, 2018. https://www.csmonitor.com/World/Middle-East /2018/0117/Libya-crisis-as-opportunity-Who-are-the-Madkhalis.

Lynch, Marc. "In Uncharted Waters: Islamist Movements Beyond Egypt's Muslim Brotherhood." Carnegie Endowment for International Peace, December 16, 2016. https://carnegieendowment.org/research/2016/12/in-uncharted-waters -islamist-parties-beyond-egypts-muslim-brotherhood.

Lynch, Marc, and Jillian Schwedler. "Introduction to the Special Issue on 'Islamist Politics After the Arab Uprisings.'" *Middle East Law and Governance* 12, no. 1 (2020): 3–13.

Lyons, Terrence. "Victorious Rebels and Postwar Politics." *Civil Wars* 18, no. 2 (2016): 160–74.

Madkhali, Rabi al-. "Al-taḥdhīr min al-fitan wa min al-dimoqāṭiyya wa mushtaqātih" [Warning against Strife and against Democracy and Its Derivatives]. Rabi al-Madkhali home page, March 4, 2012. http://www.rabee.net/ar/articles.php?cat =8&id=228.

Madkhali, Rabi al-. "Fatwā al-shaykh Rabi al-Madkhali biʿadam alqiāl fi lībīā maʿ aiy ṭaraf" [The Fatwa of Shaykh Rabi al-Madkhali Not to Fight in Libya with Any

Party]. Video. February 27, 2015. https://www.youtube.com/watch?v
=TOyYSJnLuaA.

Madkhali, Rabi al-. "Fatwā Rabi al-Madkhali al-jadīdat ʿan lībīā" [Rabi al-Madkhali's
New Fatwa on Libya]. Salem Salem, April 4, 2016. www.youtube.com/watch?v
=1bjR68rDGqU.

Madkhali, Rabi al-. "Jadīd al-ʿallama al-shaykh ʿamīr al-Madkhaliy ḥafiẓahu Allah
wa raʿah li-al-salagiyyīn fī Lībīā wa ʾan yakūnū taḥt rayat Haftar" [The New
Shaykh Rabi Al-Madkhali, May God Preserve Him and Protect Him—The Salafis
in Libya Need to Be Under the Banner of Haftar]. Video. February 22, 2018. https://
www.youtube.com/watch?v=4HAywsUtjF4.

Madkhali, Rabi al-. "Kalimat al-shaykh Rabīʿ al-Madkhalī ʿan fitnat lībīā biʿd
alQadhāfī" [Speech of Shaykh Rabi al-Madkhali on the Sedition of Libya After
Qaddafi]. Video. October 2, 2011. http://archive.today/2019.06.12-105450
/https://www.youtube.com/watch?v=sriMveeY9vA.

Madkhali, Rabi al-. "Kalimāt ʿan alʾahdāth w-almẓārāt w-alkhuruj ʿila al-hakām"
[A Word About the Events, Demonstrations, and Rebellion against the Rulers].
Rabi al-Madkhali homepage, March 17, 2011. http://archive.today/2020.05.19
-155744/http://www.rabee.net/ar/articles.php?cat=11&id=285.

Madkhali, Rabi al-. "Naṣīhat al-muslimīn ʿmūmān wa-l-salafīyn khaṣata fī lībīā wa-
ghīriha min al-bilad al-ʾislamīyati" [Advice for Muslims in General and Salafis
in Particular, in Libya and Other Islamic Countries]. Rabi al-Madkhali homepage, July 4, 2017. http://web.archive.org/web/20210825143838/https://rabee.net
/ar/articles.php?cat=8&id=319.

"Magariaf Calls Destruction of Tombs Illegal: SSC Denies Any Participation in Shrine
Destruction." *Al-Watan al-Libiya*, August 25, 2012. https://archive.md/f0m4z.
https://www.facebook.com/Libyantogether/posts/httpwwwalwatan-libyacom
morephpnewsid25740catid22/220533738080846/.

Maher, Shiraz. *Salafi-Jihadism: The History of an Idea*. Oxford University Press, 2016.

Maher, Shiraz, and Martyn Frampton. "Choosing Our Friends Wisely: Criteria for
Engagement with Muslim Groups." Policy Exchange, March 8, 2009. https://
policyexchange.org.uk/publication/choosing-our-friends-wisely-criteria-for
-engagement-with-muslim-groups/.

Mahmoud, Khalid. "Libyan Muslim Brotherhood Condemns Haftar 'Coup.'" *Asharq
Al-Awsat*, May 23, 2014. https://english.aawsat.com/2014/05/article55332524
/libyan-muslim-brotherhood-condemns-haftar-coup.

Majdi Hafala, *Nasīḥa ilā al-shabāb al-salafīy li-al-shaykh Abū Musʿab Majdī* [Advice to the
Salafi Youth by Shaykh Abu Musab Majdi Hafala]. Video. YouTube, November 21,
2012. https://www.youtube.com/watch?v=knimBlmycIo.

Mandaville, Peter. *Islam and Politics*, 3rd ed. (Routledge, 2020).

Mangan, Fiona, and Matthias Nowak. "The West Africa–Sahel Connection: Mapping
Cross-Border Arms Trafficking." Briefing Paper. Small Arms Survey, December 8,
2019. https://www.smallarmssurvey.org/resource/west-africa-sahel-connection
-mapping-cross-border-arms-trafficking.

Markoff, John. *Waves of Democracy: Social Movements and Political Change*. 2nd edition.
Routledge, 2015.

Marks, Monica. "Did Egypt's Coup Teach Ennahda to Cede Power?" *Transnational Diffusion and Cooperation in the Middle East, POMEPS Studies*, August 24, 2016: 54–57. https://pomeps.org/wp-content/uploads/2016/09/POMEPS_Studies_21_Trans national_Web-REV.pdf#page=54.

Maru, Mehari Taddele. "On Unconstitutional Changes of Government: The Case of the National Transitional Council of Libya." *African Security Review* 21, no. 1 (2012): 67–73.

Marullo, Sam. "Frame Changes and Social Movement Contraction: US Peace Movement Framing After the Cold War." *Sociological Inquiry* 66, no. 1 (1996): 1–28.

"Maṣādir takshif zīāratan qiādiy majmuʿāt musalahat lībiā l-al-sʿaudīa" [Sources Reveal the Visit of Leaders of Libyan Armed Groups to Saudi Arabia]. Al-Araby, April 15, 2018. http://archive.today/2021.12.17-092633/ https://www.alaraby.co .uk/مصادر-تكشف-زيارة-قيادي-مجموعات-مسلحة-ليبية-للسعودية.

Masry, Sarah el-, and Neil Ketchley. "After the Massacre: Women's Islamist Activism in Post-Coup Egypt." *Middle East Law and Governance* 12, no. 1 (2020): 86L–108.

Mayar, Ashraf al-. "Ashraf al-Mayār yaqul inna al-ḥākim al-sharʿiy li-Lībyā howa majlis al-nuwāb wa man yakhruj ʿanh yuʿtabar min al-khwārij wa yajib qitāluh" [Ashraf al-Mayar Says That the Legitimate Ruler of Libya is the House of Representatives and Those Who Do Not Think So Are Considered Kharijites and Must Be Fought]. Video. October 19, 2018. https://www.youtube.com/watch?v=moocXdH4M5c.

"MB Calls on Arab League to Intervene in Libya." Ikhwanweb, March 7, 2011. http://archive.today/2020.05.05-083626/https://www.ikhwanweb.com/article.php?id=28173.

"MB Calls on Libyan Factions to Unite and Draft Modern Constitution." Ikhwanweb, November 21, 2011. http://archive.today/2020.05.05-082544/https://www .ikhwanweb.com/article.php?id=29080.

"MB Chairman: We Are Confident Jihad Is the Path to Liberate Al-Aqsa Mosque." Ikhwanweb, November 1, 2009. http://archive.today/2020.05.05-090001/https:// www.ikhwanweb.com/article.php?id=21441.

McCarthy, Rory. "When Islamists Lose." *Middle East Journal* 72, no. 3 (2018): 365–84.

McConnell, Dugald, and Brian Todd. "Libyan Leader's Embrace of Sharia Raises Eyebrows." CNN, October 26, 2011. https://www.cnn.com/2011/10/26/world/africa /libya-sharia/index.html.

McDowall, Angus. "Libya's Dbeibah: The Ambitious Politician Who Promised Not to Be." Reuters, February 10, 2022. https://www.reuters.com/world/africa/libyas -dbeibah-ambitious-politician-who-promised-not-be-2022-02-10/.

McGregor, Andrew. "Radical Loyalty and the Libyan Crisis: A Profile of Salafist Shaykh Rabi' bin Hadi al-Madkhali." *Militant Leadership Monitor* 7, no. 12 (January 11, 2017).

McQuinn, Brian. "History's Warriors: The Emergence of Revolutionary Battalions in Misrata." In *The Libyan Revolution and Its Aftermath*, edited by Peter Cole and Brian McQuinn, 229–56. Oxford University Press, 2015.

Mees, Ludger. *Nationalism, Violence and Democracy.* Palgrave Macmillan, 2003.

Meijer, Roel, ed. *Global Salafism: Islam's New Religious Movement.* Columbia University Press, 2009.

Meijer, Roel. "Politicising *Al-Jarh Wa-l-Ta'dil*: Rabi' B. Hadi Al-Madkhali and the Transnational Battle for Religious Authority." In *The Transmission and Dynamics of the Textual Sources of Islam: Essays in Honor of Harald Motzki*, edited by Nicolet Boekhoff-van der Voort, Kees Versteegh, and Joas Wagemakers, 375–99. Brill, 2011.

Meijer, Roel. "The Problem of the Political in Islamist Movements." In *Whatever Happened to the Islamists? Salafis, Heavy Metal Muslims, and the Lure of Consumerist Islam*, ed. Olivier Roy and Amel Boubekeur, 27–60. Columbia University Press, 2012.

Meijer, Roel. "Taking the Islamist Movement Seriously: Social Movement Theory and the Islamist Movement." *International Review of Social History* 50, no. 2 (2005): 279–91.

Meleagrou-Hitchens, Alexander. *Incitement: Anwar al-Awlaki's Western Jihad*. Harvard University Press, 2020.

Meleagrou-Hitchens, Alexander. "Salafism in America: History, Evolution and Radicalisation." *Program on Extremism* (October 2018).

Melucci, Alberto. *Challenging Codes: Collective Action in the Information Age*. Cambridge University Press, 1996.

Meyer, David S., and Suzanne Staggenborg. "Movements, Countermovements, and the Structure of Political Opportunity." *American Journal of Sociology* 101, no. 6 (1996): 1628–60.

Mezran, Karim. "Conspiracism in and around Libya." *International Spectator* 51, no. 2 (2016): 113–18.

Mezran, Karim, and Arturo Varvelli. "Libyan Crisis: International Actors at Play." *Foreign Actors in Libya's Crisis*. Italian Institute for International Political Studies (ISPI), July 26, 2017. https://www.ispionline.it/en/publication/foreign-actors-libyas-crisis-17224.

Mihr, Anja. "Semi-Structured Interviews with Non-State and Security Actors." In *Researching Non-State Actors in International Security*, edited by Andreas Kruck and Andrea Schneiker, 65–80. Routledge, 2017.

Milton-Edwards, Beverley. *The Muslim Brotherhood: The Arab Spring and Its Future Face*. Routledge, 2015.

Milton-Edwards, Beverley, and Stephen Farrell. *Hamas: The Islamic Resistance Movement*. Polity, 2010.

Mitchell, Richard Paul. *The Society of the Muslim Brothers*. Oxford University Press, 1993.

Mitchell, Timothy. "Everyday Metaphors of Power." *Theory and Society* 19, no. 5 (1990): 545–77.

Mittelstaedt, Juliane von. "German UN Envoy Martin Kobler on Spread of IS in Libya." *Der Spiegel*, February 4, 2016. https://www.spiegel.de/international/world/german-un-envoy-martin-kobler-on-spread-of-is-in-libya-a-1075475.html.

Mneimneh, Hassan. "The Spring of a New Political Salafism?" Hudson Institute, October 19, 2011. https://www.hudson.org/national-security-defense/the-spring-of-a-new-political-salafism-.

Morris, Aldon, and Carol McClurg Mueller, eds. *Frontiers in Social Movement Theory*. Yale University Press, 1992.

Moussa, Mohamed ben. "From Arab Street to Social Movements: Re-Theorizing Collective Action and the Role of Social Media in the Arab Spring." *Westminster*

Papers in Communication and Culture 9, no. 2 (2013): 45–69. https://doi.org/10.16997 /wpcc.166.

Mozaffari, Mehdi. "What Is Islamism? History and Definition of a Concept." *Totalitarian Movements and Political Religions* 8, no. 1 (2007): 17–33. https://doi.org/10.1080 /14690760601121622

Mufti, Malik. "Elite Bargains and the Onset of Political Liberalization in Jordan." *Comparative Political Studies* 32, no. 1 (1999): 100–29.

Munson, Ziad. "Islamic Mobilization: Social Movement Theory and the Egyptian Muslim Brotherhood." *Sociological Quarterly* 42 (2001): 487–510.

Murphy, François. "Muslim Brotherhood Goes Public with Libya Summit." Reuters, November 17, 2011. http://web.archive.org/web/20191226163827/https://www .reuters.com/article/us-libya-muslim-brotherhood-idUSTRE7AG2OY20111117.

Musgrave, Nina. "Hamas and the 'Trap' of Sectarianism?" *Global Discourse* 6, no. 4 (2016): 697–708.

"The Muslim Association of Britain (MAB) Is in Agreement with the Enforcement of the No-Fly in Libya, by Britain and Its Allies in Order to Protect Libyan Civilians from Being Murdered by Its Cruel Dictator Qaddafi." Ikhwanweb, March 22, 2011. http://archive.today/2020.05.05-083141/https://www.ikhwanweb.com/article .php?id=28273.

"Muslim Brotherhood Condemns Egypt Coup Regime Aggression on Libya." Ikhwanweb, May 29, 2017. https://web.archive.org/web/20190301081510/https:// www.ikhwanweb.com/article.php?id=32702.

Nahed, Sumayta al-. "Covering Libya: A Framing Analysis of Al Jazeera and BBC Coverage of the 2011 Libyan Uprising and NATO Intervention." *Middle East Critique* 24, no. 3 (2015): 251–67.

Najjair, Sam. *Soldier for a Summer*. Hachette, 2013.

Nasr, Vali. "The Rise of 'Muslim Democracy.'" *Journal of Democracy* 16, no. 2 (2005): 13–27.

Nassar, Hala Kamis, and Marco Boggero. "Omar al-Mukhtar: The Formation of Cultural Memory and the Case of the Militant Group That Bears His Name." *Journal of North African Studies* 13, no. 2 (2008): 201–17.

National Transitional Council. "Founding Statement." March 5, 2011. https://web .archive.org/web/20110310051658/http://ntclibya.org/english/founding-state ment-of-the-interim-transitional-national-council/.

Naurin, Elin. *Election Promises, Party Behaviour and Voter Perceptions*. Palgrave Macmillan, 2011.

Nawas, John. "Mihna." *Oxford Bibliographies*, last modified July 30, 2014. https://doi .org/10.1093/obo/9780195390155-0205.

Nawawy, Mohammed el-, and Sahar Khamis. "Cyberactivists Paving the Way for the Arab Spring: Voices from Egypt, Tunisia and Libya." *Cyber Orient* 6, no. 2 (2012): 4–27.

Nesser, Petter, Anne Stenersen, and Emilie Oftedal. "Jihadi Terrorism in Europe: The IS-Effect." *Perspectives on Terrorism* 10, no. 6 (2016): 3–24.

Nicholson, Linda. *Identity Before Identity Politics*. Cambridge University Press, 2008.

Nielsen, Richard A. *Deadly Clerics: Blocked Ambition and the Paths to Jihad*. Cambridge University Press, 2017.

Nissenbaum, Dion, and Maria Abi-Habib. "Islamic State Solidifies Foothold in Libya to Expand Reach." *Wall Street Journal*, May 8, 2015. https://www.wsj.com/articles /islamic-state-solidifies-foothold-in-libya-to-expand-reach-1431989697.

North, Douglass, John Joseph Wallis, and Barry R. Weingast. *Violence and Social Orders: A Conceptual Framework for Interpreting Recorded Human History.* Cambridge University Press, 2009.

Nugent, Elizabeth. "Rethinking Repression and Islamist Behavior After the 2011 Uprisings." In *Evolving Methodologies in the Study of Islamism*, edited by Marc Lynch. POMEPS Studies 17. Project on Middle East Political Science, 2016. http://pomeps .org/wp-content/uploads/2016/03/POMEPS_Studies_17_Methods_Web.pdf.

Oakes, John. *Libya: The History of Gaddafi's Pariah State.* History Press, 2011.

Obeidi, Amal. *Political Culture in Libya.* Routledge, 2001.

Okruhlik, Gwenn. "Making Conversation Permissible." In *Islamic Activism: A Social Movement Theory Approach*, edited by Quintan Wiktorowicz, 250–68. Indiana University Press, 2004.

Olidort, Jacob. "The Politics of 'Quietist' Salafism." Analysis Paper 18. Brookings Institution Project on U.S. Relations with the Islamic World, 2015. https://www .brookings.edu/wp-content/uploads/2016/07/Brookings-Analysis-Paper_Jacob -Olidort-Inside_Final_Web.pdf.

Oliver, Pamela, and Hank Johnston. "What a Good Idea! Ideologies and Frames in Social Movement Research." *Mobilization: An International Quarterly* 5, no. 1 (2000): 37–54.

Omrani, Shaykh Nader al-. "Mudākhalat faḍīlat al-Shaykh Dr. Nadir al-Omrani bikhuṣūṣ al-mūqif min fatwā al-Shaykh Rabi al-Madkhali aldāʿiat lilqitāl ʾilā jānib Haftar!" [Intervention of His Eminence Shaykh Dr. Nader al-Omrani Regarding the Fatwa of Shaykh Rabi al-Madkhali Calling for Fighting Alongside Haftar!]. Video. *Dar al-Ifta Libya*, July 11, 2016. http://web.archive.org/web/20220323101825 /https://www.facebook.com/IFTALibya/videos/1163447350372023/.

Opp, Karl-Dieter. *Theories of Political Protest and Social Movements: A Multidisciplinary Introduction, Critique, and Synthesis.* Routledge, 2009.

"Ousted Libyan PM Flees," *Deutsche Welle*, December 3, 2014, https://www.dw.com/en /libyan-ex-premier-zeidan-flees-to-europe/a-17492737.

Pack, Jason, and Haley Cook. "The July 2012 Libyan Election and the Origin of Post-Qadhafi Appeasement." *Middle East Journal* 69, no. 2 (2015): 171–98.

Pahwa, Sumita. "Pathways of Islamist Adaptation: The Egyptian Muslim Brothers' Lessons for Inclusion Moderation Theory." *Democratization* 24, no. 6 (2017): 1066–84. https://doi.org/10.1080/13510347.2016.1273903.

Pall, Zoltan. *Salafism in Lebanon: Local and Transnational Movements.* Cambridge University Press, 2018.

Pantucci, Kristina. "Britain on Alert: The Attacks in London and Manchester and the Evolving Threat" *CTC* [Combating Terrorism Center] *Sentinel* 10 no. 7 (2017), https://ctc.westpoint.edu/britain-on-alert-the-attacks-in-london-and -manchester-and-the-evolving-threat/.

Pargeter, Alison. *The Muslim Brotherhood: From Opposition to Power.* Saqi, 2013.

Pargeter, Alison. "Qadhafi and Political Islam in Libya." In *Libya Since 1969*, edited by Dirk Vandewalle, 83–104. Palgrave Macmillan, 2008.

Pargeter, Alison. *Return to the Shadows: The Muslim Brotherhood and An-Nahda Since the Arab Spring*. Saqi, 2016.

Parveen, Nazia. "Bomber's Father Fought Against Gaddafi Regime with 'Terrorist' Group," *The Guardian*, May 24, 2017, UK News, https://www.theguardian.com/uk-news/2017/may/24/bombers-father-fought-against-gaddafi-regime-with-terrorist-group.

Perry, Damon L. "The Islamic Movement in Britain." Report. International Centre for the Study of Radicalisation, September 2020. https://icsr.info/wp-content/uploads/2020/09/ICSR-Report-The-Islamic-Movement-in-Britain.pdf.

Pickvance, Christopher. "Democratisation and the Decline of Social Movements: The Effects of Regime Change on Collective Action in Eastern Europe, Southern Europe and Latin America." *Sociology* 33, no. 2 (1999): 353–72.

Pidd, Helen. "How Family and Libya Conflict Radicalised Manchester Arena Bomber." *The Guardian*, March 2, 2023. UK News. https://www.theguardian.com/uk-news/2023/mar/02/how-family-libya-conflict-radicalised-manchester-arena-bomber.

Piven, Frances Fox, and Richard A. Cloward. *Poor People's Movements: Why They Succeed, How They Fail*. Vintage, 1977.

"Political Isolation Law: The Full Text." *Libya Herald*, May 14, 2013. http://web.archive.org/web/20130609174823/http://www.libyaherald.com/2013/05/14/political-isolation-law-the-full-text.

Pollock, Katherine, and Frederic Wehrey. "The Sufi-Salafi Rift." Carnegie Endowment for International Peace, January 23, 2018. https://carnegieendowment.org/middle-east/diwan/2018/01/the-sufi-salafi-rift.

"President Obama: Libya Aftermath 'Worst Mistake' of Presidency." BBC News, April 11, 2016. https://www.bbc.com/news/world-us-canada-36013703.

Qaddafi, Muammar. *The Green Book*. Ithaca, 1999.

Raghavan, Sudarsan. "Libya's Civil War Creates Opening for ISIS Return as Counterterrorism Effort Falters." *Washington Post*, November 24, 2019. https://www.washingtonpost.com/world/middle_east/libyas-civil-war-creates-opening-for-isis-return-as-counterterrorism-effort-falters/2019/11/21/e78745c0-056c-11ea-9118-25d6bd37dfb1_story.html.

Raghavan, Sudarsan. "A Year After ISIS Left, a Battered Libyan City Struggles to Resurrect Itself." *Washington Post*, January 8, 2017. https://www.washingtonpost.com/news/world/wp/2018/01/08/feature/a-year-after-isis-left-a-battered-libyan-city-struggles-to-resurrect-itself/.

"Raghm muʿāraḍat al-ʾamn w-al-baladīati. al-ʿtībiy yaṣil tibriq waṣt hirāsat mushadada" [Despite the Opposition of the Security and the Municipality, Al-Otaibi Arrives in Tobruk Under Heavy Security]. Al-Wasat, February 14, 2017. https://web.archive.org/web/20210126002934/http://alwasat.ly/news/libya/124686.

Rasheed, Bani. "Man yuṭālib bāsqāṭ al-ikhwān fālyusquṭ al-fasādi awla" [Whoever Demands the Overthrow of the Brotherhood Must Drop Corruption First]. Ammon News, November 23, 2012. https://archive.md/kBmsG.

Rasheed, Madawi al-. *Contesting the Saudi State: Islamic Voices from a New Generation*. Cambridge University Press, 2007.

Rasheed, Madawi al-. *A History of Saudi Arabia*. Cambridge University Press, 2010.

Rasheed, Madawi al-. *A Most Masculine State: Gender, Politics and Religion in Saudi Arabia.* Cambridge University Press, 2013.

Rayment, Sean. "How the Special Forces Helped Bring Gaddafi to His Knees." *The Telegraph,* August 28, 2011. https://www.telegraph.co.uk/news/worldnews/africaa ndindianocean/libya/8727076/How-the-special-forces-helped-bring-Gaddafi -to-his-knees.html.

Roberts, David. "Qatar and the Muslim Brotherhood: Pragmatism or Preference?" *Middle East Policy* 21, no. 3 (2014): 84–94. https://doi.org/10.1111/mepo.12084.

Roberts, Kenneth. *Deepening Democracy? The Modern Left and Social Movements in Chile and Peru.* Stanford University Press, 1998.

Robertson, Nic, and Paul Cruickshank. "Islamic Militants Among Prisoners Freed from Libyan Jail." CNN, August 26, 2011. http://www.cnn.com/2011/WORLD /africa/08/26/libya.militants.analysis/index.html.

Robinson, Glenn. "Can Islamists Be Democrats? The Case of Jordan." *Middle East Journal* 51, no. 3 (1997): 373–87.

Ronen, Yehudit. "Qadhafi and Militant Islamism: Unprecedented Conflict." *Middle Eastern Studies* 38, no. 4 (2002): 1–16.

Rootes, Chris. "Shaping Collective Action: Structure, Contingency and Knowledge." In *The Political Context of Collective Action: Power, Argumentation and Democracy,* ed. Ricca Edmondson, 81–104. Routledge, 1997.

Roy, Olivier. *The Failure of Political Islam.* Harvard University Press, 1996.

Roy, Olivier. *Holy Ignorance: When Religion and Culture Diverge.* Columbia University Press, 2010.

Saadi, Sami al-. "CV." Sami al-Saadi homepage. http://archive.today/2021.12.15 -144727/https://www.samiassaadi.ly/cv.

Sadiki, Larbi. "Libya: Testing Tolerance." Al Jazeera, September 4, 2012. https://www .aljazeera.com/opinions/2012/9/4/libya-testing-tolerance.

Salem, Paul, and Amanda Kadlec. "Libya's Troubled Transition." Carnegie Endowment for International Peace, June 14, 2012. https://carnegieendowment.org /research/2012/06/libyas-troubled-transition.

Salih, Kamal Eldin Osman. "The Roots and Causes of the 2011 Arab Uprisings." *Arab Studies Quarterly* 35, no. 2 (2013): 184–206. https://doi.org/10.13169/arabstudquar .35.2.0184.

"Al-Sallabi, al-Sheikhi wakhrūn yuqdamūn mashruʿan limīthāq wa-ṭanīn antiqālīn" [Al-Sallabi, al-Sheikhi and Others Present a Draft for a Transitional National Charter]. Al-Manara, March 28, 2011. http://archive.today/2021.12.15-084548 /http://almanaramedia.blogspot.com/2011/03/blog-post_3481.html.

Sallabi, Ali, al-. "Al-Sallabi: lā yumkin-u tajāwuz-u islamiyiyy Lībīā" [Al-Sallabi: The Islamists of Libya Cannot Be Bypassed]. Al Jazeera, September 15, 2011. http://archive.today/2020.04.30-104730/ https://www .aljazeera .net /news /reportsandinterviews/2011/9/14/الصلابي-لا-يمكن-تجاوز-إسلاميي-ليبيا.

Salwen, Sarah. "Faith in Moderation: Islamist Parties in Jordan and Yemen." *Journal of Church and State* 49, no. 2 (2007): 353–55.

Sandbakken, Camilal. "The Limits to Democracy Posed by Oil Rentier States: The Cases of Algeria, Nigeria and Libya." *Democratisation* 13, no. 1 (2006): 135–52.

Sanín, Francisco Gutiérrez, and Elisabeth Jean Wood. "Ideology in Civil War: Instrumental Adoption and Beyond." *Journal of Peace Research* 51, no. 2 (2014): 213–26.

Sarrar, Salah. "Ex-Islamists Walk Free from Libyan Jail." Reuters, August 31, 2010. World News. https://www.reuters.com/article/us-libya-prisoners-release -idUSTRE67U5U420100831.

Sawan, Muhammad. "Raiy Sawan fī al-ʿuzl alsiyāsiy w-al-muqtarah al-adhiy ʿuriḍ ʿal-mutamar" [Sawan's Opinion on Political Isolation and the Proposal Presented to the Congress]. Video. Magdi Mokhtar, March 21, 2013. https://www.youtube .com/watch?v=hbBozdRGp_M.

Sawani, Youssef Mohammad. "Post-Qadhafi Libya: Interactive Dynamics and the Political Future." *Contemporary Arab Affairs* 5, no. 1 (2012): 1–26.

Schwedler, Jillian. "Can Islamists Become Moderates? Rethinking the Inclusion-Moderation Hypothesis." *World Politics* 63, no. 2 (2011): 347–76.

Schwedler, Jillian. *Faith in Moderation: Islamist Parties in Jordan and Yemen.* Cambridge University Press, 2006.

Schwedler, Jillian. "Islamists in Power? Inclusion, Moderation, and the Arab Uprisings." *Middle East Development Journal* 5, no. 1 (2013): 1–18.

Shafai, Mohammed al-. "Muasis hizb al-umat al-lībīā la al-sharq al-awsat: lam natawaqaʿ tarājuʿ al-ʾislāmīyn bihadhi al-ṣuwra" [The Founder of Libyan Party al-Umma to Al-Sharq Al-Awsat: We Did Not Expect the Islamists to Retreat in Such a Way]. *Asharq al-Awsat,* July 11, 2012. https://archive.aawsat.com/details.asp ?section=4&issueno=12279&article=685881.

Shaiter, Mohammed. "Hiwār maʿ Mohammed Shaiter, āmir al-shuwun al-aʿskarīa fī Saraya al-Thuwwar" [An Interview with Mohammed Shaiter, the Commander of Military Affairs of the Revolutionary Brigades]. Al-Manara, August 15, 2011. http://archive.today/2021.02.15-131315/http://almanaramedia.blogspot.com /2011/08/blog-post_5220.html.

Sharif, Khaled al-. "Liqāʾ khāṣun maʿ Khaled al-Sharif wakīl wizārat al-difāʿ" [Interview with Khaled al-Sharif, Deputy Minister of Defense] Al-Nabaa TV, August 25, 2014. https://www.youtube.com/watch?v=FJvZz7_XIwU.

"Shatm al-Salafi al-Saʿadī alQadhāfī ʿala al-hawaʾ" [The Salafi Saadi Qaddafi Is Insulted Live]. YouTube.

Sheikhi, Salim al-. "Dawr al-ikhwān al-muslimīn fī 17 fibrāīr" [The Role of the Muslim Brotherhood on 17 February]. Facebook, May 14, 2013.

Siggins, Lorna. "Muslim Cleric Welcomes Irish Support for Libyan Council." *Irish Times,* September 10, 2011. https://www.irishtimes.com/news/muslim-cleric -welcomes-irish-support-for-libyan-council-1.595357.

604th Battalion. "Isdār fa hal tara lahum min bāqiya" [Issuance Do You See Anything Remaining From Them]. Video. January 11, 2018. https://www.youtube.com /watch?v=Ytd4sZzAzgo.

604th Battalion. "Jawlat ʿadasat katībat 604 mushāh fī mustashā bn sīnā li-al-ittilāʿ ʿlā mustajaddāt al-syāna bi-al-mustashfā" [A Tour of the 604th Infantry Battalion at Ben Sena Hospital to See the Latest Developments in the Hospital Maintenance]. Video. March 17, 2017. https://www.youtube.com/watch?v=RcwPd9O3yws.

Sizer, Lydia. "Libya's Terrorism Challenge: Assessing the Salafi-Jihadi Threat." Policy Paper 2017-1. Middle East Institute, October 2017. https://www.mei.edu/sites/default/files/publications/PP1_Sizer_LibyaCT_web_0.pdf.

Smith, Rhiannon. "Libya's Political Isolation Law: Confusion and Charade." Open Democracy, May 15, 2013. http://www.opendemocracy.net/rhiannon-smith/libyas-political-isolation-law-confusion-and-charade.

Smith, Rhiannon. "Political Fault Lines Threaten Libya's Stability." OpenDemocracy, October 26, 2013. https://www.opendemocracy.net/en/north-africa-west-asia/political-fault-lines-threaten-libyas-stability/.

Snow, David A., Sarah A. Soule, and Hanspeter Kriesi. "Mapping the Terrain." In *The Blackwell Companion to Social Movements*, edited by David A. Snow, Sarah A. Soule, and Hanspeter Kriesi, 3–17. Blackwell, 2006.

Special Deterrence Force Tripoli. *Bism allah al-rahman al-rahīm hadha alfīdīu yuaḍih kaīfīat takhzīn mādat mukhadirat nawʿ hashīsh tama ẓabatuha* [In the Name of God, the Most Gracious, the Most Merciful] June 21, 2015. Facebook, http://web.archive.org/web/20220323101530/https://www.facebook.com/100069149021618/videos/1124346214326210/.

St. John, Ronald Bruce, ed. *Libya: Continuity and Change.* Routledge, 2015.

Staniland, Paul. "Violence and Democracy." *Comparative Politics* 47, no. 1 (2014): 99–118.

Steenkamp, Christina. *Violent Societies: Networks of Violence in Civil War and Peace.* Springer, 2014.

Storm, Lise. "Exploring Post-Rebel Parties in Power: Political Space and Implications for Islamist Inclusion and Moderation." *Open Journal of Political Science* 10, no.4 (2020): 638–67. DOI: 10.4236/ojps.2020.104038.

Tagar, Michal Reifen, G. Scott Morgan, Eran Halperin, and Linda J. Skitka. "When Ideology Matters: Moral Conviction and the Association Between Ideology and Policy Preferences in the Israeli–Palestinian Conflict." *European Journal of Social Psychology* 44, no. 2 (2014): 117–25.

Tamimi, Aymenn Jawad al-. "Islamic State's Appointment of New Leader: Translation and Notes." http://www.aymennjawad.org/2019/10/islamic-state-appointment-of-new-leader.

Tanter, Raymond, and Manus Midlarsky. "A Theory of Revolution." *Journal of Conflict Resolution* 11 (1967): 264–80.

Tepe, Sultan. "Moderation of Religious Parties: Electoral Constraints, Ideological Commitments, and the Democratic Capacities of Religious Parties in Israel and Turkey." *Political Research Quarterly* 65 (2012): 467–88.

Tezcür, Günes Murat. *Muslim Reformers in Iran and Turkey: The Paradox of Moderation.* University of Texas Press, 2010.

Thomas, David. "A General Inductive Approach for Qualitative Data Analysis." *American Journal of Evaluation* 27, no. 2 (2003): 237–46.

Thomas-Johnson, Amandla. " 'Sorted' by MI5: How UK Government Sent British-Libyans to Fight Gaddafi." *Middle East Eye*, July 11, 2018. https://www.middleeasteye.net/news/sorted-mi5-how-uk-government-sent-british-libyans-fight-gaddafi.

Tilly, Charles, and Sidney G. Tarrow. *Contentious Politics.* Oxford University Press, 2015.

Todeschini, Vito. "Libya: The International Community's Bet over Holding Elections in 2023," Tahrir Institute for Middle East Policy blog, July 3, 2023, https://timep.org/2023/07/07/libya-the-international-communitys-bet-over-holding-elections-in-2023/.

Trauthig, Inga Kristina. "Assessing the Islamic State in Libya." Paper presented at the 3rd Conference of the European Counter Terrorism Centre (ECTC) Advisory Network on Terrorism and Propaganda, April 9–10, 2019. https://www.europol.europa.eu/publications-events/publications/assessing-islamic-state-in-libya.

Trauthig, Inga Kristina. "Gaining Legitimacy in Post-Qaddafi Libya: Analysing Attempts of the Muslim Brotherhood." *Societies* 9, no. 3 (2019): 65. https://doi.org/10.3390/soc9030065.

Trauthig, Inga Kristina. "Is the Term 'Terrorism' Still Useful for Understanding Conflicts in Libya?" *International Affairs*, blog post, Medium, September 27, 2021. https://medium.com/international-affairs-blog/is-the-term-terrorism-still-useful-in-understanding-conflicts-in-libya-bed87ef642a7.

Trauthig, Inga Kristina. "SSR and Elections: What Role for the Security Sector in 2021?" In *The Road to Stability: Rethinking Security Sector Reform in Post-Conflict Libya*, edited by Emadeddin Badi, Archibald Gallet, and Roberta Maggi, 29–38. DCAF–Geneva Center for Security Sector Governance, 2021. https://www.dcaf.ch/road-stability-rethinking-ssr-post-conflict-libya.

Trauthig, Inga Kristina. "'This Is the Fate of Libyan Women': Contempt, Ridicule, and Indifference of Seham Sergiwa." *Conflict, Security & Development* 24, no. 2 (2024): 149–73. https://doi.org/10.1080/14678802.2024.2334832.

Trauthig, Inga Kristina, and Emaddedin Badi. "Islamist Parties in Libya After Gaddafi: Old Networks in New Shapes." In *The Rule Is for None but Allah*, ed. Joana Cook and Shiraz Maher, 79–101. Hurst, 2023.

Trauthig, Inga Kristina, and Guy Robert Eyre. "'Quietist' Salafis After the 'Arab Revolts' in Algeria and Libya (2011–2019): Between Insecurity and Political Subordination." *Mediterranean Politics*, October 29, 2023: 1–24. https://doi.org/10.1080/13629395.2023.2272474.

"25 qatīlan wa 45 jarīhan saqaṭū amām dirᶜ lībīā 1" [25 Dead and 45 Wounded by the Libya Shield 1], Quryna News, June 8, 2013. https://archive.md/dVKKP#selection-955.0-959.154.

UK House of Commons. "'Political Islam,' and the Muslim Brotherhood Review: Sixth Report of Session 2016–17." Foreign Affairs Committee report, November 1, 2016). Written evidence ISL0030, http://data.parliament.uk/writtenevidence/committeeevidence.svc/evidencedocument/foreign-affairs-committee/political-islam/written/32527.html, and ISL0040, http://data.parliament.uk/writtenevidence/committeeevidence.svc/evidencedocument/foreign-affairs-committee/political-islam/written/32764.html.

UK House of Commons, Foreign Affairs Committee. "Libya: Examination of Intervention and Collapse and the U.K.'s Future Policy Options." September 14, 2016. https://publications.parliament.uk/pa/cm201617/cmselect/cmfaff/119/119.pdf.

United Nations. "Abuse Behind Bars: Arbitrary and Unlawful Detention in Libya." Human Rights Office of the High Commissioner, April 2018. https://www.ohchr.org/Documents/Countries/LY/AbuseBehindBarsArbitraryUnlawful_EN.pdf.

United Nations. "The Destruction of Cultural and Religious Sites: A Violation of Human Rights." Human Rights Office of the High Commissioner, September 24, 2012. https://www.ohchr.org/en/stories/2012/09/destruction-cultural-and -religious-sites-violation-human-rights.

United Nations. "Libya: UN Experts Call for a Swift and Rigorous Response to the Destruction of Sufi Sites." Press release. Human Rights Office of the High Commissioner, September 10, 2012. https://www.ohchr.org/en/press-releases/2012/09 /libya-un-experts-call-swift-and-rigorous-response-destruction-sufi-sites .

United Nations Security Council. "Final Report of the Panel of Experts on Libya Established Pursuant to Resolution 1973 (2011)." S/2018/812. https://www .securitycouncilreport.org/atf/cf/%7B65BFCF9B-6D27-4E9C-8CD3-CF6E4FF96 FF9%7D/s_2018_812.pdf.

United Nations Security Council. "Final Report of the Panel of Experts on Libya Submitted in Accordance with Resolution 2644 (2022)." S/2023/673. September 15, 2023. https://documents-dds-ny.un.org/doc/UNDOC/GEN/N23/234/61/PDF /N2323461.pdf.

United Nations Security Council. "UNSMIL: Report of the Secretary General, S/2018/780." August 24, 2018. https://unsmil.unmissions.org/sites/default/files /sg-report-on-unsmil_s_2018_780_e.pdf.

United Nations Support Mission in Libya. "SRSG Abdoulaye Bathily's Remarks to the Security Council Meeting on Libya." February 27, 2023. https://unsmil.unmissions .org/sites/default/files/srsg_abdoulaye_bathilys_remarks_to_the_security _council.pdf.

United Nations Support Mission in Libya. *Skhirat Agreement in English*, December 17, 2015. https://unsmil.unmissions.org/sites/default/files/Libyan Political Agreement - ENG .pdf.

United Nations Support Mission in Libya. "UNSMIL Deplores Enforced Disappearance of Elected HoR Member Ms. Sergewa." July 18, 2019. https://unsmil.unmissions .org/unsmil-deplores-enforced-disappearance-elected-hor-member-ms-sergewa -calling-her-immediate-release.

United States Agency for International Development. "Libya Community Pulse: Web Survey Results." June 23, 2021. https://app.box.com/s/jw7lp254oqj4wzk1tdcu0t unbqpzurdo.

U.S. Department of State. "Accountability Review Board Report." December 18, 2012. www.state.gov/documents/organization/202446.pdf.

U.S. Department of State. "The United States and UN Sanction Libyan Militia Leader Salah Badi." Office of the Spokesperson, November 19, 2018. https://ly.usembassy .gov/the-united-states-and-un-sanction-libyan-militia-leader-salah-badi/.

U.S. Library of Congress. "Al-Qaeda in Libya: A Profile." August 2012. https:// freebeacon.com/wp-content/uploads/2012/10/LOC-AQ-Libya.pdf.

U.S. Senate. Committee on Foreign Relations. "The Path Forward in Libya." Hearing 114-784, March 3, 2016. https://www.govinfo.gov/content/pkg/CHRG-114shrg 30552/html/CHRG-114shrg30552.htm.

Van der Heijden, Hein-Anton. "Globalization, Environmental Movements, and International Political Opportunity Structures." *Organization & Environment* 19, no. 1 (2006): 28–45.

Vandewalle, Dirk. "After Qaddafı: The Surprising Success of the New Libya." *Foreign Affairs* 91, no. 6 (2012): 8–15.

Vandewalle, Dirk. *A History of Modern Libya.* Cambridge University Press, 2012.

Vandewalle, Dirk. *Libya Since Independence.* Cornell University Press, 2018.

Vest, Nathan. "Heretics, Pawns and Traitors: Anti-Madkhali Propaganda on Libyan Salafi-Jihadi Telegram." *Jihadology* blog, February 25, 2019. https://jihadology .net/2019/02/25/guest-post-heretics-pawns-and-traitors-anti-madkhali-propa ganda-on-libyan-salafi-jihadi-telegram/.

Vidino, Lorenzo. *The Muslim Brotherhood in the United Kingdom.* George Washington University, 2015.

Vidino, Lorenzo. *The New Muslim Brotherhood in the West.* Columbia University Press, 2010.

Wagemakers, Joas. "Between Exclusivism and Inclusivism: The Jordanian Muslim Brotherhood's Divided Reponses to the 'Arab Spring.'" *Middle East Law and Governance* 12, no. 1 (2020): 35–60.

Wagemakers, Joas. "Legitimizing Pragmatism: Hamas' Framing Efforts from Militancy to Moderation and Back?" *Terrorism and Political Violence* 22, no. 3 (2010): 357–77.

Wagemakers, Joas. *The Muslim Brotherhood: Ideology, History, Descendants.* Amsterdam University Press, 2022.

Wagemakers, Joas. *A Quietist Jihadi: The Ideology and Influence of Abu Muhammad al-Maqdisi.* Cambridge University Press, 2012.

Wagemakers, Joas. "Revisiting Wiktorowicz: Categorising and Defining the Branches of Salafism." In *Salafism After the Arab Awakening,* edited by Francesco Cavatorta and Fabio Merone, 7–24. Hurst, 2016.

Wagemakers, Joas. *Salafism in Jordan: Political Islam in a Quietist Community.* Cambridge University Press, 2016.

Ward, Sharron. "Libya Uprising One Year On: Remembering the Zawiyah Massacre." *The Guardian,* February 16, 2012. World News. https://www.theguardian.com /world/video/2012/feb/16/libya-uprising-one-year-on-zawiyah.

Watanabe, Lisa. "Islamist Actors: Libya and Tunisia." Center for Security Studies, 2018. https://css.ethz.ch/content/dam/ethz/special-interest/gess/cis/center-for -securities-studies/pdfs/Watanabe-06282018-IslamistActors.pdf.

Watanabe, Lisa. "Libya: In the Eye of the Storm." *CSS Analysis in Security Policy* 193, June 2016. https://css.ethz.ch/content/dam/ethz/special-interest/gess/cis/center-for -securities-studies/pdfs/CSSAnalyse-193-EN.pdf.

Wegner, Eva. *Islamist Opposition in Authoritarian Regimes: The Party of Justice and Development in Morocco.* Syracuse University Press, 2011.

Wegner, Eva, and Miquel Pellicer. "Islamist Moderation Without Democratization: The Coming of Age of the Moroccan Party of Justice and Development?" *Democratization* 16, no. 1 (2009): 157–75.

Wehling, Elisabeth. "Politics and Framing: How Language Impacts Political Thought." In *The Routledge Handbook of Language and Media,* edited by Collien Cotter and Daniel Perrin, 136–50. Routledge, 2017.

Wehrey, Frederic. "As Their Influence Grows the Quietist Salafis Are Anything but Quiet." *World Politics Review,* December 11, 2018. https://www.worldpoliticsreview

.com/articles/26962/as-their-influence-grows-the-maghreb-s-quietist -salafists-are-anything-but-quiet.

Wehrey, Frederic. *The Burning Shores: Inside the Battle for the New Libya*. Farrar, Straus & Giroux, 2018.

Wehrey, Frederic. "The Conflict in Libya." Testimony before the U.S. House of Representatives Foreign Affairs Committee, May 17, 2019. https://carnegieendowment .org/2019/05/15/conflict-in-libya-pub-79160.

Wehrey, Frederic. "Quiet No More?" Carnegie Endowment for International Peace, October 13, 2016. https://carnegie-mec.org/diwan/64846

Wehrey, Frederic. "When the Islamic State Came to Libya." Carnegie Endowment for International Peace, February 8, 2018. https://carnegieendowment.org/2018/02 /10/when-islamic-state-came-to-libya-pub-75541.

Wehrey, Frederic, and Emad Badi. "A Place of Distinctive Despair." Carnegie Endowment for International Peace, August 8, 2018. https://carnegie-mec.org/diwan /76997.

Wehrey, Frederic, and Anouar Boukhars. "Salafism and Libya's State Collapse: The Case of the Madkhalis." In *Salafism in the Maghreb: Politics, Piety, and Militancy*, edited by Frederic Wehrey and Anouar Boukhars, 107–38. Oxford University Press, 2019.

Wehrey, Frederic, and Anouar Boukhars. *Salafism in the Maghreb: Politics, Piety, and Militancy*. Oxford University Press, 2019.

Wehrey, Frederic, and Peter Cole. "Building Libya's Security Sector." Carnegie Endowment for International Peace, August 6, 2013. https://carnegieendowment.org /posts/2013/08/building-libyas-security-sector.

Westcott, Thom. "New Libyan Ambassador to the UK Presents Credentials to the British Monarch." *Libya Herald*, December 13, 2012. https://libyaherald.com/2012 /12/new-libyan-ambassador-to-the-uk-presents-credentials-to-the-queen/.

Wester, Karin. *Intervention in Libya: The Responsibility to Protect in North Africa*, new edition. Cambridge University Press, 2020.

Wickham, Carrie Rosefsky. "Interests, Ideas and Islamist Outreach in Egypt." In *Islamic Activism: A Social Movement Theory Approach*, edited by Quintan Wiktorowicz, 231–49. Indiana University Press, 2004.

Wickham, Carrie Rosefsky. *Mobilizing Islam: Religion, Activism, and Political Change in Egypt*. Columbia University Press, 2002.

Wickham, Carrie Rosefsky. "The Path to Moderation: Strategy and Learning in the Formation of Egypt's Wasat Party." *Comparative Politics* 36, no. 2 (2004): 205–28.

Wikileaks, "[OS] Libya- Muslim Brotherhood, Salafist Said Moving Towards Political Islamization of Libya." released on February 20, 2013. https://web.archive.org /web/20201015094650/https://wikileaks.org/gifiles/docs/15/154065_-os-libya -muslim-brotherhood-salafist-said-moving-towards.html.

Wiktorowicz, Quintan. "Anatomy of the Salafi Movement." *Studies in Conflict & Terrorism* 29, no. 3 (2006): 207–39.

Wiktorowicz, Quintan. "Introduction." In *Islamic Activism: A Social Movement Theory Approach*, edited by Quintan Wiktorowicz, 1–31. Indiana University Press, 2004.

Wiktorowicz, Quintan. *The Management of Islamic Activism: Salafis, the Muslim Brotherhood, and State Power in Jordan*. SUNY Press, 2001.

Wiktorowicz, Quintan, and Suha Taji-Farouki. "Islamic NGOs and Muslim Politics: A Case from Jordan." *Third World Quarterly* 21, no. 4 (2000): 685–99.

Willard-Foster, Melissa. *Toppling Foreign Governments: The Logic of Regime Change.* University of Pennsylvania Press, 2018.

Willi, Victor J. *The Fourth Ordeal: A History of the Muslim Brotherhood in Egypt, 1968–2018.* Cambridge University Press, 2021.

Wilson, Chris. "Ideological Motives in Spoiler Violence: Post Conflict Assam, Northeast India." *Nationalism and Ethnic Politics* 23, no. 3 (2017): 280–96.

Wilson, Lachlan, and Jason Pack. "The Islamic State's Revitalization in Libya and Its Post-2016 War of Attrition." *CTC* [Combating Terrorism Center] *Sentinel* 12, no. 3 (2019): 22–31. https://ctc.westpoint.edu/islamic-states-revitalization-libya-post -2016-war-attrition/.

Winter, Charlie. "Apocalypse, Later: A Longitudinal Study of the Islamic State Brand." *Critical Studies in Media Communication* 35, no. 1 (2018): 103–21. https://doi.org/10 .1080/15295036.2017.1393094.

Wintour, Patrick. "Isis Loses Control of Libyan City of Sirte." *The Guardian*, December 5, 2016. World News. https://www.theguardian.com/world/2016/dec/05/isis -loses-control-of-libyan-city-of-sirte.

Wolf, Anne. "An Islamist 'Renaissance'? Religion and Politics in Post-Revolutionary Tunisia." *Journal of North African Studies* 18, no. 4 (2013): 560–73.

Wolf, Anne. *Political Islam in Tunisia: The History of Ennahda.* Oxford University Press, 2017.

Wollenberg, Anja, and Carola Richter. "Political Parallelism in Transitional Media Systems: The Case of Libya." *International Journal of Communication* 14 (2020): 1173–93.

Woodward, Mark, Muhammad Sani Umar, Inayah Rohmaniyah, and Mariani Yahyal. "Salafi Violence and Sufi Tolerance? Rethinking Conventional Wisdom." *Perspectives on Terrorism* 7, no. 6 (2013): 58–78.

Yadav, Stacey Philbrick. "Understanding 'What Islamists Want': Public Debate and Contestation in Lebanon and Yemen." *Middle East Journal* 64, no. 2 (2010): 199–213.

Yan, Holly. "US Launches Airstrikes on ISIS Targets in Libya." CNN, August 2, 2016. https://www.cnn.com/2016/08/01/politics/us-libya-isis-airstrikes/index.html.

Yenigün, Ibrahim. "The Political and Theological Boundaries of Islamist Moderation After the Arab Spring." *Third World Quarterly* 37, no. 12 (2016): 2304–21. https:// doi.org/10.1080/01436597.2016.1227683.

Yildiz, Hamdi. "Libyan Muslim Brotherhood Converts into NGO." Anadolu Agency, May 3, 2015. http://web.archive.org/web/20210615222008/https://www.aa.com .tr/en/middle-east/libyan-muslim-brotherhood-converts-into-ngo/2227616.

Yılmaz, İhsan. "An Islamist Party, Constraints, Opportunities and Transformation to Post-Islamism: The Tajik Case." *Uluslararası Hukuk ve Politika* 18 (2009): 133–47.

Ying, Robert. *Case Study Research: Design and Methods.* Sage, 2009.

Zahar, Marie-Joëlle. "Reframing the Spoiler Debate in Peace Processes." In *Contemporary Peace Making*, edited by John Darby and Roger MacGinty, 159–77. Palgrave Macmillan, 2008.

Zajac, Anna. "Between Sufism and Salafism: The Rise of Salafi Tendencies After the Arab Spring and Its Implications." *Hemispheres: Studies on Cultures and Societies* 29, no. 2 (2014): 97–109.

Zakaria, Fareed. "Islam, Democracy, and Constitutional Liberalism." *Political Science Quarterly* 119, no. 1 (2004): 1–20.

Zald, Mayer N., and John D. McCarthy. "Social Movement Industries: Competition and Cooperation Among Movement Organizations." Center for Research on Social Organization Paper 201. University of Michigan, 1979.

Zaptia, Sami. "HoR Grants Fathi Bashagha Government Vote of Confidence with Majority of 92." *Libya Herald*, March 1, 2022. https://libyaherald.com/2022/03 /breaking-hor-grants-fathi-bashagha-government-vote-of-confidence-with -majority-of-92/.

Zaptia, Sami. "Rada Raids Comic Con, Arrests over 20 Organisers, Participants and Spectators." *Libya Herald*, November 4, 2017. https://www.libyaherald.com/2017 /11/04/rada-raids-comic-con-arrests-over-20-organizers-participants-and -spectators/.

Zaptia, Sami. "UN Secretary General Calls for Stability, Early Elections, and Critical Decisions to Be Taken in a Transparent and Consensual Manner." *Libya Herald*, February 25, 2022. https://www.libyaherald.com/2022/02/un-secretary-general -calls-for-stability-early-elections-and-critical-decisions-to-be-taken-in-a -transparent-and-consensual-manner/.

Zelin, Aaron Y. "The Islamic State's Burgeoning Capital in Sirte, Libya." PolicyWatch 2462. Washington Institute for Near East Policy, August 2015. https://www .washingtoninstitute.org/policy-analysis/islamic-states-burgeoning-capital -sirte-libya.

Zelin, Aaron Y. "Know Your Ansar Al-Sharia." Blog post. *Foreign Policy*, September 21, 2012. https://foreignpolicy.com/2012/09/21/know-your-ansar-al-sharia/.

Zelin, Aaron Y. "The Others: Foreign Fighters in Libya," Washington Institute, January 16, 2018. https://www.washingtoninstitute.org/policy-analysis/others -foreign-fighters-libya.

Zelin, Aaron Y. "The Rise and Decline of Ansar al-Sharia in Libya." Hudson Institute, April 6, 2015. https://www.hudson.org/research/11197-the-rise-and-decline-of -ansar-al-sharia-in-libya.

Zelin, Aaron Y. *Your Sons Are at Your Service: Tunisia's Missionaries of Jihad.* Columbia University Press, 2020.

Zemni, Sami. "The Extraordinary Politics of the Tunisian Revolution: The Process of Constitution Making." *Mediterranean Politics* 20, no. 1 (2015): 1–17. https://doi .org/10.1080/13629395.2013.874108.

Zollner, Barbara. *The Muslim Brotherhood: Hasan al-Hudaybi and Ideology.* Routledge, 2009.

Zurutuza, Karlos. "The Sect Quietly Uniting a Divided Libya—Under Salafism." *Libya Tribune*, July 4, 2018. https://en.minbarlibya.org/2018/07/04/the-sect-quietly -uniting-a-divided-libya-under-salafism/.

Index

Page numbers in *italics* indicate figures.

armed groups: al-Asema TV channel
attacked by, 210n25; E. Badi on,
206n149; elections and, 104–7; GNC
and, 115–16; Libyan Muslim Brotherhood establishing, 50; locally
embedded, 4; in Tripoli, 192n47. *See
also specific armed groups*
Asharq Al-Awsat (newspaper), 51
Ashour, Omar, 41, 155, 197n117
ASL, 207n163, 219n146
Asmar, Abd al-Salam al-, 127
authoritarianism, 10; collapsing, 17;
external actors and, 145; Islamists
replacing, 148; social movement
opening, 55. *See also* Gaddafi regime
authority, of spokesperson, 178n76
Awlia al-Dam. See 106th Brigade
awqāf. See Islamic endowments

Bab al-Azizia military compound, 99
Badi, Emaddedin, 205n128, 206n149
Badi, Salah, 91, 138, 209n10
Baghdadi, Abu Bakr al-, 31
Banani, Emad al-, 150, 224n19
Bani Walid, 114–15
Banna, Hasan al-, 23
Barassi, Awad al-, 94
Barqawi, Abu Moaz al-, 180n20
Bashagha, Fathi, 3–4, 151
Bathily, Abdou-laye, 18
Bazaza, Kamal, 138
behavioral moderation, 15
Belhadj, Abdelhakim, 37–38, 65, 81, 93,
116, 118; Muslim Association of
Britain and, 53; Tripoli Military
Council spearheaded by, 192n48
Belhaj, Alamin, 55
Ben Ali, Zine el-Abidine, 86
Benford, Robert, 57
Benghazi (Libya), 29–30, 53, 141, 151
Benghazi attacks, 29, 211n42
Benghazi Defence Brigades, 220n148
Berlin (Germany), 7, 25
bida'. See sinful innovations
Biden, Joe, 153
bin Laden, Osama, 25, 27

bin Qumu, Abu Sufyan, 29
Bishr, Hashim, 101, 105n122, 126
"Black Saturday," 120
Bonnefoy, Laurent, 197n117
book burnings, 30
Boukhars, Anouar, 40
Brachman, Jarret, 108
Brinton, Crane, 174n45
Brocker, Manfred, 14
al-Bunyan al-Marsous coalition. *See* Solid
Wall coalition
Bygne, Susanne, 123

Caliphate, 23, 32
Cavatorta, Francesco, 55, 73, 157
Central Bank of Libya, 133
Central National Party (*al-Umma
al-Wasat* Party), 25, 34, 37–38, 119
CFA. *See* Crime Fighting Apparatus
chaos (*fitna*), 61, 64, 100, 113, 144, 167
Christmas Market terror attack, in
Berlin, 7, 25
civil war, Libyan, 11, 17, 100, 102, 105,
120–24; Arab Spring and, 5, 6, 14;
Libyan Muslim Brotherhood
influencing, 110; Libyan Salafi-
Madkhalis during, 215n91; SDF and,
106
Clark, Janine, 158–59
Cloward, Richard, 49
Cole, Peter, 41
collective action, 173n38
Collombier, Virginia, 106
community morals (*hisba*), 44
compromise, 11, *15*, 55, 112, 144, 159;
advanced moderation signaled by,
143, 158; by Libyan Muslim Brotherhood, 49
conflated self-perception, 19
Constitutional Declaration (Libya), 120
consultative council (*majlis al-shūrā*), 168
conviction of righteousness, 145–48
cooperation, 11, *15*, 16, 55, 77, 156–58;
Libyan Muslim Brotherhood
avoiding, 81, 88, 118, 144; Libyan
Salafi-Madkhalis and, 96, 97

GPSR Authorized Representative: Easy Access System Europe, Mustamäe tee 50, 10621 Tallinn, Estonia, gpsr.requests@easproject.com

www.ingramcontent.com/pod-product-compliance
Lightning Source LLC
Chambersburg PA
CBHW032120020426
42334CB00016B/1021